ERNEST RENAN

RENAN IN HIS STUDY, AFTER THE ETCHING BY ANDERS ZORN

ERNEST RENAN

BY

LEWIS FREEMAN MOTT

PROFESSOR OF ENGLISH IN THE COLLEGE
OF THE CITY OF NEW YORK

D. APPLETON AND COMPANY
NEW YORK   LONDON
1921

COPYRIGHT, 1921, BY

D. APPLETON AND COMPANY

PREFACE

A STUDY of Renan's life emphasizes the fact that his works, even when apparently most abstract and erudite, are in a surprising degree the product of his character and his experience; and in this experience the external is inseparably blended with the internal. Events, books, friends, dreams, meditations, travels, little incidents and observations, diligent and minute investigations, all combine into a unity amid diversity, which makes up our general impression of this eminent personality. There is an autobiographical tone to all his thoughts, and the ''I'' and the editorial ''we'' are copiously employed in his writings, though without producing the effect of egotism. His religion was not a logical system, but an experience and an outlook upon life, and his social and political philosophy also sprang rather from his observation of current and past happenings than from abstract reasoning. His moral and religious nature lay at the bottom of his thinking and gave rise to his seeming contradictions. Which of us does not find in himself antithetical feelings, mingled pleasures and regrets, changing perspectives and varying lights and colors? Renan's unusual frankness in giving vent to his unstable moods, instead of measuring his expression by a fixed, and therefore artificial, standard, is one secret of the charm, the vivacity, and the actuality of his writings. It is also a reason why a review of his life is of exceptional interest.

He saw in the development of the individual an epitome of the development of the human race. Biography, like history, is a *becoming*. Inclined by nature and by reflection to

v

attach supreme importance to origins, he has himself studied his two earlier epochs in his charming *Recollections of Childhood and Youth*. This work is accurate enough, considered as the picture of experiences viewed across the interval of forty years. The general perspective is excellent, though some lines are dimmed and some colors softened by distance. For details and for distribution of emphasis, as the author himself declares, it needs to be supplemented. The material is at hand in notes set down at the moment and in letters written in the heat of the conflict.

CONTENTS

ERNEST RENAN

CHAPTER I

EARLY YEARS; SAINT SULPICE; BREACH WITH THE CHURCH
(1823-1846)

JOSEPH ERNEST RENAN was born at Tréguier, Côtes-du-Nord, France, at 6 A. M., February 28, 1823, the son of Philibert-François Renan, grocery merchant, aged 49, and Madeleine-Josèphe Feger, aged 39, dwelling at Tréguier.[1] He was baptized March 2. The father was an unpractical Breton seaman, the grocery store being kept by the mother, a vivacious villager with Gascon blood in her veins. Their house was halfway between the port and the cathedral on the Grand' Rue, now rue Renan. The family included a brother, Alain, born in 1809, and a sister, Henriette, born in 1811. His relatives, among whom were several aunts, were humble people. The boy often visited them at Lannion, Bréhat and other nearby places. As an infant, he was cared for by a nurse and his health was very delicate. His death was averted, it was thought, by prayers to the Virgin. To discover whether or not he would live, an old sorceress, named Gode, threw one of his tiny shirts into a sacred spring and, as the garment did not sink, life was promised. Henriette early adopted him and became his little mother. In July, 1828, the father was mysteriously drowned, perhaps committing suicide, leaving debts greater than the value of his house. Finding Tréguier too sad, the family moved to Lannion, where the mother had relatives, the brother, Alain, going to Paris for a business career. At Lannion Ernest went to school. They were very poor, but the creditors did not press them, and ultimately Henriette and Alain paid all the debts. Before March, 1831, the Renans returned to

---

[1] See the record of birth printed (p. 81) in *Ernest Renan en Bretagne*, by René d'Ys, Paris, 1904. The date usually given, February 27, appears to come from Renan himself, as Mme. Darmesteter tells us. Henriette, however, writes him a letter on his twenty-second birthday, February 28, 1845.

1

their house at Tréguier, and Ernest had a very serious illness which left traces from which he suffered in later life. Mme. Renan reopened her little shop and Henriette started a small school, which was not successful. There was at Tréguier a college or seminary, officially known as the Ecclesiastical School of Tréguier. For this college Mme. Renan furnished groceries to the amount of three or four hundred francs a year. One of the masters, l'Abbé Pasco, became interested in her son, who wanted to be a priest, and secured for him a scholarship. Renan entered the school in 1832. Though some reports mention lateness and inattention in church, he is usually characterized as docile and diligent, and there was much mutual affection between him and the priests who taught him. The principal studies were Latin and mathematics, and these were thoroughly mastered. Every year Renan gained either first or second prize or honorable mention in every subject. His two chief rivals and schoolboy friends were Liart and Guyomar, both of whom died young. In 1835, Henriette, who had been educated by some nuns and by a returned émigrée aristocrat, went to Paris as underteacher in a school for girls. In 1838, Renan carried off first prize in every one of the nine subjects of his school. This fact was brought to the attention of Dupanloup, head of the seminary of Saint-Nicholas-du-Chardonnet, and he offered the boy a scholarship to last until he was twenty-five. An urgent letter, written by Henriette on August 31, conveyed the information that an unexpected providence had provided for her brother's whole future and offered to pay the expenses of the trip. On September 7, Ernest arrived at Saint Nicholas, where he remained for three years, studying chiefly classic and French literature, the rhetoric of the French schools. At this time Mme. Renan gave up her shop and rented all of the house except one room for herself. In 1839, Renan secured places in the school for his comrades, Guyomar and Liart, for both of whom he had great affection; but the first died in 1840, and the second returned to Brittany, where he also died immediately after entering the priesthood in 1845. Having obtained more prizes than any other boy in his class, Renan passed the summer of 1839 at Tréguier. The summer of 1840, after he had won five prizes, he spent at Gentilly, the country house of Saint Nicholas, just beyond the walls of Paris. The summer of 1841 he was again in Brittany, Henriette supplying the money. In January, 1841, Henriette went to Poland as governess in the family of Count André Zamoyski. In the autumn of 1841, Renan entered the seminary of Issy for two years of philosophy, and here his first doubts appear. Owing to shortage of funds, he spent the summer of 1842 at Issy, but, having received money from Alain and Henriette, he passed the vacation of 1843 with his mother in Brittany. In the autumn, he entered Saint Sulpice in Paris for theology, and here began the study of Hebrew under the learned Le Hir. In the first year, after much hesitation, he received the tonsure at Christmas and minor orders in June; in the second year he absolutely refused the subdeaconate. Both at Issy and Saint Sulpice he lived in almost complete isolation. The summers of 1844 and 1845 were both passed in Brittany. They were a period of inward struggles. He had ceased to be a Catholic, and on October 9 he left Saint Sulpice and abandoned all thought of an ecclesiastical career.[2]

I

Renan describes Tréguier, in which his childhood was passed, as a vast monastery, without commerce or industry, a place to which no sound from the outer world penetrated, where the pursuits of ordinary men were called vanity and where what the world calls illusions were regarded as the only reality. The cathedral dominated the town, and whole streets were formed by the long, high walls of convents, while the secular quarter and the port were insignificant. Not only in these physical surroundings, but in his education, the ecclesiastical influence was complete, for though there was nothing clerical about his father and his uncles,—the freethinking watchmaker and the ne'er-do-well Pierre, for example—these men were without influence on his childhood, the care of his early years being in the hands not of men, but of women, his sister and his mother, and in the background his maternal grandmother, whom he describes as intensely royalist and Catholic.

[2] In his various published recollections, Renan is surprisingly inexact in dates. This inexactitude his biographers have imitated in a degree suited to the temperament or the carelessness of each. The foregoing facts are based upon letters contemporary with the events and upon the thoroughly accurate book of the author whose pseudonym is René d'Ys.

His grandfather on his father's side was a mariner,[3] who, after accumulating a small property, had established himself at Tréguier. This property his father lost. Having served in the fleet of the First Republic, the elder Renan was later a ship captain on his own account, but he was drawn into commerce, for which he was unfitted both by his weak and sentimental nature and by his lack of business skill. In the commercial crisis of 1815, his little fortune disappeared. Though oppressed with melancholy, he continued his life on the sea, until in July, 1828, his ship, coming from Saint-Malo, entered the harbor of Tréguier without him. The crew had not seen him for several days, but a month later the body was found and buried in the sand beneath the washing of the tide.[4]

Renan's maternal grandfather was from Bordeaux, and to this component in his blood the genial author of the eighties ascribes his joyous and ironical temper, just as he ascribes his idealism and his unfitness for commerce and industry to his Breton ancestry. Perhaps his auto-anthropology should not be taken too seriously. But whatever he may or may not have owed to race, he certainly owed much to the surroundings of his early years. The vividness and permanence of Renan's impressions of his childhood are remarkable; sermons, legends of local saints, Breton festivals, persons, localities, little incidents of everyday life remained in his mind fresh and unimpaired to the end. "I have seen the primitive world," he says. "In Brittany before 1830 the most distant past still lived."[5]

Gascon cheerfulness and Breton provincial tradition were excellently combined in his mother. "My mother was in her feelings and her recollections entirely of that old world. She spoke Breton admirably, and knew all the sailors'

---

[3] Those interested in genealogy may consult the tables given by René d'Ys.

[4] For the uncertainties of this story, see René d'Ys, pp. 89–92.

[5] *Souvenirs*, p. 87.

4

proverbs and a quantity of things that nobody any longer knows to-day. She was entirely of the people, and her natural vivacity gave surprising liveliness to the long stories she told, stories which she was almost the only one to know. Her sufferings hardly at all affected her astonishing gayety; she still jested on the afternoon of her death."[6]

At the age of five Renan was put in charge of Saint Yves. "At the death of my father," he tells us, "my mother led me to his chapel and made him my patron. I cannot say that the good Saint Yves managed our affairs wonderfully well, or that he gave me any remarkable understanding of my own interests; but I owe him something better than that; he gave me a contentment that passes wealth, and a natural good humor that has kept me happy to the present day."[7]

The boy was a student and a dreamer, often lost in his visions during divine service in the cathedral. When six, in declaring a childish ambition, he proclaimed that he would be a writer of books. Weak in body and unfit for violent physical exercise and boyish games, he preferred the companionship of the little girls, a preference that earned him the sobriquet *Miss* and subjected him to all sorts of persecutions from juvenile masculinity. "As a child," he says, "it was hard for me to move; I never played, but tended to sit down and be satisfied. Twice a day I covered the distance from house to college without turning one step to right or left. I already had the rheumatism that now makes walking so difficult."[8]

Renan's elder brother, Alain, who left home in 1828 at the age of nineteen to begin a life of labor that was never fully recompensed, naturally counted for little in his development, but his sister, Henriette, was one of the cardinal

---

[6] *Souvenirs*, p. 21.
[7] *Ibid.*, p. 10.
[8] *Discours et conférences*, p. 215.

5

shaping influences in his life. Born at Tréguier, July 22, 1811, her early life was sad and filled with austere duties. The father's melancholy disposition, with no portion of the mother's liveliness, was her inheritance. To the end, she had little taste for vulgar distractions. Instead of courting the world, she withdrew within herself, gave her best to a small circle only, and made her life a succession of acts of devotion. The special object of this devotion was her younger brother, to whom, even in the precocious maturity of her girlhood, her relation was more that of mother than sister. She took upon herself the responsibility of his future, renounced entering a convent to which she had an inclination, refused an offer of marriage which would have detached her from her charge, and when a little school that she had started in Tréguier failed, she accepted in 1835 a place as underteacher in an institution for girls in Paris, where she served a cruel apprenticeship, harassed by deadly homesickness amid unworthy, frivolous and sordid surroundings. Working sixteen hours a day, she soon became director of studies in a good school, went through all the public tests and gained a knowledge, particularly in history, that Renan calls exceptional. Until she went to Paris, the boy was her constant personal care and even in absence his interests were always the anxious subject of her most affectionate thoughts.

Renan's schooling up to the age of fifteen was obtained from ecclesiastics in the college at Tréguier. According to his own statement, they taught him love of truth, respect for reason, and an appreciation of the seriousness of life, the only things in him that never varied. "These worthy priests," he says, "were my first spiritual teachers, and I owe them whatever good there is in me. All their words seemed to me oracles; I had such respect for them that I never had a doubt concerning anything they told me up to the age of sixteen, when I came to Paris. . . . At bottom, I feel that my life is still governed by a faith I no longer possess.'' [9]

His fellow pupils were mostly young peasants from the neighborhood, who were studying for the priesthood, and whose intellectual state was equivalent to that of the Germans at the time of Charlemagne. To the whole school the life of the spirit furnished the only noble career, and every lucrative profession seemed servile and unworthy. Morality was, of course, regarded as inseparable from dogma. In politics, strict legitimacy prevailed, and the Revolution and Napoleon were objects of horror. On the whole, the education was that of the seventeenth century. Latin and mathematics were thoroughly studied; but history was confined to good old Rollin and natural science did not exist. French literature ended with the pious successors of the age of Louis XIV. *"La Morale en action,"* says Renan, "was in my childhood the book that had the greatest influence on me after *Télémaque."* [10] By instinct, these teachers distrusted Chateaubriand; Lamartine, who troubled them with his religiosity, they sneered at; of Victor Hugo they were entirely ignorant; the writing of French verse was frowned upon as almost immoral, but Latin verse was cultivated with diligence.

Such was the "crypt lighted by smoky lamps" in which Renan's intellectual life began. If he had not been exposed to the sun, what would have been the outcome?

Persuaded by my teachers of two absolute truths: the first, that any one with self-respect can labor only at an ideal task, that other things are secondary, base, almost shameful, *ignominia seculi;* the second, that Christianity is the complete summation of the ideal; it was inevitable that I should believe myself destined to be a priest. This idea was not the result of any reflection, impulsion or reasoning. It was in a way a matter of course. The possibility of a profane career did not come into my mind.

---

[9] *Souvenirs,* p. 11.
[10] *Feuilles détachées,* p. 34.

Having indeed accepted with the most perfect seriousness and docility the principles of my teachers, like them looking on every bourgeois or lucrative profession as inferior, base, humiliating, good at the most for those unsuccessful in their studies, it was natural for me to want to be what they were. They became the model for my life, and I had no other dream than to be, like them, a professor in the college of Tréguier, poor but exempt from material cares, esteemed and respected as they were.[11]

Such is Renan's oft-repeated judgment, but we may be permitted to doubt whether, even had he not been taken from these honest, but limited surroundings, he would have preserved throughout life the faith that had appeared from the first the absolute expression of truth. Speculation, however, is useless. From the most obscure little town of the most hidden province, he was thrown, without preparation, into an animated Parisian environment, and the world was revealed to him.

II

The Abbé Dupanloup, having been appointed head of the minor seminary of Saint-Nicholas-du-Chardonnet in Paris, desired to call to this institution, in addition to the wealthy sons of the capital, the most brilliant students of provincial schools as scholarship pupils, so as to unite fashion and scholarly ability in emulation for the good of both society and the church. Henriette, always on the lookout for her brother's advancement, brought his school record to the attention of her physician, Dr. Descuret, a friend of Dupanloup.[12] As the scholarship would continue till the holder's twenty-fifth birthday, it seemed a godsend to the impoverished family. The rest of the story may best be given in Renan's exact words:

---

[11] *Souvenirs*, p. 140.
[12] Cognat says the scholarship was obtained partly through a Breton canon, M. Tresvaux du Fraval. *Correspondant*, May 10, 1882.

In the year 1838, I won in fact at the college of Tréguier all the prizes of my class. The prize list came to the attention of one of the enlightened men whom the ardent captain employed to recruit his young army. In a minute my fate was decided. "Bring him," said the impetuous superior. I was fifteen and a half years old; we had no time for reflection. I was spending my vacation with a friend in a village near Tréguier; on the fourth of September in the afternoon, a messenger came for me. I remember my return as if it were yesterday. There was a league to walk across country. The bells sounding the evening Angelus and answering one another from parish to parish, filled the air with something calm, sweet and melancholy, an image of the life I was going to quit forever. The next day I left for Paris; on the seventh, I saw things as new to me as if I had been flung suddenly into France from Tahiti or Timbuctoo.[13]

The school to which Renan was thus transferred differed in every respect, except neglect of natural science, from the college of Tréguier. Here the atmosphere of the epoch flooded into the cloister. The history teacher read the class pages from Michelet which filled the boy with enchantment. Hugo and Lamartine were subjects of eager discussion, literary glory was prized, and the highest value was attached to humanism and good breeding. The religious tone, though thoroughly devout, was that of fashionable society, "a perfumed, beribboned piety, a young ladies' theology far removed from scholastic barbarism and mystical jargon." The faith of the masters, though sincere, troubled itself little with the dogmas it was bound to accept. The education, indeed, was purely literary and rhetorical, as though all the pupils were to be poets, authors or orators.[14]

Dupanloup was the school, and he was an educator with-

---

[13] *Souvenirs*, p. 171.

[14] Cognat emphasizes Renan's piety in 1838 and his fervent devotion to the Virgin. The boy always added a cross to his signature. He not only performed every duty, but showed eagerness in his work, and excelled in Latin verse on light subjects. A Greek hymn to Mary by him was found among the school papers. *Correspondant*, June 10, 1882.

out an equal. Every evening, in the half hour set aside for
the reading of a book of piety, he substituted himself for
the book, and gave the boys an inimitable talk either about
school affairs or about some personal incident concerning
himself or one of the pupils. The remarks made on Fridays
in connection with their notes held the whole school in sus-
pense. A word from him was the only punishment ever inflicted short of the extreme penalty of expulsion. "He was
an incomparable awakener; no one could equal him in his
ability to draw from every boy the full sum of what he
could give. Each one of his two hundred pupils had a distinct existence in his thoughts; for each of them he was the
ever present inspirer, the motive force of life and work. He
believed in talent, and made it the basis of his faith. He
often repeated that the worth of a man is in proportion to
his faculty for admiration. His own admiration was not
always sufficiently enlightened by science, but it sprang from
great warmth of soul and a heart truly possessed with the
love of the beautiful." [15] This distinguished master exercised a dominant influence over the docile country boy. Toward the close of his third year in the school, after hearing
Dupanloup's opening address as professor at the Sorbonne,
Renan wrote to his mother: "He is the most beautiful soul
and the most lofty mind that I have so far known." [16]

The first weeks in Paris were embittered by homesickness.
Though he found both teachers and fellow pupils affable
and though Henriette visited him every week, he is sad to
be separated from his mother and the good priests at Tréguier, to whom he constantly sends affectionate remembrances.
"Ah, I was happy at Tréguier," he exclaims; but he will
submit to the will of God. His affection toward his aunts
and his friends, especially toward his comrades Guyomar
and Liart, whom he later induced to come to Saint Nicholas,

[15] *Souvenirs*, p. 139.
[16] Letter, May 9, 1841.

is very marked in his early letters, and his deep love for his mother is copiously reiterated from first to last. It was in fact an expression of this love that first attracted to Renan the special attention of Dupanloup. It is characteristic that the homesick boy finds everybody about him good and kind. He is, moreover, comforted by the Virgin, and a retreat a month after his entrance brings him the peace of God. "How good is God and how powerful the Holy Virgin!"[17] His letters are much occupied with the daily routine of the school. He regrets that there is no mathematics, he gives a list of Latin and Greek authors he is reading, he finds the study of literature interesting and good for composition. He is especially occupied with his class standing. In the Latin exercises, he is fifth, then tenth, seventh, again fourth and twelfth; then he clears his honor by attaining third place and finally he announces that he has won the coveted first place. At the end of the year, he had obtained more prizes than any other boy in his class. Thereafter there are apparently no more low grades; he and two others, Foulon and Henri Nollin, are the only rivals for high rank, and Renan soon outdistances even these competitors.[18]

The routine of class work was varied by walks to the country establishment at Gentilly belonging to Saint Nicholas. On such excursions Renan took his work with him, but not when a visit was paid to the Jardin des Plantes, where there was so much to see. Wherever there was anything interesting, he was interested; he delights in travel, moonlight over Cancale, the towns and country he passes through,

---

[17] Letter, May 30, 1839.
[18] The letters show that Renan's recollections on this point when he wrote the *Souvenirs* were a trifle faulty. Still, in a letter to Liart, February 5, 1841, he calls rhetoric "tedious, pedantic, monotonous, absurd, execrable" (*Fragments intimes*, p. 160). As soon as he gets to Issy, he regards Saint Nicholas as mediocre (letter to same, October 31, 1842). Cognat combats the opposition between Saint Nicholas and Saint Sulpice, but Renan's contemporary letters are proof of his impressions.

the architecture of the churches;[19] when the school "Academy" makes a trip around Paris, he discourses on the architecture of the public buildings; he is delighted with Notre Dame, but is not so greatly pleased with the Madeleine or other modern structures; he sees the king in the Bois de Boulogne, takes great interest in the porcelain at Sèvres; even, against his mother's warnings, risks a ride on the railroad. "You see," he remarks, "one can travel by rail without losing an arm or a leg."[0] Then he goes to see the funeral car prepared for to-morrow's 'comedy,'[21] and at another time he describes with much detail the baptism of the Count of Paris in Notre Dame, where he saw "one of the finest assemblages in the world." If, to adopt his own analysis of his dual nature, the Breton part in him got lost in all sorts of melancholy, the Gascon part perceived that this new world was very curious and really worth getting acquainted with.

The effect of all these new experiences upon the youth was disquieting. The germ in him was fertilized, the seriousness of his faith shaken. He was as yet unaware of the change, but the contrast between the solid, rigid, narrow, antiquated training of Tréguier and the brilliant, free, modern education of Saint Nicholas was decidedly unsettling. In *The Future of Science* (page 296), Renan maintains that the poetry of Hugo and Lamartine presupposes all the work of modern critical scholarship, the last word of which is literary pan-

---

[19] Letter, October 1, 1839.

[20] Letter, July 25, 1840.

[21] Letter, July 27, 1840. On July 28, 1840, the bodies of those who had fallen in the Revolution of July, 1830, were placed in a vault under the recently completed Column of July erected in their honor in the Place de la Bastille. The funeral car seen by Renan was the one used in this ceremony. The procession, including ministers of state, the Institute, city officials, and a large military escort, passed from Saint-Germain-l'Auxerrois, where mass had been sung, through the Place de la Concorde and the boulevards to the Place de la Bastille, where there were further religious and civic exercises. The word "comedy" emphasizes Renan's legitimism at this epoch. For a full account of the ceremonial see *Annuaire historique universel* for 1840.

theism. As these poets, without having read the works of erudite investigators, yet propagated the influence which we call the modern spirit, so the youth absorbed this influence with no clear consciousness of its nature.

"For three years," says Renan, "I underwent this profound influence, which brought about in me a complete transformation. M. Dupanloup had literally transfigured me. From the poor little provincial boy encased in his heavy sheath, [22] he had drawn out an active and open mind. Something to be sure was lacking in this education, and as long as I had nothing else, there was a void in my mind. What was lacking was positive science, the idea of critical search for truth. That superficial humanism stilled my reasoning power for three years, at the same time that it destroyed the first naïveté of my faith. My Christianity underwent a serious diminution; but there was nothing yet in my mind that could be called doubt." [23] The ground was, however, unquestionably well prepared for the seed.

III

In the autumn of 1841, Renan, according to the regular procedure, went for his two years' course in philosophy to Issy, the country annex of the Seminary of Saint Sulpice.

---

[22] "Pale and sickly, his wretched body bore a big head; his eyes, almost always cast down, seemed, as he said of his criticism, to read below the surface, and were never raised unless to glance sideways. Timid to awkwardness, meditative to dumbness, never mingling in games, he was self-obstructed during the recreation periods, talked little and with very few friends. If to the situation thus created are added the recollections of his homeland, the separation from his mother and, above all, the natural mortification of being no longer at Paris, as at Tréguier, the first in his class, it will be readily understood that he was seized with an almost fatal homesickness." Cognat, *Correspondant*, June 10, 1882, p. 792. The last sentence shows, what one so often feels in reading Cognat's articles, the rancor of a defeated competitor in schoolboy exercises, curiously surviving through forty years.

[23] *Souvenirs*, p. 195.

In this institution, which was devoted exclusively to training for the priesthood, he found grave and good priests who recalled his first teachers. Of these first teachers he writes: "I cannot tell you how often their remembrance comes to my mind and how much gratitude I retain for them. After God and you, my dear mother, there is no one to whom I owe more. If I possess any greater ability than others in study, I owe it to the excellent principles I received from them."[24] The spirit of Saint Nicholas was here reversed. A school of solid doctrine and of virtue, Saint Sulpice repudiated brilliance, talent, worldly success and literature. The *Télémaque* of Fénelon was the limit of what was allowed to the muses. Here M. Dupanloup was never named; his favorite disciplines were looked upon as childish; scholastic philosophy, theology and the Bible were the only studies held in esteem. The sudden jolt given by this opposition of ideas further unsettled Renan's faith.

The youth found pleasure in renewing his acquaintance with mathematics. He also had lessons in physics and natural history, which, although the teacher of these subjects cared less for science than for mysticism, furnished a foundation for Renan's philosophic thought. "Mathematics and physical induction," he says, "have always been the fundamental elements of my mind, the only stones of my structure that have never changed base and that still serve."[25] Yet philosophy, "the finest of studies and the most worthy of man,"[26] was his favorite subject. Seated on a bench under the trees of the park in which the seminary was situated—"after the cathedral of Tréguier, the second cradle of my thoughts"—he read uninterruptedly for hours at a time. "O, he will study, he will study," mocked the mystic instructor in science, who found him one day on his

[24] Letter, February 26, 1842.
[25] *Souvenirs*, p. 251.
[26] Letter, January 12, 1842.

14

bench, "and when the care of poor souls calls for him, he will still study. Wrapped up in his overcoat, he will say to those who come to him, 'O, leave me alone, leave me alone!'" [27] "I abandoned myself thus without scruple to my taste for study. My solitude was absolute. In the course of two years, I did not once visit Paris, though permission was readily granted. I never played: I passed the recreation periods seated, trying to defend myself against the cold by triple coverings. The teachers, wiser than I, called my attention to the harm to my health that would result at my age from this régime of immobility. My growth was hardly complete; I had acquired a stoop. But my passion carried everything before it. I gave myself to it with the greater assurance since I believed it good. It was a sort of fury; but could I believe that the ardor of thought, praised as I saw in Malebranche and so many other illustrious and holy men, was blameworthy, and would lead me to a result that I should have rejected with all my strength, if I could have foreseen it?" [28]

The spiritual director Renan had chosen, M. Gosselin, head of the house, was a man of erudition, as well as a model of polish and affability. "He knows everything," wrote the boy to his mother. [29] Disliking mysticism and exaltation, Gosselin leaned always toward good sense and reason. He contributed largely also toward the development of his pupil's innate tendency to erudition. His orthodoxy was so sure that he did not discourage the habitual reading of Malebranche, Locke, Leibnitz, Reid and Dugald Stuart. The philosophy officially taught, however, was scholasticism in a mitigated form as fixed in the eighteenth century in three volumes known as *Philosophy of Lyons*. "The problems were at least well stated, and this syllogistic dialectic

---

[27] *Souvenirs,* p. 242.
[28] *Ibid.,* p. 244.
[29] Letter, January 12, 1842.

made up an excellent bit of mental gymnastics."[30] Cousin, Jouffroy and Pierre Leroux were known through the arguments employed to refute their doctrines, and many heterodox modern ideas came to the pupils under the rubric *Solvuntur objecta,* where they were stated in order that they might be disproved. Malebranche in particular was the perpetual subject of Renan's meditations, a priest who had not felt obliged to relinquish his office, though professing ideas hard to reconcile with creed and catechism.

To the young student the contradiction between his philosophy and his faith was not yet apparent, yet his faith was already seriously undermined. He finds that philosophy leads to universal doubt, and writing to Henriette, he expresses fears for his mother's peace of mind.[31] This is the result of some six months at Issy. He is now learning the elements of German, borrowing books from a fellow student. He did not, it is true, make much progress at this time, yet in September he writes: "I much love the ways of the German thinkers, although they are a bit skeptical and pantheistic. If you ever go to Königsberg, I charge you to make a pilgrimage to the tomb of Kant."[32] His knowledge, in fact, came from Mme. de Staël. He is now troubled about his future. He confesses that his convictions are somewhat shaken by his first studies in philosophy. Some of his colleagues are men he could not bear to be associated with, nor could he bow to authority; on the other hand, he is not made for the world or the salon, but for an independent life of study. How to obtain such a career outside the church is an enigma. He begs Henriette not to tell his mother of his hesitations.[33]

It is obvious that a year's study of philosophy had re-

[30] *Souvenirs,* p. 246.
[31] March 23, 1842. See also Letters to Liart of this year, *Fragments intimes,* pp. 186, 197, 207.
[32] September 15, 1842, to Henriette.
[33] *Ibid.*

duced Renan's faith to a feeble and tremulous flicker.[34] He goes ahead rather by habit than by conviction. Revelation he can admit in a general sense, as was done by Malebranche and Leibnitz. "You are not a Christian," said one of his more ardent teachers after an argument. Renan was shocked and horrified, and wept at the feet of the Virgin in the chapel,[35] but it did not require any special illumination to perceive so patent a fact, any more than special keenness was demanded of the mystic who saw the sacerdotal uselessness of the student on the bench. Henriette, already an unbeliever through her reading of history, was evidently aware of her brother's condition, though she does not plainly state the case to him or in any way argue it, but only urges prudence and careful consideration before he should take any step committing himself irrevocably to an ecclesiastical career.

What attracted Renan in this direction was the example of Thomas Reid, a clergyman and at the same time a philosopher, and Malebranche, a hardy thinker, yet a priest. His taste is for a retired, tranquil life, a life of study and reflection. "All the ordinary occupations of men," he writes, "seem to me tasteless and insipid, their pleasures are tedious to me, the motives that govern them in their conditions of life inspire nothing but disgust: whence I conclude without hesitation that I am not made for such things." [36]

In April came the test. He was invited to take the tonsure. This is not an irrevocable act; it is a promise, he tells his mother in a letter filled with indecision, not a vow; but a promise to God, if broken, would be a life-long reproach. The matter is left to M. Gosselin, his director, who

---

[34] Cognat is undoubtedly right in asserting that Renan's religious skepticism was a consequence of his rational skepticism.
[35] Letter to Liart, June 20, 1843.
[36] January 17, 1843.

decides in favor of the measure. [37] Then Renan withdraws in fear; his renunciation is the will of God, but it is merely a delay till he has greater maturity; he has the approval of M. Gosselin, and he is sure the step will ultimately be taken. In every line of this letter can be read his anguish over his mother's expected grief, [38] but she replies with cheerful approval, the delay is nothing, he must have courage, all she asks is that he consult his conscience and his superiors. [39]

The whole story is told in a letter to Henriette:

The end of my stay at Issy has brought the time when the custom of the house is to call to the tonsure those who are judged worthy; and I am of the number of those whom the directors have invited to take this first step in the ecclesiastical career. You can believe that this is not a command, hardly even a piece of advice: it is merely a permission left by custom to the reflections of each and to the advice of his special director. You can feel, but I cannot express to you, all the uncertainties and perplexities in which such a proposal has plunged me. I do not believe I have either exaggerated or dissimulated the importance of the step that has been the subject of my reflections. The engagement proposed is not irrevocable: it is not a vow, but a promise, a promise given upon honor and conscience, a promise made to God: now, such a promise approaches closely to a vow. I have therefore thought that it demanded the most serious meditation before I made it, and my conscience does not reproach me for having omitted any means at my disposal for my enlightenment.

I have not lacked advice: God has furnished me a rare and inestimable treasure in a director of remarkable wisdom and goodness. In him I have found a simple and true character, perfectly in harmony with my own, and above all I have found in him refined and practical tact, apt to understand and feel what can be only half said in such delicate matters. His advice at first leaned toward an affirmative decision; once his instructions were really positive; but my temptations and uncertainties seemed to redouble as I regarded more fixedly a determination of such great import.

I have in addition the example of several friends, who have

---

[37] May 12, 1843.
[38] June 6, 1843.
[39] June 8, 1843, from Mme. Renan.

decided to wait for their stay at Saint Sulpice and the period of their theological studies (according to the generally established practice), to take their first engagement. In a word, all the difficulties that have filled my thoughts have returned in crowds: your advice, my own reflections, everything has contributed to my anxiety. I owe it indeed to the truth to say that the idea of taking a backward step in my sacerdotal career has not come to me: I have never regarded the question as anything but one of delay, and my director has engaged me not to look upon it otherwise. But I could not conceal from him the fact that this delay had become almost a necessity for me. Finally the new considerations I presented altered his first judgment, and he declared that, since there was no impropriety in delay and since the act might be precipitate in my present state of mind, he would consent to the postponement I asked for. "But always," he added, "separate the question we have before us from that of your ecclesiastical calling: they are entirely and absolutely distinct, and you know my decision on the second." . . . It needed all my courage to follow the voice of conscience against that of blood and of tenderness (mother's disappointment) in an occasion when I feared to cause deep pain to the dearest of mothers. . . . For the rest, my good Henriette, you will perhaps be surprised when I tell you that my ideas on the ecclesiastical state have never been more fixed than since this first test to which I have just been subjected. I have never believed more in my heart, my superiors have never assured me with more complete agreement that the will of God was that I should be a priest. It is not that I build up an ideal of human happiness in such a life. Neither my character nor my experience leads to that. But after all, my good Henriette, it is folly to run after such a chimera, since it does not exist here below. Duty, virtue and the delights inseparable from the exercise of noble faculties, that is all it is permissible and reasonable for man to seek; delight, in the broadest sense of the word, is not made for him; he exhausts himself in vain in pursuit of it. Christianity once admitted, as it reasonably can be, he has another end to fulfill. Nothing better proves to me the divinity of the Christian theory of man and of happiness than the very reproaches that the modern schools cast upon it, its obliging man always to come out of himself, to flow, so to speak, against his nature, to place his happiness outside of himself and of pleasures. Truly I forgive them willingly for not admitting Christianity; man is not Christian of himself, but of God; it is then only half their fault;

but I do not forgive them for not having seen that this theory is only the expression of a fact, the downfall and present misery of man; a simple experimental study of man ought to have brought them to this.

This point established, Christianity proved, and the will of God manifested, as I have reason to believe it has been for me, the logical consequence is, it seems to me, inevitable. It is nevertheless a difficulty that has often occupied my thoughts. Supposing even, as I believe, that the fear of depriving myself of some comforts and perhaps of drawing upon myself many sufferings, should not be a sufficient reason for drawing back, at least, I have said to myself, could not the desire of conserving the sweet liberty and honest independence so necessary for the full action of the intellectual and moral faculties, suffice to keep me from embracing a career in which I feel sure I could not find these?

This is my reply: There are two sorts of independence of mind, one bold, presumptuous, criticizing everything worthy of respect; that is forbidden by my priestly duties, but, even if I embraced another path, my conscience and my sincere love of truth would still forbid this; it is not then this sort of independence that is in question. There is another, wiser sort, respecting what deserves respect, despising neither beliefs nor persons, examining calmly and with good faith, using reason since God has given it for use, never rejecting nor adopting an opinion simply on human authority. Such is permitted to all, and why not to the priest? On this point, it is true, he has a duty beyond that of others. This duty is to be able to keep proper silence and to keep his thought to himself: for the number of those frightened by what they do not understand is infinite. But, after all, is it so hard to think for oneself; and is it not through a secret motive of vanity that people are so eager to communicate their reflections to others? Does not every man who would live in peace have to impose on himself the law of silence just spoken of? "It is necessary to have a hidden thought," says Pascal, "and judge everything by that, speaking, however, as the people do." This is what the clever director I have told you of said, and he dwelt on this point as though speaking from experience. "My dear fellow," he said, "if I knew that you had not the strength to keep silent, I should beg you not to become a priest." "Sir," I answered, "I have thought it over, and I believe I can promise to find the strength." [40]

---

[40] June 16, 1843.

This is the language of a man who has forced himself into an untenable position. Sooner or later this position must be abandoned; how long it shall be held depends upon circumstances. In some cases uncertainty gradually hardens into clear-cut negation; in the case of Renan, the study of the Hebrew Bible added to philosophic doubt positive evidence of the fallibility of the infallible church, and further anticipation of an ecclesiastical career on his part became impossible.

IV

The struggle, of which he seems to have been rather the victim than a participant, lasted two years, with occasional later sporadic outbreaks after the decisive act. Though aware that his faith had vanished, he strove eagerly to believe that he believed. In October, 1843, he entered the main Seminary of Saint Sulpice in Paris, where he was assigned a room on the fourth floor so that he might have the exercise of climbing the stairs. The atmosphere was that of the seventeenth century, permeated with a particular Sulpician honesty, piety, good sense and taste for order. The superior, M. Garnier, a man of prodigious theological learning, was too aged for active management of the house, and these functions devolved upon M. Carbon, good, jovial, straightforward, but by no means a distinguished intellect. The great scholar and teacher was M. Le Hir. "There was not a single objection made by rationalism that he did not know. He, however, made no concession to them; for to him the truth of orthodoxy was never an object of doubt. . . . The supernatural caused him no intellectual repugnance. His balance was most just; but in one of the scales there was an infinite weight, an unshakable faith. Whatever might have been put in the other scale would have seemed light, all the objections in the world could not make him

21

vacillate." [41] Profoundly acquainted with German exegesis and theology, he appropriated so much of these only as was compatible with his orthodoxy. In grammar he was familiar with the best and latest theories, and he possessed the critical spirit in everything that did not concern matters of faith. Being a Breton, as well as a scholar of vast learning, he was particularly sympathetic to Renan, who at once began under him a course in Hebrew grammar and was enchanted with his exact philology and his admirable exposition of Semitic idioms. "M. Le Hir fixed my life," he says; "I was a philologist by instinct. I found in him the most capable man for developing this aptitude. All that I am as a scholar, I am through M. Le Hir. It even seems to me sometimes that what I did not learn from him I have never known well." [42]

At first, as usual, Renan found everything delightful. A ray of novelty could always dispel the winter of his discontent. He is pleased with the admirable buildings, the kindness and affection of the masters, the piety and intelligence of the pupils. It was only later that some of these pupils, happily only a few, showed themselves unworthy of his confidence, just as some had poisoned his last months at Issy by their envy and their petty spirit. Among his fellow students at Saint Sulpice he had no personal friendships. Though his heart had an imperious need of true and disinterested affection, he was alone with his books and his thoughts. His solitude was even greater than at Issy. Absorbed in his work and without an acquaintance in Paris, he spent two years without passing through any other street than the *rue de Vaugirard* that he traversed once a week on a trip to Issy.

Immediately after the arrival at the Seminary, the postponed question of the tonsure again became pressing. "It

[41] *Souvenirs*, p. 274.
[42] *Ibid.*, p. 288.

is a decision; the word is terrible."[43] But further delay became impossible, the solicitations of his individual director gave him the assurance he needed. With about one hundred and fifty others he went through the ceremony performed by the archbishop of Paris in the chapel of the Seminary at Christmas time, and for a season his consecration to God brought calm and joy in place of incertitudes and struggles. This is what he told his mother; to Henriette his language is somewhat different. "I took the step because I saw that not to take it was to start in the opposite direction, to which, after all, I felt more opposed. . . . In consecrating myself to God and to what I believe the truth, in taking it for my share and the portion of my heritage, according to the words I had to pronounce, in renouncing for it the vanities, superfluities, silly delights, and what are called pleasures, I have, after all, done only what I have always without hesitation wanted to do. I have never hesitated except to know where the truth *was*, or if it required me to serve within the church, in spite of the human difficulties that I could not hide from myself. But whether or not I embraced the ecclesiastical career, I had said, whatever might be the sentiment about the religion in which I believed I found the truth, a serious and retired life, far removed from superficialities and pleasure, would always be my settled choice: that is all I have promised, and this promise seemed to me the necessary preamble of all truly serious research, the indispensable initiation into a life consecrated to truth and virtue."[44]

In *Principles of Conduct,* some notes written for his own edification just after he had received the tonsure, is found the same view of a desirable future:

"In a word, a calm, simple, poor, humble life, having

[43] To Henriette, November 27, 1843.
[44] To Henriette, April 16, 1844. The fact that his faith was not unimpaired is proved by his letter to Liart of March 29, 1844, *Fragments intimes*, p. 251. "It was in the foundations themselves, in my faith that I was attacked."

friends, a chance to think and study, and at the same time to be useful to the church, loftiness of sentiment, goodness of heart, elevation of thought, tenacious and inductive researches, lofty piety, simple and tender, and above all truth in everything, in my sentiments, never exaggeration in my conduct, acting as though I were alone in the world, always ready to die, looking at things directly and without spectacles, seeking in all and above all truth, never having reputation for an essential motive, in a word, and it is the word that sums all up: truth, truth, truth, unity, simplicity, such is my type, and all this *per Dominum nostrum Jesum Christum, Deum et hominem."* [45]

The second step, the acceptance of minor orders, which, however, added no further obligations, was taken according to the precise and repeated decisions of his director, without the worries or doubts that had accompanied the tonsure. As there was no choice there was no procrastination or debate. His ordination, in company with two hundred and fifty others, took place early in June, in the main church of Saint Sulpice, and it was a magnificent and beautiful ceremony which lasted seven hours. When Renan writes to his mother about it, he hopes God will finish what he has thus begun; [46] when he writes to his sister, he cannot think of the irrevocable next step without fear, and he calls upon God to take this cup from him, but hopelessly adds, "His will, not mine, be done." [47] Doubtless both expressions are sincere, each from its own angle. His vacillation during the whole period of his stay at Saint Sulpice was continuous and distressing. It was a struggle between heart and head, in which the heart often deluded the head with agreeable sophistries and subterfuges, only to be again inexorably brought to terms by implacable reason. The experience was by no

---

[45] *Fragments intimes,* p. 289.
[46] June 5, 1844.
[47] July 11, 1844.

means exceptional, though his situation made it unusually cruel.

The special study in the Seminary was of course theology, the philosophic side of which, involving as it did "analysis of man and society, critical discussion and experimental researches," Renan liked, while he had a distaste for the dogmatic side, with its "subtleties, scholasticism, abstract and empty formulas of the schools." [48] But what determined his religious belief, as well as his future career, was his course in Hebrew. From the beginning, he finds the subject full of charm and without difficulty after mastery of the alphabet. It is a credit to the Germans that the study of this language has been made a true science, leading to important linguistic laws.[49] In retrospect Renan writes: "At that time, I had an extraordinary power of assimilation, I absorbed everything I heard my master say. His books were at my disposal, and he had a very complete library. The days of the walk to Issy, he took me to Solitude Hill, and there taught me Syriac." [50] When Renan returned from the summer vacation of 1844, the teaching of the elementary course was assigned to him with a stipend of 200 francs which, on his objection, was made 150 francs. [51] From this little course and the obligation it imposed to clarify and systematize his ideas, sprang his future career as a philologist.

---

[48] To Henriette, November 27, 1844.
[49] November 6, November 27, 1844.
[50] *Souvenirs*, p. 288.
[51] The occasional inexactitude of the *Souvenirs* is illustrated by this incident. There Renan says that he was offered 300 francs, which appeared to him colossal, and that his refusal was on the ground that he did not need such an enormous sum. Of course he might have said this to M. Carbon, who made the offer, but it was not his real objection. In a letter to Henriette at the time, December 1, 1844, he says that the sum offered was 200 francs, that he refused because he feared its acceptance meant an implicit promise to become a future member of the Society of Saint Sulpice, that under pressure he consented to accept 100 francs for books, and that finally the amount was fixed at 150 francs.

During this same year, 1844-45, he was also allowed to follow courses at the Sorbonne and the Collège de France, where he came under the influence of the prodigious oriental erudition of Quatremère. What was the effect of all this? On the technical side, it taught him the comparative method, which revealed the fact that the Bible was full of human errors, contradictions, fables, myths and legends, and in detail it taught him that the second part of *Isaiah* was not by Isaiah, that the book of Daniel was apocryphal, and that the Pentateuch was not by Moses. The foundations of his Catholicism, already weakened by philosophic doubt, were completely destroyed by philological science, and the structure of his faith fell in ruins. At the same time, on the practical side, his relations with the University showed him that there could be a career of study and thought outside of the ecclesiastical orders.

Many plans for the future presented themselves for his consideration. He might teach at Saint Nicholas; he might become a private tutor in Germany; since his director realized that he was not adapted to the parochial ministry, he might join the Society of Saint Sulpice; he might become professor of Hebrew at a new theological faculty to be founded by the Archbishop of Paris; he even called to mind, when he began to give his course in Hebrew grammar, that the present professor at the Sorbonne had begun his career in the same way. At any rate, he wants his mother and his sister with him. "I can never be in my normal state," he writes, "unless I can join with my study and thought the joys of the heart and of love." [52] Meanwhile he continued his studies at Saint Sulpice.

Among these studies was German, which he took up seriously during this second year at the Seminary, being assisted by a fellow student from Alsace. He began with

---

[52] December 1, 1844.

Lessing's *Fables*, [53] not having progressed very far in his previous attempt, and by summer he had advanced sufficiently to get into the spirit of the literature. This reading marked an epoch in his life. "I seemed to enter a temple, when I contemplated this literature, so pure, so lofty, so moral, so religious, this word being taken in its highest sense. What a lofty conception of man and of life! How far they are from those miserable points of view in which the end of humanity is brought down to the wretched proportions of pleasure and utility! They seem to me to constitute in the history of the human spirit an immediate reaction against the eighteenth century, in substituting pure moral ideas and the ideal for its too realistic conceptions and its material positiveness. . . . In truth, life would be worthless if man's faculties were limited to what he can touch. What still more charms me in them is the happy combination they have succeeded in bringing about of poetry, erudition and philosophy, a combination that in my eyes constitutes the true thinker. Herder and Goethe are the ones in whom I find the highest realization of this intermingling; they therefore above all attract my sympathies. The second, however, is not moral enough. *Faust* is admirable for its philosophy, but desolating in its skepticism; the world is not like that; there is absolute truth and absolute good; the first must be believed, the second practiced." [54] He finds that the painting of the agony of doubt in *Faust* is in places like his own autobiography. The decisive step was at hand.

V

The subdeaconate, to which he should have been ordained in April, he had refused. To Henriette he writes that this refusal was owing to the fact that he does not sufficiently

<hr>

[53] Letter, December 1, 1844.
[54] To Henriette, September 22, 1845.

believe; his reason, claiming its rights and sincerely undertaking rational verification of dogma, had shown that, while Christianity was not false, it was not absolute truth; hence he had ceased to be a Catholic, yet strangely enough, he clings to the idea that the change is only temporary, and that he may return; since he only hesitates, he may conscientiously remain in the Seminary. [55] To his mother he is more disingenuous, emphasizing the point that, if he were subdeacon, the breviary would take an hour and a half daily from his studies, and declaring that, as his age obliges him to put some intervals between the grades of the priesthood, the delay had better come at this point. [56] To his friend Liart, who, in spite of his doubts, had become a priest, he writes [57] : "I have fully decided not to accept the subdeaconate at the next ordination. That cannot appear singular to any one, since my age obliges me to put an interval between my orders. But what is opinion to me? . . . I do not need to ask your silence. You understand that my mother must have every consideration. I had rather die than give her a minute of pain." [58] Like many others, he grasped at straws to save himself in the shipwreck of his faith, but he could not accept the illusion of the liberal Catholics, who think they are privileged to select certain dogmas for belief, while rejecting others. What he had been taught, scholasticism, theology, Hebrew, he took seriously, so that, while his inward sentiments were unchanged, each day a link in the chain of his faith was broken, and a single broken link was enough to destroy the whole chain. The process was achieved, not by metaphysical, political or moral, but by philological and critical reasoning. No self-imposed fiction could keep up his belief in the supernatural. How little his spiritual di-

---

[55] April 11, 1845.
[56] May 2, 1845.
[57] March 22, 1845.
[58] *Souvenirs*, pp. 308-310.

rectors comprehended his case is shown by their advice that he should pay no attention to his doubts, but regard them as temptations of the enemy, which were unworthy of notice. It is not by such wornout formulas that the modern critical spirit is to be exorcised.

The vacation of 1845, spent in Brittany, gave the freedom needed to assure the final separation of Renan from the Church. How far he had gone is shown by the fact that he ceased taking the sacraments. [59] On September 6, he wrote a long letter to his director announcing his final renunciation of the priesthood. Returning to Paris, on the evening of October 9, with the expectation that he could tide along for some time with half measures, he found that Archbishop Affre had transferred him to the Carmelite school of higher studies, which had just been founded. [60] Instant decision was thus forced upon him; when the presence of the Archbishop was announced a little later that same afternoon, he avoided an interview, announced to his directors that he would not continue at the Seminary, took cordial leave of them, and passed from Saint Sulpice to a neighboring hotel. He carried with him the esteem and affection of his former teachers, who were vainly persuaded that he would soon return. [61]

Throughout this whole period of painful uncertainty, Henriette had been through her letters his constant support. In the indecisions that played over the surface of a fundamentally steadfast nature, Renan somewhat resembled one

---

[59] According to Cognat, Renan still went to confession on November 12.

[60] See letter of November 12 to Abbé Cognat in appendix of *Souvenirs*. Cognat also was transferred to this school on the order of the Archbishop.

[61] To Henriette, October 13, 1845. October 6, the date of his departure given in *Souvenirs*, p. 324, is one of the slight inaccuracies in which the book abounds. The letter of October 13 is dated, not from the hotel described in *Souvenirs*, but from *rue du Pot-de-fer*, which is some distance from Saint Sulpice.

conception of Hamlet, and Henriette, with her practical good sense and self-sacrificing affection, was far more to him than ever Horatio was to the Dane. The principles of action and the plan that was finally carried out were, however, entirely Renan's; encouragement, moral support, financial aid and helpful suggestions were contributed by Henriette. The result was a program, intelligently conceived and tenaciously adhered to. The basic idea was that the present should be sacrificed to the future, and that the future was to be a life of independent study and research, with sufficient income to allow brother, sister and mother to live together. From this idea Renan never deviated, and his persistence was crowned with the most astonishing success. Whatever vacillation he displayed was momentary and superficial; at heart and in essentials, he never wavered.

Henriette echoed his thought. Not one word from her ever urged him to renounce his belief; not one argument did she advance against creed or priestly career. She is glad that he is seriously considering his future, concerning which he must not be precipitate in taking obligations. How can you expect independence in the Church? she asks, merely posing the question and leaving him to decide. [62] The final step, she tells him, while he is still hesitating on the brink, should come, not from external influences, but from enlightened and free will. [63] She does not believe that he will return to his faith, [64] though it is true she is often afraid that he will not persist in his resolutions. Other later friends also sometimes spoke to Renan as though he were without will power; but how many lives do we find proceeding so undeviatingly across obstacles and discouragements to a clearly perceived goal? In following his aim, he was neither irresolute nor unpractical, however often he is will-

---

[62] October 30, 1842.
[63] February 28, 1845.
[64] June 1, 1845.

ing to entertain us with this fiction. As early as September 15, 1842, he had determined on an independent life of study, and he never afterward thought of entering the priesthood, except on this condition. He later toys with Henriette's idea of travel in Germany, but ultimately rejects it. He is distinctly averse to adopting secondary teaching as a profession, [65] and he always clings obstinately to this resolution. He will accept no position unless it allows him ample time for study, for it is bad calculation to sacrifice fruitful years for a little money. He will take his degrees, with his eye on the Collège de France and the École Normale, but for support during the period of preparation, he will not be a teacher, but a pensionary giving service. Every step that he took was the result of his own reflection, and in every step, after he had decided it, he had the approval and sympathy of Henriette. This sympathy was necessary to him— "Her exquisite letters," he says, "were at this moment decisive for my life. They were my consolation and support." [66] His sister's introductions to people of influence were useful, and the 1500 francs [67] she sent him on September 16, 1845, though he used little of the money, gave him financial peace of mind. Her practical efforts to secure him lodgings came to naught, and we do not know whether he followed her advice about the color of his lay clothes, though he probably did. [68]

---

[65] April 16, 1844.

[66] *Ma Sœur Henriette*, p. 29.

[67] In the letters it is 1500: in *Ma Sœur Henriette* and *Souvenirs*, 1200.

[68] In *Quatre Portraits*, Jules Simon, who was from Brittany, tells of his first meeting with Renan. The younger man, still in ecclesiastical costume, visited his compatriot in his room. "I no longer believe," said he tragically. "Drop that costume," said Simon. But Renan protested that his uncle, the abbé, had paid all the expenses of his education. "If I go, I rob him," he said. Thereupon Simon laughed, and the two went in search of a frock coat. This uncle is supposed to be the Abbé Mignot, but there is no mention of him in the published correspondence. Simon's explanation is that Renan

Henriette's love for her brother was extraordinary. To her mother, she calls him "our good and dear child." [69] "I have mingled my life in yours, my dear Ernest," she writes. "Be assured that I will never separate it from yours." [70] She was, in fact, his second mother, and the one in whom he had the closest confidence.

His relations to his mother herself were of the most tender affection. Never was there a more considerate and loving son. It was this feeling, indeed, that made his separation from the Church so painful, and it also involved him in a considerable network of deceit. When writing to her, he always emphasizes the approval of his directors, his agreement with the Church, and the pious exercises in which he takes part. After the tonsure, and until he left Saint Sulpice, he invariably adds to his signature the words "tonsured clerk," though this form never appears in his letters to Henriette. His spiritual directors knew of his doubts while his mother was kept in ignorance. He begs Henriette to keep his secret, which she faithfully does, and they often write one another letters which the mother may see without harm, at the same time putting the part to be concealed from her on a separate sheet. All this was natural enough, but it was useless. The mother's intuition perceived some undefined change in her Ernest, and she once vented her irritation on a volume he was reading,[71] though this particular volume happened to be by de Bonald, one of the pillars of the Church. More definite was the impression she received from a letter Renan had written to Liart, which ar-

---

was saying to him what he wanted repeated to common Breton friends and thus spread broadcast. It may be added, however, that Jules Simon's memory is sometimes at fault. He says, for example, that Taschereau took Renan at the Library in 1848: Taschereau himself was not appointed till 1852.

[69] July 1, 1840.

[70] February 28, 1845.

[71] This story is repeated by Renan half a dozen times in different writings.

rived at Tréguier after his friend's death and thus fell into his mother's hands. [72] What must she have thought of such a passage as this: ''I am consoled in thinking of Jesus, so beautiful, so pure, so ideal in his sufferings, that under any hypothesis I shall always love him. Even if I should abandon him, it ought to please him, for it would be a sacrifice to conscience, and God knows what it would cost me.'' Perhaps even more disquieting would be some words toward the close: ''I need not ask you to keep silent. You understand that there must be precautions on account of my mother. I had rather die than cause her a moment of pain.'' After this, it would seem as though hypocrisy were futile, but Renan labored under the mask for another six months. At length, Henriette sensibly cut the knot and ended all tergiversations by a frank but tempered statement of the facts. [73] The mother's heart was not broken, and Renan had no further painful waverings. Perhaps this experience was the basis of his sister's convincing argument against lying, which led him to renounce the practice entirely in 1851. [74]

Renan's habitudes, affections, interests, ambitions were all bound up with the Church. No one who has been placed in a situation even slightly similar will be surprised at his twistings and turnings, and his alternations of hesitation and fixed purpose. He would have been glad to stifle the voice of his reason, but he was unable to do so. This voice called him out of the comfortable shielded fold into the wilderness—for to him the world was unknown, repellant, appalling—and he obeyed the inexorable call.

---

[72] See letter to Henriette, June 1, 1845. This is the letter published in *Souvenirs,* p. 308.
[73] March 15, 1846.
[74] *Souvenirs,* p. 363.

CHAPTER II

On leaving the Seminary, October 9, 1845, Renan passed a few days in the neighboring "hotel of Mlle. Céleste," kept exclusively for people connected with Saint Sulpice. M. Dupanloup and Renan's former superior, M. Carbon, procured him a place as supervisor of studies under the Abbé Gratry, Director of the Jesuit Collège Stanislas. Though expecting to remain a year, Renan left in about a fortnight, because he was obliged to wear the ecclesiastical habit. About November 2, he went to a pupils' boarding house kept by M. Crouzet (rue des-deux-Églises, now rue de-l'Abbé-de-l'Épée), which was attached to the Lycée Henri IV. Here, in consideration of reviewing lessons for two hours every evening, he was allowed board and lodging and laundry. He also had a private pupil in mathematics three hours a week, for which he was paid 25 francs a month.[1] In this place he remained until March, 1849. He attended courses at the Sorbonne and the Collège de France, which were given gratis, and he studied in libraries, having special permission to take books from Sainte Geneviève. On encouragement from M. Le Hir of Saint Sulpice, he began writing a Hebrew grammar. The friendship between Renan and Berthelot began at Crouzet's in November, 1845. On January 26, 1846, Renan passed his examinations for the baccalaureate. Berthelot, having completed his studies at the Lycée, left Crouzet's at the end of the academic year and went to reside at his father's, across the Seine, but there was no interruption in the intimacy between the two young men. During this period, Renan was much occupied with preparation for the examination for the *licence*, in addition to his oriental studies. He also filled several notebooks with his reflections. The examination for the *licence* he passed October 23, 1847, after a summer spent in Paris. The term that

---

[1] Regarding money values, it is interesting to note that this was the monthly rent paid by Sainte-Beuve for his two rooms in the hotel de Rouen, where he lived till 1840.

followed, he studied Sanscrit and comparative philology under Burnouf, and was profoundly influenced by his learning and his character. He became a member of the Société Asiatique [2] (received in the *séance* of August 13, 1847), qualifying as a student in the school of oriental languages.

This same year he took the *Prix Volney* of 1,200 francs with an essay: "Histoire générale et système comparé des langues sémitiques." The summer of 1847 was spent in Brittany. In 1848 Renan was deeply impressed by the insurrections in Paris, though the street fighting did not interrupt his studies. Up to May he was working on a mémoire, "The Study of the Greek Language in the West of Europe from the End of the Fifth Century to the End of the Fourteenth," for the prize (2,000 francs) of the Academy of Inscriptions and Belles Lettres. His work was crowned by the Academy on September 1. In September, too, he stood first in the competition for *agrégé* in philosophy, and soon after he was offered a position in the Lycée at Vendôme, which he declined, having been nominally professor from September 17 to October 7. At this time (October, 1848-March, 1849) he wrote *The Future of Science*. At the Lycée of Versailles, from April 13 to May 27, 1849, he lectured to the class in philosophy in place of M. Bersot, who was making a campaign at Bordeaux for election to the *Assemblée Législative*.[3] He was also working on both his Latin and his French thesis for the doctorate. He published several important articles in *La Liberté de Penser* and he contributed also to the *Journal général de l'instruction publique et des cultes*, the *Gazette de l'instruction publique* and the *Journal Asiatique*. The summer of 1849 was spent in Brittany, where he found valuable material for his work on Averroism in the libraries of Saint-Malo and Avranches. Soon after his return to Paris, he was sent by the government on recommendation of the Academy of Inscriptions and Belles Lettres on a mission to examine and report on oriental manuscripts in the libraries of Italy.

I

The Collège Stanislas, where Renan found his first posi-

---

[2] The dues of the society were 30 francs, but he gained access to a library of oriental books, obtained publications at a reduced price, and, above all, became personally acquainted with the leading oriental scholars of the day.

[3] See Hémon, *Bersot et sès amis*, pp. 93, 94.

tion after leaving Saint Sulpice, was a regular school of the University, a connection which would facilitate his taking his baccalaureate degree. At the same time the institution was entirely under ecclesiastical control, and this fact he counted upon to make his step seem less awful to his mother. The ecclesiastical character of the place, however, made his situation intolerable. Wearing the garments of a churchman was an outward profession of a faith he had relinquished. The director, moreover, though kind and good, was of a type of mind that Renan could not get along with. "I feel," he writes, "that my reasons have no weight with him; for he is persuaded, and he protests to me, that at the end of a few months of intellectual relations with him, I shall have changed my mind. But I, knowing how things stand, can no longer accept such reasoning. This puts us both in a peculiar situation, in which it is as impossible for us to understand one another as two men who speak different languages." [4]

His complete emancipation was accomplished only when he transferred himself to the institution of M. Crouzet, a move which he concealed from his mother for two months and which he misrepresented after revealing it to her: "Certain artifices which it was perhaps wrong for me to adopt." [5] Those passages in his letters dealing with this deception are most unpleasing and are to be condoned only because the motive was an extreme sensitiveness over giving pain to one he so deeply loved. His mother, on her part, seems to have displayed such good sense as to make any double-dealing unnecessary, a point that the straightforward

[4] To Henriette, October 31, 1845. To objections (*e. g.*, story of Samson) the theologians reply that these have been reduced to dust a hundred times, referring you to books they are sure you will not read. They are superficial men resting on the superficiality of others. "Jesus, I have nevertheless received thee this morning, but this is for my rational part." Dimanche, 20 juillet 1845. By "this" Renan seems to mean his note. *Cahiers de jeunesse*, p. 99, note 39.
[5] *Souvenirs*, p. 330.

Henriette soon perceived. She is in fact chiefly concerned about her son's health and comfort, his relinquishment of his neat room with a fire to poke for enjoyment rather than for heat, the danger she thought he ran of being knocked down by ruffians in the street when coming at night from the library. "No, my child," she writes, "you will not be placed in the cruel alternative of deciding between your conscience and my earnest wishes. I put the scepter in your hands, persuaded that you will not let it fall in the mud." [6] In fact, she bears her disappointment without complaint and the poignancy of desperate grief seems to be rather in the son's imagination than in the mother's heart. After matters had been cleared up by Henriette's letter, she was relieved of her suspicions, and Renan was able to go ahead untroubled by the entanglements of a false position.

While it cannot be said of Renan, as La Rochefoucauld said of himself, that he never knew a trouble that a half hour's reading would not console, yet there can be no doubt that books, and meditations upon books, now furnished a potent medicine for his moral distress, as in later life they helped to alleviate intense physical suffering. His situation at Crouzet's often humiliated and exasperated him, but he could hardly have found elsewhere such comfort combined with so much freedom. He had a room on the third floor, overlooking the garden of an institution for deaf-mutes across the street and commanding an extensive view. All he had to do, in addition to three private lessons a week for which he was paid 25 francs a month, was to superintend the studies of seven boys from seven to nine each evening, a task that was at first a sort of rehearsal for his own examinations. The rest of his time from eight in the morning to midnight was devoted to study in his room or in libraries and to attendance at lectures at the Sorbonne and the Col-

---

[6] Letter, February 3, 1846.

lège de France. Two evenings a week he gave to recreation: Wednesdays he visited his sister's friend, Mlle. Ulliac, where there were "magnetic séances," and Sundays he looked over the journals in the reading room.

For the baccalaureate, since Renan had no certificate from a state college, the formalities caused ten times more trouble than the preparation, but this difficulty was overcome, though not without some slight, but customary, evasions, assisted by influence. An important choice had to be made between the faculty of letters and that of the sciences. Science he would have preferred, his mind being in his judgment more scientific than literary; but philosophy, to which he was dedicated, fell, improperly as he thought, under literature. He consoled himself with the reflection that history and the higher criticism might save him from the empty and pedantic rhetoric which excited his aversion. [7] At this time he followed regularly the courses in letters at the Collège de France and the Sorbonne, in addition to continuing his oriental studies under Quatremère. Some of these courses were almost intimate, being taken by but a handful of students. At his examination for the degree in January, his committee, headed by Ozanam, consisted exclusively of distinguished professors of the Sorbonne. He was thus becoming personally known to the best scholars of France, several of whom began to manifest a special interest in his career.

His ambition was a chair in some branch of oriental scholarship at the Collège de France, a dream, he admits, but a dream that he obstinately clung to. The only such chair was that occupied by Quatremère, who had already adopted his successor, and even if competition had been possible, Renan would not have been willing to supplant any one. To teaching modern oriental languages, with the aim of favoring commercial relations, he could not conse-

---

[7] Letters, November 5 and December 15, 1845.

crate himself. For a time the École Normale, with a career as professor in a *lycée*, was considered, but this was soon definitely abandoned, and he devoted himself to a life of research, keeping a close watch for any opening that might present itself. Already he had several works sketched, the publication of which might bring him to the attention of competent judges. He had great hopes especially for the Hebrew grammar,[8] suggested by Le Hir, on which he was engaged with all his fire, and which was to be adopted in the Sulpician Seminaries of France. He was, in fact, working at many tasks besides preparation for his examinations. Even thus early it was his rule to have, in addition to his principal or dominant study, some secondary work to fill up the intervals left by the main subject, a practice which, like all the chief developments of his youth, remained with him to the end.[9]

From childhood Renan seems to have exercised a peculiar fascination of manners and mind. The old Breton priest, Pasco, even while the fuss about the *Life of Jesus* was at its height, prayed as he lay dying that God would bring back his best loved pupil to the Church. For a year after the break and while there was yet hope of a reconciliation, Dupanloup continued to be a friend and adviser, and Le Hir received Renan's visits every week. His pupils were fond of him and his professors seem to have been always helpful and often very friendly. Mlle. Ulliac,[10] a close friend of Henriette and herself of Breton origin, was also most cor-

---

[8] The manuscript of this grammar consists of sixteen copy books. See *Nouveaux Cahiers,* p. 133, note 2. The first chapter is complete, the rest consists of observations and notes. There are also a preface and an introduction. See René d'Ys, pp. 355, 356. Another interesting manuscript of youthful days is the volume of Psalms mentioned in *Souvenirs,* p. 313. This is a complete breviary, containing not only the Psalms, but also the prayers and hymns in Hebrew. *Revue d'histoire des religions,* vol. xxvii, p. 355.

[9] For all these points see letter to Henriette, December 15, 1845.

[10] Born, 1794, at Lorient, she was a person of considerable literary importance in her day.

dial and serviceable; but the relationship that above all influenced his thinking and brought a fresh, invigorating and unfailing stream into the current of his life, was his intimacy with Marcelin Berthelot.

Writing to his mother, February 24, 1846, Renan tells of a fine neighbor who occupies the opposite room at Crouzet's. "He is a young man who is preparing to take his degrees in science, after having obtained the most brilliant success at the Lycée Henry IV and at the general competition. He is the son of one of the most celebrated physicians of Paris, Monsieur Berthelot. I have known few young persons so distinguished, so religious, so serious; it seems as though we were cut out for each other. So, after having studied one another for a time, keeping within the limits of politeness, we recognized that we were worthy to be friends."

Berthelot was eighteen, Renan twenty-two, yet Berthelot had the wider experience of life. Their ardor for study was equal, while their fields were diverse. Thus one supplemented the knowledge of the other, and their ideas were shared without question of priority or ownership. They visited each other's rooms, walked together, studied together, each giving the other instruction in his own specialty. To Renan there were thus opened the vast and exact perspectives of natural and physical science. The discussions of the two friends were endless, covering the universe and leading them toward the new conception of collective reason and the scientific evolution of human society. Devoted to exact knowledge and free thought, they were inflamed with a common disinterested ardor for goodness and truth. The friendship, begun on this high plane, was continued without decline or diminution till Renan's death. With the opening of new prospects through these conversations and with the confirmation of his historical views by every advance in his studies, it is little wonder that, after Renan had been one year away from Saint Sulpice, he could scarcely understand how he could ever have believed the orthodox theology.[11]

II

Much of Renan's spiritual life from June, 1845, to June, 1846, approximately is presented in a group of nine copy books of identical form, written in the same ink, and each provided with a Hebrew or Greek title. These titles betoken, as the contents also indicate, that the notes in question were begun as jottings of reflections provoked by his studies ("Harvest," "New Harvest"), and were continued as furnishing a basis for future literary work ("Useful for Many Things"), and as constituting a personal record of some of the battles fought out in his mind and heart ("Wrestlings," "Myself"). When the warfare was practically over, this journal of intellectual experiences simmers down again to a purely reflective tone ("My Life," "Thoughts," "The Cistern of Joseph," "Present for a Child"). In this last group it is not clear what meaning is to be assigned to the titles. In none of these pages, it may be observed, is there any mention of Berthelot, and the influence of talks with him is nowhere obvious. "Harvest," written before Renan left the seminary, is chiefly philological, the philosophical notes being few, and these few being largely attached to a single book, *La Philosophie morale* of the Abbé Louis E. Bautain (Paris, 1840). The main interest in the philological notes lies in their presentation of certain details of the process, a process of constant comparison, under which the idea of the Hebrew Bible as an inspired book crumbled to pieces in Renan's mind. Closely connected with

---

[11] Renan went to confession as late as March, 1846: see *Cahiers*, p. 351, n. 39. As note 50 speaks of a letter of March 22, the incident must be about that date. His breach with Cognat came in 1847, after a discussion in which he said to the young priest, "You don't believe Jesus is God. You have too much sense for that." *Correspondant*, January 23, 1883.

these Bible studies are a half-dozen entries dealing with primitive man, unconscious of himself and unaware of natural law. On the other hand, the metaphysical speculations center on the conception of substance as manifested in body and soul. Sometimes we catch the very motion of the thought, with its involuntary recoils. He writes:

Instinct sees God everywhere and law nowhere; observation sees law everywhere (hence its tone of mockery and pride) and God nowhere. True philosophy sees God everywhere, acting everywhere freely through laws, which are invariable because they are perfect.—Here is real providence, more beautiful, more true, less poetical perhaps than that of our fathers, but more rational and more worthy of God; I will say even more active and vast.— The ancients, busying God with man and certain great matters, eliminated him, in their gross conception at least, from little occurrences, which it seemed could happen very well without him. As for us, we put him everywhere. Of necessity he acts in the motion of an atom. Act! a word entirely relative.

Especially interesting is the final entry, for it contains in germ the essential idea of *The Future of Science:*

M. Bautain has luminous ideas about certain branches of research to be created in the sciences. . . . He gives an idea of a true new science to be created, a science of which I too have had an idea. It is a sort of general physics, a physiology of the world, dealing, not with the analysis of elements, but with their synthesis in the world, which would be in relation to physics and chemistry, as they now exist, what physiology is to anatomy.— This was the point of view of the ancients; it led them into fallacy, for one must not begin here; but we ought now to finish here. In a word, there are relations of the composite, as there are relations of the simple; chemistry studies the relations of the simple; physics the relations of the composite; but what I speak of would deal with the relations of composites of composites.[12]

The "New Harvest" is, in contrast, almost exclusively speculative, there being but two linguistic notes. The young thinker is much concerned with the universe, with substance,

---

[12] *Cahiers,* pp. 50, 51, n. 57.

force, monads, atoms; he meditates on psychological experiences and problems, and is still much occupied with Bautain and with the Scotch school; yet he finds a thousand facets to the world, a thousand points of view, a thousand operations of science, all equally true. (16.) The theory of the spontaneous and of progress from instinct to reflection begins to emerge. But what is most significant is the break after entry 42: "Five months' interval—Vacation. Departure from the seminary."

Just before this crisis come some notable entries, which manifest his agitation. He states his fundamental principle of the inward religious life to be that it is not a separate faculty, a pigeonhole apart, but a face of all things, of every duty, of every exertion, there being no sacred and profane objects, but merely sacred and profane outlooks. (35.) He longs to embrace everything from every point of view. "O God, give this to me, and I will suffer all. But not to be sure is the sad thing; and even if sure about oneself, can one be sure of what is outside?" (36.) Above all, his mission presents itself, though by no means in clear outline. It is, at any rate, seen to be a religious mission, and it is hostile to orthodoxy. "Such is their tone (the apologists), declamatory generalities; where analysis is required, a silly *a priori*, resolved not to yield to all the difficulties shown them. O Germany! who will transplant thee to France! Heavens, can I do what I want to do? I, so feeble, so poor, alone in the world, knowing no one? But Luther was as I am. Jesus sustain me!" (38, p. 97.) And again: "My God, my God, express my thought for me, or give it to me as well expressed as you give it strong and true!" (39, p. 98.)

When he resumes his jottings, however, he is purely intellectual again, and he congratulates himself. "It is a consolation to note that, in the midst of these cruel realities that torment me I have enough courage and faith in science to pursue so coolly my line of speculation." (43, p. 102.)

43

The third Notebook, "Useful for Many Things," is mostly concerned with the courses Renan was taking at the University and with his general reading, though he also deals with psychology, especially with dreams, and continues to meditate on substance. Particularly to be noticed is a further expression of some fundamental ideas, all of which are found in *The Future of Science*; certain reflections, for example, which are still not much developed: synthetic scientific beauty after analysis (33), the curious and the useful not scientific aims (42), the idea of law not proved by any one experiment, but a result of the spirit of all (45). The constantly repeated notion of the many faces of things appears again: Why do the learned quarrel? Because they speak different languages and hence though each tells the truth, they do not understand one another. (65, 69.) But the most persistent and characteristic tone in this group of notes is the preference expressed for primitive literature—impersonal, embodying the true life of the people, therefore holy—over the literature of artificial society and of the salon, which is treated with utter contempt. (1, 4, 31, 35, 36, 44, 46, 60.)

III

Quite different is the general trend of the fourth Notebook, which is called "Nephthali" or "Wrestlings," and which was begun March 7, 1846. Here we have indeed many entries of the same philosophical and literary character as those already mentioned, together with records of visits to professors and of university doctoral disputations; but what in general distinguishes these notes from those of the preceding copy books is the definite effort to construct a group of beliefs destined to fill the place of the discarded dogmas of Catholicism. This effort transpires in the motto from the book of Genesis, "I have fought the fights of God and have prevailed," a motto which Renan wishes to stand for his epitaph. (9.) All the important thoughts, even when not a part of his religious project, are either in origin or application personal. If he views action and reaction in the universe, his eye is fixed on his own functionings (7, 113); if he weighs the value of erudition, the determining factor is the use he himself can make of it (61). When he holds that everything must be sacred, he suggests "my heart, my mother, my books," and he insists on mysticism for his own part, in the sense that all belongs to God and to the ideal, but this mysticism must be positive and subject to the scientific method. (84.)

Christianity he rejects, but still loves; it is an old friend (53); logic carries him to a hard and sharp-cut antagonism, but a higher instinct holds him back; he calls himself Christian, he admits and explains Christianity. "I seek," he adds, "the true point of view." (29.) When he hears some of his professors utter stupid remarks about Christian superstition, he is seized with the desire to write a book showing definitely how Christianity should be regarded. "I would praise it, exalt it, cover it with kisses, but humanize it. Man or God, it is all one, even without pantheism. I shall react against all these men when the time comes." (50, p. 235.) A book is already forming in his mind and heart. "They will be surprised when they see me come forth armed from head to foot." (51.) God he cannot represent; all our notions are confounded, all our words froth (127), but negatively he finds psychological anthropomorphism as absurd as material anthropomorphism (120), and he devotes it to destruction. Providence and liberty, for example, are only human expressions, without meaning when applied to God. "All is law, nothing but law; a free hand, with the exception of man, has not been interposed in the world since its creation. . . . And yet, at bottom, the fact of providence is true. It is the words *providence, governing,* etc., that are

45

false. For the establisher of laws acts through his laws, and in this sense God does everything." (132.)

What we get here are but glimpses of the workings of Renan's mind and no consecutive view. There is, for instance, not one word of the animated discussions with Berthelot, so decisive for the development of both, although this was the epoch of their daily meetings. The Notebooks contain, indeed, what may be regarded as almost casual fragments of thought, yet they yield evidence that Renan was reflecting more or less methodically on the articles of his creed. After God, immortality. "I have just considered immortality at a moment when, vividly penetrated with lofty thoughts and with the suprasensible aim of man, I perceived that all this had no meaning without immortality. That is my proof." (142.)

His central problem is already fixed. "The secret of organic life, the passage from the raw material to the vital is that which has always most preoccupied me. For me the problem of science is there. I cannot believe that the organic is nothing but a physical and mechanical arrangement. Life is there. This is my fixed idea; I love to lose myself in it." (67.)

Some other of the fundamental notions of *The Future of Science* are also first developed here. The doctrine that science should be useful stirs Renan's wrath. "It is the useful that I abhor. Blasphemy to submit science to anything useful. . . . How I detest those commonplace philosophers who assign a value to living, to activity, to commerce, that eighteenth century, for example, and its offshoots. Ah! I should prefer my monks and my ascetics, if they fully realized their type." (52.) "Every science has its full value only for the philosopher who does not make it a specialty, but who absorbs its results. . . . The truth is that there is a vital science, which is the whole of man, and that this science needs to be based upon all the individual sciences,

which are its members and are besides goodly in themselves." (101.) As all sciences melt into one, so all classi-
fications only serve to show the unity of nature. There are
no geometrical divisions. "The world is not divided into
pigeonholes with fixed boundary lines; it is a picture in
which all the colors vary in a hundred ways and by insensible gradations." (13.) Every separate species merges into
its neighbor, whether it be the case of languages, races, animals (13, 109), or men of genius (6), or parts of speech
(147).

It is interesting to observe this unfolding of Renan's ideas.
In all sacred books he discovers primitive syncretism. (19.)
In history he sees, not alternating epochs of stability and
transition, but a continuous progress, nothing but transition,
and though humanity lingers long on certain ideas as though
to hatch them, it is a bird of paradise that hatches while
flying. (36.) Even such little comparisons are preserved
in *The Future of Science.* For Renan was seeking not only
to stabilize his ideas, but to clothe them in adequate expression. "I have not succeeded in defining my thought,"
he remarks. "It has not the necessary sharpness; I see it
sketched like the point of a dagger under a veil, a statue
under a veil." (79.) At another time he has even less
success: "This old criticism takes hold of a work like—
an image that I cannot find." (105.) All this effort is leading toward his characteristic style. "There is a certain point
of thought impossible to render in words, at least in the
ordinary kind of speech. . . . When I reach these various
tones or points of thought, I get irritated. Then I seek the
vaguest words, tone, point, scheme, form, to render my
thought; for these words, having the least definite meaning,
are the least inexact, and are the least calculated to oppose
to my meaning a clear and definite contrary meaning." (122.)

The animating spirit is the spirit of youth, an enthusiasm
checked by sudden turns of reflection.

'Ah! why have I only one life! Why can I not embrace everything! When I think that for certain forms I must say: Never, Never! (117.) At this age how joyously and fully life is grasped; irretrievably, indeed, and without reflection. . . . I am all fire, hope, life and future. Life lies there before me and excites my appetite: a bird of prey enticed by the quarry. There is an emptiness that calls for repletion and seeks to swallow, to draw things to itself. I do not speak of the material. Ideal, God. Then when one is filled, I imagine one turns away. (171.) Dreams! but how many great things have not dreams led to, without speaking of the sweet moments they have produced. The ideal carries you away, you do not attain it, but you mount to the heights. If my dreams did nothing but make me forget M. Crouzet and his brats, that would still be much. (74.)

Once he is seized with horror lest he may be on the point of losing his lofty ideal in his effort to obtain a position, a pigeonhole in the world, but the horror itself reassures him, the life he contemplates appearing "hideous and dry as a dusty courtyard in summertime." (14.) On the other hand, he lectures himself on his idealistic exclusiveness: "Ernest, you fall perhaps into the fault of those who, being partial, deny that which they do not possess. Assuredly none is broader than I within the ideal; but what is outside I declare to be vanity. I almost scruple to use the word. Perhaps nothing is vanity." (123.) Might not a perspicacious applied psychology almost predict some of the works that forty years would ripen?

The contents of the copy book labeled "Myself," also written in March, 1846, [13] is in consonance with the title, for a large proportion of it is given to self-analysis. It furnishes admirable illustrations of the intimate interrelation in Renan's intellectual production of experience, emotion and reflection. "I have," he remarks, "an excessively reflective nature, and as soon as I have spontaneously experienced a sentiment or movement, I turn back upon myself to study

---

[13] See Note 50.

and debate it." (8.) A good example of this procedure is furnished by his remarks on affectation:

> I suffer horribly as soon as I find in myself anything affected, any tone assumed, above all when it relates to the good or the sublime. Oh! then everything looks suspicious to me, and as I had a thousand times rather die than renounce what is grand, I find myself in a cruel alternative. It is remarkable that I fear affectation in regard to the beautiful more than I ever do in regard to the good. I never reproach myself for deliberately moralizing as I should for deliberately and factitiously poetizing. As to truth, the thing would have no sense. I must decidedly take my stand on this matter, and willy-nilly go forward to the beautiful. What if I have really been affected for a moment? And indeed, what harm is there in it, understood in the sense I assign to it? This affectation is nothing but the considered and deliberate will to aim at something great and beautiful. The vulgar mock it, as they mock so many other things, and here again the laughers have the incredible advantage of being believed on their word. Frightful tyranny exercised by these people! They are all men without ideals, common, without elevation, infected with positive ideas and without poetry, and it is to such that the scepter is awarded to judge if such or such a thing is pure gold or not. Let them mock the naïve efforts a soul makes to rise. They are not capable of such an effort, and their laugh proves nothing. Arm thyself against this laugh, for thou canst be sure they will laugh much at thee. (23.) [14] In spite of myself I am always on my guard for fear of exposing myself on some side to ridicule. . . . But what arms me against this is that I never feel myself less exposed to ridicule than when I mock myself or take my censorious critical tone. Being exposed to ridicule or not has then nothing to do with intrinsic value. (60.)

Thus he arrives at a whole theory of mockery and the fear of being duped (17, 18), but the starting point is the inward experience, not the abstract proposition.

His antipathy to the practically useful—"foolishness and occupation for idiots" (38)—is also a matter of emotion and experience, reënforced by reflection. That science, for ex-

---

[14] See also 85.

ample, should be regarded as material for instruction springs
from this wretched view of utility. "Misery! science is an
end in itself. It may indeed lend itself to the college, and
dwarf itself to enter those doors, but this is a condescension
on its part." (77.) Here science seems to be largely, and
perhaps unconsciously, identified with Renan himself. "It
seems to me that teaching is death to science, and whoever
gives himself fully to teaching kills himself for science. It
is a poor *caput mortuum.*—I mock teaching, though apparently proceeding in that direction. For me it is only a
breadwinner for a few years." (27 bis.) When writing this
passage, he had in view a particular institution, the college
attended by his own pupils. "I never saw anything more
silly, more pedantic, of a more exasperating insipidity than
those professors at the Collège Henri IV. . . . O God! how
I suffer! I pray thee to express my thought with the fire
and the bile that gnaw my soul in conceiving it, while unable to fling it forth!" (27.) Some of his university teachers, too, are unsatisfactory because their aim is merely to
form good professors; but he is not one of these products.
He will indeed be a professor for his bread, but he is willing
to take oath before a notary as to his contempt. It is not
textbooks that he meditates, but works dealing with religions,
man, morals, the direction and aim of life; and although he
sees that he can make no worldly fortune, it does not matter,
he will hold fast and the world will come to him. (93.)

This confidence in his powers, very frequent in these
notes, is perhaps nothing extraordinary in a young man,
but it is always of interest when justified by the sequel.
"What consoles me when I grow desperate of success, seeing
how greatly I differ from the intellectual world around me,
is that the world will not always remain the same. How
many times has it not changed in the past forty years! It
is certain that it will change quite as much in the forty years
to come. And perhaps I shall be one of those to bring about

a revolution. For this reason, do not change thyself by system, let thyself go and let the age come to thee, without going toward it.'' (84.)

Nothing could be more characteristic than his love for Jesus and the influence of this feeling on his moods. The mixture of emotionalism and reason is very curious.

I have just confessed and I am well content, though a little troubled. It seems that I am entirely out of my sphere. I have spoken very clearly to Jesus, in the host; for I cannot fancy, after having believed so long, that it is only ordinary bread. In this there is a very remarkable psychological fact: literally I cannot fancy it. But I have preferred to speak to the Jesus of the Gospel. O this time he has penetrated me, and I have seen in what an astonishing position I stand in relation to him. He is the only man before whom I bow. I have told him this and I think it must have pleased him. The truth is, for nothing in the world would I pay homage to the superiority of any man, whoever it might be, present or past, scarcely even of the future. But for him, O I do so heartily. I have said to him: Thou art my master in moral ideas, which is the capital matter; thou art a God in comparison with me. I have indeed an idea in addition to thine, that thou couldst not have and oughtest not to have had; it is *science,* which also has its rights; for after all, while the child is lovable and sublime, science ought nevertheless to be maintained. But Heavens! how thou surpassest me in the great vital science! O if I had only known thee! how I should have been thy disciple! Love me, I pray, yes, bend me, if thou wilt, I will do thy will to please thee. Dost thou wish me to make myself a little child, to renounce even science? I am content, but I cannot believe that thou demandest it of me. How I long to know if thou lovest me! for, after all, thou canst not be dead. What art thou? So much the better if thou art God; but then cause me to know it. Ah! if I could see thee, O God! I would willingly consent to pass the rest of my life without consolation. Make me believe concerning thee all that I must believe to please thee. Do what will make thee love me: tell me now, wilt thou be my friend? My God, why canst thou not answer? Thou wilt tell me at least what I must do to be thy friend. For thou art not disdainful, repulsing those who would share thy friendship. Thou findest me perhaps stiff and too much tainted with science. But what can I do? That is what we are like now, and I swear that I love thee for the sake of loving thee. I have even simplicity and purity in my spirit, science does not dry me up or deflower me; yes, truly, I believe our hearts are made for one another. Thou knowest well that when I hear the stupid men of our time, who know thee not, speak ill of thee, or speak not of thee at all, which is more ridiculous and more superficial, I shrug my shoulders. I have never blasphemed thee; appear to me once in my life and I will be content. At my death, at least. I hope that in the other life we shall be friends and reunited sensibly. Thou wilt then pardon me all, is it not so? But I must believe that henceforth thou lovest me. (39.)

At another time he has a dream in which he defends Jesus at his trial (89), a dream that for a whole day held him rapt, and also formed the basis for an argument in favor of immortality, [15] since he is sure that Jesus could not have been a mere aggregation of molecules that have since been dispersed [16] .(89 bis).

This vision is closely associated with remembrances and images of Tréguier, for Renan's feelings are so bound together that they do not come singly, but in groups. Home and family belong in the group with the religion of his early days.

My heart twinges at the recollections of my dear Brittany, above all in springtime. I dream of the little back roads, the banks of the Guindy, the road of Saint Yves, the chapel of the Five Wounds, the three pines on the hill, the poplar close by the spring, where mother snatched from me a book of philosophy.[17] Even the least

---

[15] See also 2. The *Essai psychologique sur Jésus-Christ,* though scholastic in tone and method, expresses much the same feeling. Written during the ordination retreat, May, 1845, it calls upon Jesus to reveal what he is by yes or no. ''I have been to the chapel,'' says Renan, ''to pray to Jesus, and He said nothing to me.'' *Revue de Paris,* 15 September, 1920, p. 260.

[16] See also letters to Liart and Cognat, *Souvenirs,* and to Henriette, April 11, 1845.

[17] See p. 318 and also *Souvenirs d'enfance et de jeunesse,* p. 313. The same incident appears in *Fragments intimes, Avenir,* and elsewhere.

attractive places are those that please me best. The dry and arid spots are colored by regret. And to say that it is forever, to say that the cruel opinion exists there which will keep me forever exiled. And yet I shall never be attached to any other region. Come, my soul, let us be attached to heaven. Think that it is for virtue and duty that thou hast sacrificed thy Brittany and thy mother. O God, was that what thou shouldst demand of me? Wilt thou not give it back? Jesus, thou oughtest to love me. (72.)

If he had possessed the mechanism of verse-making, he would have written a little poem advising the swallows that nest near his mother's window not to fly to Paris to lodge under the eaves or in the chimneys of the Tuileries (81), but verse-making is not his talent. "I have a certain reflective and psychological turn that always comes back on me and prevents me from being largely or easily poetical. It is only the lofty, firm and grand poetry of man in which I am in my ready element. Elsewhere my habitual (acquired) turn of mind is opposed to the wholly external ways of poetry." (82.)

He was born romantic, requiring soul, something bordering on the abyss (15), yet for him poetry needs a mingling of science and criticism (13); the literature of pleasure is an abomination (22); the Chatterton apes are utterly ridiculous (79). Once he is tempted to devote himself to natural history (73); at another time he conducts a metaphysical analysis so rigidly that it leads to the annihilation of thought (48); there appear to him to be two ways of judging—absolutely and eclectically—each of which he adopts in turn (103); eclecticism in a large sense is the formula of the good method, no absolute negation, no positive opinion (59); all are right and all are wrong (112); yet eclecticism dulls the point of every proposition and gives no result—better the round, firm manner that warms up and takes fire, yielding much error but also much truth (28)—in such entries we find Renan sounding for firm ground, and finding the bottom

53

all in flux, he has abandoned every rigid formula. Orthodoxy, a tortoise shell that cramps, had been at the same time
a protection; nevertheless, at whatever cost of pain, it must
be removed by criticism, so as to give free air to the living
tissues it had crushed. (37.)

This freer spirit it is not easy to harness in words. He
feels that his thought molts and cannot speak. (85.) He
has undertaken to express what is really inexpressible, the
inward image that accompanies every thought and sentiment.
"For what makes the ease or difficulty of any style is not
a subjective quality of the writer, but the objective quality
of what he tries to express; the attempt to express what in
the soul is mysterious, confused, obscure, that is what brings
difficulty and obscurity." (89.)   And this is not all; for the
finest part of himself, flaming into sentiments that surpass all
expression, is not contained in these pages; he does not even
try to write such things. (109.)

In spite of his antipathy to the practical, he consents to
consider politics, since it acts so strongly on things of the
mind and enters so largely into the progress of the world.
(38.) It is not yet, however, a topic of much importance to
him. His views, he realizes, have been influenced by the
profound European peace during the period of his education
(58) : liberty, therefore, seems natural enough, but unfavorable to original production (64) : he feels that absolute
power as a kind of ownership is horrible (44) : on the other
hand, constitutional ideas seem the application of the scientific inductive method in politics—the king as representative
of God being the *a priori* view, the king as the first functionary of the state being the experimental view (91) : socialism, he thinks, has revolutionary possibilities, since hollow
and superficial men have heretofore succeeded in starting
great movements in the world (63). All the while, the con-
tinent was seething with discontent. Assuredly Renan was
little sensible of the imminent eruption.

IV

The remaining Notebooks, published as *Nouveaux Cahiers,* represent very much the same type of experiences and reflections, excepting that the struggle is over, and we have here simply jottings to serve as a sort of commonplace book. The change of tone is manifested by the formula that begins so many entries: "It is a singular fact that," or its equivalent. "In this notebook," says Renan in "My Life" (VI), "I put only my most superficial results. My deeper and more solid, often more brilliant acquisitions, which have reached the state of *habitual,* I do not utter except when occasion demands." (24.) Yet one is constantly coming upon entries that reappear in the pages of *The Future of Science.* The idea of a philosophical treatise seems already to have occurred to him: "On the collection of matters that occupy philosophy—substance, God, soul, body—I have a series of ideas that I shall try to unite in a whole; for they truly make an organic whole and include everything. But so far as concerns the old scholastic concepts, I feel that I have gone beyond them once and for all." (2.) Particularly to be noted as reappearing in *The Future of Science,* are certain thoughts about humanity: It is not synchronous in all the parts of its development (3), it marches like an army with great men as scouts (7), each nation is one of its faculties (10), it develops like the individual, the psychology of its childhood being different from that of its maturity (30), it is attached to a stake and with each turn it unwinds the chain and enlarges its circle (51).

In "Thoughts" (VII) the subject of government becomes more prominent than in the previous books: His intellectual, moral and political system is well woven together, but he finds the function of government to be purely that of repressing disorder (1); men perform disagreeable tasks because they work in a mass (19) ; an opposition party, having gained its point, becomes conservative, and therefore the day after a revolution, a new revolution is beginning (21, marked *very good*) ; rulers have never governed on moral principles (30) ; an oppressive government that crushes and smothers progress is monstrous (31) ; so is one that regards the people as its possession (62) ; logic is of doubtful application in political matters (92) ; the sovereignty of the people is in politics analogous to the experimental method in the sciences (112). These ideas, together with others of a literary and philosophical character, are fixed acquisitions to be used in his book.

In "The Cistern of Joseph" (VIII) he concludes from the political outlook that there will be a terrible overturning and also a religious regeneration. (27.) Such predictions are, however, not to be considered unusual. On the whole, in spite of its motto, "I have found heart and fire for several lives," this collection seems to have no special feature. Yet for their interest in connection with Renan's feelings about his work, two passages may be quoted :

(*a*) Adieu individual glory! What a pity to see poor individuals struggling in this great chaos! Impossible to be heard, at least for any length of time. The whole begins to exist; adieu poor little members. It is sad, but who of us will in truth speak to the future? (42.)

(*b*) There is an original way of drawing inspiration from the books of one's literary predecessors. For after all, if the inspiration drawn from the beauty of nature does not destroy originality, why should not intellectual beauty also be an occasioning cause in the creation of the beautiful? But they must be only occasioning causes and not themes to copy or imitate or extract. You are lighted by contact with them; but do not steal their flames, a torch lit by a torch. (113.)

Assuredly it was in this spirit that Renan later treated German biblical scholarship.

Least important of all the ''Notebooks'' is the ''Present for a Child'' (IX). One entry, however, presents a favorite view, which has not been previously given in these selections:

Liberty might reproduce among us what religious enthusiasm has accomplished in past ages. Crusade of liberty. It will be seen, I am sure. These ideas are now the only powerful ones. If five hundred thousand heads exalted to this pitch should rise, imagine what would happen. It would be a religious movement. (30.)

V

The bits of self-analysis that Renan jotted down from time to time are of considerable interest: for example, his discomfort in a crowd that manifests signs of unrestraint (*Nouveaux Cahiers,* p. 133, n. 76), or his instinctive tendency toward conformity with what people think of him (*ibid.,* p. 182, n. 13; p. 189, n. 24). In what he says about his associations of ideas, we are introduced to a matter of prime importance. ''A result is not completely acquired by me until I have gone over the matter twice. It needs a sort of knot, a first end that escapes, and awaits a second to be tied to it.'' (*Ibid.,* p. 108, n. 40.) He never heard a music lesson at Crouzet's without renewing the sadness he felt on first entering that house (*ibid.,* p. 108, n. 42); a bell on a cart in the street calls up a picture of a Breton vehicle (*ibid.,* p. 123, n. 60); because there was an odor of ether in Pinauld's classroom at Issy, he smells ether when he opens the book on physics he had used there (*ibid.,* p. 193, n. 30); the scent of new wood from a box calls up his vacations in Brittany (*ibid.,* p. 196, n. 35). These particular cases are perhaps not extraordinary, but they are worth noting, for in studying Renan's writings, we find that one of the marked characteristics of his mind was the strength and permanence of its associations.

At first the attractions of his lost faith were not entirely overcome. "I admire *adoration,* but I can scarcely rise to it. . . . Here I am, erect in the temple, listening to sounds from every side. Ah! when shall I fall on my knees? It will not be when I wish it, but when I do it spontaneously." (*Cahiers,* p. 203, n. 144.) "How I wish I were a poor little nun, wholly simple and pure, praying, loving, not thinking. But I barb my life with a bitter and hard science or a terrible philosophy. How happy is Beatrix; to-day, holy Thursday, she is there in the church, devoutly kneeling by a pillar with her book. And I in the midst of my Hebrew accents, Gesenius, Buxtorf, Leibnitz. . . . My beautiful, pure and poetic life is all there, farewell forever! . . . I shall never forget the day when I sat there near the Chapel of the Five Wounds, at the foot of a tree and read De Bonald: mother, with her maternal instinct, took the book from my hands. The tone frightened her and she saw from the way I took it that it was turning my head. 'Read nice things,' she said." (*Ibid.,* p. 353, n. 40.) Renan even began to write a confession of faith for an opening lecture in some course he expected to give, but he does not get very far in his curious task, and terminates the fragment with the words, "The rest can wait." (*Ibid.,* p. 353, n. 40.) He realized that he had passed through the faith which is based upon last chances and the safest way, and that he had ended in unbelief. (*Nouveaux Cahiers,* p. 126, n. 67.) Yet even this conviction is disturbed by the old associations. "My poor friend, your idea is now to come back into Christianity bravely, strong-armed, lance in hand: perhaps you will return like a little girl." (*Ibid.,* p. 126, n. 67.) But there is also the other side: "Doubt is so excellent that I have just prayed God never to deliver me from it: for I should be less excellent, though happier." (*Ibid.,* p. 232, n. 96.) Doubt thus turned him to belief, and belief turned him to doubt.

Such revulsion from a dominant idea, which was one of the principal features of Renan's intellectual and moral character throughout life, is a marked trait in these Note-books. "Where shall I find a man that pleases me? These superficial men attract and then repel me. It is like electricity when the alder wood ball is saturated. Even my good Germans have the same effect on me. Well, I shall be alone, but I shall be what I am." (*Cahiers*, p. 238, n. 51.) Even within himself he finds these repulsions. "When I have remarked anything affected in myself, I react vigorously against it by a calm, cold, veracious, inward tone, to such an extent that what is really not affected, but might merely seem so, nauseates me." (*Ibid.*, p. 260, n. 76.) For a moment, pleasantry directed against erudition pleases him, but he immediately afterwards takes sides with the scholars. (*Ibid.*, p. 281, n. 111.) He admires the strict logic of Hobbes, yet revolts against it. (*Ibid.*, p. 294, n. 131.) This sort of revulsion he notes particularly in the case of personalities, both in life and in books; at first enthusiasm, love, the formation in his mind of an ideal type; then disappointment, faults and weaknesses becoming apparent, experience spoiling the too favorable picture. (*Nouveaux Cahiers*, p. 51, n. 50.) Much of Renan's surface inconsistency is explained by this trait.

Throughout these Notebooks there is frequent recurrence of agitation, even of irritability. Ennui he never feels—it is only for children and empty minds (*Cahiers*, p. 199, n. 12) —though he often suffers (*ibid.*, p. 410, n. 95). It even pains him terribly when a professor expresses an idea that he had himself developed and that seemed his own property. (*Ibid.*, p. 118, n. 2.) On every sort of occasion impatient and angry exclamations burst forth. "I have just undergone an unspeakably painful attack of impatience. I know nothing that makes me suffer more." (*Ibid.*, p. 227, n. 45.) Stupid or insincere ideas excite him quite as much as people or occurrences. His rage at the Czar is almost comical. "I would cuff him, spit in his face, have him scoffed at and

judged, condemned to death by the populace, drowned amidst
hootings." (*Nouveaux Cahiers*, p. 97, n. 27.) We cannot
understand Renan aright if we exclude this savagery. However much it might be tamed, it always seethed potentially
under the layers of calm and courtesy added by training,
reflection and years.

VI

Both his impatience and his proclivity to revulsion are
manifested in his feelings toward his professors at the Sorbonne and the Collège de France. For all, he has moments
of admiration, all stimulate his thought, but only one, Ozanam, is uniformly the subject of his approval, excepting
only his uncompromising orthodoxy. Renan never issues
from Ozanam's lectures without feeling "stronger, loftier,
more decided on great things, more courageous and joyous
for the conquest of life and of the future." (*Cahiers*, p. 256,
n. 71.) Villemain generally pleases him for his elevated
views and delicate criticism, but is sometimes felt to be too
pretentiously literary. The philosophers, particularly Garnier, he finds superficial in their treatment of religious questions. Ozanam, though dealing with literature, seems more
philosophical, and is certainly more to Renan's taste. "I
can imagine what that imbecile Garnier would say, if any
one spoke to him of Jesus Christ." (*Ibid.*, p. 304, n. 145.)
Yet almost always Garnier is treated with entire respect.
The erudite Le Clerc and Gerusez arouse admiration for their
vast learning, but something approaching contempt for
their narrowness and pedantry. Gerusez is found insipid;
Le Clerc is a rhetorician, one who knows simply for the sake
of knowing and of shining by his scholarship, exasperatingly
exclusive in his interests, miserable and petty. But Renan's
chief aversion is Saint-Marc Girardin. For him he has
hardly a good word. "He laughs, he pretends to be clever;
ah! the foolish progeny of men of the equivocal, who never

take life whole, because they are neither strong enough nor true enough." (*Ibid.*, p. 171, n. 58.) "That imbecile Saint-Marc Girardin, the most nauseating creature I know. . . . I rage against them all. Germany! Germany! Goethe, Herder, Kant." [18] (*Ibid.*, p. 310, n. 151.)

Germany was to Renan's imagination the antithesis, not only of the narrow theology of Saint Sulpice, but also and more particularly of the fashionable frivolity of the Parisian salon and the superficiality of French men of letters. It seemed superior in philosophy, moral ideas and scholarship. He speaks of "a secret instinct, a love without acquaintance that bears me toward Germany to see if I may there find my form." (*Ibid.*, p. 253, n. 66.) Outside of oriental scholarship, indeed, his acquaintance with German literature does not appear to have been extensive. "The important thing is not here and there to glean particular ideas, but to seize the *spirit* that implicitly includes all. I have read but a few lines of the Germans, and I know their theories as though I had read twenty volumes, for I put myself at their point of view. . . . A spirit, when made for you, is divined in a word, and the whole follows. For the Germans, whom I knew almost entirely from Mme. de Staël, I inferred all their theories. Any one who had heard me talk would have thought I had read fifty volumes of German criticism." [19] (*Nouveaux Cahiers*, p. 211, n. 59.) At any rate, he had read *Faust* and *Werther*; Kant and other philosophers apparently came to him through French commentators; what is more surprising is that all his references to Herder—"*my king of thought*, reigning

---

[18] Garnier and Le Clerc were later among Renan's most helpful friends (see Chapter V), but Saint-Marc Girardin was never sympathetic.

[19] One of Renan's primary notions is found in Mme. de Staël: "Where one rises to the infinite, a thousand explanations may be equally true, although different, since questions without limit have thousands of faces, one of which is sufficient to fill the duration of a lifetime." *De l'Allemagne*, Pt. III, Ch. V.

over all, judging all, and judged of none" (*Cahiers*, p. 243, n. 30)—are to the translation of the *Poetry of the Hebrews* by Mme. de Carlowitz.

Among the French writers who largely occupied his thoughts, the most important is perhaps Cousin, particularly in his course of 1818, which is very frequently cited.[20] Poetry is represented by Lamartine, Victor Hugo being scarcely mentioned. It is *Jocelyn* that looks like a new variety of masterpiece. The chief historians are Guizot and Michelet. In fact, Renan could not have had the leisure for any extensive commerce with contemporary literature. Especially worthy of remark are the references to Sainte-Beuve, whose *Portraits littéraires* seems to have been read with active attention.[21] Sometimes Renan is attracted, but he is just as often repelled. The critic, who in one matter presents a perfect bit of feeling, a delicate appreciation or a luminous reflection, becomes in another a type of that witty frivolity which makes one's flesh creep (*Cahiers*, p. 158), one of our fine critic-skeptics, with their mocking tone, affectation of superiority and pretension of a thousand delicacies and

---

[20] Renan knew Cousin's course of 1818 under the shades of Issy: "The impression on me was such that it could not be deeper; I knew his winged phrases by heart; I dreamed over them. I have a consciousness that several bits of the framework of my mind are thence derived, and this is why, without ever having been of Cousin's school, I have always had for him the most respectful and deferential sentiments. He has been not one of the fathers, but one of the exciters of my thought." *Feuilles détachées*, p. 299. A typical note is the following: "M. Cousin has one clearly defined characteristic, which completely represents him. It is that he grows enthusiastic over other great men and rises to their ideas. This explains in the first place all his philosophic travels, and it gives besides the key to his idea of eclecticism. Indeed, when one has thus successively admired all great men, one tends to find truth in them all, to embrace all, as one loves all; and is not this pure eclecticism? Moreover, he has philosophic erudition, and the learned man must seek to give value to all the objects of his studies. Every philosopher thus acquires some value. I myself have the same tendency." *Cahiers*, p. 264, n. 80. In the brief *Essai psychologique sur Jésus-Christ* Cousin is quoted half a dozen times.

[21] An early edition is found in the catalogue of Renan's library.

reserves (*ibid.*, p. 319). This irritation even leads to the bracketing of Sainte-Beuve with Saint-Marc Girardin.

There are pretentious men of letters, who always appear to have some reservation in their thought. You can never wholly accept what they say: nothing makes me more impatient. This petty worldly tone of the man who affects the clever is in the highest degree unphilosophical and without truth. M. Saint-Marc Girardin, M. Sainte-Beuve, for example. Always the attitude of only half giving out their soul, and from time to time the half avowal, which seems to say that their bottom is mud, pleasure, vanity, money, that the rest is mere shell, exhibited for the sake of imposing on the silly. (*Nouveaux Cahiers*, pp. 291, 292, Appendix.)

This dissatisfaction was the result of dwelling exclusively, one may say too exclusively, with the ideal: yet the tenacity with which Renan clung to his plan for an unworldly life, when seconded by his great ability, achieved the success that ultimately crowned his career. He was often lonesome in that Paris which was like a forest of walking trees, and wretched enough; "shoes with holes, every penny to be reckoned, frightful external life in that house with brats and an ogre." (*Cahiers*, p. 226, n. 44.) Nevertheless, he kept his aim fixed on the higher scholarship. The career offered by teaching in a lycée would be death to science; it could at best become a mere temporary breadwinner. "Ozanam, Fauriel, Damiron, etc., these are my types, to this I proceed." (*Ibid.*, p. 341, n. 27 bis.)

Awaiting whatever rewards the future might provide, he would be "pure, moral, and a good analyst." (*Ibid.*, p. 298, n. 132.) "Learned man, yes; college professor, pish!" (*Nouveaux Cahiers*, p. 115, n. 49.) "I see myself professor of oriental literatures in the Faculty of Letters, seated at the table surrounded by a semicircle of benches, discussing, criticizing, admiring." (*Cahiers*, p. 256, n. 71.) However much he might be attracted to other topics—and, as a matter of fact, he was attracted to every subject he essayed (*Cahiers,* p. 285, n. 117; *Nouveaux Cahiers,* p. 140, n. 85)— the aberration was but momentary, a mere velleity, and he always really held firmly to his work in linguistics and philosophy, with his eye on the Collège de France. "We had confidence in our energy and power of work," writes Berthelot concerning this period. Both young men regarded the promotion of science as more important to them than a worldly career and, with a determination to preserve their personal independence, they refused to enter any of the great schools, though these provided the ordinary line of advancement. They chose the wiser part: at the fixed hour of destiny, place and fame came to both.

CHAPTER III

The amount of work accomplished by Renan between 1845 and 1849 was stupendous. He pursued his studies at the University, the School of Oriental Languages and the Collège de France; he passed his examinations for the *licence* and for *agrégé*, he prepared the ground for his doctor's dissertations, he carried off two prizes for erudite linguistic memoirs, he contributed extensively to periodicals, both lay and learned, and he wrote *The Future of Science*.

I

No other scholar made such an impression on Renan as Burnouf,[1] under whom he studied Sanscrit and Indo-European grammar. In the solidity of his learning, in his devotion to thankless tasks, in his care for the minutest details, all animated by a broad and profound philosophy, this master seemed to the ardent pupil the ideal of a man of science in the field of philology. Under his inspiration, Renan immediately proceeded to apply the method of Bopp to his own specialty, the Semitic tongues. The result was a first sketch of his *Histoire générale et système comparé des langues sémitiques,* which he presented in 1847 to the Institut in competition for the Volney Prize, 1,200 francs awarded by the Academies for a work in the domain of comparative philology. This prize he won, and his brilliant success opened new prospects.

Meanwhile he had undergone the difficult examination for the *licence*. The whole summer of 1846 was passed in dreary

---

[1] See Dedication to *Avenir,* p. 4, and essay on Burnouf in *Questions contemporaines.*

isolation and under pressure of the unattractive labor of preparation for this test.[2] Master of Latin that he was, Renan found it irksome to distort his ideas by forcing them into the strict *Tullianism* that was required. "O what a heartbreaking work," he exclaims, "to strive thus to *dis-originalize* one's thought! You devilish grammarians, how I rage against you!"[3]

While the stupidity of such requirements annoyed him, his loneliness and the uncertainty of his situation often caused actual suffering. "Yes," he writes in his notebook, "to keep him from going mad, a thinker needs a mother, a sister, a friend, a modest sort of life, nice and simple and with few worries."[4] The charm of such family life he found again on visiting his mother in Brittany during the summer of 1847, though he now felt himself out of tune with the narrow mediocrity of the social environment at Saint-Malo.[5] The sister was still in distant Poland, and though the modest competence was not yet in sight, he still in almost every letter begs Henriette to come to Paris. He is sure, even if he cannot secure an official position, that, without touching their reserve fund, they can get along on what he can pick up from substitute teaching, private coaching lessons, and articles in periodicals. A five-franc piece went a long way with the Renans.[6] The needy young student had never exhausted, in fact had hardly touched, the 1,500 francs put at his disposal by Henriette when he left the Seminary. He regarded the sum as not for use, but for assuring tranquillity of mind. Indeed, Renan, poor as he was, never underwent such privations, as, for example, his compatriot, Jules Simon, who shivered in his

---

[2] Letter to Cognat, September 5, 1846, *Souvenirs*, Appendix.
[3] *Nouveaux Cahiers*, p. 15, n. 5, also p. 132, n. 74.
[4] *Ibid.*, p. 9, n. 2. See also letter to Cognat, September 5.
[5] Letter to Berthelot, August 28, 1847.
[6] See letters October 13 and November 6, 1843.

fireless garret while lecturing in place of Cousin for 1,000 francs a year. He was, however, lonely. His sister and Berthelot are the only ones to whom he can impart his confidences. With all others he assents, through long habit, to everything they say, reserving his true thought for his writings,[7] and even in his writings avoiding practical applications and keeping to theory.

A character sketch in the manner of La Bruyère, which he inserted, without much relevancy, in *The Future of Science*, is plainly intended to represent his conception of himself at this period (for "Hermann," we should of course, substitute "Ernest"):

Hermann has lived only with himself, his family and a few friends. With these he is frank, true, full of spirit; he touches the sky. In society he displays insufferable stupidity and is condemned to silence by the entire course of conversation, which does not allow him to get in a word. If he makes up his mind to try, the strange sound of his voice causes everybody to look up; it is incongruous. He cannot deal in small change; if he wants to repay, he takes from his pocket gold, not pennies. At the Academy or the Porch, he would have been thoroughly at home; he would have been one of the favorite disciples, he would have figured in a dialogue of Plato as Lysis or Charmides. If he had seen Dorothea, beautiful, brave and proud, by the fountain, he would have dared to say to her: Give me to drink. If, like Dante, he had seen Beatrice coming out of a church in Florence with her eyes on the ground, perhaps a ray of light would have been flung across his life, and perhaps the daughter of Falco Portinari would have smiled at his troubled state. Well, before a young lady, he feels and causes only embarrassment.—Your Hermann, you say, is a country lout, let him go back to his village.—Not at all. In the village he will find coarseness, ignorance, lack of appreciation of everything delicate and beautiful. Now, Hermann is polished and cultivated, more refined than even the men of the salon, but not with an artificial and factitious refinement. There is in him a world of sentiment that neither coarse stupidity nor frivolous skepticism could understand. He is a true and sincere man, taking

---

[7] To Henriette, July 30, 1848.

his nature seriously and adoring the inspirations of God in those of his own heart.[8]

In all his views, Renan's thought is personal, generalized from his own experience. "A thinker needs a mother, a sister, a friend"; the dictum results from his own longing for his mother and his sister. The friend he had near him, there in Paris, working with the same lofty purpose, albeit in a different field.

Berthelot, having left the Crouzet house on the completion of his studies at the *lycée*, was now living with his father by the Tour Saint-Jacques on the other side of the Seine. The intimacy of personal friendship was, however, in no way relaxed.

When he came to see me evenings at the rue de l'Abbé-de-l'Épée [says Renan] we talked for hours; then I would accompany him to the Tour Saint-Jacques; but, as usually the question was far from being exhausted when we reached his door, he would return with me to Saint-Jacques-du-Haut-Pas. Then I would go back with him, and this movement to and fro would be continued several times. Social and philosophical questions must have been difficult indeed if we did not solve them in our desperate effort. The crisis of 1848 stirred us deeply. No more than ourselves could this terrible year solve the problems that it set. But it showed the decrepitude of a multitude of things considered solid; for young and active minds, it was like the dissipation of a curtain of clouds that hid the horizon.[9]

The elder Berthelot, a physician of high standing and of multifarious beneficent activities, was a liberal in politics and a Gallican of the old school in religion. The religion of the two youths came to be "the worship of truth, and by truth is meant science,"[10] an idealism based on a

---

[8] *Avenir*, pp. 467, 468.

[9] *Souvenirs*, pp. 335, 336. The church of Saint-Jacques-du-Haut-Pas was at the corner of the street on which Renan lived. The distance is more than a mile.

[10] Speech at banquet in honor of Berthelot, November, 1885: *Discours et conférences*, p. 232.

realization of the reign of law, admitting no supernatural intervention and no plenary revelation. Their political ideas involved the acceptance of the Revolution—"our holy Revolution," Renan calls it [11]—as the starting point of a new era of emancipation, an era which was to be continued by the application of scientific methods to government and social reforms. Some notion of their discussions may be obtained from three letters that Renan wrote to Berthelot from Saint-Malo in 1847 and 1849, and the conclusions they reached are embodied in *The Future of Science*.[12]

This book, indeed, is the acknowledged product of both, though only one held the pen. It was in companionship that they began to think. "We owe too much to one another," writes Renan, "ever to be separated, at least in heart and thought; the more so, since the results we have reciprocally lent one another are so intertwined that no power could ever analyze this network and discern the property of each."[13] And thirty years later, in the dedication to Berthelot of his *Philosophical Dialogues,* Renan speaks of ideas that they had talked over more than a thousand times, till it had become as impossible to distinguish what belongs to one or to the other as to divide the members of a child between father and mother. Berthelot, too, says of *The Future of Science,* "This volume represents the first unripe product of the effervescence of our young heads; a mixture of current views of the philosophers and scholars of the epoch with our personal ideas, which though later developed, were at that time merely confused sketches."[14]

These confused sketches, which were later developed,

---

[11] Letter to Berthelot, August 27, 1847.
[12] The ideas in these letters and even many phrases are identical with passages in the book. The same is true of letters written to Henriette in 1848; *Revue de Paris,* April 15, 1896.
[13] Letter to Berthelot, August 28, 1847.
[14] Introduction to the Renan-Berthelot Correspondence.

represent, indeed, one side of Renan's intellectual activity, the side that he soon began, and never ceased, to exhibit to the wide public of general readers; but under the more obvious effervescence, there was a deep and persistent current of arduous specialized labor. For 1847, and again for 1848, for some reason postponing the award, the Academy of Inscriptions and Belles-Lettres proposed for its annual prize of 2,000 francs the subject, *"L'Histoire de l'étude de la langue grècque dans l'occident de l'Europe, depuis la fin du Ve siècle jusqu'à celle du XIVe."* [15] Renan presented his essay in May and on September 1 his work was crowned in a séance at which his favorite professor, Burnouf, presided. Simultaneously, and throughout the summer, he was preparing for the competitive examination for *agrégé* in philosophy, a test which was held in September and in which he ranked first, delivering a lecture on Providence, which caused some stir. [16] This success secured him the regular stipend of 500 francs a year and made him eligible to a professorship in a *lycée*.

Such an appointment he received in the little country town of Vendôme, but he begged for a leave of absence and enlisted in his favor the influence of the great Cousin. "Excuse the liberty I take in writing," he says, "when I have not the honor of being known to you. It is my duty at the opening of my career, to offer my homage to him to whom I owe my calling in philosophy, and whose writings have had such a profound influence on my thought." What he wants is Cousin's influence with the ministry of public instruction to secure a leave of absence in order that he may finish his theses in Paris, because the work would be im-

---

[15] Académie des Inscriptions, *Mémoires*, vol. xvi, pp. 153, 154.
[16] Caro, the prize pupil of the École Normale, stood second. The fourth was also a Breton. See article by Quellien, *Revue encyclopédique*, 1892. In this article the dates of Renan's residence at Crouzet's are given from November, 1845, to March, 1849.

possible in the provinces. "I hope to show in these two works," he adds, "how I proceed in making philology tributary to philosophy." [17] The situation appealed to Cousin and the request appears to have been granted; at any rate, Renan did not go to Vendôme. He supplied for some weeks the place of a friend, Bersot, in the Lycée of Versailles, where he lectured on æsthetics, changing the announced subject of the course in order to avoid religious controversy. For odd lessons from time to time he had already taken the place of Amédée Jacques and other Parisian professors.[18]

His studies were now especially directed to his dissertations for the doctorate. As early as 1846, he had already made researches toward a history of incredulity within Christianity,[19] the starting point of his work on Averroës, and in 1848 he speaks of a study he had undertaken on the history of Hellenism among the orientals, the subject of his Latin thesis, a dull and dry task by means of which he hopes to throw some light on the history of the human spirit.[20] During the summer of 1847, he found in the libraries of Brittany, especially at Avranches, most valuable manuscripts and incunabula, including Aristotle with the commentaires of Averroës, and here he composed several chapters of his book.[21] Both Le Clerc, dean of the Faculty of Letters at the University, and Cousin, all-powerful member of the Royal Council of Public Instruction, were interested in this investigation and eager to aid the young author.

---

[17] September 25, 1848, Barthélemy Saint-Hilaire, *Victor Cousin*, vol. iii, p. 456. As the letter was sent from Rue de l'Abbé-de-l'Epée, Renan was still at Crouzet's.

[18] See Letters to Berthelot, April 10 and 17, 1848.

[19] See letters to Cognat, September 5 and 11, 1846, *Souvenirs*, Appendix. In the letter to Cousin, just quoted, he speaks of having already given a year to the task.

[20] *Avenir*, p. 185.

[21] Letter to Berthelot, August 28, 1847, and *Feuilles détachées*, pp. 101, 102. "The library of Mont-Saint-Michel, now at Avranches." *Mélanges religieux et historiques*, p. 267.

II

Renan's mind was agitated, but his studies were not interrupted, by the revolution of 1848. On February 25, he crossed the barricades with Burnouf to go to the Collège de France, where they found the lecture room occupied by guards, who looked upon them with suspicion.[22] As all the college rooms continued to be used for clubs and soldiers, Burnouf held his classes thereafter at his home.[23] During the disturbances in June, Renan visited the barricades and saw the fighting in the streets. He was even for twenty-four hours in the hands of the insurgents. One evening, on going out to mail a letter, he was driven back by a fusillade. He also saw the horrors enacted in the Luxembourg gardens, where prisoners were shot in squads; and his sympathies went out to the poor wretches. "I am always for those who are massacred," he writes, "even when they are at fault."[24]

Both heart and mind had broadened since 1839, when on the occasion of the revolt of Blanqui and Barbès, the smug little seminarist had written to his mother:

You have doubtless heard of the troubles that have agitated Paris. Do not be disquieted about me; for I assure you that they do not disturb us. A truly remarkable fact is that we were all infinitely gayer that day than usual; we were doing composition Monday, when the riot had not been entirely quelled, and our excellent professor urged us to work well, saying that in these times of rioting we seemed to touch the earth only with the soles of the feet, and indeed it is certain that the mind is much freer than usual. Nevertheless, I feel horror on account of these troubles, for one shivers to think that each cannon shot you hear has

---

[22] Dedication of *Avenir*.
[23] Letter to Henriette, March 21, 1848. *Revue de Paris*, April 15, 1896.
[24] To Henriette, July 16, 1848.

brought death to many of our brothers who perhaps were not prepared for it (May 30, 1839).

This boyish effusion represents, not only immaturity, but medievalism of spirit. When Renan left the seminary years later, he was "old in thought, but as inexperienced, as ignorant of the world as it is possible to be." [25] In his conversations with Berthelot, he acquired more humane and larger views. In politics, he at first sided with the left, being repelled by the selfish narrowness of the bourgeoisie and the reactionary stubbornness of the clericals. Now socialism had sprung, as it were, out of the earth. He could not decidedly espouse either extreme. "If Cavaignac and Changarnier had been as critical as I," he writes a few months later, "they would not have saved us in June; for I avow, that since February, the question has not been posed clearly enough to my eyes for me to hazard myself on either side. For, I said, perhaps my brother is on that other side; perhaps I shall be killed by one who wants what I want." [26] The musket, moreover, was not his weapon; any street gamin could beat him in a shooting affray. In general, he favors the party of order, for the present form is better than chaos, but he sympathizes with the sufferers and hates the bloody excesses of military repression exercised upon the brutes that society itself has created. He perceives that the movement is premature, that socialism is a pure Utopia, true in principle but false in forms, that the real solution is to destroy the lower class by giving it moral education and sufficient material well-being. The bourgeoisie, he notes, is a spirit, not a caste, an obnoxious spirit because impervious to ideas. The ends of the revolutionists, on the other hand, are good, but the means are not yet found; these will spring at length from the force of things. When the Triumph

---

[25]-*Sœur Henriette*, p. 29.
[26] *Avenir*, p. 447.

is achieved, it will be that of neither party, but of humanity conquering a more advanced form. France, taking a new road, stumbling and ridiculed by others, who themselves never venture, but who nevertheless follow her lead, France, he hopes, will march first to the accomplishment of the divine destinies of humanity.[27] "If I should see humanity in tatters and France dying," he writes (June 26), "I should still say that the destinies of humanity are divine and that France will march in the van for their accomplishment." And again, to quiet Henriette's fears: "I am not a socialist; I am convinced that none of the theories advanced as capable of reforming society can triumph in their absolute form. Every new idea is obliged to take the shape of a system, a partial, narrow shape, which never comes to practical realization. Only when it has broken this first shell, and become a social dogma, can it become a universally recognized and applied truth" (July 1).

These experiences and reflections are all worked into the political parts of *The Future of Science*, which he composed in the autumn and winter of 1848-1849. At the same time, he was producing many articles, both learned and popular, which were published in various periodicals. To Henriette he writes (July 1, 1848) that he is contributing to the *Journal officiel de l'instruction publique*,[28] the *Revue philosophique*, the *Gazette de l'instruction publique*, and the *Journal Asiatique*, to which last he sends only anonymous notices. In this list one is surprised at first to find that he omits the most important of all, *La Liberté de Penser*, but this magazine is surely meant by *Revue philosophique*, its subtitle.

---

[27] See various letters to Henriette, *Revue de Paris*, April 15, 1896.
[28] Egger, professor of Greek, procured the publication of Renan's articles in this journal. His most important contribution was "Eclaircissements tirés des langues sémitiques sur quelques points de la prononciation grècque," reprinted by Franck from the issues of July 7, 18, 21 and 25, 1849. Vicaire, *Manuel*.

LA LIBERTÉ DE PENSER

Founded by Jules Simon, professor of philosophy at the Sorbonne, and by Amédée Jacques, *maître de conférences* at the École Normale, *La Liberté de Penser, revue philosophique et littéraire,* was a serious periodical of about one hundred pages a number, appearing on the fifteenth of each month. The original idea had been to make the *revue* technically philosophical, but, considering that philosophy had a political and social task to perform, it was decided that there should be included articles of a wider interest, comprising religious and philosophical polemics, philosophy proper, politics, history, literary criticism and book notices. While of no single philosophical school, the writers are in general accord on the spiritualist doctrines; they are, above all, defenders of the absolute rule of reason and hostile to everything opposed to liberty of thought. Standing for no political party, though sympathizing with the left, they have neither sought nor obtained partisan or official support. They are men of letters, who will treat contemporary disputes, as well as all other questions, from a philosophical standpoint, asking the authorities for neither money, nor advice, nor support.[29] Among the contributors, besides the editors, were Charles Baudelaire, Ernest Bersot, Adolphe Garnier, Carnot, Eugène Sue, Quinet, Michelet, Henri Martin, Ratisbonne, E. Deschanel, Isidore Geoffrey-Saint-Hilaire, Paul Janet and numerous other writers of note. Even Thiers contributed one article in denunciation of the Minister of Education, Falloux, leader in the clerical assault upon the University, against whom the review was particularly bitter. These young men were animated by ardent hopes, soon to be cruelly disappointed. Writing in the issue of May 15, 1848, Paul Janet says, ''Triumphant democracy, after so many disappointing illusions, cruel downfalls, useless victories, may aspire at last, not to the reign of a moment, a

---

[29] Program in the first number, December 15, 1847, signed by Amédée Jacques.

new surprise, a new terror to the world, but to a definitive reign, which it will establish without obstacle, by its moderation, its magnanimity, its beneficence." But the clouds were not long in gathering. In April, 1850, Jules Simon, who had written for each issue the political leading article on the national assembly, withdrew because of political disagreement, and Jacques proceeded alone. In the same year, Jacques himself was suspended from his university functions and prohibited from all teaching on account of an article on the religious instruction of children. The Coup d'État ended the publication, sending Jacques into permanent exile in South America and suppressing all freedom of speech.

It is obvious that Renan was in thorough sympathy with this group and with the tendencies of their *revue,* particularly in its attitude toward religion. The program might almost have been his own. To this magazine, during 1848-1849, he contributed seven signed articles, which may be considered his *début* in the world of letters. Five of these seemed to him of such importance that he afterwards reprinted them as worthy of permanent preservation in his works.

An essay, "On Clerical Liberalism," the first article of Renan to appear in *La Liberté de Penser,* was published on May 15, 1848, in the sixth issue of that periodical. Here he maintains that such liberalism is a sham and that it is contrary to the teachings of the Church. If the orthodox favor the Revolution of 1848, it is because they hate the Revolution of 1830, and see in the new movement a chance for the restoration of legitimacy. The Church has always taken its stand against the sovereignty of the people, against the participation of all in government. Its internal movement has been away from a primitive democracy to the oligarchy of the bishops and then to the absolutism of the Pope. As for tolerance, the Church is, from the necessities of its dogmatic teachings, an oppressor and a persecutor, demanding liberty only for itself and, when possessed of power, crushing all freedom of thought. Evidence is given from the Fathers, the councils, and from modern writers, as well as from the facts of history. Renan's attack is both learned and vigorous. Those who read the reprinted article in *Questions contemporaines* do not by any means get the full combative energy of the original. All the facts remain, all the thoughts, all the quotations, but the evidences of feeling have been carefully removed. Hardly more than a third of the sentences stand as they were originally printed. The others have been mostly toned down by omissions and verbal changes. Almost all the insulting expressions, particularly those implying bad faith, have been suppressed. Often the vigor is lost, but many alterations are improvements in style, tending toward definiteness in syntax and lucidity and exactness of statement. On the other hand, absolute assertions are frequently qualified and all the italics used for emphasis are deleted. A few of the changes, moreover, bring the ideas into harmony with Renan's later attitude toward democracy. The revised article is not a genuine example of the *verdeur* of his youth, however satisfactory it may be as a testimony to the excellence of his theology.[30]

All the other essays that he republished from *La Liberté de Penser* underwent a like revision. Only to a reader who has examined these pieces in their original form can the strenuous—one is almost tempted to say, the bumptious—young Renan be really known. This form is preserved, indeed, in *The Future of Science,* a guarantee of its authenticity, and a multitude of phrases in these essays are identical with phrases in that book. The style is vigorous, but crude; positive in manner, dogmatic in tone, unsparing

---

[30] *Questions contemporaines,* Preface, p. xix.

in unfavorable implications attached to opponents. In the rewriting, all this harshness and exaggeration are moderated, as in the case of the essay just discussed: irritating expressions are softened or omitted, personalities are dropped, absolute statements are qualified, some views are corrected, and the sentences throughout are recast for exactness and neatness of phrasing. No single feature is more striking than the substitution of substantives for pronouns where there might be the slightest danger of ambiguity. In general, juvenile inexperience has been replaced by mature skill. A close study of these alterations would indeed furnish a superb lesson in the art of composition.

As an example of Renan's adult urbanity, take the opening of his essay, "Les historiens critiques de Jésus," as it appears in his *Studies in Religious History:*

"It is said that Fra Angelico of Fiesole always knelt while he painted a head of the Virgin or Christ: it would be well if criticism did the same, not braving the brightness of certain figures before whom centuries have bowed, until it has adored them."

The same essay in *La Liberté de Penser* opened with these harsh words: "Criticism knows no respect; it judges gods and men. For it there is neither prestige nor mystery, it breaks all charms, tears aside all veils."

The eight years intervening between the two versions had changed, not only Renan's style, but his mental attitude also, and it seems strange that in the Preface to his *Studies,* he should speak of this essay as though it still retained its original character (pp. ii, iii). As a matter of fact, not a single paragraph remains intact, and transpositions, omissions and additions are so extensive as to go far beyond what can normally be called editing.

The essay appeared in two installments in *La Liberté de Penser* for March 15 and April 15, 1849, and differed from his other articles by being signed E. R., instead of Ernest

Renan. This discussion is a first step toward the *Origins of Christianity*, a work already projected. Its purpose is to present to the French public the methods and results of German biblical studies, the principal theme being an appreciation and criticism of Strauss. The points most insisted upon are the universal reign of law, the consequent rejection of the supernatural, and the testing of sacred texts by the same methods as are applied to other writings. While, on the one hand, the views of orthodoxy are dismissed as untenable, on the other hand, the aggressive and doctrinaire hostility of the eighteenth century is held to be equally far from the truth.

"It is, once for all, time," he says, "that criticism should get used to taking its proper subject matter wherever this may be found; not discriminating between the works of the human mind, when concerned with making inductions or bestowing admiration. It is time that reason should cease to criticize religions as foreign works, set up against it by a rival power, and that it should at last recognize itself in every product of humanity, without distinction or contradiction." [31]

It is interesting to observe that Renan already distinguishes between the creative age of German thought and the succeeding period, many tendencies of which he did not approve.

The great fault of the intellectual development of Germany is the abuse of reflection, that is to say, the conscious and deliberate application to spontaneous productions of laws recognized in former phases of thought. . . . This weakness, peculiar to the German genius, explains the singular progress of ideas in that country during the last quarter of a century, and the ways in which, after the lofty and ideal speculations of the great school, Germany is now going through its eighteenth century, hard, crabbed, negative, mocking, dominated by the instinct of the finite as in our French

---

[31] *Liberté de Penser*, vol. iii, p. 451. The passage is entirely rewritten in *Études*, p. 197.

epoch. For Germany, Voltaire has come after Herder, Kant, Fichte and Hegel. The writings of the young school are precise, blunt, realistic, materialistic, boldly and absolutely denying the beyond (das Jenseits), that is to say, the suprasensible, the religious in all its forms, declaring that it is an abuse to make man live in such a fantastic world. This is what has followed the most ideal literary development presented by the human spirit, and it has come, not by logical deduction or as a necessary consequence, but by deliberate contradiction and in virtue of the premeditated principle that, since the great school was idealistic, we intend to react toward realism.[32]

Previous to this contribution, there had appeared in the issues of September 15 and December 15, "De l'origine du langage,"[33] the purpose of the essay being to show that language was not formally created and then revealed to man in complete form (the theological view), and that it was not artificially manufactured according to a plan worked out by the reflective faculties (the eighteenth-century view), but that it resulted according to permanent psychological laws from the spontaneous exercise of the human powers amid conditions that specially stimulated creative linguistic activity. The methods of comparative philology are applied to the study of the *embryogeny* of the human mind, and while the actual steps in the beginnings of speech naturally remain an unexplored mystery, it is maintained, according to Renan's general theory of evolution, that the earliest language, like all products of primitive psychology, is characterized by syncretism, a confused grasp of the whole, and that its exuberance, variety and complexity were afterwards simplified and unified by analysis. When this essay was republished as a volume ten years later, some completely

---

[32] *Ibid.*, pp. 438, 439. Omitted from *Études*. This passage refutes the German allegation that all Renan's unfavorable views of Germany arose after 1870.

[33] There was a reprint selling for six francs: "De l'origine du langage" par M. Ernest Renan. Extrait de la *Liberté de Penser, revue philosophique*, Paris, au bureau de la Revue, 1848, in-8° 32pp. *Manuel de l'amateur de livres du xixe siècle*, par G. Vicaire, Paris, 1907,

new topics were introduced (Chapters X and XI), there were many omissions and a few additions in detail,[34] and the style was revised throughout, though perhaps not so extensively as in the preceding article.

Another essay, the only one of his signed contributions that he did not think fit or opportune to reprint,[35] was published in the issue of November 15, 1848. This is "Cosmos de M. de Humboldt," a review based on the same ideas of science and philosophy as are found in *The Future of Science*. Lying outside Renan's field, the article is of slight interest, and appears to have been written with effort. It nevertheless exhibits considerable learning and contains some excellent and uncommon remarks.

III

On July 15, 1849, was published "De l'activité intellectuelle en France en 1849," with an editorial footnote which reads: "These pages are extracted from a book which will appear in a few weeks with the title: *The Future of Science*." The article is not, however, a single chapter, but a series of selections taken here and there without regard to their original order from various parts of the book, and carefully rearranged so as to give consecutive sense. In this way is constructed a fervent essay in favor of the revolution and against conservative and self-interested timidity. The argument is entirely philosophical, the application of universal principles to questions of the day. Chaos is crea-

---

[34] One of these added sentences gives a new turn to Renan's view of miracles: "A miracle, far from being a proof of divine power, would be rather a confession of weakness, since by it the divinity would be correcting his first plan, thus showing its insufficiency." "*De l'origine du langage*," p. 239.

[35] Renan republished all of his early writings that he considered worth preserving. (See preface to *Nouvelles Études*, 1884.) The specimens collected in *Mélanges religieux et historiques* convince us that his judgment was correct.

tive. It is revolution, agitation, not regulated liberty, not repose, that furthers the things of the mind. What is needed is new ideas. Shameful hedonism may tremble, the amateur may lose his collections, the salon may be dispersed, but youth will not be suppressed; it *will* think for itself, despite its ancestors, and overturn the dogmas and the limits of the past. The aim of humanity is not happiness, but perfection; life is to be devoted not to enjoyment, but to the ideal. Culture, science, philosophy are to be conceived as religious. Thinkers, not politicians, are called upon to conduct the needed revolution, for instead of being political, it should be moral, and its result is to be the scientific organization of mankind.

This essay was republished, with the one ''On Clerical Liberalism,'' in *Questions contemporaines* (1868), when the reactionaries were again attempting to form a coalition to suppress liberty of thought. The changes made in it—omissions, verbal substitutions, punctuation—are almost insignificant, being far fewer than the corrections in any other of these pieces from *La Liberté de Penser,* with one exception.

This exception is his last contribution, an unsigned review, which appeared September 15, 1850.[36] The title is that of the book reviewed, ''Qu'est-ce que la religion dans la nouvelle philosophie allemande? Par Hermann Ewerbeck,'' a volume of translations chiefly from Feuerbach. In opposition to the school represented by this writer, which finds everything Christian ugly, atrocious or ridiculous, Renan asserts the beauty of Christianity, not antique beauty, which was that of the finite, but a new manner of beauty,

---

[36] The article was promised on June 15 for the next number. It was to be a comparison of Ewerbeck's book with *Les mémoires d'un enfant d'ouvrier*. What finally appeared from Renan's pen was only half of what was promised. The other book was reviewed by Amédée Jacques. Later Ewerbeck's translations were the subject of three articles by Jacquemard.

a new mode of feeling, sprung from human nature at the appointed time and disclosing the longing for the infinite. With the exception of the introductory paragraph and the final page, which, though a quotation from the book, has nothing to do with the main topic, the whole essay is reprinted in *Studies in Religious History* under the title, "M. Feuerbach et la nouvelle école hégélienne." The omissions and corrections, while not very numerous, are of the same character as those already mentioned. Of special interest is the quotation of a considerable passage from *The Future of Science,* a quotation that is increased by a few sentences in the republished essay.[37]

This final contribution to *La Liberté de Penser* is somewhat out of harmony with the general tone of that periodical, now bitterly fighting the clerical reaction. Both in date and in spirit, the essay belongs to Renan's new epoch. Eighteen months in Italy had modified his outlook, and he was now permeated with the sentiment of Italian art. He even thinks pictorially. "The representation of the *Incoronata,* where Mary, placed between the Father and the Son, receives the crown from the hands of the former and receives the homage of the latter, are the true Trinity of Christian piety."[38]

Still more significant is the following passage:

M. Feuerbach should have been plunged into livelier springs than those of his exclusive and haughty Germanism. If, seated amid the ruins on Mount Palatine or Mount Cælius, he had heard the sound of the everlasting bells lengthen out and die on the deserted hills where Rome once stood, or if from the lonely shore of the Lido, he had heard the carillon of Saint Mark die away on the lagoons; if he had seen Assisi and its mystic marvels, its

---

[37] The passages are: *Que si vous pratiquez,* etc.; *Liberté* 341, *Études* 418, *Avenir* 474, 475; *Le mot Dieu,* etc.; *Liberté* 347, 348, *Études* 418-419, *Avenir* 475-476: *à ceux qui,* etc.; not in *Liberté, Études* 418, *Avenir* 476.

[38] *Liberté,* p. 344; *Études,* p. 411.

double basilica with the great legend of the second Christ of the Middle Ages traced on the walls of this holy of holies by the pencil of Cimabue and Giotto; if he had been cloyed with the long, sweet gaze of the virgins of Perugia or had seen in San Domenico at Siena the ecstasy of Saint Catherine, no, M. Feuerbach would not then cast opprobrium on one-half of human poetry and shriek as though he were exorcising the ghost of Judas Iscariot.

The rigid Breton enthusiast had obviously seen unfamiliar sights and breathed an unaccustomed atmosphere. His views had been enlarged and his manner of speech softened by the experience. Though not different, he was substantially modified. Before discussing this experience, however, it is necessary to give an account of *The Future of Science*, the epitome and consummation of Renan's epoch of origins.

CHAPTER IV

"THE FUTURE OF SCIENCE"

I

AT about the age of twenty-five young men of genius are apt to spread their wings in some characteristic work. Such works have a freshness and enthusiasm of inward experience, not yet troubled with much contact with the actual world. They have the fragrance of the springtime when originality is in blossom, unripe but promising. In 1848 Renan felt the impulse of this creative agitation, and he produced *The Future of Science* (*Hic nunc os ex ossibus meis et caro de carne mea,* is the motto), embodying the results of his religious struggles and of his meditations both on his studies and on the newly disclosed field of politics.

The year 1848 [he tells us in the preface] made upon me a most vivid impression. Till then I had never reflected upon the problems of socialism. These problems, springing as it were out of the earth and coming forth to frighten the world, took hold of my mind and became an integral part of my philosophy. Up to the month of May, I scarcely had the leisure to listen to sounds from without. A memoir on the *Study of Greek in the Middle Ages,* which I had begun in answer to a question of the Academy of Inscriptions and Belles-Lettres, absorbed all my thoughts. Then I passed my examination for the degree in Philosophy in September. Toward the month of October,[1] I was face to face with myself. I felt the need of reviewing the new faith that had replaced my ruined Catholicism.

---

[1] The writing must have occupied four or five months, for, though Renan says in his preface that it took ''the last two months of 1848 and the first four or five months of 1849,'' the dedication to Burnouf is dated March, 1849.

This new faith he called science, for "to know is to be initiated into God."⁵ (P. 17.)

What he has to say of politics is mostly recent, though it has its roots in his previous meditations: for his reflections on religion and on his studies he had recourse to his "Notebooks" of 1845-1846, which he reread on this occasion.² In no case, however, did he copy anything directly from these "Notebooks" into *The Future of Science;* his intellectual and emotional associations were vivid and permanent; his mind was permeated not only with the ideas he had wrested from the formless infinite, but even with the verbal expressions and the images into which he had molded these ideas. His repetitions furnish a most interesting subject of study.

The Future of Science, while frequently in form abstract and general, is, as a confession of faith, largely personal, yet it is personal in a sense far different from the manner of the "Notebooks." These represent experiences, soul-struggles, meditations, and efforts to reduce thought to language; *The Future of Science* presents the product of such struggles and efforts prepared for the public. "Thought," says Renan, "presents itself to me in a complex way; the clear form comes only after a labor analogous to that of the gardener, who cuts his tree, trims it and sets it up as a fence." (Preface, p. iv.) The cutting and trimming had been done in the "Notebooks"; the building of the fence—certainly a more formal procedure, even when the inclosure zigzags instead of running in a straight line—was the task of the volume.

A few illustrations will show how the author utilized the jottings he had made two years before. His isolated remarks are, as might have been expected, elaborated and fitted into the consecutive thought of some passage in the book.

---

²See the date 1848 to a note added to 89 *bis, Cahiers de jeunesse,* p. 406.

THE FUTURE OF SCIENCE

Singular revolutions that result from the apotheosis of the classics and the mania of rhetoricians, Molière, so hostile to the learned in *us*, etc.; becoming the delight of the erudite, etc. The same may be said of many ancients, Horace, Homer, for example. What would be their surprise to see themselves thus become *objects* of erudition.

Nouveaux Cahiers, p. 197, n. 37.

Criticism is often more serious than its object. A madrigal or a frivolous novel may be seriously commented upon; austere learned men have consecrated their lives to productions whose authors thought of nothing but amusement. All that comes from the past is serious; some day Béranger will be an object of science and will be exalted by the Academy of Inscriptions. Molière, so inclined to mock the learned in *us*, would he not be a bit surprised to see himself fallen into their hands?

Avenir de la Science, p. 215.

Why have we no longer in our modern society the type of the ancient philosopher, who did not write, but fulfilled a social function, Socrates, Stilphon, Antisthenes, Pyrrho, etc. . . . They talked and kept school, that is all.—It is because 1st, Christianity; 2nd, *books* kill *the school.*

Nouveaux Cahiers, p. 238, n. 105.

We have nothing analogous to the ancient *school.* Our schools are exclusively designed for children and hence devoted to semiridicule, like everything pedagogical; our club is wholly political, and yet man needs spiritual reunions. The ancient school was a gymnasium of the mind for every age. The sage, like Socrates, Stilphon, Antisthenes, Pyrrho, writing nothing, but speaking to disciples or habitués (Οι συνοντες), is now impossible. The philosophic conversation, such as Plato has preserved for us in his dialogues, the ancient *Symposia,* can no longer be conceived in our days. The Church and the press have killed the school.

Avenir, p. 466.

Sometimes the elaboration is not altogether happy.

He who would go by sea from Panama to Carthagena is nearer Carthagena at Cape Horn than at Panama, and yet he has turned his back under full sail on his destination. The same for humanity. For it, to retire is to advance.

Cahiers de jeunesse, p. 222, n. 37.

ERNEST RENAN

A ship sailing from the wild western coast of the United States to reach the eastern, civilized coast, would apparently be much nearer its destination at the point of departure than when it struggled with the tempests and snows of Cape Horn. And yet, looking at things aright, this ship is at Cape Horn nearer its destination than it was on the shores of the Oregon. The fatal circuit was inevitable. In the same way, the human spirit has been obliged to traverse deserts to arrive at the promised land.

Avenir, p. 306.

Notes suggested by his reading—and to Renan books were elements of experience quite as real as persons and incidents—appear in impersonal form.

The *Apologie pour tous les grands hommes qui ont été faussement soupçonnés de magie,* of Naudé (1625), was then a book of circumstance, of living controversy, even courageous. I imagine that, in a few centuries, the same will be said of a book written to-day to directly combat supernaturalism.[3] They will laugh at it from their point of view, they will find it idle to have taken the trouble to make a frontal attack with a direct purpose. They will think that the writer should have taken the contrary for granted, and not even have discussed it, at the same time that they note the fact as characteristic of the epoch. So things go; when a result is achieved, we no longer conceive how difficult it was to accomplish. Nothing seems simpler. It is the egg of Columbus. Cf. article on Naudé by M. Sainte-Beuve, *Portraits litt.,* I. p. 473.

Nouveaux Cahiers, p. 20, n. 13.

How many works there are which, though having no absolute value, have had in their time and in consequence of established

---

[3] In writing this entry Renan had in mind his own views about miracles. In *Nephthali,* note 11, he says: ''Cruel destiny that binds the thinker to the acquired results of his time, and forces him at his own risk to conquer more advanced views. Hereby the noblest intelligence often exhausts its powers to win a truth which will in a few centuries be in the domain of children. For example, if I should criticize Christianity, I should in five centuries be outside the circle, I should have no further value, for the problem will be solved in everyday opinion. But it is nevertheless honorable. The statue remains, when everything about it has been brushed away.'' *Cahiers de jeunesse,* p. 199. Five hundred years! The young man was truly ambitious for glory.

prejudices, a serious importance! The *Apologie* of Naudé *pour les grands hommes faussement soupçonnés de magie* does not teach us much and yet it might in its time have exercised a real influence. How many books of our century will be thus judged by the future! Writings designed to combat an error disappear with the error they have combated. When a result is achieved, we do not picture the trouble it has cost. It has needed a giant to conquer what becomes later the domain of a child.

Avenir, p. 216.

See in *Portraits littéraires* of M. Sainte-Beuve, vol. i, p. 407, some very luminous reflections on the Wertherians. One may be Wertherian in theory without being so in practice, and this too without any farce, for that would be too ridiculous. No, one can be this well enough without the pistol shot. It means having a penetrating mind capable of taking an interest in thought. Goethe, for example, do you believe he wanted to kill himself? No, indeed. I am a little the same; I cannot help admiring Werther, because by one of his sides he is a philosopher; but to imitate him, thanks; for life is full of color for me; I hold fast moral ideas and truth, even when I am skeptical; and then there is so much pleasure in describing it all that one ceases to suffer in describing his sufferings.

Cahiers de jeunesse, p. 372, n. 61.

Life, always life. This explains how science formed an essential part of the intellectual system of Goethe. To seek, discuss, inspect,—in one word, speculate, will always be most pleasant, whatever may be the reality. However much of a Werther one may be, there is so much pleasure in describing it all, that life becomes full of color again! Goethe, I am sure, was never tempted to shoot himself.

Avenir, p. 449.

It is not that I do not admire Télémaque, but what I admire in it is precisely the modern genius (for that too is admirable), but not the ancient form; for example, I admire the Christian spirit that dictates the Elysian fields, I admire the advanced political ideas of Fénelon. But I cannot admire this description or that comparison taken from Homer or Virgil. All I can say is to add coldly and without admiration: Here is a man who was gifted with a very delicate taste for the antique.

Cahiers, p. 356, n. 41.

ERNEST RENAN

What do we admire in *Télémaque?* Is it the perfect imitation of antique forms? Is it this description, that comparison borrowed from Homer or Virgil? No; this makes us say coldly and as though it were a matter of stating a fact: "This man has acquired a very delicate taste for the antique." What arouses our admiration and sympathy is precisely what is modern in this fine book; it is the Christian genius which has dictated to Fénelon the description of the Elysian fields; it is those political ideas, so moral and so rational, divined by miracle amidst a Saturnalia of absolute power.

Avenir, p. 191.

But what is of still greater interest, because profoundly characteristic of Renan's most typical thinking, is the actual experience, often a matter of vivid personal suffering, carried over into the calm region of philosophy as though it were a subject for purely abstract discussion.

The note, part of which follows, is concerned with the humiliations one has to suffer in one's earthly career. The first characters to be considered are the mediocre who realize their insignificance and bear every insult without a murmur. They are estimable. Then come the mediocre who think themselves distinguished and fire up at the first offense. These are ridiculous and blameworthy. Another group are the distinguished who are proud and would kill themselves rather than bend.

For example, they would die of hunger rather than accept a vulgar and apparently humiliating position that would give them bread, or serve to lead them ultimately to their aim. These are to be pitied, and they have not attained the *summum philosophicum.* Add that they are on the edge of the highest degree of the ridiculous. For if they are not geniuses as they think (and who can assure them of it, for how many others have so believed without being geniuses?) they are the most silly, the most ridiculous, the most insipid of fops, like all these types à la Chatterton, these *young people of genius* who find everything beneath them and fulminate against society because it has not awarded them a fit portion to permit them to give themselves up to their sublime thoughts (Heavens! what a horrible type and how it inspires me

90

with prodigious horror! Add to this that they are commonly lazy, glory in doing little work, and would be fed in order to smoke and do nothing, and find that good form. Ah! if they were serious workers, yes), and who would not for the world accept any vulgar, humiliating, hard, but not dishonorable employment that does not keep one from thinking, feeling, and developing one's genius.

Then there are true geniuses who are aware of it, esteem themselves and are *inwardly proud*. But outwardly they attach importance to nothing. If Providence has refused them the necessary fortune, they suffer, but bow without a word, do all that is demanded, suffer all that is demanded, insults, contempt, whims, without a word, but retaining all their inward dignity. They have made a complete sacrifice of what is not themselves. They despise the caprice of a master and the master himself too much to feel the weight. Exalted in themselves, they despise everything and would regard it as too great an honor paid to these vulgar creatures to consider themselves humiliated by their outrages. They mock the one they serve and thereby are superior to him: but they are careful to be silent and not to act like the superficial man who feels offended and is foolish enough to react against such miseries. Feeble soul, do you not see that you put yourself on a level with him in doing him the honor to react against him? We put ourselves on a level with him against whom we get irritated and to whom we attach importance. We do not feel the insult of the crazy man, because we know ourselves too far superior to him. Only those of the populace feel the insults of blackguards, because they are their equals. Surely a man of brains is less offended by the insult of a passing drayman than by that of a man of education.—Come now! pride of the sage, wholly inward. It is there that he rises superior to all, outside he is servant to everything and everybody, yet mocking them all. Thereby also he will direct his life well, he will reach his aim, a modest independence, and he will avoid the horrible type of Chatterton apes.

My friend Ernest, regulate thyself according to these principles. Despise these mediocre and positive men, who for money pass through every path, every depressing humiliation; for example, the one who found it ill that thou shouldst seek a place that left thee much time for thinking and work, who held himself up as a model, a man who, as he said, had accepted in his youth a place that left him only one free hour a day, which he found to be a great deal. Despise also those young hot-heads who think themselves geniuses because they wish to do nothing, and who look on thee with pity, thee, poor usher in a boarding school. I am sure that, at the sight of thee, if they happened to compare themselves to thee, they would make an eloquent protest. And if they knew M. Crouzet, what wouldn't they say? They would treat thee as low and debased to suffer all that *without a word*. And I, I think that I should be silly if I spoke. Well, well! The day will come when these Chattertons will be nothing, will be *immorally poor*, obliged in order to live to have recourse to immoral means, for not having been willing to do what is permissible, when above all they will amount to nothing in estimation and in science, and when thou, thou wilt be in the ideal regions. O God! O God! What consolations thou reservest for those who suffer for thee. Yes, it is for thee that I suffer. Ah! if I had wished, I should have been there at the Carmelites, petted, the first in all and everywhere, full of hope. Well, no! I am here on the lowest step of the social ladder, annoyed by a real tyrant, plaything of his caprices, never mind. It is for my conscience. *Dominus pars hereditatis meae et calicis mei; tu es qui restitues hereditatem meam mihi.*

Cahiers, pp. 385-389, n. 79.

Discussing the possibility of uniting manual labor and the intellectual life in *The Future of Science,* he continues:

There are men eminently endowed by nature, but little favored by fortune, who become proud and almost intractable, and would die rather than accept for a living anything that general opinion regards as an outward humiliation. Werther quits his ambassador because he finds silly and impertinent people in his salon; Chatterton commits suicide because the Lord Mayor has offered him a position as valet.[4] This extreme sensibility to externals shows a certain humility of soul and demonstrates the fact that those who feel it have not attained the lofty summits of philosophy. They are even on the edge of the highest degree of the ridiculous, for, if they are not really geniuses (and who can assure them of it! How many others have like them so believed without being geniuses?), they risk resembling the most silly, the most ridiculous, the most foppish of all men, those would-be Chattertons, those young people of unrecognized genius, who find everything beneath

---

[4] Renan's knowledge of Chatterton is, it is clear, wholly derived from de Vigny's drama.

them, and anathematize society, because it has not awarded a fit portion to those who devote themselves to sublime thoughts. Genius is not at all humiliated by manual work. Certainly it must not be required to give its whole soul to a trade, that it be absorbed in its office or workshop. But dreaming is not a profession, and it is an error to think that great authors would have thought much more if they had had nothing to do but think. Genius is patient and full of life, I might say almost robust and rustic. "The force of life is an essential part of genius." It is through the struggles of an external situation that great geniuses have been developed, and, if they had had no other profession but that of thinkers, perhaps they would not have been so great. Béranger was a clerk. The truly lofty man has all his pride within. To pay attention to the outward humiliations is to show that one still gives some consideration to things that are not of the soul. The brutish slave, who felt himself inferior to his master, bore stripes as a matter of fatality, without a dream of reacting in anger. The cultivated slave, who felt himself equal to his master, must have hated and cursed him, but the philosophic slave, who felt himself superior to his master, could not have felt himself in any way humiliated though serving him. To have been irritated against him would have been to put himself on his level; better despise him inwardly and be silent. To have haggled over matters of respect and submission would have been to take them seriously. We feel only the offenses of our equals; the insults of a black-guard touch his like, but do not reach us. Thus those whose inward excellence has made them susceptible, irritable, jealous for an outward dignity in proportion to their worth, have not yet passed beyond a certain level, nor understood the true royalty of men of mind.[5]

Avenir, pp. 401, 402.

From the previous examples it might seem that Renan worked over his notes with the systematic purpose of turning the personal into the impersonal, but this is not so. What he designed for publication is often quite as personal as

---

[5] In the thoughts on Werther cited above, Renan refers to a passage in an essay by Sainte-Beuve. The essay is the one on Charles Nodier and the remarks in question are in Sainte-Beuve's usual tone of complete detachment. In Chatterton and the Wertherians he simply views an interesting literary phenomenon. Renan, on the other hand, is giving the result of a bitter experience.

what he wrote for his own edification; it is only less intimate, better adapted to the eyes of strangers.

What is regarded as the real in knowledge is nothing but the puffed up. When you push on to the bottom, continually generalizing and abstracting, you reach really A=A, which is nothing. To seize the real, you must go up to a certain protrusion that covers this; here you believe yourself at the positive; then, if you go beyond, you fall into nothingness. What then is knowledge? This thought has often made me suffer, when I have seen it thus melt away. In mathematics too; such a thing seems positive, and, being pressed, all disappears; you reach A=A, which is horribly empty. This result has come to me a hundred times in a hundred different matters. Ah! That I could say the thing just as it seemed to me! Melting away, dissolution, the knot alone has value, untie it, nothing remains. This is explained perhaps by the ideas of Kant: That reason is only form, and that you will find only emptiness if you do not put in the positive element of fact.

Comparison that marvelously presents my thought; an equation that, at bottom, is identical, but which, in its actual form, contains a great complication of terms. The *seizable* is only there; push on, you reach A=A, which is nothing.

Cahiers, pp. 265, 266, n. 82.

If you place yourself at the point of view of substance and ask: This God, is he or is he not?—Heavens! I answer, it is he who is, and all the rest that seems to be. If the word *being* has any meaning, it is surely as applied to the ideal. What, you admit that matter is, because your eyes and your hands tell you so, and you doubt the divine being that your whole nature proclaims from the very beginning? And what is the meaning of the phrase: "Matter is?" What does it leave in the hands after rigorous analysis? I don't know, and to tell the truth, I think the question impertinent; for we must stop at simple notions. Beyond lies the gulf. Reason carries only to a certain medium region; above and below, it is confounded, like a sound that, by becoming too low or too high in pitch ceases to be a sound, or at least ceases to be perceived. I like, for my individual use, to compare objects of reasoning to those foamy or frothy objects, in which the substance is slight and which have being only through puffing up. If you too closely pursue the substantial ground, there remains nothing but fleshless unity; as mathematical formulas, pressed too far, all yield a fundamental identity, and mean something only on condition of not being too greatly simplified. Every intellectual act, like every equation, reduces at bottom to $A = A$. Now at this limit there is no longer any knowledge, there is no longer an intellectual act. Science begins only with details. For exercise of mind, surface is needed, the variable, the diverse, otherwise you are drowned in the infinite One. The One exists and is perceptible only through development in diversity, that is, in phenomena. Beyond is repose, is death. Knowledge is the infinite poured into a finite mold. The faces of unity are alone the object of science.

Avenir, pp. 476, 477.

Oh! read the letter of Fichte in which he describes to his friend his mode of life, his happiness in his poverty, etc.; his exuberance of joy, the absence of ennui, the taste he finds in life, etc. Oh! how well I understand this! It has touched my system of life. It is admirable. He is superior to me inasmuch as he has far less reflection about himself, more spontaneity, and goes straight to the truth; true stoic, true and without any mental reserve about personal matters.

Nouveaux Cahiers, pp. 20, 21, n. 14.

That Mary (contemplation) has the better part, is literally true of science. One of the noblest souls of modern times, Fichte, assures us that he had reached perfect happiness and that at times he tasted such joy as to make him almost afraid. Poor man! at the same time he was dying of poverty. How often in my poor room amid my books, have I tasted the fullness of happiness and defied the whole world to procure for any one purer joys than those I found in calm and disinterested thinking! How often dropping my pen and abandoning myself to the thousand sentiments whose intermingling produces an instant elevation of the whole being, I have said to heaven: Only give me life, I will take care of the rest!

Avenir, p. 450.

One calls himself a disciple of Plato, of Descartes, etc., without adoring them; why not a disciple of Jesus without adoring him, regarding him as the greatest of men, the moralist *par excellence,* and attaching oneself to him? In this way, every man ought to be a Christian.

Cahiers, p. 406, n. 90.

There have been made heretofore two categories of men from the point of view of religion: religious men, believing a positive dogma, and the irreligious, placing themselves outside all revealed belief. This is unbearable: henceforth one must class thus—religious men, taking life seriously and believing in the holiness of things; frivolous men, without faith, without seriousness, without moral ideas. All who adore something are brothers, or certainly less hostile than those who adore only self-interest and pleasure. It is indubitable that I more resemble a Catholic or a Buddhist than a skeptical mocker, and my proof of this is my inward sympathies. I love the one, I detest the other. I can even call myself a Christian, since I recognize that I owe to Christianity most of the elements of my faith, about as M. Cousin has a right to call himself a Platonist or a Cartesian without accepting the whole heritage of Plato and Descartes, and above all without being obliged to regard them as prophets.[6]

Avenir, pp. 482, 483.

Aristotle's remark that some men are naturally slaves, has an interesting development. The point came up in a university disputation for a doctorate;[7] later the quotation appears in some reflections on the rights of man and the French Revolution.[8] In *Avenir* its truth is denied (p. 339) in connection with a passage on democracy, with the moral

---

[6] References to a few further passages for comparison are subjoined. It need hardly be said that the list is merely casual and makes no pretense to exhaustiveness:

Cahiers,	p. 249,	n.	59	*Avenir,*	p.	269
"	" 260,	"	78	"	"	380
"	" 346,	"	34	"	"	463
"	" 17,	"	23	"	"	58
"	" 349,	"	37	"	"	60
"	" 291,	"	124	"	n.	169
"	" 356,	"	42	"	"	183
"	" 249,	"	59	"	p.	270
"	" 221,	"	36	"	"	376
"	" 370,	"	58	"	"	421
Nouveaux Cahiers	" 3,	"	1	"	n.	47
"	" " 303,			"	p.	380
"	" " 184,	"	15 bis	"	n.	14 and p. 221

[7] *Cahiers,* pp. 206, 207.
[8] *Ibid.,* p. 260.

that we must elevate the masses in order to avoid the new barbarism. The procedure illustrates one kind of action of Renan's mind: like a magnet, it seized from the environment whatever belonged to it, and held this fast till it was needed.

II

The Future of Science is a series of twenty-three essays, setting forth Renan's general ideas, together with a good many special applications. He seems to have tried to get in pretty much all of his philosophy as it stood at the date of composition. "Here will be found, without any diminution," he wrote forty years later, "the little conscientious Breton who, one day, fled in fear from Saint Sulpice, because he believed he had found that perhaps a part of what his masters had taught him was not wholly true." [9] As a result of the attempt at completeness, there is no exact sequence of thought, for though there is a general progress, this is by no means definite. The earlier chapters may be said to deal with the character of science and its tasks; these chapters are followed by a group devoted more particularly to his own science, philology, with his theory of human progress from syncretism through analysis to synthesis; then comes an application of his ideas to socialism; and finally there is a return to the idea of science as the new religion. Never is a chapter limited, however, to a single topic, for the views are so interrelated that they spring up together as luxuriously and inextricably as the vegetation of a tropical forest. Rarely does a chapter grow out of that immediately preceding it, and the order could often be interchanged without detriment. In fact, Renan himself seems to have been rather undecided about his arrangement, for he transferred long passages from one position to an-

---

[9] Preface, p. vi.

other, as is evidenced by the fact that, in several instances, the Table of Contents does not correspond with the text.[10]

This lack of definite order results from the incompatibility between the author's ideas and the processes of scholastic definition and division. In Renan's view distinctions are like lines of demarcation between tints that fade into one another at the edges and are fully perceptible as decidedly different colors only as you approach the center. Arrangement in pigeonholes would falsify the thought. Furthermore, he tries to express the whole, rather than to build it up out of the separate parts, from which indeed a whole can never be constructed. He looks therefore now on one face of this whole, now on another, each view being confessedly imperfect, yet all combined giving as nearly as possible his conception in the only manner in consonance with our faculties, a series of partial views. For these partial views there is obviously no absolute arrangement required. Which should precede, which follow, is largely a matter of convenience or of personal inclination, or of psychological accident, if there be such a thing. Apparent lack of rigor in general forms, combined with intense rigor in the analysis of details, is therefore characteristic of Renan's method from the very beginning.

The fundamental idea of *The Future of Science* is the substitution of science for the Church, of investigation for revelation, of criticism for dogma. It is a wider interpretation of Christian doctrines, a translation of Catholicism into terms of the modern spirit, a removal of shackles from the idea of God. A new faith, a new religion, this is what he had in view. "The more I advance," he writes to Ber-

---

[10] In Chapter XVII is found matter assigned by the Table of Contents to Chapters IV, XVI, and XVIII, matter assigned to Chapter XXII is found distributed in two places in Chapter XXIII, and there is further redistribution within chapters. These changes may, of course, have been made at the time of publication, but this hardly seems probable.

thelot, "the more I see dawn in the present the elements of a new religion." (August 28, 1847.) He even thought of writing the lives of the Saints of Science.[11]

The book opens with the distinction between the vulgar, the practical, the egotistical, on the one hand, and, on the other, the ideal, the religious, the divine, the infinite; this, the one thing needful, not limited by dogma or confined to morality, as in the customary narrow belief, but embracing and expressing the whole. (Chapter I.) To know is the least profane act of life. Humanity, moving toward perfection, impelled by a divine force, works spontaneously to construct both beliefs and such mechanisms as church and state, which are regarded as sacred, but this notion must be overthrown and the systems built by instinct must be reconstructed by reason, by science, which is to take the place of religion. Humanity is to be scientifically organized, and then reason must organize God. (Chapter II.) Science is of human value only as seeking what revelation pretends to teach. Supernaturalism is destroyed by modern criticism, not through logical or metaphysical argument, but from taking a new point of view. Scientific truth regards the whole, and is not fixed in formulas. If the intelligent seem weaker than the barbarians, progress is nevertheless a fact. There is no decadence in humanity, viewed in its entirety, and we must have faith in the future. (Chapter III.)

Indifference and speculation are enemies of science. Industrialism, too, may be an enemy, if taken as an end, but as a means it is useful to progress. The heroes of the disinterested life stand against materialism. (Chapter IV.) The inevitable progress of science destroys consoling beliefs, such as that in personal immortality, but the new temple will be more magnificent than the old. In the true religion schools will be the churches and philosophers the

---

[11] *Nouvelles Études d'histoire religieuse,* p. 29.

priests, for it demands universal culture. (Chapter V.)
Science, however, is not for mere instruction; it has a value
in itself, and must not lose itself in pedantry or pedagogy.
(Chapter VI.) Nor is the mere satisfaction of curiosity
the aim of science; erudition is useful as a means. We
adore God by knowing. (Chapter VII.) Philology is not
simply a form of erudition, though erudition is needed:
Philology is the science of humanity, of the human spirit,
not abstract, but based on patient critical study of facts,
requiring finesse rather than logic. (Chapter VIII.) A
critical philosophy into which all sciences shall enter will
study human origins and constitute the real science of humanity. (Chapter IX.) It will study embryogeny, the child
and the savage, primitive productivity and the laws of creation and progress. Philology is the only means of studying
race psychology, which is not a group of pigeonholes but a
becoming. We must realize the spirit of each age and cherish historical admiration, for, though great men play their
part, humanity is the great author, and a mere discussion
of literary faults is absurd. (Chapter X.) Philology is
not simply a means of culture, though we French must study
Latin for a comprehension of analytical and synthetic languages. (Chapter XI.) The minute investigations of philology are like those of natural science; in the future, works
of genius will be reduced to a few pages and literary history
will take the place of reading the originals. Happy the
classics, though the moderns are just as good. (Chapter
XII.) Specialization and monographs, valuable only in view
of later generalizations, are the task of the present. The
products are so vast that a scientific workshop is needed.
(Chapter XIII.) The state should patronize, but not control, science, giving it what was previously given to religion,
but the compensation must not be large enough to attract
self-seekers. (Chapter XIV.) Critical philosophy shows
two stages in humanity, primitive spontaneity and the age

of reflection, revealed by the detailed comparative study of languages and religions, a study in which all human works must be treated without distinction of sacred and profane. We find two sorts of religions, those with and those without sacred books. (Chapter XV.) There are three epochs in human progress toward perfection: Syncretism, a confused unity; Analysis, the distinction of parts, and Synthesis, a combination of these parts into a new unity, which is God. (Chapter XVI.) The new belief is satisfying, but is deficient in that it is for the few. We must open the eyes of all, for men must advance even if they suffer for it. Brutal force and revolutions will solve problems, thousands will perish, but at length paradise will be established here below. Society and the State must elevate and educate, not suppress, for all social evil springs from lack of culture. Universal suffrage and liberalism are dangerous for the ignorant. The only divine right is reason, not majorities. The ideal government would be a scientific government. At present we halt between two dogmatisms, but liberty is not needed for new ideas, which have always made their way in spite of persecution. (Chapter XVII.) The aim being the highest human culture,—that is, the most perfect religion,—society owes the individual the possibility of life. The Socialist solution is imperfect, for the aim of life is not well-being or pleasure, but perfection. Rights are not absolute, but become, and must be won at the sacrifice of some for the good of all. Absolute equality is impossible in any unity, and it is not the individual, but humanity that must become perfect: and humanity itself is but a part of a larger whole. (Chapter XVIII.) The destruction of modern civilization by barbarians is improbable; the modern spirit has come to stay: even Rome might conceivably have tamed the barbarians, who returned ultimately to Roman culture. We will civilize our barbarians by giving to all the intellectual life. While not now practicable, there may some day come a combination of high culture and manual labor, and all may be scholars. If this is a chimera, such hopes yet lead humanity on. (Chapter XIX.) The science for the masses must not be "popular science," which is not true science. The populace must be elevated, not science degraded. Plutocracy is an enemy of the ideal and wealth must come to be regarded as insignificant. (Chapter XX.) Revolutions are favorable to science, for chaos is productive, and crises give birth to both sublimities and follies. The aim is not repose, but perfection. (Chapter XXI.) The aim of this book is to present faith in reason and in human nature. Some mock us, others flee to the accepted beliefs. Mockery is good for nothing and, while the simple faith of the peasant is admirable, the conventional creed of gilded catholic youth is contemptible. There will come a century dogmatic through science, not narrow, but critically dogmatic. The critic is eclectic, sees truth in all human systems, embraces all. The real revolution will be, not political, but moral and religious, conducted by men of thought. Science must take hold. (Chapter XXII.) The heroes will be, not kings and generals, but philosophers. Thought has led even conquerors. There are two parts of life, the religious and the profane, but the religious is the whole, the grand unity of life, a necessity of our nature. The word God is still to be used, interpreted by each in his own way: it is the category of the ideal, the innate cause of adoration. Not the dogmatic, but those who take life seriously, are the religious; yet for the majority it is the established cult that represents the ideal. For the people, the temples; for us, science. We are looked upon as impious; it is a grief, but we cannot help it. And so, in conclusion, still adoring, Renan bids farewell to the God of his youth.

III

This brief abstract, giving imperfectly even the thread
of the argument, is entirely inadequate to render the impression one receives—and this impression is an essential
feature of Renan's thinking—that every idea advanced is a
part or a phase of every other idea. Whatever the topic
of any page may be, it is sure to be brought into relation
with a group of constantly recurring motives—the ideal,
science, humanity, progress, perfection, the unity of all
things, the infinite. The fundamental ideas of Renan flow
in and out of one another in such varied cross currents
that it is impossible to distinguish which is the source and
which the derivative. There are no fixed channels, no separating dikes, only a general movement away from restriction
into freedom. This freedom is limited only by the bounds
of human capacity, man being localized in space and time
and developed to a stage far short of perfection. With
these limitations Renan looks out upon the world about him
and perceives that, like himself, it is not fixed and stable,
but in a condition of *becoming*. The stars in their courses,
land and sea, plants and sentient creatures, man, in whom,
so far as we know, the universe first becomes conscious of
itself, are all moving forward toward some unknown, infinite perfection. This movement is the evolution of God,
and the contemplation of it, instinctive in the uncultured,
narrowed by dogma in the theological, free and elevated in
the devotees of divine philosophy, constitutes the ideal,
which is but another term for religion.

Renan's hatred of indifference and frivolity, as well as
of industrialism, springs from his devotion to ideas. His
aversion to the salon and the school is caused by the superficial artificiality of the one and the lifeless pedantry of
the other. Those who are not serious irritate him. To the

industrialist, he prefers the fanatic, because the fanatic is governed by an idea instead of by material interests. Extreme asceticism is often a subject of admiration, and even the sacrifice before the Juggernaut is defended as a moral force, though in excess. Yet, from another angle, asceticism is blamed as ascribing overmuch importance to the things of which we deprive ourselves. We should live the life of the spirit so energetically that gross and sensual temptations have no meaning. In themselves, external objects are indifferent. "Things have value only according to what humanity sees in them, the sentiments attached to them, the symbols drawn from them." (P. 190.)

No thought or feeling is more permanent and pervasive in Renan's philosophy and more firmly rooted in his character than his exaltation of the ideal and his aversion and contempt for the practical. This racial and inherited trait was reënforced, as we have seen, by his education; and here, as in other cases, he found arguments to justify his instincts. The ideal life is the life of ideas and sentiments, in contrast with the life of material satisfactions; it is the higher life, the disinterested life, as distinguished from the life of self-interest and pleasure; it is devotion to the divine, the infinite, in other words, to "God himself, touched, perceived, felt under his thousand forms, by the understanding of all that is true and the love of all that is beautiful." (P. 7.) Even the narrowest asceticism is preferable to blatant egotism, though the true idealist of to-day is the man of science who devotes himself, not to practical utility, but to enlightenment. For utility is the opposite of the ideal, and industrialism is the archfoe of the soul. Bread is indeed necessary, and a moderate supply of vulgar accessories may be helpful to the philosopher, but to seek riches is to substitute the means for the end. The aim of humanity is not repose, well-being, wealth or pleasure, but intellectual and moral perfection.

THE FUTURE OF SCIENCE

Heroes of the disinterested life! [he cries] Saints, apostles, mounis, hermits, cenobites, ascetics of all countries, sublime poets and philosophers, who wished no heritage here below; sages who went through life with the left eye fixed on earth and the right eye on heaven, and thee, above all, divine Spinoza, who remained poor and forgotten for the worship of thy thought and the unimpeded adoration of the infinite, how much better have you understood life than those who take it as a narrow calculation of self-interest, as an insignificant struggle of ambition or vanity! It would doubtless have been better not to have withdrawn your God so far, not to have placed him in those cloudy heights which required for the contemplation of him such a tenuous position. God is not only in heaven, he is near each of us; he is in the flower you tread upon, in the breeze that blows upon you, in the tiny life that buzzes and murmurs everywhere, above all, in your own heart. But how much more do I find in your sublime follies the suprasensible needs and instincts of humanity, than in those pale existences that the ray of the ideal has never traversed, who, from their first moment to their last, have unfolded day by day, exact and methodical, like the pages of a ledger! (Pp. 84, 85.)

These heroes of the disinterested life have one aspect of the true religion. It is not belief, but faith; not a collection of traditional doctrines and practices, but enthusiasm, devotion, sacrifice, lofty and divine emotion. Intellectual culture in the highest sense—art, science, literature, philosophy—is of the soul and therefore holy; but for those not yet capable of such culture, for the disinherited of the world bent under heavy daily toil, the Church, with its festivals, its saints, its gorgeous temples, its consoling liturgies, is still the essential medium of religious feeling. In these simple souls the divine is still in its instinctive stage, almost untouched by reflection. To a certain extent they correspond to the epoch of syncretism in the life of humanity, an epoch marked by a general confused view of the whole. The skeptics represent the second stage, which is confined to a distinct analytic view of the parts. The true philosopher will, with a sufficient knowledge of the parts, consciously construct a synthetic recomposition of the whole and thus attain a higher level of religious experience. For the critical thinker, the old faith, now become impossible, must be replaced by faith through science, a science that looks upon the whole universe and perceives under the diversified phenomena presented to the view a unity of substance, which is God. Science will thus tear down the fixed boundaries set up by dogma; it will look on every face of things and, for God, the soul, the moral life, it will have many varied and flexible formulas in place of the exact, and therefore false phrases which senselessly attempt to define and limit the infinite.

Science, then, is to take the place of religion, for "perfection is impossible without science" and "the way to adore God is to know and love what exists." (P. 126.) Science alone can furnish vital truths. "If it could be supposed that these truths could spring from anything but the patient study of things, the higher science would have no meaning; there would be erudition, curiosity of the amateur, but not science in the noble sense of the word." (P. 38.) Nor is such science utilitarian; nor is it metaphysics, or mere good sense: it is the result of a universal experiment with life.

When I question myself on the most important and most definitely acquired articles of my scientific symbol, I put in the first rank my ideas on the constitution and mode of government of the universe, on the essence of life, its development and the nature of its phenomena; on the substantial basis of things and its eternal delimitation in passing forms, on the appearance of humanity, the primitive facts of its history, the laws of its progress, its aim and its end; on the meaning and value of esthetic and moral elements, on the right of all beings to enlightenment and perfection, on the eternal beauty of human nature blooming toward all points of space and time in immortal poems (religions, art, temples, myths, virtues, science, philosophy, etc.); finally on the portion of the divine which is in everything, which constitutes the right to exist, and which, properly expressed, constitutes beauty. (P. 147.)

Having lost his belief in the teachings of revealed religion, Renan turned to the universe, and particularly to humanity, to seek a new religion by means of rational research.

The first effect of rational research is the removal of artificial limits and the enlargement of the horizon. The world of ideas becomes fluid, instead of standing as a resisting solid mass. The essential difference between the religious results of science and those of orthodoxy is that every conception, instead of being sharply outlined, spreads out into the vague and the undefined, and that every dogma, instead of professing itself the final expression of a complete truth, becomes an approximate statement of perceptions that are recognized as partial and subject to variation.

God, for example, is no anthropomorphic personality. To say he is spirit is meaningless, and to say he is wise and good is limiting the notion almost as much as to say he has hands or feet. As the soul is the individual *becoming,* so God is the universal *becoming.* (P. 181.) God exists in all things, or rather is the sum of all things, grows conscious in humanity, and is subject to evolution toward the perfect. It is the task of reason to take in hand the work hitherto accomplished by blind tendency and, after having scientifically organized humanity, to organize God. (P. 37.) The simplest act of intelligence involves the perception of God, for it involves the perception of being and of the infinite. This is innate. Though dulled by vulgar facts, the infinite is in all our faculties. Behind the visible, man finds the invisible, and the belief in something beyond the finite is universal. (P. 478.) Argument on the subject is futile. "If your faculties, resounding simultaneously, have never given out that great, unique tone that we call God, I have nothing more to say to you: You lack the essential and char-

107

acteristic element of our nature." (P. 475.) But why not call this vague idea by some other name?

The word God, being in possession of the respect of mankind, having a long right of prescription, and having been used in beautiful poetry, to suppress it would be to lead mankind astray. . . . God, providence, soul, so many good old words, a little heavy, but expressive and respectable, that science will explain but can never replace to advantage. What is God to mankind, if not the transcendant résumé of its suprasensible needs, the *category of the ideal,* that is to say, the form under which we conceive the ideal, as space and time are the categories, that is to say, the form under which we conceive bodies? All is reduced to this fact of human nature: Man in face of the divine comes out of himself, is suspended by a celestial charm, annihilates his miserable personality, is exalted, absorbed. What is this but adoration? (P. 476.)

Thus the anthropomorphic limits are removed from the idea of God; no less are they removed from the idea of Providence. To Renan the will of God is replaced by natural law, the world-machine by living forces. "The formation and preservation of the different planetary systems, the appearance of organized beings and of life, of man and of consciousness, the first facts of humanity, these are but the development of a collection of physical and psychological laws established once for all, and the superior agent who models his activity within these laws has never interposed his will with any special intention in the mechanism of things. (Pp. 169, 170.) Bossuet conceived history as the unrolling of a particular plan in which God assigned to this individual or to that nation a definite task to be accomplished toward the working out of the general purpose. The divine power constantly interfered to aid those who were carrying on the scheme and to confound their opponents. In Renan's view, on the contrary, history merely displayed a spontaneous tendency toward an ideal aim, toward perfection, a movement produced by an active, living force in things and without any external help. "Perfect autonomy, self-creation,—in a word, life—such is the law of humanity." (P. 173.)

When the supernatural is thus banished from history, it is banished from the lives of saints and prophets; Jesus, a son of God, if you choose, becomes a natural human phenomenon, and all sacred books are mere examples of primitive literature. Revelation must yield to investigation, arbitrary tenets to reality. Christian asceticism, admirable as it is in its high-mindedness, is pronounced narrow because it regards the good as consisting in obedience to imposed rules, and because it mutilates human nature by excluding the true and the beautiful. Exclusion is indeed the besetting sin of orthodoxy. "The first philosophical victory of my youth," says Renan, "was to proclaim from the depths of my consciousness: 'All that is of the soul is sacred.' " (P. 9.) Moral sentiments should replace the sacraments. The spirit is all; positive dogma insignificant. In contrast with theology, science has no creed, its principles being nothing but a way of looking at things. For those who have no science, indeed, the established cult continues to represent the ideal part in human affairs; but the mind aspiring to high reflective culture must free itself of Catholicism, a shell that the living creature has outgrown, but that still retains the contours of the vanished life.

The study of this shell, and of other similar shells, political, philosophical, literary, is valuable, not because it gives curious information about certain convolutions, which is mere erudition, but because it reveals the secrets of the life that wrought them, which is critical philosophy. The subject of such study is the science of humanity, and its chief instrument is philology, the exact science of the things of the spirit. "The true philologist should be at once linguist, historian, archæologist, artist and philosopher." (P. 130.) Erudition, to be sure, he must possess, not for its own sake, but as a prerequisite to the history of the human spirit. "The science of the human spirit ought above all to be the history of the human spirit, and this history is only possible through the patient philological study of the works that this spirit has produced in its different epochs" (Dedication, p. 5), for "History is the necessary form of the science of all that is in the state of *becoming*" (p. 174). As a result of modern critical scholarship, there is seen in humanity a self-developing consciousness from the spontaneous workings of instinct, through reason and reflection, to some still unperceived, but surely more perfect future. As represented in works of the mind, the primitive stage is that of syncretism, a general confused view of the whole, comprehensive, but obscure and inexact; this is followed by analysis, a distinct view of the parts, partial, exact, uncreative, negative, skeptical; and finally will appear synthesis, a recomposition of the whole with distinct knowledge of the parts, a restoration of unity by the combining force of intelligence. "All is noble in view of the great definitive science, in which poetry, religion, science, morals will again find their harmony in complete reflection. The primitive age was religious but not scientific; the intermediate age will have been irreligious but scientific; the last age will be at once religious and scientific. Then there will be a new Orpheus and a new Trismegistus, no longer to sing their ingenious dreams to an infant people, but to teach humanity grown wise the marvels of reality." (P. 308.)

The science that is to take the place of religion must be ideal and not practical science. But, though not practical in the ordinary sense, it must nevertheless be applied, as has hitherto been the case with religion, to the reorganization of society. It should therefore receive from the state the support previously granted to the church. There should be established lay chapters, lay benefices, lay monastic orders, for the maintenance of critical Benedictines, of scholars who have renounced the worldly life. Thus science, its pedagogical bane removed, would have its priests and saints, who would labor to advance knowledge and to make the present life, "the theater of that perfect life that Christianity places in the beyond." "There is nothing exaggerated in the spiritualism of the Gospel, nor in the exclusive preponderance it assigns to the higher life. But it is here below, and not in a fantastic heaven, that the life of the spirit is to be realized." (P. 81.) The future will say: "We hold God quit of his paradise since celestial life is brought here below." (P. 406.) The pagans of the new age will be the orthodox. The real skeptics are those who deny the modern spirit, and the atheists are the indifferent, the superficial and the frivolous.

Such are the main ideas underlying the various reflections embodied in *The Future of Science*, ideas which remained practically unchanged to the end. When Renan wrote the preface in 1890, his religion was still "the progress of reason, that is to say, of science": He still believed that nothing is created, but that everything becomes, according to a design that we see obscurely, an immense development, the first links of which are given by cosmological science, and the last by history. His chief youthful illusion had been an exaggerated optimism.

IV

The buoyant fervor, the unabashed self-assurance, the eager seriousness of *The Future of Science*, characterize the period of its production. To this youth nothing is more important than the search for truth. "Science and science alone can give to humanity that without which it cannot live, a symbol and a law." (P. 31.) "Science is thus a religion; science alone will henceforth construct the symbols; science alone can solve for man the eternal problems the solution of which his nature imperatively demands." (P. 108.) This science is no agreeable pastime, no ornament of the salon, no mummy for the museum. "Science becomes degraded the moment it lowers itself to please, to amuse, to interest, the moment it ceases to correspond directly, like poetry, music, religion, to a disinterested need of human nature." (P. 413.) The scholar amusing himself learnedly leads a vain existence. "To live is not to glide over an agreeable surface or play with the world for amusement; it is to accomplish many noble things, to be the traveling companion of the stars, to know, to hope, to love, to admire, to do good. That man has most lived who by mind, heart and act, has most adored." (P. 123.) Surely it is a very strenuous young man who is thus preaching to the world.

God grant that I may have brought some beautiful souls to understand that there is in the pure worship of the human faculties and the divine objects they reach a religion just as suave, just as rich in delights as the most venerable cults. I tasted in my childhood and in my early youth the purest joys of the believer, and I say from the bottom of my soul, these joys were as nothing compared with those I have felt in the pure contemplation of the beautiful and in the passionate search of the true. I wish for all my brothers who have remained orthodox a peace comparable to that in which I have lived since my struggle ended and the pacified tempest has left me in the midst of this great calm ocean, a sea without waves or shores, where the only lodestar is reason and the only compass is the heart. (P. 318.)

The lodestar is reason, not logic: for in the sciences of humanity logical argumentation is nothing, and finesse of mind everything.

In reasoning logically one may in the moral sciences reach absolutely false conclusions from sufficiently true premises. . . . When our logic leads to extreme consequences, have no fear: for facts delicately perceived are here the only criterion of truth. (P. 153.) Logic, understood as the analysis of reason, is but a

branch of psychology; looked upon as a collection of procedures
to conduct the mind to the discovery of truth, it is entirely useless,
since it is not possible to give recipes for finding truth. Delicate
culture and the multiple exercise of the mind are from this point
of view the only legitimate logic. (P. 155.)

Conceptions reached by such culture are freer and at bottom more exact in their vagueness than rigorous definitions
and precisely limited propositions. The supernatural, for
example, is not a question for argument; its negation results from the ensemble of modern science. "What converts is science, philology, the wide and comparative view
of things, in a word, the modern spirit. . . . The results of
criticism are not *proved*, they are perceived; they require
for understanding a long exercise and culture in finesse."
(P. 298.) It is not the function of philosophy to answer
particular questions. Instead of proving positive statements, it insinuates a spirit, inoculates a new sense. The
truths of criticism it is almost impossible to communicate.
In such matters, minds must be led to the same point of
view, so that they will see the same face of things. "I am
persuaded that, if minds cultivated by rational science
should question themselves, they would find that, without
formulating any proposition susceptible of being phrased,
they would have views on vital matters sufficiently fixed,
and that those views, diversely expressed by each, would
come to about the same thing." (P. 60.) Renan's rationalism is "the recognition of human nature, consecrated
in all its parts; it is the simultaneous and harmonious use
of all the faculties; it is the exclusion of all exclusion."
(P. 66.)

As this point of view is essential to an understanding of
Renan, an understanding in which many of his critics have
sadly failed, some further passages may be quoted:

We equally reject frivolous skepticism and scholastic dogmatism; we are critical dogmatists. We believe in truth, although

we do not pretend to possess absolute truth. We do not wish to shut humanity up forever in our formulas: but we are religious in so far as we are firmly attached to the belief of the present and are ready to suffer in view of the future. Enthusiasm and criticism are far from being mutually exclusive. We do not impose ourselves on the future, any more than we accept the heritage of the past without control. We aspire to that high philosophic impartiality that attaches itself exclusively to no party, not because it is indifferent, but because it sees in each a portion of truth alongside of a portion of error; an impartiality that has neither exclusion nor hate for any one, because it sees the necessity of all these various groupings and the right that each of them has, by virtue of the truth it possesses, to make its appearance in the world. (P. 445.)

"I see the sea, rocks, islands," says he who looks out of the northern windows. "I see the trees, fields, meadows," says he who looks to the south. It would be wrong for them to dispute; they are both right. (Note 30.)

When we find Renan in one passage maintaining that men of thought and not men of action are the motive force in revolutions, and in another passage proclaiming that thinkers are impotent and that the masses are moved only by one-sided partisans and narrow-minded fanatics, we feel that he has turned away from the north window to gaze toward the south. Often, indeed, a single view offends him by its lack of completeness. Spiritual extravagance is in fact the only excess against which he does not react with a sort of irritation, and such a reaction always impels him to look out of the opposite window. When, for example, he sees patient erudition piling up minute details by exact research, he is inclined to pay it honor and to pour contempt upon empty metaphysical speculations; but when erudition in its turn grows exclusive and becomes the sole aim of life, he turns to the ideal standpoint and overwhelms the spiritless pedant with vigorous reprobation. To curiosity he denies moral value, but he finds it useful as a means of progress. Dogmatism is the constant object of his assaults, yet he prefers the narrowest formulas of dogmatism to frivolity. In such cases, and in all his other contradictions, he is looking at the object from a different angle. If we would understand Renan, we must always put ourselves at the right window.

Renan thus gives us what he sees, sometimes looking in one direction, sometimes in another. Often enough he speaks dogmatically, but the reader should not be led astray by the inevitable limitations of language. Aware that the author is expressing only one phase of his topic, we should consider the general lines of thought, not the absolute formula. We are indeed specifically warned against such error: "I beg the reader's pardon for a multitude of partial and exaggerated views that he will not fail to discover in the preceding chapters, and I beg him to judge this book not by an isolated page, but by its general spirit. The spirit can be expressed only by sketching successively diverse points of view, each of which is true only in the ensemble. A page is necessarily false, for it says but one thing, and truth is only a compromise amid an infinity of things." (P. 433.)

It is the infinity of things, and this infinity in constant progressive motion, that constitutes reality. Of course the whole, or any vast amount of the whole, is beyond human capacity; but the more we free ourselves from mechanical limitations, the closer we approach to truth in its living freedom, as it actually is, and not distorted by compression into lifeless forms. The attainment of this view is the triumph of modern criticism. "The great progress made by modern reflection has been to substitute the category of *becoming* for the category of *being,* the conception of the relative for that of the absolute, movement for immobility." (P. 182.) The perception of reality in the universal and the unstable pervades Renan's thinking on every subject. Religion is a human need; while its forms are destined to disappear, they will be replaced by something else. Let us not be too definite. There is a religious way of taking things, understood by "those who once in their lives have breathed the air of the other world and tasted the ideal nectar." (P. 56.) "All who adore something are brothers." (P. 482.) In morals, rules are a poor substitute for the moral sense, for intimate spontaneity. In literature, "the only rule is to elevate your soul, to feel nobly and say what you feel" (n. 66): praise and blame are here evidences of a petty method and the idea *fault* should be banished from the critical vocabulary. In science, the separate sciences are less special subjects than different ways of looking at things. If analysis had no ulterior aim, it would be inferior to primitive syncretism, which seized life whole. All our mechanism is indeed a result of spontaneous action, but it has become petrified. In the primitive period the sacred book united religion, science, poetry, philosophy, history, law into something that was one and indivisible. Religion was indeed the whole of life. But time and analysis separated the expression of emotion from the study of fact, abstract speculation from political maxims, knowledge from worship. Each was assigned to its own fenced-off field, and the intuition of the infinite was fossilized in the forms of orthodoxy. It is the task of the modern spirit to break down the barriers and to reunite all in a harmonious culture. If the perfect man cannot be realized, he can at least be pictured.

The perfect man would be he who should be at once poet, philosopher, scholar, example of virtue; and this not at intervals and at separate moments (only a moderate approach indeed to perfection), but through an intimate compenetration at every moment of his life, being poet at the same time that he is philosopher, philosopher when he is scholar,—in a word, having all the elements of humanity united in a higher harmony, as in humanity itself. (P. 11.) Man's end is not simply to know, to feel, to imagine, but to be perfect, that is to say, to be a man in the widest acceptation of the word; it is to offer in an individual type an epitome of complete humanity, and to display united in a

powerful unity all the faces of the life that humanity has portrayed in various times and places. . . . The model of perfection
is given us by humanity itself; the most perfect life is that which
best represents humanity as a whole. (P. 12.) The lives of
men of genius almost always present the ravishing spectacle of
vast intellectual capacity joined with an elevated poetic sense
and a charming goodness of soul, so that their lives, in their calm
and suave placidity, are almost always their finest achievement,
and form an essential part of their complete works. In truth,
the words poetry, philosophy, art, science, designate not so much
the diverse objects of man's intellectual activity, as the different
ways of looking at the same object, which is being itself in all
its manifestations. (P. 15.)

It was its unity and reality, quite as much as its scientific
value, that attracted Renan to primitive literature. Here
he found all humanity in each of its acts. He saw in the
period of origins certain permanent laws of nature working
in special conditions; he felt the prodigious activity, the free
play of energy, creative freedom, caprice, exuberance, the
harmony between thought and sensation, man and nature,
the faculty of interpretation, an echo answering outside
voices, a vision perceiving a thousand things at once, in short,
a creative fecundity attaining by its inward tension an
unpremeditated result. "The child who learns its language,
humanity creating science, have no more difficulty than
the plant that sprouts or the organic body that reaches its
full development. Everywhere it is the hidden God, the
universal force, that, acting during sleep or in the absence
of the individual soul, produces these marvelous effects, as
far above human artifice as infinite power surpasses limited
forms." (P. 260.)

It might be thought that the succeeding epochs marked
a decadence, but decadence is seen only by narrow minds, restricted to a single point of view. Humanity's means for
attaining its ends are inexhaustible; when one decays, another
grows. If reflection has smothered spontaneous instinct, if

creative faculties become atrophied through inactivity, the power still remains latent in man, ready to be called forth when there is a void to be filled. The force that continues life is at bottom the same force that causes birth. Even if man should lose his language, he would create a new one. Humanity tends unceasingly, fatally, though with many oscillations, toward a more perfect condition, through forces that are successively and diversely imperfect. Nothing can interrupt the march. Ultimate triumph is assured. "Often humanity in its advance has found itself stopped like an army before an impassable precipice. The clever then lose their heads, human prudence is at bay. The wise want a withdrawal to go around the precipice. But the waves behind keep pushing; the first ranks fall into the gulf, and when their corpses have filled the abyss, the last comers pass evenly over them. Thank God! the abyss is traversed! A cross is planted at the place and tender hearts come there to weep." (P. 327.)

Brutal solutions are found for impossible problems. "The world creates only in primitive periods and under the reign of chaos." (P. 422.) Crises produce sublimities and follies.

Those solemn moments when human nature, exalted, pushed to the very limit, gives out the most extreme tones, are the moments of great revelations. (P. 424.) The new faith will be born only under frightful storms, and when the human spirit shall have been subdued, derailed, if I dare say so, by events till now unheard of. We have not suffered enough to see the kingdom of heaven. When several millions of men shall have died of hunger, when thousands shall have devoured one another, when the heads of others, led astray by these deadly scenes, shall be shot out of the ordinary paths, then shall we recommence to live. Suffering has been man's mistress and the revealer of great things. Order is an end, not a beginning. (P. 426.)

The orderly age in which Renan had received his education, that of the July Monarchy, was not at all to his taste. Born under Mercury, it was marked by timidity, moral feebleness, and vulgarity of outlook. The world seemed a regularly organized machine, producing enervated souls, whose ideal of life was repose. There was nothing militant or hardy in these peace-lovers. Politics was a matter of rival ambitions, personal combats and intrigues, agitation without principle. Who should be minister was the leading question. Absorbed in administration and banished from the high regions of thought, the politician played a humiliating rôle, in which ideas and convictions must be an invincible obstacle to success.

Such complaints about the unedifying spectacle of party struggles are common enough. Doubtless Renan was right, for history has pronounced a distinctly unfavorable judgment on the French Government of this period. But it is not his criticism of contemporary politics that interests us. When he deals with such matters practically and in detail, he is often confused, almost incoherent: It is his view of government from the higher viewpoint of humanity that is significant. He sees in the state a machine for progress; government represents reason, God, humanity; the question of governmental reform is not political, but moral and religious. Here we are in the full tide of the universal. The only sovereign by divine right is reason. "To govern for progress is to govern by divine right." Such might be the sanction of a new Napoleon. Who is to judge, we are not informed. Up to the present time, indeed, revolutions have afforded the only means of destroying condemned institutions. Happy the age when such irrational and absurd means become unnecessary.

Obviously such notions are fit only for criticism, not for any practical application to problems of the day; and Renan is already an effective critic. French liberalism he finds superficial, occupied exclusively with liberty, the means rather than the end. This liberty is profitable only to agitators, not to the true progress of the human spirit. Until the masses are elevated, to preach liberty is to preach destruction; the triumph of the people as they are would be worse than that of the Franks and Vandals; universal suffrage is legitimate only when all shall have intelligence enough to deserve the name of men. Stupidity has no right to govern the world. The majority has no right to impose its opinion, unless it represents reason and enlightenment. A triumphant insurrection is often a better criterion of right than a numerical majority, for the ballot of battle measures the energy an opinion lends to its partisans. On the other hand, a petty bourgeois system of government, guaranteeing the rights and well-being of each, has produced nothing great. Better the brilliant embodiment of a phase of humanity in the court of Louis XIV, or even the monstrous structures of Ninevah and Babylon, than sluggish mediocrity. The individual may properly be sacrificed that humanity may find expression, yet the disinherited excite sympathy. Socialism, in spite of its absurdities and perversities, corresponds to a perfectly legitimate tendency of the modern spirit. It is wrong in making well-being and enjoyment its aim, instead of intellectual advancement. The problem is to conserve the conquests of civilization, yet give all a share. All, indeed, shall be ennobled, but, failing this, the tradition of the beautiful should be maintained by an élite. The oft-repeated moral of the entire discussion is: Elevate the masses.

Renan's conception of the progress of humanity involved a diminution of the importance usually attached to nationality, although his feeling of patriotism and his love of his native province were very strong. He considered the aim of nature to be enlightened man, be he French, English or German. (Note 79.) "What difference by whom the work of civilization and the good of humanity is accomplished? In the eyes of God and of the future, Russians and French are only men." (P. 73.) "Each nation is a unity, a mode of looking at life, a tone in humanity, a faculty of the great soul." (P. 175.) To destroy a nation, then, would be to destroy an organ essential to the constitution of the general life. "The perfection of humanity will consist, not in the extinction, but in the harmony of nationalities." (P. 314.) France eminently represents the analytic, revolutionary, profane, irreligious period of humanity. Having fulfilled its rôle, it may some day disappear as an obstacle in the path of progress. "To each his task, such is the law of nature. France will have been the great revolutionary instrument; will it be equally powerful in rebuilding religion? The future will know. Whatever may happen, it will be enough for its glory to have sketched one facet of humanity." (P. 318.) That he could speak thus calmly of the extinction of France should not surprise us, for he could view with equal calm the extinction of our planet. Humanity itself might perish, but the great evolution would still proceed unchecked, and philosophers would watch the process without agitation. "If the world should tumble to pieces, it would still be good to philosophize, and I am sure that, if ever our planet should fall victim of a new cataclysm, at that awful moment there would still be some human souls who, amidst submersion and chaos, would entertain disinterested and scientific thoughts, and who, oblivious of imminent death, would discuss the phenomenon and seek to draw from it conclusions in regard to the general system of things." (P. 433.)

V

A collection of detached passages will perhaps help further to elucidate Renan's social and political views:

If your religion is only for a small number, if it excludes the poor and humble, it is not a true religion; moreover, it is barbarous and immoral, since it banishes from the kingdom of heaven those who are already disinherited from the joys of earth. (P. 319.)

We must labor to advance the happy day when all men will have a place in the sun of intelligence and will be called to the true light of the children of God. (P. 321.)

For myself, I do not understand perfect happiness unless all are perfect. I cannot imagine how the rich can enjoy their riches while obliged to veil their faces before the misery of a part of their kind. My sharpest pang is to think that not all can share my happiness. There will be no real happiness until all shall be equal, and there will be no equality till all shall be perfect. What pain for the savant and the thinker to see themselves by their excellence itself isolated from humanity, having a world apart, a belief apart. Are you surprised that they are sometimes sad and solitary? If they should possess the infinite, absolute truth, how they must suffer to possess it alone, and how they must regret the vulgar dreams that they enjoyed at least in common with all. (Pp. 323, 324.)

If it were true that humanity were so constituted that there was nothing to do for the general good, if it were true that politics consisted in smothering the cries of the unfortunate and folding one's arms over irremediable ills, nothing could induce beautiful souls to endure life. If the world were made like that, we should have to curse God and commit suicide. (P. 325.)

Woe to him who makes revolutions; happy he who inherits from them! . . . Happy above all those who, born in a better age, will no longer need to bring about the triumph of reason by the most irrational and absurd means! The moral point of view is too narrow to explain history. One must lift oneself to humanity, or, better still, surpass humanity, and lift oneself to the supreme being, where all is reason and everything is reconciled. (P. 330.) [12]

I have never understood a feeling of security in a land always menaced by floods, nor moral happiness in society that presupposes the degradation of a part of the human race. (P. 333.)

---

[12] "*Malheur à qui les fait, hereux qui les hérite,*" says Lamartine in *Jocelyn*. Many of Renan's ideas on poetry, religion and humanity are expressed in this poem, a work for which he expresses high admiration.

THE FUTURE OF SCIENCE

To maintain a portion of humanity in a state of brutality is immoral and dangerous; to put back on it the chains of religious belief, which moralized it sufficiently, is impossible. There remains then only one way; it is to enlarge the great family, to give every one his place at the banquet of enlightenment. (P. 334.)

A legitimate government is one founded on the reason of its age; an illegitimate government is one that uses force or corruption to maintain itself in spite of facts. (P. 348.)

The ideal of a government will be a scientific government, in which competent specialists will treat governmental questions as scientific questions, seeking their rational solution. (P. 350.)

In primitive societies, the college of priests governed in the name of God; in the societies of the future, savants will govern in the name of rational research for the best. (P. 350.)

The end of humanity, and consequently the aim that political thought ought to propose to itself, is to realize the highest possible human culture, that is to say, the most perfect religion, through science, philosophy, art, moral ideas, in a word, through all the ways of reaching the ideal which are in man's nature. (P. 364.)

In a word, society owes to man *the possibility of life,* of that life which man in his turn ought to sacrifice to society if there is need. (P. 365.)

The wise man is angry with no one, for he knows that human nature becomes wrathful only over partial truths. He knows that all parties are both right and wrong. (P. 374.)

When the socialists say: The aim of society is the happiness of all; when their adversaries say: The aim of society is the happiness of a few; both deceive themselves, but the former less than the latter. We ought to say: The aim of society is the greatest possible perfection of all, and material well-being has no value excepting as being in a certain measure the indispensable condition of intellectual perfection. (P. 378.)

A few further remarks of a general character are here added:

123

Perfection will be the aspiration for the ideal, in other words, religion, exercised no longer in the world of chimeras, but in the world of reality. (P. 85.)

I ask whether an action is beautiful or ugly, rather than whether it is good or bad; and I think I have a good criterion; for with the simple moral code of the respectable man one can still lead a wretched enough kind of life. (P. 177.)

The altar on which the patriarchs sacrificed to Jehovah, taken materially, was nothing but a heap of stones; taken in its human significance, as a symbol of the simplicity of ancient worship and of the rough, amorphous God of primitive humanity, that heap of stones was worth a temple of anthropomorphic Greece, and was surely a thousand times more beautiful than our gilded marble temples, built and admired by people who do not believe in God. (P. 189.)

Voltaire is not in his tragedies and *La Henriade,* but in *La Fête de Bellébat* and *La Pucelle,* infamous if you choose, but it is the century, it is the man. (P. 193.)

The most sublime works are those that humanity has made collectively and without any possible proper name attached to them. The most beautiful things are anonymous. What do I care for a name placed between me and humanity? The name itself is a lie; it is not he, it is the nation, it is humanity, working at a certain point of time and space, that is the real author. . . . True nobility is, not to have a name for oneself, a genius to oneself; it is to participate with the noble race of the sons of God, it is to be a soldier lost in the immense army that advances to the conquest of the perfect. Yet criticism must assign a large part to great men. They feel clearly what the mass feels vaguely; they give voice to mute instincts. "We were mute, O sublime poet, and you have given us a voice. We sought ourselves, and you have revealed us to ourselves." (Pp. 194-196.)

It is a law of things that the forms of humanity acquire a certain solidity, that all thought aspires to become stereotyped and set up as eternal. Such forms at last become an obstacle and must be burst. (P. 383.)

Gymnastics is considered by many a useful diversion from indoor work. Would it not be more useful and more agreeable to exercise for two or three hours the trade of carpentry or gardening, taking it seriously, that is, with real interest, than to fatigue oneself thus with insignificant and aimless movements. (Note 166.)

Affected abstinence proves that one makes much of the things he deprives himself of. . . . Antagonism of body and spirit must be destroyed, not by equalizing the terms, but by carrying one of them to infinity, so that the other becomes zero. That done, allow the body its pleasures, for to refuse them would be to suppose that these poor things have some value. The device of the Saint-Simonians: "Sanctify yourself through pleasure," is abominable; it is pure Gnosticism. That of Christianity: "Sanctify yourself in abstaining from pleasure," is still imperfect. We spiritualists say: "Sanctify yourself, and pleasure will become insignificant to you, you will never dream of pleasure." (P. 404.)

The perfect man would be in turn inflexible as a philosopher, weak as a woman, rude as a Breton peasant, naïve and sweet as a child. (P. 408.)

I can without pride believe that I have as much capacity as an agent or employee. Well! the agent, by serving material interests, can live honorably. And I, who direct myself to the soul, I the priest of the true religion, I truly do not know what it is that next year will provide me bread. (P. 416.)

The critic is he who accepts all affirmations and perceives the reason of everything. He goes through all systems, not like the skeptic to find them false, but to find them true in some respects. And for this reason the critic is little adapted to proselytism. For what is partial is strong; men grow passionate only for the incomplete, or, to speak better, passion, attaching them exclusively to one object, closes their eyes to all the rest. . . . The critic sees nuances too well to be energetic in action. Even when he joins a party, he knows that his adversaries are not altogether wrong. Now, in order to act with vigor, you must be a bit brutal, believe that you are absolutely right, and that those opposed to you are blind or wicked. (P. 447.)

A recollection comes to me that saddens me without making me blush. One day at the foot of the altar and under the hand

125

of the bishop, I said to the God of the Christians: *Dominus pars hereditatis meæ et calicis mei; tu es qui restitues hereditatem meam :nihi.* I was very young then, and yet I had already thought much. At each step I took toward the altar, doubt followed me; it was science, and child that I was, I called it the devil. Assailed by contrary thoughts, tottering at the age of twenty on the foundations of my life, a luminous thought arose in my soul and for a time reëstablished its calm and sweetness: Whoever thou art, I cried in my heart, O God of noble souls, I take thee for the portion of my lot. Hitherto I have called thee by the name of a man; because told to, I have believed him who said, I am the truth and the life. I shall be faithful to him in following truth wherever it may lead. I shall be a true Nazarite, since, renouncing the vanities and superfluities of the world, I shall love only beautiful things and shall propose no other object for my activities here below. To-day I do not repent my promise; I repeat again willingly, *Dominus pars hereditatis meæ,* and I love to think that I pronounced these words in a religious ceremony. The hair has grown again on my head, but I am still a member of the holy militia of the disinherited of the earth. I shall hold myself an apostate only on that day when self-interest usurps in my soul the place of holy things, the day when thinking of the Christ of the Gospels I shall no longer feel myself his friend, the day when I shall prostitute my life to lower things and when I shall become the companion of the joyous ones of earth.

Funes ceciderunt mihi in præclaris! My lot will always be with the disinherited; I shall be of the company of the poor in spirit. Might all those who still adore something be united by the object they adore! The age of little men and little things is past; the age of saints is come. The atheist is the frivolous many; the impious, the pagans, are the profane, the egotists, those who think nothing of the things of God; withered souls that affect cleverness and laugh at those who believe; base and earthly souls, destined to yellow with egotism and to die of nullity. How, O disciples of Christ, can you ally yourselves with such men? Would it not be better for us both to seat ourselves by the side of humanity sitting sad and silent by the dusty road, so that we might raise its eyes toward the sweet heavens it no longer looks to? For us the die is cast; and even if superstition and frivolity, henceforth inseparable auxiliaries, should succeed in benumbing human consciousness for a time, it will be said that in this nineteenth century, the century of fear, there were some men who, notwithstanding vulgar contempt, loved to be called men of the other world; men who believed in truth and had a passion for research, in the midst of a century that was frivolous because without faith and superstitious because it was frivolous.

I was formed by the Church, I owe her what I am, and this I shall never forget. The Church separated me from the profane, and I thank her. Whom God has touched will always be a creature apart; whatever he may do, he is out of place among men, he is marked by a sign. For him youths have no pleasing offerings and maidens no smiles. Since he has seen God, his tongue falters, he can no longer speak of earthly things. O God of my youth, I long hoped to return to thee with flags flying and in the pride of reason, and perhaps I shall return humble and conquered like a frail woman. Formerly thou didst listen to me; I hoped some day to see thy face; for I heard thee answer my voice. And I have seen thy temple fall, stone after stone, and in the sanctuary there remains no echo, and instead of an altar adorned with lights and flowers, I have seen raised before me an altar of brass, against which my prayers are broken, severe, bare, without images, without tabernacle, blood-stained by fatality. Is it my fault or thine? I would gladly beat my breast, if I might hope to hear that cherished voice that formerly made me tremble. But no, there is nothing but inflexible nature; when I seek thy fatherly eye, I find only the empty and bottomless orb of the infinite; when I seek thy celestial forehead, I stumble against a vault of brass that coldly casts back my love. Adieu, then, O God of my youth! Perhaps thou wilt be the God of my deathbed. Adieu; although thou hast deceived me, I love thee still. (These words form the conclusion of the book.)

VI

This is obviously the style of a very young man. Along with the enthusiasm, there is throughout something of the arrogance of the neophite in scholarship, who looks with superior contempt on occupations that do not coincide with his studies, and whose pet aversion is the business man. He can get along with a peasant, a workman, an old soldier, but a vulgar bourgeois he cannot talk to: "We are not of the same species," he affirms. (P. 467.) This is frank, and the whole book is frank, even naïve. The author is thinking aloud, quite without reserve. The dominant note, indeed, is personal, often autobiographical, though without egotism, because simple and sincere. The interest of many pages is largely increased by familiarity with Renan's correspondence, notebooks and *Recollections.* With him every completely acquired experience or idea is permanent, and is apt to pop up in the most unexpected places. When his main thought suggests subsidiary reflections, he allows his mind to pursue such a train, however far it may lead, through digression after digression, much in the manner of Hamlet. As in his later works, so here, his illustrations and analogies are most effective. When precision is appropriate, he is perfectly clear-cut and accurate, while aware that a precise outline of a vague object is as misleading as a vague outline of a precise object. Whether the ideas be of the one sort or the other, he propounds them with the utmost assurance. His aggressiveness is, in fact, a little surprising to those accustomed to his later suavity. The words *puerile, superficial, pedantic, little narrow minds,* and the like are not spared. Unqualified and trenchant expressions are the rule, exhibiting a vivacity of feeling that he afterward learned to control. There is eloquence, too; we find even the poetic apostrophe, a form he was always fond of and that he possibly borrowed from Herder. In style and in matter, Renan's life work is here presented like hard, unripe fruit that needs some days of sunlight to bring it to mellowness.

The future work that is most clearly in mind is the *Origins of Christianity.* In addition to numerous illustrations drawn from the history of the early church, there are two direct references to such a project.

(*a*) A history of the *Origins of Christianity,* based on the sources and written by a critic, will assuredly be a work of some philosophical importance; with what must this marvelous history which, if executed in a scientific and definitive manner, will revolutionize our thought, be constructed? With entirely insignificant books, such as the Book of Enoch, the Testament of the Twelve Patriarchs, the Testament of Solomon, and in general the Jewish and Christian Apocrypha, the Chaldaic paraphrases, the Mishna, the deutero-canonical books, etc. (Pp. 185, 186.) (*b*) The most important book of the nineteenth century will be a *Critical History of the Origins of Christianity.* Admirable work, which I envy whoever will realize it, and which will be the work of my mature age, if death and the many external fatalities that often lead lives out of their path, do not hinder me. (P. 279.)

Perhaps even more interesting in the light of character growth is the fact that Renan already has a predilection for Job and the Song of Songs, but he feels no attraction as yet for Ecclesiastes.

All that is fundamental in Renan is to be found in *The Future of Science,* his sympathies, his antipathies, his ideas, his hopes. If his hopes faded, his ideas remained at bottom but little altered. Superficially it might seem that we have here the prerevolutionary faith in human progress and perfectability, with copious additions from German philosophy and criticism, particularly from Hegel and Herder. These influences, that of Herder above all, and many others besides, are unquestionable, and are freely acknowledged; but a great writer is not a mere collection of scraps gathered from his predecessors. He is a strong and original personality that absorbs many external influences and fuses them into an individual and genuine unity. Such a pervasive unity manifests itself throughout Renan's writings, and in a crude form it makes its unmistakable appearance in this early work.

The public, however, was as yet unaware of its new prophet. A fragment of the work, as already stated, was given out in *La Liberté de Penser* in the issue for July 15, 1849, with the announcement that the volume would appear in a few weeks; but before a publisher was found, Renan started on his mission to Italy, and when he returned, his illusions of 1848 had fallen away as impossibilities. "I saw," he says in his preface (1890), "the fatal necessities of human society; I became resigned to a state of creation in which much evil serves as the condition of a little good, in which an imperceptible quantity of aroma is extracted from an enormous *caput mortuum* of spoiled matter. I became reconciled in some respects with reality, and, in taking up again, on my return, the book written a year before, I found it crude, dogmatic, one-sided and hard." The friends he consulted about publication gave an unfavorable verdict. Augustin Thierry in particular urged that the book would be a complete failure and a heavy load for him to carry. What Renan should do, in his judgment, was to give out his ideas in small doses in the form of articles on various topics contributed to the *Journal des Débats* and the *Revue des deux Mondes*. This advice Renan fortunately followed; he put his book away in a drawer of his desk, and from 1851 to 1859 he disseminated most of the essential substance of it in a series of miscellaneous essays and reviews. These are collected in two volumes, *Studies in Religious History* and *Critical and Moral Essays*, which, had he written nothing else, are alone sufficient to give his intellectual measure. *The Future of Science* in its original form was offered to the public only in the spring of 1890.

CHAPTER V

In August, 1849, Renan visited his family at Saint-Malo. In September, he was sent by the Ministry of Education, and under instructions from the Academy of Inscriptions and Belles-Lettres, on a mission in company with Charles Daremberg to investigate the libraries of Italy and report on their manuscript collections, particularly Syrian and Arabic. Starting early in October, he passed through the south of France and by sea to Rome. At the end of December he visited Naples, spent a fruitful week at Monte Cassino, and was back in Rome by January 26. February found him in Florence, with visits to Pisa and Siena. Then Daremberg returned to Paris, and Renan went back to Rome, where he remained till late in April. Altogether he spent almost five months in the sacred city. The government having granted an additional 500 francs, he journeyed by Perugia, Assisi, and Ravenna to Bologna (early in May) and so to Venice, whence he passed by Padua, Milan and Turin (May and June) back to Paris (about July 1). In September, Renan fetched Henriette from Berlin, and the two then lived together on the Val-de-Grâce, the mother at the same time going to live with Alain at Saint-Malo. At some time after his return, he paid a short visit to the British Museum for the purpose of studying the collection of Syrian Manuscripts, which he found essential for his Latin thesis, and of which he published a notice. In 1851, Renan received an appointment as *attaché* in the department of manuscripts at the Bibliothèque Nationale. In the same year he began writing for the *Revue des deux Mondes,* his first published article being "Mahomet et les origines de l'islamisme," December 15, 1851.

In 1852, Renan took his degree of Docteur-ès-lettres (August 11) and published his two theses, the Latin thesis—approved February 7—being *De philosophia peripatetica apud Syros,* and the French thesis being his first book, *Averroës and Averroism.* In July he was elected to the Council of the Société Asiatique, to the

Journal of which he now began to contribute signed articles. On June 13 he contributed an obituary notice of Burnouf to the *Moniteur universel.* His only article of this year in the *Revue des deux Mondes* was a brief note in the *Chronique* on Augustin Thierry. In this magazine also in 1853 he published but one article: "Les religions de l'antiquité et leurs derniers historiens." (*Études d'histoire religieuse.*) A most important step in advance, however, was the beginning of his connection with the *Journal des Débats,* for which he wrote, "Les Séances de Hariri" (*Essais de morale et de critique*), published June 8, and three shorter reviews, "L'Espagne Mussulmane," August 31; "Origine et formation de la langue française," October 22; and "Voyages d'Ibn-Batoutah," December 14 (all three republished in *Mélanges d'histoire et de voyages*). In pure scholarship he published in the *Journal Asiatique* (1853), "Fragments d'un livre gnostique intitulé Apocalypse d'Adam," which was reprinted as a pamphlet the following year. On June 13, he read before the *Société Asiatique* a portion of his *Grammaire comparée des langues sémitiques.*

I

IN the summer of 1849, while Renan was at Saint-Malo, Génin, Chief of the Division of Science and Letters in the Ministry of Public Instruction, proposed to the Academy of Inscriptions and Belles-Lettres that the young scholar and his friend Daremberg be sent on a mission to examine, describe and copy manuscripts in the libraries of Italy. The proposal was, in regular order, referred to a committee consisting of Le Clerc, who made the report on September 14, Quatremère, Hase, and Burnouf, all three of whom added observations regarding the task to be accomplished. Daremberg had already been on a similar mission in 1845 to investigate Greek manuscripts of medical works. This he was to continue; both were equally to concern themselves with documents valuable for the literary history of France, and Renan was especially to fix his attention on oriental manuscripts. The task laid down was of immense scope, and, in addition, a large field was left for individual initiative on the spot. After calling attention to certain works to be examined, Burnouf, who wrote the last part of the report, concludes by saying that, beyond these instructions which are incomplete because the authors have only vague information, "there is a superior order of instructions that a man like M. Renan finds in his intelligence and his curiosity."[1]

Renan, having other projects in mind, did not want to go. He had expressed his repugnance to Génin, who paid no attention to it. Now, in his embarrassment, he even hopes that the cholera, which had broken out in Italy, will scare his companion, Daremberg, and thus prevent the consummation of the plan. In a year or two he would like the trip, from which he foresees great advantages. "I have felt so far," he writes, "only in this humid and cold climate; I have seen only these indented and rugged coasts. I imagine that under that sky, which they say reveals so much, I should experience more complete sensations and that this would make an epoch in my esthetic and physical life."[2]

Fortunately nothing happened to prevent the Italian journey. Again, circumstances obliged Renan to do what was best for him. To say nothing of scholarly advantages, his experiences transformed him. His branching horns, as he says, that scraped every side, were worn down; his rigor was softened as by a sort of warm breeze; he felt the power of plastic form. The value of beauty in life he already knew as æsthetic theory; in Italy this value became experience, and the emotion was recognized as at bottom identical with religious aspiration. "The realm of art, until then almost closed to me, seemed radiant and consoling."[3]

---

[1] Académie des Inscriptions et Belles-Lettres, *Mémoires,* vol. xviii, p. 123. Renan's companion, Daremberg, afterward professor of the history of medicine in Paris, was both physician and philologist.
[2] To Berthelot, September 5, 1849.
[3] *Avenir,* preface, p. 11.

And first Provence.

I was twenty-five [he said in 1891 in his speech to the Fé-
libres] when for the first time I passed through the land that
I had till then known only from books. Heavens, what a revelation it was for me! I had never before seen mountains. The
morning I awoke amidst the mountains of Forez, that jagged
horizon filled me with astonishment. Lyons became thenceforth
one of the towns I loved best. I descended the Rhone in one
day from Lyons to Avignon. What enchantment! At four in the
morning, the cold mists of Perrache; at Vienne the beginnings of
day; at Valence, a new sky, the true threshold of the south; at
Avignon, a luminous evening, the 5th of October, 1849.[*]

Berthelot accompanied him and, after visiting Nîmes and
Arles, they parted at Narbonne, Renan going by sea to Civita
Vecchia, and thence to Rome. Here the mass of impressions that assailed him during his first days took from him
every faculty but that of feeling. The change was as prompt
as a stroke of lightning.

This city is an enchantress [he writes]; she puts one to sleep,
she exhausts; in these ruins there is an indefinable charm; in these
churches, met at every step, there is a quiet, a fascination almost
supernatural. Would you believe it, dear friend, I am entirely
changed, I am no longer French, I no longer criticize, I no longer
get indignant, I no longer hold opinions; all I can say about
anything is: It is so, things happen so. . . . You know that with
me religious impressions are very strong, and, as a consequence
of my education, they mingle in indefinable proportions with the
most mysterious instincts of our nature. These impressions have
been awakened here with an energy I cannot describe. I had
not understood what a popular religion really is, a religion accepted by the people naïvely and without criticism; I had not
understood a people incessantly creative in religion, taking the
dogmas of it in a living and true way. . . . I came here strangely
prejudiced against southern religion, I had ready-made phrases
about this sensual, despicable, subtle worship. . . . Well, the Ma-
donnas have conquered me; I have found in this people, in its

[*] *Feuilles détachées*, p. 114.

faith, in its civilization, an incomparable loftiness, poetry and ideality. . . . Our idealism is abstract, severe, without images; that of this people is plastic, turned to form, invincibly led to translation and expression. You cannot walk a quarter of an hour in Rome without being struck with the prodigious fecundity of images. Everywhere paintings, statues, churches, monasteries; nothing commonplace, nothing vulgar, the ideal penetrating everywhere. . . . If you enter a church, you find a painting of Raphael, Domenico, Albani, a Madonna of Pietro da Cortona, a statue of Michelangelo. Take, for example, that little convent yonder. . . . Everywhere monastic life, all the poetry of the middle ages revealed in grandiose images. In the interior of the monastery, at a corner of a corridor, you stop before a celestial countenance: a Madonna, the monk tells you, of Leonardo da Vinci. . . . He who should live in such a place, renouncing action, thought, criticism, opening his soul to the sweet impressions of things, would he not lead a noble life, and should he not be numbered among those who adore in spirit?[5]

After Rome, Naples.

I told you that Rome had led me to understand for the first time a religion which is paramount and monopolizes the spiritual life of a people. I can say that Naples has led me to understand for the first time the sovereign absurdity, the horrible bad taste of a religion degenerated and debased by a degraded people. You can never imagine, no, never, what the religion of Naples actually is; God is as unknown in this country as among the savages of Oceania, whose religion is reduced to faith in genii. For these people there is no God, there are only saints. And what are these saints? Not religious or moral models: but wonder-workers, species of supernatural magicians, by whose aid one can get out of trouble or be cured of illness. There are saints for robbers, and I have actually seen some *ex-voto* in which the robber is represented as delivered by the saint, at least from the police. I cannot express the disgust I felt the first time I entered a church at Naples. It is no longer art, no longer ideality. It is the grossest sensuality, instincts too vile to name. The religion of Naples may be defined as a curious variety of sexual perversion. You are psychologist enough to understand this by analogy; but you could never imagine the thing in such vivid features unless you

[5] To Berthelot, November 9, 1849.

had seen this indescribable city. Imagine a people deprived of moral sense, yet religious, since to humanity in its lower stages religion is more essential than morality, and picture what this can be. . . . The first, the dominant effect produced by Rome (and I think by Florence too) is artistic intoxication. One is possessed, dominated, filled, overflowed by the torrent of the plastic, of forms, of the sensuous, that strikes the eyes and every sense, at each step on that sacred soil. Art is in the atmosphere, in the sky, in the monuments, I may say even in the men. Here, on the contrary, there is no trace of art, nothing worthy of the name: not a religious manifestation in the least degree poetic, churches that make you burst out laughing, a grotesque worship, monuments of supreme bad taste. . . . Naples has never produced an artist, a poet; bad taste has always reigned supreme, and, in truth, it is only here that I have understood bad taste. All this, I repeat, because the ideal could win no place: sensation smothers everything. Priapus, that is their god, that is all the art of this country. . . . The instinct for pleasure is necessary for high artistic sensibility; but, if it goes beyond its just proportion, the higher formula is violated, there is nothing but matter left, brutal pleasure, degradation, nullity; such is Naples. . . . I can never tell you what I felt amid the ruins of ancient Pæstum. Picture a Dorian city of the seventh or eighth century before the Christian era, perfectly preserved in its temples and édifices, a Greek city in its purest and most primitive type, an admirable site, on one side the mountain, on the other the sea, three temples still almost intact, in that bizarre and exceptional style that bears the name of the town, the civilization of Greater Greece subsisting there absolutely whole; and to-day, in the nineteenth century, savages living in huts in the midst of this vast enclosure that still stands. I have seen the limits of civilization and I have been frightened: like a man striking his foot against a wall he believed far distant. Yes, I felt there the saddest emotion of my life. I trembled for civilization, seeing it so limited, seated on so weak a base, resting on so few individuals even in the land where it rules. For how many men are there in Europe who are truly of the nineteenth century? And what are we, scouts, advance guard, in the presence of this inertia, of this flock of brutes that follows us? Ah! if some day they should fling themselves upon us, refusing to follow! I must see Paris to drive Pæstum from my mind.*

* To Berthelot, January 7, 1850.

136

Renan's dream of science redeeming the world was postponed to an indefinite, but assuredly far-away, future.

In general, his political prophecies go wide of the mark. A week before the triumphal reëntry of Piux IX, he is sure the Pope will never return to Rome; he is equally positive that Rome will never be a capital, only a little center like Turin or Florence. "The salvation of Italy," he writes, "will come from the monks" (January 20, 1850).

Quite as erroneous is a political forecast based on historic development:

Centralization would be the death of Italy. Rome, Naples, Florence, capitals of departments! That is all right for Dijon, Bordeaux, etc., which have never been alive. But Florence has lived, Florence would never accept such a rôle. Make Italy free, Florence would secede, Siena would secede, Genoa would secede, Sicily would secede, Venice would secede—and yet the idea of Italian unity germinates all over. Let us come to an understanding: the theorists imbued with French and cosmopolitan ideas would be the first dupes and victims and the first to be disappointed, if Italy were freed from the foreigner. Yet it is true that Italy has a common hatred of the foreigner, and even a vague feeling of intellectual and moral unity. This would be enough to create a league against the foreigner. Would it be strong enough to create a compact state? No, a thousand times no. Would it be enough to produce a confederation of Italian republics? I do not believe even this much. These cities would tear one another again with their teeth, and at the end of a year, would call in against their rival, France or the Emperor. This may be said only of the present, without speaking of the destiny a far future may reserve for this country.[7]

But it was not chiefly current politics that Renan absorbed in Italy. Wherever he went, his mind was open to every sort of impression, and these impressions were of extraordinary

[7] To Berthelot from Florence, February 5, 1850. The political ideas that Renan acquired in Italy are set forth in his essay, "Dom Luigi Tosti, ou le parti guelfe dans l'Italie contemporaine," written in 1851, and published, apparently for the first time, in *Essais de morale et de critique.*

vividness. Always a good traveler even in his latest years, with a most lively susceptibility and the keenest interest in all the varying phases of nature, art, and humanity, Renan in this first journey had in addition the buoyant flexibility of a perfectly fresh, yet admirably cultivated spirit responding unhampered to the excitement of absolute novelty. He mingled in social life, visited cafés, went to the opera, took delight in Petrarch; he never gets over his astonishment at the beauty of real ruins, temples, pavements, arches, tombs, the Colosseum, statues in their original stations instead of in museums, true monuments, not mere objects of curiosity. He is enchanted, too, with natural beauty, the Bay of Naples, the Apennines, the lagoons, the sun, the sky. The particularities of each region excite reflections, the Papal rule in Rome, the horrible tyranny at Naples, the liberalism of the monks at Monte Cassino, the local and municipal life of Tuscany and Umbria, the fatal isolation of Venice. He never tires of Rome; at his third visit, he finds it like a great poem that reveals new beauties at each successive reading. Only once is there even a touch of homesickness, which is, indeed, rather a painful longing for intimate communion with his friend (March 10, 1850). At Portici he had an interview with Pius IX, and found him amiable and good, with characteristically Italian limitations of mind. The spectacle of the Pope's return to Rome made an indelible impression of mutable popular ferocity ready for explosion. All these experiences, eagerly assimilated, became a permanent gallery of pictures and a magazine of ideas, from which he constantly drew traits for his later works.

Pisa fills him with enthusiasm, art developing in the town itself, among its own citizens, to satisfy municipal needs; and this enthusiasm is even more ardent in Perugia and Assisi.

Assisi [he writes, May 11, 1850] is incomparable, and I have been rewarded for the truly meritorious pains I have undergone to visit it. Picture to yourself the whole of this great popular medieval legend in two superposed churches by Giotto and Cimabue! The city is still older than its monuments. It is all of the Middle Ages; whole streets absolutely abandoned have remained stone for stone what they were in the fourteenth century. Six or seven churches almost as curious as Saint Francis, make this city unique in the world. The profusion of art surpasses imagination. The outside, the inside, the doors, the windows, the beams, the mantelpieces, everything is painted or sculptured. Street painting, frequent all over Italy, is the characteristic trait of Umbria. The mystical and little nationalistic tint of the Umbrian spirit (wherein lies its inferiority in comparison with Tuscany, so intellectual) is above all sensible in this place, still full of the second Christ of the Middle Ages.

And finally Venice, Milan being entirely modern, mercantile, Parisian, and, from an architectural standpoint, a transported rue de Rivoli.

Venice is the most striking example of the irremediable decadence of certain very beautiful things in humanity: Venice is certainly one of the most beautiful flowers that has bloomed in humanity. Yet Venice will not live again. Venice can live only on condition of being autonomous; and the tendency being toward agglomerations, the autonomy of a town, the antique city, and that of medieval Italy, has become impossible. The only alternative for Venice is to be rich or to perish. But all efforts to give her back her splendor will be futile; prosaic Trieste is easily worth more; and it is not even desirable for the general good of humanity, that real and present advantages should be sacrificed to historical considerations. . . . Yet these old things remain with their poetry, their charm, their reminiscences. What Venice reveals above all is the spirit of the city, the contact, the consecutiveness, the solidarity of generations, what it means to *found* institutions, *customs*. The primitive constitutions of Venice equal in poetry and harmony all that is purest in Greek origins. Venetian art, however, is much less pure than Tuscan. The source is not pure; there are reminiscences of Constantinople, of the Arab style. There is caprice, fantasy, ravishing fantasy, caprice full of charm. But it is not pure beauty without mannerism, as in the Parthenon and at Pisa. (May 23, 1850.)

Everywhere in his reflections the character of the art is as prominent as the character of the life of the people. Indeed, art has become so essential to Renan that he advises it to Berthelot as a remedy for a fit of the blues, not art as the handmaid of thought, but unadulterated beauty and poetry of the antique stamp, free from any disturbing philosophic idea.

But while appreciation of art was the capital addition to his equipment which Renan brought back from Italy, it was a by-product, and not the main object of his endeavors. His time was chiefly spent in libraries, seeking and examining manuscripts. Little as this task appears in the letters to Berthelot, we yet know that it was accomplished in such a manner as to add to his stock of learning and to increase his reputation as a scholar. At Naples everything was under seal, but at Rome, Florence and Monte Cassino valuable treasures were found. In addition to Syriac manuscripts, catalogued and described, he discovered an unpublished fragment of Abelard and an important Arabic text of Averroës.[8]

His thesis for the doctorate was, indeed, constantly in mind. Writing of his trip to Venice, he says: "I have there the seat of my Averroistic philosophy, whose history I want to write, and about which my ideas have been much enlarged in Italy. It will be the history of incredulity in the Middle Ages."[9] Two letters from Rome addressed to Reinaud, his teacher of Arabic in the *École des langues orientales*, and published in the *Journal Asiatique*,[10] show how laboriously he worked, sometimes copying as much as a hun-

---

[8] The manuscript of Abelard, that of Averroës and others of a philosophical interest in Florence and Pisa are the subject of a long letter to Cousin written from Rome, February 17, 1850. Renan offers to copy anything Cousin may desire and he signs himself, "Your respectful disciple." *Revue d'histoire littéraire de la France*, 1911, p. 197.

[9] To Berthelot, March 31, 1850.

[10] December 10, 1849, and February 27, 1850, series iv, vol. xv.

dred pages of Syrian or Arabic text. To the Academy of Inscriptions and Belles-Lettres, a letter written jointly by Renan and Daremberg was read by Le Clerc, January 18, 1850; on March 15, Burnouf read a second letter, this time solely by Renan; and the official report was presented, the first part from both on May 24, and the second part from Renan alone on September 6.[11]

At some time shortly after his return, Renan went to London to examine the Syrian manuscripts in the British museum, but his time for this investigation was sadly limited.[12] He found, however, much material for use in his Latin thesis on Aristotle in Syria. Without these manuscripts, indeed, his argument in that work would have lacked its decisive weight.

While in Italy, Renan had begun to embody his experiences in the form of a novel. The reflections of the hero and his situation—loss of faith, abandonment of the seminary, trip to Italy—are his own; the author has simply added the love of a pious Breton maiden and placed the episodes in the epoch of the French Revolution. There are two fragmentary forms, one *Patrice,* a series of letters almost purely reflective, and the other, *Ernest and Beatrix,*[13] in which there are scraps of the sketch of a story. The chief interest

---

[11] Renan's troubles in finding manuscripts in the disorderly collections in Rome are echoed in his review of Ozanam's *Documents inédits pour servir à l'histoire littéraire de l'Italie* in the *Journal des Savants,* April, 1851; *Mélanges religieux et historiques,* p. 319 et seq. See particularly the story of a miracle and Renan's interpretation, pp. 321-323. A curious feature of this article is that Renan repeats almost verbatim a passage from an earlier review. Cf. pp. 328, 329 and pp. 265, 266.

[12] See letter from him to Reinaud in *Journal Asiatique,* April, 1852, of which there was a separate reprint; "Lettre à M. Reinaud sur quelques Manuscrits syriaques du Musée Britannique contenants des traductions d'auteurs grecs profanes et des traités philosophiques. Extrait du *Journal Asiatique,* 43 pp. Imprimerie Nationale.''

[13] Balzac had written a story *Beatrix,* the scene of which is in Brittany, but Beatrix seems to have been a general name for an ideal maiden. It is often thus used by Sainte-Beuve.

of these documents lies in their presentation of the romantic and sentimental element in the young Renan. Like St. Augustine, he was in love with love, and he felt the need to express, not only his philosophical and scientific side, but the whole of his nature. His heart was full of vague longing. "I love in general," he says, "I have constructed a Beatrix, I see her, I adore her. But this Beatrix has no real person to whom she corresponds. Every woman I see ravishes me to heaven; but passes, and her trace is soon effaced. My timid modesty, my external position permit nothing more. Alas! my golden age will pass perhaps without my being able to do more than dream of happiness."[14]

His dreams, however, cannot long detach him from his reflections upon his impressions of Italy and upon things in general, the same ideas as are found in his correspondence and in *The Future of Science.* Often, it is true, we find a view from a fresh angle. "The time has come when Christianity should cease to be dogma and become poetry."[15] "Science aspires to be true; religion seeks above all to be beautiful."[16] After Rome and Naples, he is impressed with the necessity of Catholicism for the masses, with its fitness for its place in the world.

Nothing equals the grandeur of Catholicism when looked upon in its colossal proportions, with its mysteries, its ritual, its sacraments, its mythical history, its patriarchs, prophets, apostles, martyrs, virgins, saints, immense accumulation of eighteen centuries, where nothing is lost, mountain always growing, gigantic temple, where each generation places its layer. . . . Humanity needs poetry. The priest is not the philosopher and scholar, the man of the truth; but he is the man of this great system of confused and intertwined idealism that humanity creates for itself under the name of religion. So complex a creation is assuredly open to criticism, and science cannot accept it all of a piece. But

---

[14] *Fragments intimes et romanesques,* p. 104.
[15] *Ibid.,* p. 33.
[16] *Ibid.,* p. 34.

when, in these vast constructions, science finds diverse elements, straw, mud, worthless materials, it has no right for that reason to condemn the whole edifice, nor to claim that this is not fitted for its social purpose.[17]

It is only the dogmatic doctors of theology who revolt him. "I would gladly climb the Scala Santa on my knees, if I were dispensed from believing in the authenticity of the Book of Daniel or in the Messianic interpretation of this or that Psalm."[18] The reality lies, not in the fact, but in the idea. "What do I care whether this man, of whom history tells almost nothing, has or has not trod this ground? Would Cephas be any the less the cornerstone of humanity? What do I care about that obscure fisherman, who doubtless never suspected the exalted destiny to which he was called! The true Peter, the Peter to be revered, is the one created by humanity, the Peter who, for ten centuries, has been the master of souls, before whom emperors have bowed, to whom humanity has paid tribute, and whose bronze foot is worn by the kisses of pilgrims."[19]

There are interesting passages in these pages, but, judging from the fragments as they stand, it is fortunate that Renan never completed his novel, whether *Patrice* or *Ernest and Beatrix*. In both we find an inharmonious jumble of exaggerated sentimentalism and philosophic reflection, of romantic unreality and his own personal experience. Thirty years later he returned to the plan of self-expression through fictitious characters, but by the time he wrote his dramas, he had ripened; his tendency to prolixity was restrained by the stricter form, and his tendency to gush was chastened by years and wisdom. He had grown to be, what could not be claimed for the youth of 1849, a literary artist.

---

[17] *Ibid.*, pp. 34, 35.
[18] *Ibid.*, p. 38.
[19] *Ibid.*, p. 65.

II

Late in September [20] Renan went to Berlin for Henriette, who had developed in Poland a chronic affection of the larynx that necessitated her return. She had paid her father's debts, and the house at Tréguier was now unincumbered in the hands of the mother. Her task was accomplished, but age had prematurely wrinkled her brow and withered her personal charms, though her expression of ineffable goodness remained.

Brother and sister took a small apartment at the end of a garden on Val-de-Grâce.

Our solitude was absolute [writes Renan]. She had no social ties and sought to form none. Our windows looked on the garden of the Carmelites of the rue d'Enfer. During the long hours I spent at the library, the life of these nuns in a way regulated hers and constituted her single distraction. Her respect for my work was great. I have seen her for hours by my side of an evening, scarcely breathing for fear of interrupting me; she just wanted to see me, and the door between our rooms was always open. Her love had become so ripe that the secret communion of thought sufficed. She, so exigent in matters of the heart, so jealous, was content with a few minutes a day provided she felt assured of being the only object of love. Thanks to her rigorous economy, she conducted with singularly limited resources a household in which nothing was ever lacking and which even had its austere charm. . . . She was an incomparable secretary for me; she copied all my works and entered into them so deeply that I could rely on her as on a living *index* of my thought. For my style I owe her more than I can say. She read proofs of all I wrote, and her precious criticism hunted out with infinite delicacy the negligences I had overlooked. . . . She convinced me that everything might be said in the simple and correct style of good writers, and that neologisms and violent images always spring from misplaced pretension or ignorance of our real riches. Thus,

[20] Berthelot addressed a letter to Renan at the Hôtel des Mines, rue d'Enfer, Paris, on the 16th.

from my reunion with her dates a profound change in my way of writing. I got used to composing in view of her remarks, hazarding many points to see what effect they would produce on her, and ready to sacrifice them at her demand. . . . One quality that offended her in my writings was a love of irony that beset me and that I mingled in my best things. I had never suffered, and I found in a discrete smile, provoked by the feebleness or vanity of man, a certain philosophy. This habit offended her and little by little I sacrificed it to her.[21]

Their means were slender and precarious. Henriette wrote for Mlle. Ulliac's magazine, the *Journel des jeunes personnes*, under the pseudonym Mlle. Emma du Guendy, and Renan wrote book reviews for various periodicals, among them the *Journal général de l'instruction publique* and the *Athenæum français*,[22] and probably gave lessons and supplied the places of absent professors. In 1851 [23] he was appointed by Hauréau *attaché* in the department of manuscripts of the Bibliothèque Nationale [24] under Hase, a humble position paid by the day;[25] but giving time and opportunity

---

[21] *Ma Sœur Henriette*, pp. 31-34.

[22] *L'Athenæum français*, an imitation of the London weekly, was published from 1852 to June, 1856. For it Renan wrote only two signed reviews, one of Egger's book on comparative grammar, December 18, 1852, and one of the refutation of Spinoza by Leibnitz, April 29, 1854. (*Mélanges religieux et historiques.*) He wrote one signed and a half dozen unsigned notes. See Strauss, *Politique*, p. 341. Although his name was still carried in the list of principal contributors, he ceased writing for this paper when in 1854 it published a poem to la Montijo, a bit of servility that filled him with contempt. (Letter to Bersot, Strauss, *ibid.*) The chief scholarly support of the *Athenæum* was Maury, who was a very frequent contributor.

[23] In the list of members of the Société Asiatique for 1851 Renan appears as Élève de l'école des langues orientales; in the list for 1852 as attaché. On January 14, 1852, he writes to Bersot as though he had been settled for some time at the library.

[24] Hauréau says the appointment was made by his free choice; *Histoire littéraire de la France*, xxxi.

[25] It seems that his pay was five francs a day. He writes to Bersot, May 17, 1852, "If five hours of erudition at five francs a day were not beneath you, I should ask you to share in the cataloguing of our Latin manuscripts," *Bersot et ses amis*, p. 109.

for study and reading in the intervals of cataloguing.[26] In the same year he was introduced by Augustin Thierry to the *Revue des deux Mondes,* to which he contributed for a time one article or, at most, two a year.

The story of his initial contribution rejected by the editor is told in the preface of *New Studies in Religious History* (1884), where the essay, with some changes and additions, was first published. "The article on Buddhism was composed during the last months of the life of Eugène Burnouf. It was destined for the *Revue des deux Mondes* and was the first piece of work presented by me to that magazine. M. Buloz, the least Buddhistic of men, praised certain minor points, but would not believe that the substance of the article was true. A real Buddhist, in flesh and bones, seemed to him incredible. To all my proofs, he answered inflexibly, 'It is not possible that there are people so stupid as that.' " Possibly Buloz had other reasons for the rejection, for the article is one of the author's least interesting compositions.

Renan's actual collaboration began with the issue of December 15, in which was published "Mahomet et les origines de l'islamisme," republished in the *Studies in Religious History* with changes and corrections, which, though not so numerous as those in the essays from *La Liberté de Penser,* are still considerable. The modifications of style are generally in the direction of exactness, exemplified in the frequent substitution of nouns for pronouns where the antecedent was at all vague.[27]

In spite of Buloz, Renan managed to work into this essay

---

[26] For a reminiscence of this work under the direction of Hase, see Preface to the General Index of the *Origins of Christianity,* p. ii.

[27] There was a reprint of this article, a pamphlet of thirty-nine pages, from the press of Gerdès, publisher of the *Revue des deux Mondes.* See G. Vicaire, *Manuel de l'amateur de livres du XIX siècle,* where many such reprints are listed. For one of these the author is thanked by Bersot, who regards the essay with fervent admiration, "a true piece of French erudition and of philosophy à la Burnouf," *Bersot et ses amis,* p. 105.

about two pages (pp. 237-238) from the rejected article on Buddhism. The reflections suggested by the story of Mahomet are identical with ideas in *The Future of Science*. The author inculcates his conception of critical method; he expresses the principle of spontaneous birth, at a given moment and under invariable law, as opposed both to creation and to the work of reflective reason, the delicate task of science being to divine origins by means of traces which remain; he maintains that things are beautiful only by what humanity sees in them, that sentiments have their value independently of the object that excites them, that a race produces its masterpiece and retires as though used up by the effort, that man is too weak long to bear the divine mission and those alone are immaculate whom God early frees from the apostolic burden; ideas never long absent from his religious studies. He clings to the theory of the monotheism of the Semites, stating it in the striking phrase, which he did not hesitate to repeat elsewhere: "The Semitic race has never conceived the government of the universe otherwise than as an absolute monarchy." Scattered here and there we find sly digs at the theologians. "It is clear," he remarks, "that Buddha, a son of God, an exalted wonder-worker, was beyond the temper of this race." (P. 234.) The implication throughout is that religions, not excluding Christianity, belong to a class of human products which pass through certain phases and may be studied by the same comparative method that applies to all historical phenomena. And he concludes with a statement of the right of nations, as of individuals, to perfect freedom of conscience.

Mohammedanism indeed was not the subject that was chiefly agitating Renan's spirit in December, 1851. The Coup d'État, validated as it was by the enormous majority given by universal suffrage, achieved the repression of thought begun in 1849, when the reactionary forces dominated the legislature and the ministry. The education law put through the assembly by Falloux at the behest of the clericals (March 15, 1850) was a serious blow to the University, already wounded by his administration.[28] Candidates for professorships who did not please the minister of public education or his advisers failed of appointment and a goodly number already teaching were deprived of their chairs, among these being Renan's friend, Amédée Jacques. With the Coup d'État, reaction seemed completely in control. The young liberals were filled with shame; they felt humiliated, even disgraced. As Renan wrote in later years: "The youth of to-day can hardly understand the character of those years of reaction that followed 1848, years in which the enemies of the human mind reigned as masters."[29] "Those gloomy years 1849, 1850, 1851," as he calls them on another page, "when the human mind was governed by its enemies, and the first ten years of the Empire, when everything not mediocre or frivolous was considered dangerous."[30] Jules Simon, "my intimate and proved friend,"[31] gave up his chair at the Sorbonne and went into temporary exile in Belgium, and Amédée Jacques buried himself for good and all in South America. The situation was disheartening. The liberals of France needed all their philosophy. For consolation they must mount to heights of historical contemplation, from which the miseries of the day should sink into insignificance because viewed in their relation to the whole. "To him who has so many times seen unfolded the apparent caprice of human affairs," wrote Renan of Augustin Thierry, "what is one incident more? For him who so eminently possesses the experience of the past, the

---

[28] Dupanloup wrote that the law of 1850 was not only directed against the University, but was intended to ruin the École Normale. Barthélemy Saint-Hilaire, *Victor Cousin*, vol. i, p. 531.
[29] *Feuilles détachées*, p. 299.
[30] *Mélanges d'histoire et de voyages*, p. xiii.
[31] Letter to Bersot, December 28, 1852.

experience of the present, it seems, should count for little." [32]

Under the new constitution, every functionary of the state—and teachers were such functionaries—was called upon to swear fidelity both to the constitution and to the president. About forty professors refused and lost their positions, and in this number were several of Renan's friends and acquaintances, such as Barthélemy Saint-Hilaire, administrator of the Collège de France, Hauréau, keeper of manuscripts in the Bibliothèque Nationale, and, more modest, Bersot, professor in the Lycée at Versailles! Thinking that this was carrying a scruple too far, Renan wrote to Bersot urging him to reconsider his determination. Only members of a former administration and those who had a settled intention to conspire against the government were bound to refuse the oath. The refusal of others would be regrettable, "for," says he, "besides depriving the public service of those who could best fill the positions, it implies that everything done and everything that happens is to be taken seriously. For my part, I should have desired that, with the exception of five or six men, easy to pick out, every one without distinction should have taken the oath." As for himself, he has not been asked, and, if asked, he is too unimportant to make himself an exception among his colleagues. "If your decision is irrevocable," he adds, "I beg to press your hand and say that you have sinned by excess of virtue." [33]

As usual, Renan accepted what he could not help, but he ceased for a quarter of a century to be a democrat. In a review of Garnier's *La Morale sociale*, published in May, Renan had maintained, in the spirit of *The Future of Science*, that the multitude never governed, the sovereignty

---

[32] *Revue des deux Mondes*, July 1, 1852, p. 198, a notice in the *Chronique* of Thierry's *Collection of Monuments of the Third Estate*.
[33] Letter to Bersot, May 17, 1852. Hémon, *Bersot et ses Amis*, p. 108. Cousin, though deprived of office, gave the same advice to his former pupils, and the young Taine took much the same view.

of the people being at bottom merely the rule of public reason, expressed, not by the crowd, but by that part of the nation especially given to administrative studies.[34] This theory was entirely upset by the Coup d'État. He would now forever repudiate universal suffrage, because it had played such a trick. If Napoleon III is the consequence of '89, he would even repudiate '89. Indeed, in the fever of the first days after the catastrophe, he was almost tempted to become a legitimist, and he would still incline that way, if hereditary transmission of power should be found to be the only means of escaping Cæsarism, for he is convinced that civilization can not last fifty years under such a régime.[35] It is civilization that he cares for, not this or that form of government; yet, though no longer a democrat, he is always a liberal.

III

However excited Renan may have become at times over the political situation—and he was often violently excited in talk, though not in print—he always had at his disposal another world into which such troubles could not enter. The year 1852 was one of prodigious labor in linguistic and historical scholarship.[36] In January Taschereau was named adjunct administrator of the Bibliothèque Nationale and director of catalogues, charged with the task of publishing a full account of the treasures of that institution. Reinaud, president of the Société Asiatique, became keeper of the section of oriental manuscripts, and among his assistants was Renan, to whom the Syrian, Sabean and Ethiopian manuscripts were assigned. This work was still in progress in

---

[34] *Mélanges religieux et historiques*, p. 70, article reprinted from the *Journal de l'instruction publique*, May 7, 1851.
[35] To Bersot, January 14, 1852; *Bersot et ses amis*, p. 104.
[36] His days were so occupied that he could not visit Bersot at Versailles. See letter of January 14, 1852, *Bersot et ses amis*, p. 103.

1855.[37] He also, as a specialist in medieval literature, prepared a careful and erudite study of manuscripts and church history for the use of Victor Le Clerc in the *Histoire littéraire de la France*.[38] In addition to these library tasks, he carried through the press his two theses, *De philosophia peripatetica apud Syros* and *Averroës and Averroism*,[39] and obtained his degree of Docteur-ès-lettres.[40] Meanwhile he was assiduous in his attendance at the monthly meetings of the Société Asiatique, and in July he was elected to its Council, on which he served continuously till his death.

Up to this time, Renan had brought out no book, his only independent publications having been reprints of contributions to periodicals.[41] *Averroës* was published by Auguste Durand and, as a doctor's dissertation on a nonpopular subject, it was published at the author's expense, the cost being 1378 francs.[42] This was a large sum for a poor man, but Renan was, as usual, ready to sacrifice the present to the future. The Latin dissertation made its way among specialists; the French dissertation became a standard work.[43]

---

[37] *Journal Asiatique*, vol. lxvi, p. 576 et seq.

[38] Embodied in the essay, "Joachim de Flore et l'évangile éternel," *Nouvelles Études d'histoire religieuse*, p. 217 et seq., first published in the *Revue des deux Mondes*, July 1, 1866.

[39] The first was presented to the Société Asiatique July 3, and the second September 13. On May 17 Renan told Bersot that the Latin thesis was printed and the French thesis was in press.

[40] Renan sustained his thesis before the Faculty on August 11, 1852, and received the congratulations of his judges and the doctor's degree. See *Athenæum français* for 1853, p. 5, a review of the Latin thesis by A. Charma. *Averroës* is reviewed in the following number, p. 47, and Renan is warned against skepticism.

[41] For an incomplete list of these, see G. Vicaire, *Manuel de l'amateur de livres du xixᵉ siècle, Paris*, 1907. The most notable are "De l'origine du langage," 1848, and "Éclaircissements tirés des langues sémitiques sur quelques points de la prononciation grècque," 1849, from the *Journal général de l'instruction publique*, July 7, 18, 21, 25.

[42] In a letter dated November 29, 1852, to Bersot, who is thinking of publishing his *Essay on Providence*, Renan gives this detail. See Hémon, *Bersot et ses amis*, p. 126.

[43] A second edition of *Averroës*, revised and augmented, was published by Michel Lévy frères in 1861.

Renan's Latin thesis,[44] approved by the Faculty of Letters February 7, 1852, traces the Aristotelian philosophy from Alexandria to the Nestorian Syrians, from the Syrians to the Persians and Arabs, and more slightly, from the Arabs to the Schoolmen. Working upon fragments and upon names of lost works, and piecing together indications derived from the manuscripts that have survived, Renan follows the course of philosophical studies in the Syrian schools from the fourth century to the eighth, and traces the influence of these heretical Christian teachers and physicians (Nestorians and Jacobites) in shaping the development of Aristotelian learning in Bagdad, where new Arabic translations were made by them, and not at all by the Arabs, in the ninth and tenth centuries. It was after this that the Arabs in turn became teachers of their former masters. In addition to published documents, the author makes copious use of manuscripts examined by him in Italy or in the Bibliothèque Imperiale, and especially exploits his discoveries in the British Museum, which furnish an essential link in his argument. This voyage over an obscure epoch, the finding of an uninterrupted current from Alexandria to Arabia, the marshalling of facts, the divining of the nature of lost treatises, the search for the least trace of evidence and the subtle discovery of its bearing, all shadow forth the labor of later years. The little pamphlet is, indeed, a direct precursor of the *Origins of Christianity*. Written by obligation in Latin, it avoids the Tullianism that Renan hated and even here and there presents really characteristic phrases, though most of it is sufficiently matter-of-fact for its destination.[45]

---

[44] *De philosophia peripatetica apud Syros commentationem historicam scripsit E. Renan.* Parisis, apud A. Durand, bibliopolam, 1852.

[45] The concluding sentence furnishes the most obvious example: Quod omen detestabile [that we should sink to the intellectual level of the Syrian schoolmen] Deus O. M. avertat, ac prius nos e medio tollat, quam videamus, ingravescente stoliditate, bonas artes atque humanitatis liberalem cultum pessum ire.

Averroës and Averroism, undertaken with the encouragement of Cousin and Le Clerc, is in large part the sort of monograph lauded in *The Future of Science,* an individual sacrifice to the progress of historical studies. As a patient exploration of a tedious stretch of the human spirit, it could hardly be surpassed either for the tediousness of the stretch or the patience of the exploration. Yet Renan could not regret the years spent in digging up and dusting off the mummies of metaphysical theory and tracing their uninteresting and half-effaced features. Even if his subject was useless practically, the history of the human spirit is the greatest of subjects, and the nineteenth century is the century of history. In spite of the hours spent in reading unreadable books, Renan was not infected. "Began Renan's *Averroës,*" wrote John Morley in 1897. "There is such a mixture of scholar and writer as no longer exists to my knowledge. And what a mixture it is, when the world is so lucky as to find it."[46] In the midst of the dryest enumeration will come a flash of fancy or an apt reflection. "Padua is nothing but the Latin Quarter of Venice"; "Many delicate spirits prefer belief to an incredulity that involves bad taste"; "This barbarism began to be tiresome, even at Padua"—such are specimen asides.

In no book addressed to the general public is Renan's method so exact in plan and statement. Beginning with the life and doctrines of Averroës, he proceeds to the Jewish translators of the fourteenth century—the origin of his later interest in the rabbis of France—and to the opposition of the scholastic philosophers, a topic involving a notable piece of intuition based upon erudition—his conjectural resurrection of the unknown Franciscans and masters of arts of the University of Paris against whom the great doctors fulminated. After this, we pass to the development of the legend of Averroës, the most interesting chapter in the

[46] Morley's *Recollections,* vol. ii, 67.

book, and to the prolongation of his reputation in the schools of northern Italy through the seventeenth century.

The reference to both manuscripts and early printed books must have left the examiners in a state of utter helplessness, for Renan had lived in a strange society with which they could have had only a bowing acquaintance. Every assertion is founded on a text. In addition, these notes include, as was to be expected in a thesis, references to the works of other investigators in the field, and are not entirely confined, as in his great histories, to the original authorities. Though his statements have the impartiality of scientific criticism, one feels his sympathy with incredulity, his admiration for Frederic II, and his horror of somber fanaticism, whether of Islam or Rome, when it destroys science and philosophy. Perhaps the most original passages in the book are the section in which he deals with Averroës and Thomas Aquinas in the paintings of the fourteenth century, and that in which he equates art and philosophy, contrasting Platonic Florence with Aristotelian Venice. Here, as in his *Life of Jesus,* what he saw in his travels becomes an integral factor in his book.

Although Averroism stood in a certain sense for freedom of thought, Renan finds satisfaction in the conclusion to which his study leads him, the conclusion that it was positive and experimental science which "swept away the mass of sophisms and puerile and empty queries heaped up by scholasticism." And he has a certain delight also in the irony of fate. "It was the destiny of Averroës to serve as a pretext for the most diverse hatreds in the conflicts of human thought, and to cover with his name doctrines which surely never entered his mind." (P. 432.) A sentence from the preface must also be quoted, since even at this early date it elicited reprobation: "Who knows if finesse of mind does not consist in abstaining from drawing conclusions?" [47]

[47] *Averroës* was reviewed in the *Débats* by *Daremberg* July 12, 1853; in the *Athanæum* by Alfred Maury, December 28, 1852; in the *Revue*

A copy of this book, with an accompanying letter, was sent by the author to Sainte-Beuve. This proceeding may have been prompted by Renan's helpful friend, Émile Egger, who had long been in correspondence with the great critic,[48] but such an act could not have been unusual, for we find Taine writing in 1857 and sending his *French Philosophers* to both Sainte-Beuve and Renan, neither of whom he had met.[49] To Renan Sainte-Beuve made a formal reply in which he thanks and compliments the author, utters a page of reflections on incredulity, and excuses himself for not treating the subject in the *Constitutionnel* on the ground that it is too heavy for his public.[50] This is apparently the beginning of the relations between the two, distant at first, but in the course of ten years becoming intimate. The *Revue des deux Mondes* was not the bond, for just before Renan began his connection with that periodical, Sainte-Beuve had withdrawn, nothing from his pen appearing there between September 15, 1849, and May 15, 1863. All his time was occupied with his *Causéries* and his *Port-Royal*.

IV

Hitherto Renan's friends had, as was natural, been almost wholly of the university circle. This circle, it is true, was

---

de l'instruction publique by Bersot, December 20, 1852. Bersot became a regular reviewer of Renan's books. In this same *Revue,* he wrote of the *Langues sémitiques,* the *Études d'histoire religieuse* and *Job;* and in the *Débats* of *Essais de morale et de critique, Vie de Jésus* and *St. Paul.* Renan is proud of his friendship and after each review sends a letter of thanks. He agrees in general with Bersot, there being between them, as he expresses it, only the thickness of a few words, his correspondent putting more definiteness into his philosophical language. ''I have a little less confidence,'' adds Renan, ''in the competence of human language to express the ineffable. But, after all, it is only a question of more or less,'' 1853. *Bersot et ses amis,* p. 133. It may be added that Bersot, although a freethinker, got along perfectly well with Cousin and even with Montalembert.

[48] See *Revue de l'histoire littéraire de la France* (1905), p. 107 et seq.
[49] Taine, *Sa Vie et sa correspondance,* vol. ii, p. 147.
[50] *Nouvelle Correspondance de Sainte-Beuve,* p. 130.

not entirely distinct from the literary group, for many of the leading contributors to the periodicals and most of the authors of serious works were teachers, administrators or librarians. In the journals they performed the delicate task of reviewing one another's books and, in doing so, trying to reconcile friendship with critical vigor.

Renan early perceived that success in the career he had marked out for himself depended on the good will of the leaders in the field, "the protection of the great," as he calls it.[51] Such good will and help be secured, and he was not unmindful of his benefactors. In the *Recollections of Childhood and Youth* (p. 370) he names six who, in his early years, chiefly gave him aid and encouragement: Émile Egger, professor of Greek in the Faculty of Letters; Eugène Burnouf, professor of Sanscrit in the Collège de France; Adolphe Garnier, professor of philosophy in the Collège de France; Victor Le Clerc, professor of Latin eloquence and dean of the Faculty of Letters; Victor Cousin, the greatest power in the Council of Education; and Augustin Thierry, regarded as the foremost historical scholar of his day. Cousin had done the young scholar favors, and took frequent long walks with him, expatiating on the history of various houses and their seventeenth-century owners,[52] but, surrounded by disciples who reverenced every word of the master, the great man was hard to deal with and could never be called a patron of Renan. It was quite otherwise with Burnouf and Le Clerc, who were proud to bring him forward as a promising pupil whom they had trained. Egger was even more helpful. He was not only a friend and a guide in classical studies,[53] but he introduced his pupil to the *Journal de l'instruction publique,* for which Renan wrote book reviews

---

[51] Letter to Liart, March 22, 1845; *Fragments intimes,* p. 270.
[52] *La Réforme intellectuelle et morale,* p. 15.
[53] In later life Renan used to exchange Latin verses with Egger as a summer amusement. *Débats,* September 4, 1885.

up to the time of his connection with the *Journal des Débats,* and he in all probability also presented him to the great Thierry who was his friend. Garnier's helpfulness was of a different sort. He was a delightful man socially and Mme. Garnier was a woman of noted charm and intelligence, Renan's "first object of admiration in a kind of beauty from which he had been weaned by theology." Through them the recluse was brought into contact with society. On March 21, 1848, Renan writes to Henriette: "I dined some days since at Garnier's. Profound sadness prevailed. All the frequenters of the salon were people satisfied with the past, some even personally attached to the court. M. Garnier himself is little concerned with politics. M. Saint-Marc Girardin, who was to have joined the ministry of Molé, is deeply grieved. M. Cousin speaks already of the fate of Socrates." [54] On this occasion Renan is obviously a person of small importance, but in four years things had changed. A report of another dinner at Garnier's in 1852 shows how the brilliant young men of the schools already looked up to him. Prévost-Paradol, after describing two traveling scholars who were present, exclaims that the real good fortune of the evening was his meeting "the great Renan," to whom he has become attached through a quarter of an hour's talk and whom he intends to visit at his library. [55]

Most important of these early friends was Augustin Thierry. Of him Renan writes: [56]

"M. Augustin Thierry was a true spiritual father to me. His advice is always present to my mind, and it is to him that I owe the avoidance of certain offensive faults in my way of writing, faults which I should not, perhaps, have discovered by myself. It is through him that I became acquainted with the Scheffer family, to which I owe a wife who has always been so perfectly

---

[54] *Revue de Paris,* April 15, 1896, p. 675.
[55] Letter to Gréard, November 24, 1852; Gréard, *Prévost-Paradol,* p. 204.
[56] Souvenirs, p. 371.

adjusted to the rather fixed conditions of my program of life, that I am sometimes tempted, when I reflect on so many happy coincidences, to believe in predestination."

The bond of sympathy between the unknown author of *The Future of Science* and the famous historian is made obvious by the well-known passage from the preface of Thierry's *Ten Years of Historical Studies:* "Blind and suffering without hope and almost without intermission, I can bear witness, not doubtful when coming from me, that there is in the world something better than material force, better than fortune, better even than health, and that is devotion to science."

In 1852 Thierry was living at No. 4 rue Montparnasse, where he received that society which he so much loved, friends, admirers, intelligent women, young men who came for advice and encouragement. Seated in an armchair, in which his faithful servant had placed him, he greeted all comers with voice and hand, listening to the news, questioning his visitors with unfailing interest about everything, great or small, pronouncing authoritative judgments upon the events or the books of the day, and always ready for the latest current anecdote. "Above all he loved the young men, and he would face any obstacle in order to do them a service." [57] Not only had he happily dissuaded Renan from publishing *The Future of Science,* but he had to a considerable extent launched him into the larger world of Paris by presenting him to the *Revue des deux Mondes* and acquainting him with various friends who visited his house. Renan made researches for Thierry in the library and even became associated with an intimate group, a sort of privy council, which included La Villemarqué, Egger and other scholars, to whom the historian submitted his historical doubts and scruples.[58]

---

[57] Ferdinand Valentin, *Augustin Thierry,* pp. 36, 37.
[58] *Ibid.,* p. 38.

From early manhood the Scheffer brothers, Ary and Henri, had been intimate with Augustin Thierry, with whom they had been fellows in revolutionary liberalism at La Grange, Lafayette's country home.[59] In settled age the intimacy continued. In 1840 Henri painted a celebrated portrait of his old comrade, and Ary was a frequent visitor at the house of the blind and paralytic historian.[60] Renan had therefore ample opportunity of here becoming acquainted with the Scheffer family, to whom he soon became strongly attached. The sympathy between the distinguished painters and himself, indeed, extended from art to political and moral ideas, for both brothers were enlightened liberals, in spite of Ary Scheffer's close and affectionate association with the house of Orleans.

The gain of new friends was, however, offset by the loss of his most admired teacher and patron, Eugène Burnouf, who died May 28, 1852, at the age of fifty-one. An appreciation from the pen of Renan appeared in the *Moniteur universel* for June 13, probably the only article, except his reports, ever contributed by him to that official journal. He had not as yet obtained access to the *Débats,* and a eulogy under *Nécrologie* could in no degree be thought to commit him to the political policies he abhorred. Renan's article was signed, as was usual with important obituaries in the *Moniteur.* In it Burnouf is held up as an example of great abilities consecrated to minute philological scholarship; of brilliant talents refusing publicity, and of learning heedless of its claims to the priority of discoveries; of erudition, not for show, not for the mere satisfaction of curiosity or the

---

[59] The Duc de Broglie in his *Souvenirs* tells of meeting Ary Scheffer at La Grange in 1817. The other young men in the company he does not remember. It is perhaps worth noting that about this time Thierry as a journalist contributed a few articles on painting and music of a strangely political color to the papers with which he was connected. *Revue d'histoire littéraire de la France,* 1905, p. 612.

[60] See Mrs. Grote's *Life of Ary Scheffer.*

love of difficulties vanquished, but for the advancement of the history of the human spirit.

It is easy to see that Renan is depicting the model he had chosen for his own career. With aptitudes that might readily have brought him wide popularity, Burnouf, he asserts, preferred his more serious gifts. Study was to him a duty, family life a delicious happiness. Though he had an early thirst for glory, he later attained the unalterable peace of a man who knows no judge but his own conscience. "This life wholly consecrated to higher things," the article concludes, "this example of a man possessed by the disinterested passion for truth, with a rare genius for its satisfaction, will remind us that, even if glory is not for all, yet to all are open the pure joys of study and of duty done."

Such was, indeed, the philosophic scholar prefigured in *The Future of Science;* yet in one respect the pupil was to differ from his master.

The proud and noble ways of the older masters [he remarks] rejecting as unworthy every effort to make instruction attractive and easy, suppose in the pupil a will power, a resolution, a disinterestedness, which are to-day very rare. Scientific work, besides, includes two quite distinct functions: The genius of discovery, the work of original research, and the art of making the results accessible to the public. It is only by the same person that these two rôles can be properly filled. Science is generally injured by interpreters who set themselves to speak for her without knowledge of her methods and procedures.

For his own part, Renan seems already resolved to be both an abstruse investigator for specialists and an untechnical writer who will charm and inform the general public.[61]

---

[61] This article is reprinted with very few verbal alterations, e. g., "*voilà pourquoi*" for "*c'est ainsi que,*" "*aux fonctions d'inspecteur général de l'enseignement superieur*" for "*aux plus hautes fonctions de l'enseignement,*" in *Questions contemporaines,* 1868.

V

The next important step forward in Renan's career was his connection with the *Journal des Débats,* the foremost liberal newspaper of Paris. According to his own account, the opening came in April or May, 1853. Reinaud, president of the Société Asiatique and professor in the School of Oriental Languages, and Derenbourg, a Jewish scholar of Germanic birth, but a naturalized Frenchman, had just brought out a new edition of Silvestre de Sacy's commentary on the *Séances of Hariri.* Ustazade Silvestre de Sacy, son of the great orientalist, and now director of the *Débats,* asked Reinaud to assign one of his pupils to write a review of the work for the newspaper, and Reinaud naturally selected Renan. "I went," says the story, "to present my article to M. Ustazade, and he was pleased with it, perceiving a certain care in the use of language. Consequently he was kind enough to ask me to treat in his paper subjects that pertained to my studies or such others as might suggest any ideas to me." [62] For the rest of his life Renan was a more or less regular, though not very frequent, contributor to the *Débats.* From 1853 to 1860 he wrote about forty book reviews, notices and announcements, the most important of which have been republished in various collections.

We learn from Taine that the *Débats* was an incomparable school.

On the second floor [says he, in a description of the dingy offices] is a tiled room, furnished with a screen, two ink-spotted tables, a water-jug and a glass. There you see statesmen, bankers, great writers, scholars, celebrated musicians. They come and go, talk of all sorts of things with remarkable freedom, equality and frankness; wealth and rank are left outside the door; they seek only the pleasure of discussion and thought. Here no one plays any part; pretentious phrases would be held in abhorrence;

---

[62] *Feuilles détachées,* p. 128.

the main thing is to utter your opinion with arguments and anecdotes in the shortest and least tedious possible way; it is conversation in undress. For admission only two points are required:
you should believe what you say and tolerate what is said by
others. That granted, you enter, and you find a museum of opinions. In matters of taste, of science, of philosophy and of religion, every sort of thing meets and clashes; there is no other
place where one can see and learn so much; open contradiction,
multifarious and polite, rapid and revealing words of specialists
and of illustrious men, precise recollections of eyewitnesses, little,
characteristic details of great events, a true light thrown upon
matters of history disfigured by ignorance or legend, exact and
blunt personal impressions, observations brought from every corner of Europe, authentic biography of every important personage
of the time, such was the mine, open every day, from which all
could freely draw.[63]

On its literary side the *Journal des Débats* of these years
was a remarkable periodical. "Write with five hundred
people in mind," was the tradition repeated to newcomers.
In the press it was to be analogous to the Académie Française
in literature, a paper to which the most eminent could contribute and in which collaboration was an honor.[64] De Sacy
himself and Bertin, owner and one of the chief editors, wrote
on books as well as on events. The dramatic and the musical
critics were Jules Janin and Hector Berlioz. Saint-Marc
Girardin produced a long essay almost every fortnight, sometimes even more frequently. Philarète Chasles discussed
foreign literatures, particularly English and German. Cuvillier-Fleury, Laboulaye, Michel Chevalier, Louis Ratisbonne are names constantly appearing; and everything under the press laws of the Empire had to be signed. Littré

---

[63] *Nouveaux essais de critique et d'histoire*, pp. 167, 167. This article on de Sacy, one of Taine's most charming essays, displaying an
unusual tenderness and sympathy, appeared in the *Revue de l'instruction publique*, November 18, 1858. Two such eulogists as Taine and
Renan ought to be enough to conserve the fame of this illustrious
editor.

[64] *Feuilles détachées*, p. 141.

occasionally sent an important article. In 1856 Taine became as assiduous contributor, joined in 1857 by the astonishing Prévost-Paradol, and two years later by Bersot. All these authors wrote in a department headed *Variétés*,[65] which contained usually one long book review of about four columns—such were the pieces reprinted by Renan in his *Studies* and *Essays*—and often shorter notes, besides lectures opening new courses at the University and prefaces and extracts from forthcoming volumes. In this part of the paper, as Renan tells us,[66] the principles of liberalism, banished from the political leading articles, were insinuated, and forbidden ideas were conveyed through subtle inferences. What could not be openly stated, a sharp-eyed reader could with attention read between the lines, the criticism of the book in hand being frequently but an excuse for penetrating thrusts at oppressive reaction, thrusts that could neither be parried nor resented. The tyranny of Napoleon III had, therefore, two beneficial effects on liberal journalism: it made the writers known to the public and it obliged them to acquire a delicate skill in expression too often missing in the unfettered utterance of clumsy freedom of speech.

The *Journal des Débats* was for Renan, as he himself acknowledges, an indispensable school of style. In spite of the difference in their religious views, M. de Sacy being a sort of belated Jansenist,[67] a cordial and enduring friendship sprang up between the chief editor and his young contributor. On de Sacy's side was the authority of years—he was fifty-two, Renan thirty—and of an achieved position.

[65] In the journals of the Empire the *Variétés* were distinct from the *Feuilleton*, with which some confuse them. Printed on the mid page, they were exclusively literary, generally in the form of book reviews. The *Feuilleton*, printed at the bottom of the first page, was either a novel or a dramatic, musical or art criticism. This is true at least for the *Débats*, the *Constitutionnel* and the *Moniteur*.

[66] *Feuilles détachées*, p. 143.

[67] Just in these years he was editing *Introduction à la vie dévote* de François de Sales, 1855, and *Lettres spirituelles* de Fénelon, 1856.

Although he had as yet published no volume, the first collection of his essays, *Variétés littéraires, morales et historiques* appearing only in 1858,[68] he was sufficiently celebrated as a journalist to be elected in 1854 to the Académie Française. "M. Ustazade," says Renan, "went over my articles with the greatest care. I read them to him, and on them he made remarks which formed the best lesson in style that I have ever had."[69] It was a lesson drawn from the classic literature of the seventeenth century in modern times and from Latin literature in antiquity, for such was de Sacy's taste,[70] pure but exclusive, and precisely what was needed by the scholar enamored of Hebrew, medieval mysticism and primitive archaism. Even without the *Débats*, Renan would have been a distinguished writer, but it was doubtless to this training that he owed his supreme mastery of his instrument.

---

[68] Collected from the *Débats*—Reviewed by Renan in the *Revue des deux Mondes*, August 1. See *Essais de morale et de critique*.

[69] *Feuilles détachées*, p. 134.

[70] *Essais de morale et de critique*, p. 32; Taine, *Noveaux Essais*, p. 167 et seq.

CHAPTER VI

Throughout the years 1854-1860, Renan continued to contribute articles to the *Revue des deux Mondes* and the *Journal des Débats*, most of which have been republished in collections. In 1855 he published the *Histoire générale et système comparé des langues sémitiques*, which, with his other philological papers, led to his election to the Academy of Inscriptions and Belles-Lettres December 5, 1856. On September 11, 1856, he was married to Cornélie Scheffer. Shortly after this, he was sought out by Michel Lévy, who made a contract with him to publish all his future writings. The first book to appear under this contract was *Études d'histoire religieuse* in 1857. A son, Ary, was born October 28, and Renan's mother came to live with him in Paris. He now produced studies of contemporaries, Cousin, de Sacy, and Lamennais for the *Revue des deux Mondes* and one on Thierry for the *Débats*. In the autumn of 1858 he traveled in the south of France with his wife and in 1859 in the north with Henriette to study monuments of fourteenth century art for an article in the *Histoire littéraire de la France*. A daughter, Ernestine, was born July 20, 1859, and died the following March. In 1859 appeared from the press of Lévy, *Essais de morale et de critique* and a translation of the Book of Job. An essay on Béranger in the *Débats* excited much comment. In 1860 he published his translation of the Song of Songs, and in the *Revue des deux Mondes* two articles which may be regarded as summing up his philosophy. Accepting a mission to excavate Phœnician remains in Syria, he left Paris with his sister October 18, 1860.

I

AT the age of thirty Renan was well started upon his career. He had won recognition as a brilliant, and at the same time, painstaking scholar, and though his situation at the library was modest in the extreme, his income was sufficient for his needs. He had access to the foremost review and to the foremost daily newspaper of France, and was rapidly gaining fame as a critical writer. He had published a book that was to become and remain a classic in its field. He had aroused enmity, it is true, though not bitterness, and his friendships included famous leaders in art and letters, as well as in learning. The future gave promise of literary eminence. His own plan was to complete the history of the Semitic languages, and after that to throw some light on the history of Semitic religions and on the origins of Christianity.[1] The story of his next two years is simply a record of his contributions to periodicals and of the publication of his second book. The most important of his articles for this period in the *Revue des deux Mondes* was "The Poetry of the Celtic Races"[2] (May 15, 1854), an expression of one of his strongest and most abiding sentiments, attachment to Brittany and the things of Brittany, "the region where my imagination has always delighted to roam, and where I love to take refuge as in an ideal fatherland." In writing this piece he looked, he tells us, to its moral and esthetic value rather than to any aim of erudition, and he felt that, in a way, it explained some peculiarities of his other miscellaneous essays as being the work of a Breton but little

[1] *Études d'histoire religieuse*, p. xxvi.

[2] In the magazine this essay was a review of three books, Lady Guests' *Mabinogion*, La Villemarqué's *Poèmes des bardes bretons du sixième siècle*, and E. Williams *Ecclesiastical Antiquities of the Cymry*, a fact which accounts for the special treatment of these subjects in the review. When republished in *Essais de morale et de critique*, the piece had been thoroughly revised, as Renan indeed indicates in his note on p. 419. In addition to slighter corrections, many passages, especially pp. 393, 406, 412, 418 and 433, where note 1 was originally a part of the text, were largely recast, and several pages of new matter, besides notes, were added; e. g. the whole of part iv and pp. 430, middle, to 435, top, all but four scattered sentences. For the influence of this essay on Matthew Arnold, see *Modern Language Notes*, February, 1918, p. 65.

removed from the soil.[3] Celtic enthusiasm is, in fact, the personal equation for which the reader must make allowance.

When the traveler in the Armorican peninsula leaves the region nearest the mainland, a region which prolongs the gay, but common physiognomy of Normandy and Maine, and when he thus enters the real Brittany, the Brittany deserving of the name for its language and its race, an abrupt change at once makes itself felt. A cold wind, full of vague sadness, rises, and bears the soul toward other thoughts; the tops of the trees become bare and twisted; the heather spreads afar its monotonous tints; at every step the rock pierces a soil too poor to cover it; a sea almost always somber forms at the horizon a circle of eternal moanings. The same contrast in the people: to the Norman vulgarity, to a fat and sated population content to live, full of self-interest, egotistical like all who are habituated to enjoyment, there succeeds a race that is timid, reserved, living all within itself, heavy in appearance, but with profound feeling and in its religious instincts an adorable delicacy. . . . It seems, indeed, as though you entered the subterranean strata of another age. (Pp. 375, 376.)

This poetic introduction brings us to a consideration of the qualities of the Celtic race, its isolation making it proud and timid, strong in sentiment and weak in action, expansive at home but clumsy and embarrassed with strangers; hard to win, but when once won, clinging to every cause with unfaltering fidelity and loyalty. These concentrated natures are unfit to impose themselves on the world. Feminine, if a race may be said to possess sex, and lacking aggressiveness, they yet offer an invincible resistance. They are romantic; they dwell in the imagination; to them all nature is an enchanted wonderland; with natural objects they live in close sympathy, and the animals, so often in their poetry transformed into intelligent creatures, are especially their friends and fellows.

---

[3] *Essais de morale et de critique*, p. xviii.

With these traits in mind, Renan reviews at length the *Mabinogion*, the bardic songs and legends of the Breton saints, and shows the influence of the Celts on the ideals of chivalry, the gentleness of this race being contrasted with Teutonic barbarity. Particularly emphasized is the almost mystical devotion to woman, and attention is also directed to peculiarities in the medieval treatment of the marvelous derived from Arthurian legend. "A forgotten tribe at the ends of the earth imposed its heroes on Europe and in the domain of the imagination accomplished one of the most singular revolutions known to the history of literature."

While Renan the critic is evidenced by the learning, by the scrupulous reservations and by the delicate insight displayed in the perception of relationships, Renan the ardent personality is still more prominently exhibited in the attractions and repulsions so eloquently set forth. Indeed, the author in his extraordinary way—it seems like mysticism or transcendentalism—identifies himself in some sort with the Celtic race. He observes and describes something outside of himself, yet he is a part of this object and at times he is actually identical with it, its life and its voice. This paradox is illustrated by the opening of the essay, already quoted; it is equally manifest in the closing passage:

In view of the progress, day by day more overwhelming, of a civilization which belongs to no country and can receive no other name than modern or European, it would be puerile to hope that the Celtic race should in the future attain any isolated expression of its originality. And yet we are far from believing that this race has spoken its last word. After having used up every kind of chivalry, pious and worldly, after having pursued with Peredur the Holy Grail and the fair sex, dreamed with Saint Brandan of mystic Atlantides, who knows what it might not produce in the intellectual domain, if it became bold enough to enter the world and subject its rich and deep nature to the conditions of modern thought? It seems to me that such a combination would bring forth highly original productions, displaying a delicate and discrete way of grasping life, a singular mingling of force and weakness, of the rude and the sweet. Few races have had a poetic childhood so complete as the Celtic races: they have lacked neither mythology, nor lyric or epic poetry, nor romantic imagination, nor religious enthusiasm. Why should reflection be denied them? Germany, which began with science and criticism, has ended in poetry; why should not the Celts, who began with poetry, end in criticism? The distance from the one to the other is not so great as is commonly supposed; the poetic races are the philosophical races, for at bottom philosophy is but another kind of poetry. When we realize that it was less than a century ago that Germany found her genius and that a multitude of national individualities which seemed obliterated have in our days suddenly sprung up more animated than ever, it appears an act of temerity to lay down a law for the intermittence and the re-awakening of races; and it is easy to believe that modern civilization, which seemed destined to absorb these races, will in truth be nothing but the fruit of their coöperation.

In contrast with the idealism and the imaginative visions of Brittany he found the flat materialism of Paris. The Empire and its adulators gloried in the International Exposition of 1855, with its display of textures, fabrics and machines. Renan's spirit of antagonism was immediately aroused. Such things have their value as subordinate instruments of civilization, but why all this clamor? The great ages of the world—Phidian Greece, the Renaissance—were not devoted to industrialism and comfort, but to beauty and ideas. Such impatient reflections find voice in an essay "On the Poetry of the Exposition." [4] Here the author invites meditation upon the fact that, while the Olympic Games and the medieval pilgrimages and festivals were occasions for poetic production, the Exposition had not given birth to a single stanza worth remembering. For the first time in history, he remarks, our century has brought together multitudes without any ideal aim, simply to view a display

---

[4] *Débats,* November 27, 1855, *Essais de morale et de critique.*

of merchandise. Industry is, indeed, good and honorable, but it is not liberal. "The useful does not ennoble; that alone ennobles which presupposes in man some intellectual and moral value." This sentiment, implanted in Renan during childhood, perhaps even born in him, is also the sentiment of his maturity and of his last days. "Industry," he proceeds, and how often has he repeated the thought! "Industry renders society immense services, but services which, after all, may be paid for in money. To each his recompense; to men of practical utility riches, earthly fortune, all the blessings the world can bestow; to genius, to virtue, glory, nobility, poverty." In the whole industrial movement he sees a progress away from lofty aims toward mediocrity. The young enthusiast of *The Future of Science* flares out again in this explosion, which concludes with the contemptuous words: "It does not appear that many left the Exposition Palace better than they entered it; indeed our friends, the exhibitors, would not exactly have got what they wanted if all the visitors had been wise enough to say as they came away, 'What a lot of things that I can just as well do without!'"

Art, as well as poetry, furnished matter for Renan's thought. At the studio of Ary Scheffer, so elegant and aristocratic, he not only saw and discussed the master's paintings, but he entered a musical atmosphere. Here distinguished performers rendered classical chamber music, Mme. Viardot, the opera star, often sang, and a young pianist, Günsberg, called by some a genius, but a premature victim of tuberculosis, fascinated the privileged visitors by his poetic playing.[5] Ary Scheffer was a painter who sought the expression of thought through form and color and found in art a medium for the promulgation of his ideas. It was this side of his genius, and not technical skill, that Renan pre-

---

[5] See Vitet's article in the *Revue des deux Mondes,* October 1, 1858.

sented to the reading public in "The Temptation of Christ." [6] This is a picture that meets the test; it makes the beholder better. The artist has presented in visible form Renan's favorite contract; on the one hand, the figure of Christ expressing an absorption without effort in things not of this world, and beside it and below it the tempter, already vanquished, because incapable of conceiving any motive beyond egotism, cupidity and imposture. A whole theory of religious progress is based on the tolerant portrayal of Satan. Skeptical regarding abstractions, our age has faith in essential truths. When language fails, art takes up the task, for it is the privilege of art to present moral ideas without dogmatism. "All philosophy is necessarily imperfect, since it seeks to shut the infinite within a limited framework. . . . Art alone is infinite. . . . Thus art appears to us the highest criticism; this idea we grasp when, convinced of the insufficiency of all systems, we attain wisdom, seeing that each formula, religious or philosophical, is vulnerable in its material expression, and that truth is nothing but the voice of nature, disentangled from every scholastic symbol and from every exclusive dogma." Here we have the first public expression of Renan's philosophy of art. [7]

Prophetic of the future was a review of Ewald's *Geschichte des Volks Israel,* which appeared in the *Revue des deux Mondes,* November 15, 1855. This essay, the last on his specialty to be published in this magazine for ten years, might almost serve as a general outline of Renan's later volumes on this subject, for it indicates the conflict between the prophetic and administrative forces as the central current of Israel's history. Here, at length, we find Renan master of his style, the republished article in *Studies in Religious History* differing but slightly from the original in the mag-

---

[6] *Débats,* April 25, 1855.
[7] Compare Matthew Arnold's "Poetry is a criticism of life."

azine.[8] We find, indeed, no further recasting of his periodical essays that appeared from this time forward: The first printed form is sufficiently satisfactory for permanent preservation. Here and there a superfluous phrase will be dropped or a more suitable word will be substituted, but the alterations never touch whole passages. The author is content to follow the rule laid down in the preface of *Discours et conférences* (1887, p. ii) that anything published has a date and should not be changed.[9]

II

The year of the Exposition, as Renan himself tells us,[10] a statement confirmed by a chronological study of his essays, marked the adoption of a settled manner of writing. He had always given much attention to the handling of style. The false rhetoric of Saint Nicholas had looked absurd when viewed from the sober gardens of Issy, though doubtless the schoolboy practice had been beneficial. Under the roof of Crouzet his efforts at expression had resulted in *The Future of Science* and its attendant contributions to periodicals. He was already a powerful writer. His ideas clamored for expression, while his enthusiasm, learning and vigor could not fail to attract notice. What he chiefly lacked was grace. Henriette, whose severe taste upheld an ideal of perfect fitness in diction, found his writings abrupt and negligent, often excessive and hard, even disrespectful in their treat-

---

[8] The alterations are wholly verbal in the direction of exactness or euphony: e. g. *les procédés qui ont présidé* becomes *les lois qui*, etc. The corrections in the Channing essay of December 15, 1854, are of the same nature, and but slightly more extensive.

[9] The principle stated in the preface to *Études* is less rigorous (pp. ii, iii), a writer in reprinting should not change the original character of his work and, at the same time, he should not send it forth in a form that he is able to make less imperfect. The corrections noted largely fulfill these two conditions.

[10] Preface to *Avenir*, p. vii.

ment of language. Her criticism convinced him that he could speak his whole thought without departing from the simple and correct style of the best authors.[11] Added to the influence of Henriette, and in the same direction, was the revision of his articles by M. de Sacy in the office of the *Débats*, "the best lesson in style I have ever had."[12] The result was a less dogmatic way of saying things; the fully developed phrase, with varied transitions, cadences and rhythmical units, substituted for the series of short, sharp assertions. The change coincided with a change in his habits of thinking, for with Renan, throughout, the style is the thought. "The perfect work," he says, reviewing Sainte-Beuve's *Port-Royal* in the *Débats* (August 28 and 30, 1860), is that in which there is no literary subconsciousness, in which no one can for a moment suspect that the author writes for the sake of writing; in other words, that in which there is not a trace of rhetoric."[13] "*Port-Royal* alone," he adds, "has known the simple manner of antiquity at its best, the style that leaves to each his own shape, and does not give the airs of genius to him who possesses none, but, like a well-fitting garment, is the exact measure of the thought, seeking no other elegance than that which results from a rigorous propriety."[14] It is the sincerity of Renan's style exactly fitting his thought, which gives it that precision, transparency and grace so often admired. If he can speak every language, as Pellisier says,[15] that of poetry as well as

---

[11] *Sœur Henriette*, pp. 32, 33.
[12] *Feuilles détachées*, p. 134. "It was these two organs (*Débats* and *Revue des deux Mondes*) that taught me how to write, that is to say, how to limit myself, how constantly to rub the angles off my ideas, how to keep a watchful eye on my defects" (Preface to *Avenir*). That de Sacy was the real master is proved by the fact that the *Débats* essays are never much altered when reprinted in book form, while the early *Revue* essays undergo rather extensive changes.
[13] *Nouvelles Études d'histoire religieuse*, p. 477.
[14] *Ibid.*, p. 478.
[15] *Le Mouvement littéraire au xixe siècle*, p. 321.

that of scholarship, with tones of phantasy, irony, tenderness, sublimity, it is because all these tones echoed within his soul and he had learned with unusual perfection to express, not a made-up image, but himself.

In this connection a note by Taine in 1863 is of interest: "His process of writing consists in throwing down bits of sentences, paragraph headings, here and there; when he has arrived at the sensation of the whole, he strings it all into one."[16]

It was in 1855 that Renan finally published his *Histoire générale et système comparé des langues sémitiques.*[17] This was a development of his prize memoir of 1847. Intending to do for the Semitic languages what Bopp had done for the Indo-European, he had found that his general introduction on the history of these tongues, "their rôle in time and place, their geography, the order and character of the written monuments by which they are known," had grown to a volume. A projected second volume on the internal history, the comparative grammar, work on which was interrupted by the mission to Phœnicia in 1860, was never completed, only two studies for it being published much later in learned periodicals.[18] As far as it went, however, this comparative

---

[16] Taine, *Sa Vie et sa correspondance*, vol. ii, p. 244.

[17] Ouvrage couronné par l'Institut, Première partie, Histoire générale des langues sémitiques. Paris. Imprimé par autorization de l'Empereur à l'Imprimerie impériale, 1855 (in-8°) Noms des libraires chez lesquels se vend l'ouvrage, Benjamin Duprat et Auguste Durand. Duprat was bookseller of the Institut and Durand was the publisher of *Averroës* and Renan's Latin thesis. A second edition, revised and enlarged, appeared in 1858, and a third in 1863, both published by Lévy. In May, 1855, an article by Renan, "Histoire et système comparés des langues sémitiques," appeared in the *Journal de l'instruction publique*. I have not seen this article, but I presume it was the preface of the book.

[18] A chapter on Semitic verbs in *Mémoires de la Société de Linguistique de Paris*, vol. i, and "Les noms théophores dans les langues sémitiques," in *Revue des études juives*, tome v, p. 161. A long essay published in Vol. 74 of the *Journal Asiatique*, February-March and April-May, 1859, on "Nouvelles considérations sur le caractère général

view of Semitic idioms was a new enterprise and, in spite of the slight attention given to Assyria and Chaldea, the book was a capital event in the subject and made Renan the uncontested master of Semitic studies in France. Jules Mohl, reviewing the work in his annual report to the Société Asiatique (June 20, 1855) says: "The author embraces all the Semitic idioms, with the exception of Babylonian, on which he thinks it premature to theorize in the present state of our knowledge. It may be seen how such a plan raises historical and linguistic questions, and it will be found that M. Renan attacks them with an excellent method, wisely, courageously, and sometimes hardily. He gathers what he finds true in the ideas of others, he adds his own, and thus presents an extremely interesting picture." [19] Shortly afterwards, Derenbourg, in a review of the book in the *Journal Asiatique* (August-September, 1855, p. 296), speaks of the solid qualities of the author, his exact knowledge, lucid exposition, moderate and circumspect judgment, and happy and clear expression, rare in philological books.

But the learned journals were not the only ones to notice the work. In the *Débats* for December 2 and 4, 1856, Édouard Laboulaye gives it a long notice, in which he praises the author's ardor, though he would like a little more moderation, holding up the example of Burnouf and insinuating most grateful praise by saying that, if any one could console the public for the loss of such a scholar and fill up the void, it would be Renan. The work is also the subject of a long review by Littré in the *Revue des deux Mondes* (July 1, 1857), who says: "M. Renan is a skillful writer. He exhibits not only the lucidity without which no effect can be made on the reader, but also that elegance which pleases, and, as Cicero calls them, those lights of style, *lumina di-*

---

des peuples sémitiques et en particulier sur leur tendance au monothéisme," was, however, intended to be the first chapter of the second volume.
[19] *Journal Asiatique*, vol. 67, p. 57.

cendi, which are for the page what the light of day is for the landscape.'' (P. 138.) The author, we are told, possesses erudition and the art to make it effective, and in a grammatical subject, he touches on delicate problems of psychology and origins.

It was, indeed, the treatment of such problems that aroused the chief objections to the book. In the midst of some linguistic discussion, we come suddenly upon a passage from *The Future of Science* or from one of the periodical essays. Much of this matter may be regarded as comparatively unimportant. On the other hand, there were some theories that displeased many philologists, an example of which is the hypothetical early connection of Semites and Aryans. But the theory that above all met with immediate, and, as it befell, permanent disapproval, was that of the monotheism of the Semites. Such a theory is, in Littré's opinion, not borne out by the evidence, and Mohl and others in the *Société Asiatique* at once presented their arguments against it. Curiously enough, Renan clung to this pet idea and defended it long and stoutly.[20] He had found the Semitic race characterized solely by negative qualities, having neither mythology, nor epic, nor science, nor philosophy, nor fiction, nor plastic art, nor civic life; in all, absence of complexity, of nuances, an exclusive sentiment of unity. And yet he says in his preface (1855) that he does not defend himself against those who say he has treated too exclusively the nomadic and monotheistic Semites, if they will admit that these alone

[20] In the *Journal Asiatique* for February-March and April-May, 1859, appeared ''Nouvelles considérations sur le caractère général des peuples sémitiques et en particulier sur leur tendance au monothéisme,'' also reprinted in pamphlet form, 102 pp., 3 fr. 50. This was a refutation of objections against his book. In his report for 1859, Mohl speaks of Renan's articles as follows: ''The thesis has found many to contradict it, and evidently the statement of a tendency of an entire race cannot be strictly proved,'' but Renan's idea conforms to the leading facts of the history of these peoples ''so far as such an assertion can be deduced, defined and proved.'' *Journal Asiatique,* vol. 75, p. 15.

have left written monuments and represent the Semitic spirit. Here is obviously one of those qualifications which leave little subsisting of the original doctrine.[21]

In linguistic methods Renan follows the best masters, Burnouf and Bopp, and he owes much to Gesenius and Ewald. He still speaks also of a height of spirituality known only to Germany and India. But he is fully aware of the demoralizing influences at work in German scholarship. "The great evil of philological science in Germany," he says, "is the fever for innovation, which has as its result that a branch of research, brought almost to its perfection by the efforts of penetrating minds, finds itself the next moment apparently demolished by presumptuous beginners, who aspire, from their very first attempts, to pose as creators and chiefs of schools." [22] The statement, often made, that Renan began to find fault with Germany only after 1870 is, we repeat, far from the truth.

III

His scholarly book opened to Renan the doors of the Academy of Inscriptions and Belles-Lettres. On May 26, Augustin Thierry died, and Renan was elected his successor on December 5.[23] Besides the honor of a seat in the Institut, the goal of every French scholar's ambition, he received the annual gratuity of 1500 francs attached to mem-

---

[21] In July, 1859, Renan read his thesis on this subject at the *Académie des Inscriptions*, on which occasion there were strong objections, followed by much discussion. See *Comptes rendus* for the year.

[22] P. 422, edition of 1855. The same reproach is found in a letter to the *Revue germanique*, December 15, 1857, reprinted in *Questions contemporaines*. See p. 259 in particular.

[23] Some of Renan's detractors have taken pleasure in making it appear that there was decided opposition in the Academy to his election, but of such there is no evidence. To the seat left vacant by Thierry was added that of Fourtoul, who died July 7. Thierry was replaced by Renan December 5, and Fourtoul by Renier December 12, the delay being no longer than usual.

bership, and within a year, being added provisionally in 1857 (April 17) and permanently in 1858 (November 19) to the committee on the *Histoire littéraire de la France,* one of the three standing committees of the Academy, he received further compensation at the rate of 2400 francs a year, a substantial addition to his limited resources, now still further depleted by his brother's failure in business. The other members of the committee were Paulin Paris, Le Clerc and Littré, all much older and more widely known men than himself, and assuredly good scholarly company for the new member. Few of his associates in the Academy were more active than Renan. From the very first, he was assigned to committees for proposing prize subjects and for reading the memoirs presented in competition. He was also assiduous in his attendance at the weekly meetings, a good academician, as he afterwards asserted.[24]

Meanwhile he had married, though after a severe domestic strain. From the habitude of years, his sister had come to feel a sort of proprietary right to his undivided affection. She had once proposed that he should marry, but apparently without any serious realization of what the step would mean to herself. When he announced that he had chosen Cornélie, daughter of Henri and niece of Ary Scheffer, for his bride, there was a trying scene. The story must be told in his own words:

We passed through every storm of which love is capable. When she told me that, in proposing my marriage, she had only wished to test me, and declared that the moment of my union with another would be that of her departure, I felt death in my heart. . . . When she met Miss Cornélie Scheffer, the two felt the mutual attraction that later became so sweet for both. The noble and lofty attitude of M. Ary Scheffer also captivated and overwhelmed her. . . . She wanted the union; but at the decisive moment, the

---

[24] The above information may be found in the *Comptes rendus* and the *Mémoires* of the Académie for 1857.

woman in her came again to the fore; she no longer had the strength of will to master herself.

Finally the day arrived when I felt obliged to issue from this cruel agony. Forced to choose between two affections, I sacrificed everything to the older one, to the one which looked most like a duty. I told Miss Scheffer that I would see her no more, unless my sister's heart ceased to bleed. It was evening; I came back to tell my sister what I had done. A quick revulsion took place in her heart; to have prevented a union that I wished, and that she highly appreciated, filled her with cruel remorse. Early the next morning, she hurried to the Scheffers'; she spent long hours with my fiancée; they wept together; they parted happy, and friends. After, as before my marriage, we had everything in common. It was her economy that made our new household establishment possible. Without her I could not have faced my new duties. My confidence in her goodness was, indeed, so great that the naïveté of my conduct did not strike me until much later.

Certain alternations lasted a long time; often the cruel and fascinating demon of affectionate inquietude, of jealousy, of sudden revolt, or sudden repentance, that dwells in women's hearts, revived to torture her. Often in her grieved talk she broached the idea of abandoning a home in which, during her periods of bitterness, she pretended she had become useless. But these were only the remnants of bad dreams, which were dissipated little by little. The delicate tact, the exquisite heart of the one I had given her for a sister won a complete triumph. In the midst of transient reproaches, the charming intervention of Cornélie, her gayety, full of spontaneity and grace, changed our tears into smiles; all three would end by kissing one another. . . . The birth of my little Ary obliterated the last trace of her tears.[25]

The wedding, a quiet ceremony, Berthelot, Jules Simon and a few others being apparently the only friends outside the family to be invited,[26] took place on the morning of September 11, 1856, at Saint-Germain-des-Prés and afterwards, since the Scheffers were Protestants, at the Temple de l'Oratoire. It was Renan's opinion that the Church per-

---

[25] *Sœur Henriette*, pp. 40-48.
[26] *Lettres Berthelot*, pp. 141, 142; Jules Simon, *Quatre Portraits*, p. 193.

formed a useful social function in providing appropriate ceremonies for baptism, marriage and burial. Brother, wife and sister seem to have taken an apartment in the rue des Saints-Pères, from which an invitation of this period is sent to Berthelot to dine with Ary Scheffer.[27] In 1857 Renan moved to 27 rue Casimir-Perier, where he remained two or three years. This was near the Invalides, the farthest from the Latin Quarter of any of his Paris homes, for though Renan migrated rather frequently, he usually sought the neighborhood of the University.[28]

IV

It was doubtless just about the time of his marriage that he received the visit from Michel Lévy of which he tells in his *Recollections* (pp. 350-352):

I had never imagined that the product of my thinking could have a money value. I had always wanted to write; but I did not believe that writing would bring in a cent. What was my

---

[27] *Lettres Berthelot*, p. 142.

[28] Grant Duff found him in November, 1859, in rue Casimir-Perier; in 1862 in rue de Madame, close by the Luxembourg; in 1863 in 29 rue Vanneau, not far from rue Casimir-Perier; in 1881 in rue Tournon, right in front of the Luxembourg palace. After 1883, he lived in the Collège de France. Renan must have moved to rue Madame as early as 1860, for Berthelot speaks of meeting Baby in the Luxembourg Gardens, p. 179.

The *Annuaire* of The Institut de France gives Renan's residences as follows:

1857, rue des Saints-Pères, no. 3.
1858-1860, rue Casimir-Perier, no. 27.
1860-1863, rue de Madame, no. 55.
1864-1876, rue Vanneau, no. 29.
1877-1879, rue Saint-Guillaume, no. 16.
1880-1883, rue de Tournon, no. 4.
1884 et seq., au Collège de France.

Only once did he emigrate to the right bank of the Seine, and this was in January, 1871, to avoid the German shells. See Goncourt *Journal*, p. 186, under date of January 10, 1871. Brandes is in error when he says he visited Renan in 1870 in rue de Vannes; he means rue Vanneau, where Renan lived, three flights up.

astonishment when I saw come into my garret a man with an intelligent and agreeable countenance, who complimented me on some of my articles and offered to collect them in book form! A stamped paper he had brought stipulated conditions that seemed to me astonishingly generous; so that, when he asked if I was willing to have all my future writings included in the same contract, I consented. I thought for a minute of making some observations; but the sight of the stamp forbade; I was checked by the idea that such a fine sheet of paper would be lost. It was well that I desisted. M. Michel Lévy must have been created by a special decree of Providence to be my publisher. A self-respecting literary man ought to write only for a single newspaper and a single review, and he ought to have only one publisher. M. Michel Lévy and I had only the best of relations with one another. Later, he called my attention to the fact that the contract he had offered me was not sufficiently to my advantage and he substituted another still more liberal. I have been told that, after all, it was not a poor piece of business for him. I am delighted. On the whole, I can say that, if I represented any capital in the line of literary production, justice required that he should have his large share in it; he, indeed, discovered it, for I should never have suspected it myself.

Allowing for humorous exaggeration, we may accept the story as substantially accurate. The young scholar had, indeed, been paid for his articles, but his books had so far brought him nothing. He had written for several periodicals, yet after his introduction to the *Débats* and the *Revue des deux Mondes,* he almost wholly confined his untechnical contributions to these two; and though Durand had published *Averroës* and was the distributor of the *Histoire générale* and of various pamphlets, Lévy was henceforth to take over both of these books, and to publish everything new that came from Renan's pen.[29] The absolute statement concerning the self-respecting author's relation to his medium and to his publisher is merely an instance of an habitual

[29] Flaubert found Lévy rapacious, *Revue d'histoire littéraire,* 1911, p. 364, *et seq.,* but his case seems to have been exceptional.

generalization of personal experience into moral dogma, which is one of Renan's salient characteristics.

The first volume that resulted from this collaboration was *Studies in Religious History* (March, 1857),[30] a collection of book reviews from *La Liberté de Penser,* the *Revue des deux Mondes,* and the *Journal des Débats.* Notwithstanding their diversity of origin, these essays have a unity of subject found in no other of Renan's collections. They constitute, if we add the rejected Buddha and the still unwritten Saint Francis, a rounded program of his religious studies; beginning with Greek mythology; embracing the three great Semitic systems, Israel, Jesus, Mohammed; then glancing at medieval Catholicism with the Saints and the *Imitation of Christ;* at Protestantism with Calvin; and concluding with the present, the Unitarianism of Channing, the skepticism of the neo-Hegelians, and the poetic insight displayed in Ary Scheffer's canvas. Israel and Jesus, however, were the author's chosen topics. There is a prefatory promise of a history of Semitic religions and of the origins of Christianity after the completion of the half-published work on Semitic languages. (P. xxvi.)

The preface must be viewed as one of the most important of the essays, a sort of review by the author of his own work. Herein, often in the very phraseology of *The Future of Science,* he states his general attitude toward religion. It is the highest manifestation of the human spirit, an eternal and sacred form of poetry that elevates man above vulgar life, and whose one deadly foe is materialism. But a distinction must be drawn between religion and its forms. Theological dogmatism, exacting belief, is opposed to the scientific spirit, which applies to sacred and profane literature, without distinction, the critical principles followed in history and philology, disinterested principles which substi-

---

[30] The volume was popular. Four editions appeared within a year.

tute the nuance for the system, the delicate qualification for the absolute assertion. This scientific spirit uses the inductive method, and rejects miracles, finding for every fact a rational explanation. By no means polemical, its results are given without the least regard to practical consequences, and, while ever ready to discuss problems in good faith, it is unwilling, no matter what the provocation, to answer passionate adversaries.[31]

The essays that follow are an application of the critical procedure indicated in the preface. Inspiration is drawn from the German scholarship of "the heroic age";[32] its liberal reason so strongly contrasted with both theological and rationalistic narrowness. With no vain pretension of infallibility, Renan seeks the real with every instrument provided by erudition and sympathetic intuition, such being supplied to a certain extent, it is true, but by no means completely, in the books under review. The poetic is what he seeks in past and present, aspiration toward the infinite, the identity and continuity of religious feeling in every form of adoration, from the Greek mysteries to the Catholic mass, from the worship of fabled divinities of earth and sky and sea to the worship of the Saints. Discarding an absolute standard of judgment, he portrays that which is human, and being human, is also divine. Though no specialist in Greek myth-

---

[31] Though condemning all polemic, as having been used up by Voltaire, Renan saw the need of coöperation. In a review of Jules Simon's *Le Devoir* (*Chronique* of the *Revue des deux Mondes*, March 1, 1854), he says (p. 1066), "Now above all, in the midst of the attacks directed against the modern spirit, we must unite; and union can be attained only through the great impregnable truths, by mutual sacrifice of paradoxes and individual opinions. The aristocracy needed by modern times, that of noble souls, recruited almost equally from every order of society, will be formed only when all who have a little sense and probity join hands, and, while retaining complete liberty regarding the particular forms of their belief, unite on the common ground of enlightened reason and duty." Renan, as well as a whole group of young university men, felt themselves to be crusaders in the cause of enlightened reason.

[32] Cir. 1780-1830. Strauss and Ewald must of course be added.

ology, he makes it intelligible as a "secret accord of nature and the soul." With the Aryan mood he contrasts the Semitic, sprung from the desert and insistent upon the unity of God. The question whether Mahomet was enthusiast or impostor, posed and argued by a Gibbon, has no meaning to Renan, and could not be raised by a reader of his essay. This enemy of theology is, furthermore, charmed and fascinated by the Christian Saints and he draws a most tender portrait of the author of the *Imitation of Christ*. On the other hand, he is repelled by the hardness and violence of Calvin. Protestantism appears to him both less lovely and less reasonable than Catholicism. Channing he appreciates for his honest, simple goodness, but he disparages him for his lack of critical power, fineness of intellect and high culture, for "a world without science and genius is as incomplete as a world without virtue." The essay on Scheffer's painting is thus really a fitting climax to this series, for it again emphasized the axiom that religion is not merely philosophy, but also, and above all, art.

That Renan was following Thierry's advice and giving out small doses of *The Future of Science* in periodical essays will be obvious to any attentive reader. Throughout the book the doctrines and even the words of the earlier work meet us on every page: Primitive spontaneity, age of analysis, eclecticism, man not to be happy but noble, France orthodox because indifferent, and a hundred more. As an illustration of Renan's economy—it might almost be called parsimony—may be noted a passage from *The Future of Science* which was inserted in the magazine text of the article on the religions of antiquity, but deleted from the volume because already used in another of the essays.[33] Either Renan knew such passages by heart, or, as seems more

---

[33] The passage in question is to be found on p. 413; *La vie antique si sereine*, etc. It was omitted from p. 69, after *Hereux ceux qui pleurent!*

probable, he turned to his old manuscript and copied them verbatim.

A single quotation will be added because it illustrates the personal character usual in Renan's abstract views: "To give the history of a religion, it is essential that one should have believed, but that one believes no longer: we fully understand only the worship that has aroused our first aspirations toward the ideal. Who can be just to Catholicism if he has not been cradled in its admirable legend, if in the tones of its hymns, in the vaults of its temples, in the symbols of its worship, he does not find the first sensations of his religious life?" (P. 7.)

V

M. Ary Scheffer once advised his niece, and the advice seems really to have been superfluous, to marry the most intelligent man he knew. By 1857 Renan was not only intelligent, but ripe. The dogmatic tone of the clever neophyte is now replaced by the authoritative voice of the master. He no longer shouts his doctrines, but insinuates them with the urbanity of accomplished maturity. This change of manner, the beginnings of which have already been noticed, reached an even completeness in the review of the posthumous works of Lamennais.[34] There are still, it is true, phrases verbally transcribed from *The Future of Science,* but they are transfigured by the context. The ideas are unchanged, only they are allowed to operate by their own motive force, instead of being driven in with a hammer.[35]

---

[34] *Revue des deux Mondes,* August 15, 1857.
[35] One example must suffice. In his review of Garnier's *La Morale sociale,* May 7, 1851 (*Mélanges religieux et historiques,* p. 70), Renan says: "In political and moral science, reasoning and proof are less necessary than delicate perception of the nuances of human nature." Here (*Essais de morale et de critique,* p. 189) he says: "In the moral and political sciences, in which the principles, through their insufficient and ever partial expression, rest half on the true and half

The character of the essay, moreover, displays the unmistakable influence of Sainte-Beuve, with whom Renan was now on terms of friendship.[36] A sympathetic study of an eminent personality, its purpose is to throw light "on the present state of men's souls and on the laws that preside over certain developments of thought." In the spirit of his friend, Renan maintains that "it cannot be the duty of criticism to regret that men have not been other than they were, but simply to explain what they actually were." The Breton origin and the ecclesiastical education of Lamennais —here also we observe Sainte-Beuve's method—are given full weight in the explanation of this poet of the "severe and ever irritable Muse." Out of the discussion, furthermore, a unified personality emerges, complete and invariable in spite of change of faith, a character with an "identical system of eloquent hate applied to the most diverse objects." Another hardly less marked borrowing from the master critic is the habit of allowing praiseworthy qualities to eminent persons, while the special matter in hand is the indication of their faults.[37] Here plainly the unruffled Sainte-Beuve is superposed upon the eager Renan; not, however, with any diminution of the younger man's originality. The poetic Breton, as is his custom, imputes much of himself to the object of his study; and, indeed, in his early hates and violences,

---

on the false, the results of reasoning are legitimate only when controlled at each step by experience and good sense. . . . Logic does not grasp the nuances; yet it is wholly in the nuance that truths of the moral order reside." A very striking case in point is furnished by a comparison of what he says in this essay about Catholic intolerance and what he said in *La Liberté de Penser.* See *Questions contemporaines,* the essay on "Clerical Liberalism," softened, as we have seen, when reprinted, and *Essais de morale et de critique,* pp. 159-162.

[36] In a letter of 1852, Sainte-Beuve addresses Renan as *Monsieur.* On September 27, 1857, he writes *Cher Monsieur,* and offers to support his candidacy for Quatremère's chair. *Nouvelle Correspondance de Sainte-Beuve,* p. 146.

[37] Compare *Avenir,* p. 212, p. 499, n. 51, and p. 572, n. 109, with "M. de Maistre, etc.," *Essais,* p. 154.

though never a partisan, he did approach Lamennais on this hard side. He has also the same tenderness, the same love of nature, the same antipathy to vulgarity. This special sympathy with his subject is especially manifested in an account of education at the Seminary, a passage almost in the very words of one on the same topic in *Recollections of Childhood and Youth*. The essay was no perfunctory or mercenary exercise. For years Lamennais haunted Renan's spirit. No contemporary is so frequently mentioned in the *Origins of Christianity;* and then he disappears suddenly and completely. The *History of the People of Israel* knows him no longer.

The search for the dominant trait is also shown in an article on Thierry in the *Débats* (January 5, 1857), all the qualities of the historian's genius being grouped around his special gift, "direct intuition of the sentiments and passions of the past." This gift, which enabled Thierry to discover the spirit under the dead letter of charters and chronicles, learning from his own epoch how to understand former ages and to make the past live again, this gift is one that Renan not only admires, but stands ready to imitate; and, in defending the methods of his friend, he in fact presents his own fundamental ideas as to how history should be written. An art, as well as a science, history requires perfection of form and grace of style. The Benedictines furnish one type of research, necessary, indeed, for the accumulation of facts, but incomplete and therefore misleading. Even a knowledge of texts has been the gainer by a large and free method. In fact, the details of history are mostly false, as Renan demonstrated to his own satisfaction by a futile attempt to reconstruct for himself a complete idea of the happenings of '48. "Every generalization," he continues, "is vulnerable, and the only way to escape criticism in writing history is to limit oneself to insignificant particulars. But no. This way is the most false of all, and the pretended exactitude of which it is so proud is at bottom only falsehood. Imagination, proscribed with such anathemas by exclusively learned historians, has often a better chance of finding the truth than a servile fidelity, content to reproduce the original narratives of the chroniclers. . . . It is only with love that one creates, and, if I may venture to say it, with passion; the foundations of an historical study can be laid only by being decisive on many points upon which science is far from having spoken its last word.'' Thierry had, what Renan himself was later to develop, "the double stamp of genius, hardihood in creation and finish in detail." The eminent historian who furnishes the text for this discourse on the nature of history was thus as much a model for Renan's historical composition as Burnouf had been for his scholarship; only Renan, not fully content with the personal kind of history of which Thierry was master, would assimilate to it a rival type, exemplified in Guizot, the philosophical. Thus the history lesson taught by his friend needed a complement, but none had to be added, or could be added to the moral lesson of that "almost miraculous life," that heroic struggle of a strong soul against blindness, paralysis and agony, without a moment of lassitude, of ennui, of discouragement. Renan pays feeling tribute to "that simplicity, that uprightness, that goodness, which belong only to the man of genius, and which so often made you feel, as you came from a chat with him, that even above his lofty intelligence you would be inclined to place his heart."

Two further studies of contemporaries in the manner of Sainte-Beuve appeared in the *Revue des deux Mondes* in 1858, that on Cousin (reviewing *Fragments et souvenirs,* April 1) and that on de Sacy (reviewing *Variétés littéraires et historiques,* August 1). Renan has written nothing more delightful than this little group of four essays, which stand alone as the only pieces of the kind from his pen. To pass judgment on the great Cousin was considered a bold enterprise. Worshiping disciples were scandalized, and the master himself, who did not relish criticism of any kind, was in bad humor over the polite but authoritative estimate of one whom he had seen emerge from insignificant beginnings in 1848. "His originality lies in his personal character much more than in his work": "seeking to philosophize for a large number, he was obliged to try, not so much to refine his formulas, as to make them clear and acceptable": "M. Cousin belongs rather to literature than to science": "From the moment we admit that the design is noble and elevated, the faults which this design carries with it are absolved at once, and there is no one who cannot say what the Church says of the original sin, *Felix culpa"*: such phrases, setting forth the notion that eminent faculties limit one another, and that faults are an inevitable condition of every sort of merit, implied that the master had faults, an implication by no means palatable to the inner circle, particularly when coming from an outsider like Renan. That Cousin, not content to be a philosopher, wished also to be writer, politician and founder and chief of a school, and that the popular side in him damaged the scientific, are, however, judgments now universally recognized as correct. Others might have equally well distinguished faults and merits, but Sainte-Beuve alone could have done this with such charm, and there are certain original traits that we should fail to find even in Sainte-Beuve. *The Future of Science* is still here— body and soul are as inseparable as the instrument and the music, the print on the page and the idea; the true philosophy of our age is history; philosophy is one side of life, a way of taking things, not an exclusive study; you can say all the ill you choose of the world, but you cannot prevent its being the strangest and most attractive of spectacles—yet these are no longer abstract formulas, but side remarks that spring from the subject under consideration, and furnish a graceful, fitting and unobtrusive background to the portrait.

In the opening of the Cousin essay an unfavorable contrast is drawn between the generation that came to maturity in 1848 and its predecessor that matured in 1815. Something of the same spirit is found in the treatment of de Sacy, who had for the old a taste that Renan shared. "What constitutes the interest and beauty of things," he says, "is the stamp of man, who has lived, loved and suffered among them. A little town of Umbria, with its Etruscan walls, its Roman ruins, its medieval towers, its Jesuit seventeenth century churches, will always have more charm than our incessantly rebuilt cities, in which vestiges of the past seem to remain, not by any right, but by favor, and in the nature of theatrical decoration." One of the features of de Sacy was his old-fashioned taste in literature and his strict old-fashioned morality. Uprightness is selected as his master quality. Aware of his own prejudices, he yet clings to them with perfect honesty. Indeed, the mind of the moralist, Renan maintains, ought to be closed against innovations, since the principles he deals with are settled, while the critic, the man of open and free intelligence, requires ever widening views and fresh and larger sympathies. Here again the quality involves the defect, for de Sacy is found to excel rather as moralist than critic. Yet what nobility, what absence of vulgarity in his taste for the seventeenth century and for books of devotion, what excellence of classic style! This excellence we have an opportunity to examine in the passages quoted from de Sacy, and it is a good test of the classic character of Renan's own style that, however different in certain elements of technic, it is hardly distinguishable in tone from these quotations.

The first part of the essay just discussed treats of de Sacy, the moralist; the second, after a glance at de Sacy, the critic, is devoted to the Liberal School. Here Renan sets forth his political views, soon to be still further elaborated in his article "Concerning the Philosophy of Contemporary History, as suggested by the *Mémoires* of M. Guizot."[38] Though himself a liberal, Renan finds fault with the Liberal School, his chief objection being against its attitude toward the French Revolution. In his view, the history of France resolves itself into a conflict between the Latin spirit of administrative centralization and the Germanic spirit of individual liberty. The French nobility, who should have stood against the king for their own rights, and therefore for the rights of all, as the English nobles had done, abdicated their function, and, under Louis XIV, became mere servants of a royal tyrant. Hence, the only way out was revolution; but the Revolution itself was doomed to failure, for liberty can be founded only on institutions that have long endured, and not on abstract theory. Moreover, the movement fell into incompetent hands, and resulted in an even greater burden of centralized administration, its code disdaining personal rights, moral obligations and liberal culture, and leading, under the despotism of material interests, to mediocrity. Neither the Restoration nor the February monarchy had appreciated its task, which should have been the establishment of a legitimate hereditary dynasty, in the hands of a family set apart to protect the rights and liberties of all by preventing any group, large or small, from exercising undue and oppressive authority, either by republican tyranny or praetorian Cæsarism. The government should never itself interfere with freedom of assembly or freedom of thought and speech, unless these attack the very foundations of government itself, and it should have no concern whatsoever with the subject-matter of education or with religious belief. The liberalism of Re-

---

[38] *Revue des deux Mondes*, July 1, 1859. Reprinted in *Questions contemporaines*.

nan much resembles the liberalism of Edmund Burke, though he seems to have known of Burke only the *Essay on the Sublime and Beautiful*. At any rate, he thinks on these subjects like a statesman, and the substantial character of his political philosophy, its method and its applications support Talleyrand's view of the value of theological studies as a preparation for statecraft.[39]

VI

Meanwhile, other cares occupied Renan's attention. In 1857, the death of Quatremère left vacant the coveted chair in the Collège de France. To this Renan felt himself called both by his abilities and by his attainments. It had been the goal of his ambition since his seminary days. More recently, in an article on Ramus (*Débats*, January 5, 1856), he had expounded the rôle of the Collège as a propagator of new ideas, the bulwark of liberty of teaching, the suitable home for branches of science not yet complete, but in the making. When Quatremère died, he gave an analysis of his merits and defects (*Débats*, October 20, 1857), his vast learning and his lack of philosophical views, his indefatigable labors and his antiquated philology. ''He did not perhaps observe delicately enough the essential shade of difference that should distinguish a chair of Hebrew, Chaldaic and Syrian Literature at the Collège de France from a chair of 'Holy Scriptures' in a faculty of theology. . . . In a course in which Hebrew literature was treated, as Hindoo literature is in a course in Sanscrit or Chinese literature in a course in Chinese, that is, as an implement for the study of the origins of a portion of humanity, such questions (i.e., as to whether or not the sun actually stood still at Joshua's command) could never arise.''[40] Conciliation of the cleri-

---

[39] See Morley's *Life of Gladstone*, vol. i, p. 515.
[40] Both essays are reprinted in *Questions contemporaines*.

cal party at the expense of his scientific conscience is obviously far from Renan's thought. Caring nothing for the attitude of the ministry, he made every effort to secure the vote of the Academy of Inscriptions and of the Faculty of the College,[41] but the Minister of Public Instruction postponed the call for candidates and the chair remained vacant for five years.[42]

Simultaneous with these happenings in the outer world were some changes in Renan's home life. On October 28, 1857, was born his first child, a son whom he named Ary. The babe was baptized November 11 in the church of Saint-Thomas-d'Aquin, the officiating priest being the Abbé Saint-Paul Taillandier, vicaire de garde. Renan's mother came to Paris to act as godmother in this ceremony, and thenceforth until her death resided with her son. The bright old lady and the bright young wife seem to have been very companionable; and Henriette, finding a new object of devotion in the baby, grew more contented and felt that she was not a superfluous member of the family. All three women were devoted to the abstracted scholar, who often hardly noticed the attentions of which he was the object. For his mother, however, he had a particular solicitude, and he spent the twilight hour with her every day. This tenderness she reciprocated. She liked to talk with every comer about her Ernest and any one who would talk to her of him became her friend. Sainte-Beuve, who had once been received by her in Renan's absence (1862), says that she had a veritable cult for her son, which she manifested as she

---

[41] See Berthelot *Correspondance*.

[42] When a chair at the Collège de France fell vacant, the procedure was for the minister to call for two nominations each from the Faculty of the Collège and from the appropriate Académie of the Institut. From the possible four, often only two, names presented, he made his choice for the appointment, but if the same name headed both lists, he was practically obliged merely to confirm the selection thus made. Renan seems to have felt sure of the Académie, but to have had some doubts about the Faculty.

showed her visitor the rooms of the apartment and the study.[43] Henriette, Sainte-Beuve had only seen once casually when she opened the door for him.[44] The friendship of these two great critics was, it is evident, one of public places apart from the domestic circle.

In the autumn of 1858, we find Renan making a trip to the south with his wife, and in 1859 one to the north, though not very far from Paris, with his sister, both trips having in view a study of fourteenth-century art that he was writing for the *Histoire littéraire de la France*. Henriette, indeed, was his indispensable helper in this work, for she examined many books, collected all the materials from the archæological journals, and even contributed her own judgments, which her brother often adopted.[45] The southern trip covered Avignon and the Comtat Venaissin, in search of monuments contemporary with the pontifical court in that region. From Lyons the young couple traveled on a freight boat. "The discomfort," said Renan in 1891, "surpassed anything that could be imagined, but we were ravished."[46] With Henriette he visited le Vexin, le Valois, le Beauvoisis, and the region of Noyon, Soissons, Laon and Reims.[47] The resulting essay clearly shows that the author had not only gathered information from books and manuscripts, but that he had studied the objects with his own keen and well-trained eyes. The death of Ary Scheffer, July 17, 1858, cast a shadow over these pleasant investigations but did not by any means interrupt them.

Writing the gossip of Paris to Édouard de Suckau under date of April 29, 1858, Taine says: "Renan is manufacturing books, one with his *Language* from the *Liberté de*

---

[43] Letter of June 21, 1868, in *Nouvelle Correspondance*.
[44] *Ibid.*, June 2, 1863.
[45] *Sœur Henriette*, p. 36.
[46] *Feuilles détachées*, p. 114.
[47] Académie des Inscriptions, *Comptes rendus*, vol. iii.

Penser, another with short articles. The one on language is a typographical curiosity, an octavo made up of two Review articles!" [48] The *Origin of Language,* just out when Taine wrote, is not quite so absurd as he would have it. The *Book of Job,* which appeared in December, is a work of moment, and was called in the *hommage* at the Academy of Inscriptions an "exegesis as intelligent as it is eloquent." [49] More important still is the collection of articles from the *Revue* and the *Débats, Moral and Critical Essays,* the high-water mark of Renan's production in this line. Many collections appeared later, and each of these contains admirable work, but never again did he attain such a level of felicity in both subject-matter and treatment as is here exhibited. This is one of the half-dozen volumes that represent Renan at his best.

The emphasis in these essays is on moral, social and political questions. Unity the book does not claim, unless it be the unity of tendency. Liberty and idealism furnish the thread upon which are strung discussions which range from contemporary leaders of thought, through Italian politics, Procopius, *Patelin,* the Academy, to their culmination in the essay on Celtic Poetry. Whatever the subject, it offers the occasion for wide views and, almost without exception, for a stab at the Empire, with its materialism and tyranny. Is it *Patelin,* we see the close of the Middle Ages, and the debased century this piece represents provides the moral: "If you wish to succeed, be a rascal; but if you wish to be still more certain of success, try to be or to appear a fool." Is it Hariri, we perceive the qualities of the Mussulman world, with a final glance at the value of freedom of thought, teaching us that false rhetoric is a result of the interdiction of such freedom: "And it is a great error to believe that

---

[48] Taine, *Sa Vie et sa correspondance,* vol. ii, p. 163.
[49] *Comptes rendus,* December 24, 1858.

the degrading of intellect has ever been a guarantee of repose." Is it Procopius, we are introduced to the Empire of Justinian and secret calumny is traced to the suppression of free speech: "The lie of hatred answers the lie of adulation; there is a simple means of avoiding both, respect for human character and for liberty." Though indirect, such thrusts are scarcely veiled. "Every despotism," the author casually remarks, "is founded by persuading societies that it will conduct their affairs better than they can themselves. Each people has thus in its history a moment of temptation when the seducer says, showing all the good things of the world: "I will give you all these if you will worship me." Materialism is still the archfoe. In the preface our attention is chiefly directed to the moral life. "Good is good; evil is evil. To hate the one and love the other requires no system, and it is in this sense that faith and love, though apparently unconnected with intelligence, are the true foundation of moral certitude and the unique means possessed by man for understanding something of the problem of his origin and destiny. . . . Like the perfumes on the Erythræan Sea, which lingered over the waves and were wafted afar to the ships, this divine instinct is for me an augury of an unknown land and a messenger of the infinite."

Such moral ideas, it is obvious, are akin to the poetic, and the preface, like the volume itself, leads up to the two essays on poetry. As he closes his introduction, the author is rapt in Celtic enthusiasm:

O fathers of the obscure tribe at whose hearth I imbibed my faith in the invisible; humble clan of husbandmen and seamen, to whom I owe it that I have preserved the vigor of my soul in an extinct land, in a century without hope; you are doubtless wandering on those enchanted seas where our Father Brandon sought the land of promise; you contemplate the fresh isles whose verdure is washed by the waves; you traverse with Saint Patrick the circles of that world which our eyes can no longer see. Sometimes I regret that your bark, in leaving Ireland or

Cambria, did not submit to other winds. I see in my dreams those peaceful cities of Clonfert and Lismore, where I should have dwelt, poor Ireland, nourished by the sound of thy bells, by the tale of thy mysterious odyssies. Useless both thou and I in this world, which understands naught but what subdues or serves it, let us flee together toward the splendid Eden of the joys of the soul, even that country which our saints beheld in their dreams. Let us seek consolation in our illusions, in our nobility, in our disdain. Who knows if our secret dreams are not truer than the reality? God is my witness, ancient fathers, my sole joy is to dream at times that I am yourselves made conscious and that through me you come to life and find again your voice.

Writing to Renan, March 17, 1858, Sainte-Beuve said: "Keep on without allowing yourself to be troubled by the insults and declamations that have for some time past raged about you: such howlings are only a sign of what you are worth and what those people fear." An echo of these bitter attacks is found in the opening pages of the preface to the *Moral and Critical Essays,* where the author refuses to enter into the controversy, having learned from de Sacy the wise policy of simply stating his case and refraining from recrimination.

The first decree of the Congregation of the Index entered against a work of Renan was that on April 11, 1859, condemning his translation of the *Book of Job*.[50] For this Hebrew poem he very early expressed his admiration and sympathy. Writing to Cognat (August 24, 1845), he says: "The reading of Job carries me away; I find there all my feelings; there dwells the divine spirit of poetry, I mean of the higher poetry. It makes you touch those mysteries which you feel in your own heart and which you struggle to formulate."

In the *Débats,* December 8, 1858, at the end of a review of

---

[50] René d'Ys, p. 212.

Cahen's version of the *Pentateuch*,[51] he states his principles of translation as follows:

The French language is puritan; it does not admit conditions. You are at liberty not to write it; but, as soon as you undertake the difficult task, you must pass with bound hands under the Caudine Forks of the authorized vocabulary and the grammar consecrated by usage. . . . Every translation is in its essence imperfect, since it is the result of a compromise between contrary obligations: on the one hand, the obligation to be as faithful as possible to the turns of phrase of the original; on the other, the obligation to be French. But one of these obligations admits no middle course, and this is the second. The duty of the translator is fulfilled only when he has brought the thought of his text into perfectly correct French. If the work he translates is wholly foreign to our spirit, it is inevitable that his translation should offer, in spite of all his efforts, singular traits, images little in harmony with our taste, peculiarities that need explanation; but what is absolutely forbidden is an offense against the obligatory rules of our language.

These are the principles adhered to in the translations of *Job* and the *Song of Songs*, published respectively December, 1858, and May, 1860. Both are studies in the development of Hebrew ideas, preliminary to his life work. In the critical essays prefixed to each, Renan disclaims original interpretations, and he very freely cites his authorities. When a choice is offered, he prefers the conservative view. In discussing the question of dates, he insists that not only grammatical evidence shall be admitted, but also historical and literary considerations, and especially the dictates of taste. In *Job* he attempts by varied rhythmical lines to reproduce "the sonorous cadence that gives such charm to the Hebrew text." In the *Song of Songs* he divides the poem into acts and scenes, with copious stage directions; at the same time giving another version without this parapher-

---

[51] *Nouvelles Études d'histoire religieuse*, pp. 179-181. The passage is reprinted verbatim in the preface to *Job*, pp. ii and iii.

nalia, so that the reader may suit his own fancy. We have, at any rate, an arrangement representing what might have been, and based upon exhaustive study and contemplation. The principles he follows are the same that guided him in his vaster historical works, of which these versions may be regarded as precursors. At all events, the primitive grandeur of *Job* and the idyllic charm of the *Song of Songs,* each representing one of Renan's own instincts, are presented to the public in a form that constitutes a distinct addition to the treasures of French literature.

The contradictory impulses so characteristic of Renan find curious expression in two articles of 1859, one on "The Academy" (*Débats,* January 29),[52] and the other on "The Theology of Béranger" (*Débats,* December 17).[53] In the former we find a new spirit, traceable, it seems, to Saint-Beuve; in the latter, the old hardness of the spiritual crusader. The great merit of the Academy is seen in the injection of the spirit of polite society, of the man of the world, into science and literature. Purging the language of the dross of pedantry, it insists that the model for good writing is found in the people who talk well. Recalling that he used to curse the shackles that prevented him from saying what he wanted to, Renan has finally come to see the advantages of such limitations. "Full intellectual maturity," he says, "is not really reached until it becomes plain that everything may be said without any scholastic apparatus and in the language of people of the world, and that the *Dictionary of the Academy* contains all that is necessary for the expression of every thought, however delicate, however new, however refined."

On the other hand, the old Renan bursts out, and poor Béranger is clubbed over the head in the most savage fash-

---

[52] *Essais de Morale et de Critique.*
[53] *Questions contemporaines.*

ion. He is guilty of artificiality, pretentious declamation, false gayety; coquetting with immorality, he plays the rôle of a spurious drunkard and libertine; orthodox in his revelry, he bows, glass in hand, before his God, the God of prostitutes and topers, the God who is slapped on the back and treated as a comrade and a good fellow. Renan, bowing before the mystery of the infinite, is scandalized at this vulgarity; and his irritation is increased when he reflects on the general alliance of dogmatism with frivolity. Béranger, in fact, becomes the scapegoat for the bourgeois spirit of France, suffering a vicarious castigation. The pitiless blows rained upon him aroused public sympathy and protest, almost a storm, but Renan, offended in one of his cherished sentiments, remained obdurate, and, though he later spoke more gently of the poet, he never really retracted or made amends.

Toward the close of 1859, Renan was led to rehearse his philosophical ideas for the first time in public. The occasion was a review of *La Métaphysique et la science, ou principes de métaphysique positive,* by Étienne Vacherot, the article appearing in the *Revue des deux Mondes* for January 15, 1860,[54] with the title "De la Métaphysique et de son avenir." The praise of the author, whose independent thinking had cost him his position as master of studies at the École Normale, is significant in view of what Renan himself was soon to undergo, but for the substance of the book there is little approval. Since 1830, Renan thinks, philosophy has been dead. The official brand taught in this state institution he finds entirely sterile, producing pedants and iterators rather than scholars and thinkers. "If I had been cut out for chief of a school," he remarks, "I should have shown a singular inconsistency; I should have loved only those of my disciples who severed themselves

---

[54] *Dialogues Philosophiques.*

from me." (P. 271.) For the natural and historical sciences he sees a vast future; for metaphysics, none at all. Philosophy, indeed, is not a separate science, but a side of all sciences. Here we are on the ground of his still unpublished book of a decade before. What he proceeds to say of erudition, philology and humanity (pp. 295-309) consists word for word, comparisons and examples included, of sentences from various pages of *The Future of Science* (Chapters IX-XIII). The phrases are the same, but the total effect is more moderate, the emphasis is modified. God, he proclaims, is revealed, not in Nature,—which is wholly unmoral, showing no favor to virtue, inflicting no punishment on wickedness, in fact often favoring the wicked,—but in the moral sentiments of man, for without God, duty, devotion and self-sacrifice are inexplicable. It is indeed not reason, but sentiment, that determines God, who can thus be better expressed by poetry than by philosophy. "Every proposition applied to God," says Renan, still repeating his earlier work, "is impertinent, with a single exception: He is." "The glory of philosophy is not to solve problems, but to propose them, for to propose them is to attest their reality, and that is all man can do in a matter in which, from the very nature of the subject, he can only possess fragments of truth." (P. 332.)

"O Heavenly Father, I know not what thou reservest for us"; thus he concludes with a prayer that simply expresses in a new form the thoughts that persisted unchanged from his early days. "The faith that thou dost not permit us to efface from our hearts, is it a consolation granted to render our fragile destiny endurable? Is it a beneficent illusion wisely wrought by thy pity, or a deep instinct, a revelation that suffices for those who are worthy? Can it be despair that is right, and will the truth be sad? Thou hast not willed that such doubts should receive a clear answer, to the end that faith in goodness should not remain

201

without merit and that virtue should not rest on calculation. A clear revelation would have removed the barrier
between the noble and the vulgar soul; evidence in such
matters would have struck at our liberty. It is upon our
inward inclinations that thou hast made our faith depend.
In everything that is the object of science and of rational
discussion, thou hast delivered truth to the most intelligent;
in moral and religious things, thou hast judged that it should
belong to the virtuous. It would have been iniquitous that
here genius and brains should constitute a privilege, and
that the beliefs that ought to be the common possession of
all, should be the fruit of reasonings more or less well conducted, of researches more or less favored. Blessed art thou
for thy mystery, blessed for thy concealment, blessed for having preserved full liberty to our hearts!'' (Pp. 332-334.)

The translation of orthodox formulas into free idealism
in harmony with a scientific and critical spirit is here, as
it was in *The Future of Science* and as it will continue to
be in *The Examination of Philosophic Conscience,* the abiding basis of Renan's perception of existence.

VII

It is curious how little Renan's family experiences affected his writings. A daughter, Ernestine, born July 20,
1859, lived but seven months. Her death in February, 1860,
moved him deeply, as the *Invocation to Ernestine* [55] shows,
but in his writings of the time there is no trace of his emotions. *Titine chérie* fitted into his philosophy, no less than
every other phenomenon. ''Thy passage in our transitory
life was short; but thy vestige will endure long in our hearts
and be eternal in the bosom of God. . . . If the ocean, in
which everything that is individual has its origin and its
end, seems to us like vacuity, that fact comes from the veil

[55] *Fragments intimes.*

which covers our eyes and the narrow horizon of this earth on which thou didst not care to linger.''

By this time the scholar and critic had become one of the Parisian notables, sought out by foreigners who visited the capital. In 1859 Matthew Arnold met him and found in him a congenial spirit,[56] and Grant Duff, whose specialty was making the acquaintance of eminent men, sought him out at The Library as one of the persons he most desired to know. Bersot writes (May 1, 1858): ''It is with great pleasure that I see you take your place in the world; it is one of the things that console me the most for being nothing myself.''[57] In an article on Thierry in the *Revue des deux Mondes* in 1858, the author speaks of Renan as ''an eminent critic.'' Taine's letter of January 3, 1857, shows the admiration of a slightly younger contemporary for his colleague on the *Débats,* to whom he pays homage as a critic and philosopher. In a letter of January 25, 1858, he predicts that Renan will be one of the great men of the century. Nevertheless, Renan felt that he had just begun. ''You have constructed your monument,'' he writes Berthelot, who had just published his *Organic Chemistry,* ''but I have as yet built only the porch to mine''; and he resolves to be ''an owl,'' parsimonious in correspondence and conversation, until he has finished his *Origins of Christianity.*[58]

When this letter was written, he was on the point of starting for the East to obtain the experiences which made that work what it is. As early as 1857 (October 9 and December 11), he had read before the Academy of Inscriptions a mémoire on ''The Origin and true Character of the Phœnician History that bears the name of Sanchoniathon,''[59] and in a note near the end, he had expressed the

---

[56] *Letters,* December 24, 1859.
[57] *Bersot et ses amis,* p. 177.
[58] October 4, 1860.
[59] *Mémoires de l'Académie des Inscriptions,* tome xxiii; reprint 94 pp. from the Imprimerie Impériale, 1858. A preliminary essay on this

hope that excavations might be made at Byblos to find the record of Phœnician cosmogony on sacred steles which he was sure must be there. Mme. Hortense Cornu, Louis Napoleon's playmate in childhood, had attended practically all the meetings of the Academy since 1856,[60] and her great influence with the Emperor was often used to advance philological science. It was through her that the excavations were determined upon by the government and Renan selected to conduct them.

The Empire was rapidly becoming liberal. The fête of August 15, 1859, the prominent themes of which were Imperial glory and the return of peace, led to the proclamation on the following day of amnesty for political offenses and the annulment of warnings given to the press under the decree of February 17, 1852. While Victor Hugo, Quinet and a few others refused all offers of reconciliation, Sainte-Beuve, Nisard, Gautier and Augier were now found in the court circle. The *Journal des Débats* acquiesced in the situation on the principle of taking the best one could get. Renan, therefore, after some hesitation, accepted the appointment and, taking Henriette with him as secretary, he left Paris October 18, 1860.[61]

same subject appeared in the *Journal Asiatique* for January, 1856. About a dozen technical philological articles, some rather lengthy, others of only a page or two, appeared from 1850 to 1860. Renan was always a prodigious worker.

[60] Article on her in *Feuilles détachées*.

[61] There was still much petty oppression in the department of education. Writing to Suckau, April 29, 1858, Taine tells him that the minister had forbidden Weiss and Talbot to write for the *Revue de l'instruction publique*, a journal that, like the *Débats*, had, at the Coup d'État, eliminated politics, but put liberalism in book reviews. See *Bersot et ses amis*, p. 125. The *Revue germanique* was also dangerous to write for, and of Buloz, proprietor of the *Revue des deux Mondes*, the minister said: "I will not permit our professors to write for that fellow." Taine himself had to suppress a phrase in his book on the Pyrenees—"in spite of myself, I thought of the vanished religions which were so beautiful"—as insulting to Christianity, in order that the censor should permit the volume to be sold on the railroads. *Correspondance*, vol. ii, pp. 163-166. On the other hand, the clericals

His wife, and "Baby," as Ary is always called, remained with his mother in the Paris apartment. His brother Alain was not far off, as he had moved to Neuilly, Professor Egger and Baron d'Eckstein, a distinguished Sanskritist, royalist and Catholic journalist, often called, and Berthelot was a constant visitor, whose letters never fail to give pictures of the family group, especially "Baby." Another subject of the first part of this correspondence is the reception accorded to the translation of the *Song of Songs*, recently published,[62] and to an article, "Concerning the Religious Future of Modern Societies," which came out in the *Revue des deux Mondes* for October 15. This was the first article from Renan's pen that headed the table of contents of the magazine, a position which manifests the importance attached to both the article itself and its author.

The "Religious Future of Modern Societies," is the most formally constructed of the essays of this period and, with the exception of that on metaphysics, the most dogmatic in manner, a reversion to type.[63] Berthelot finds that "There is in it less phantasy and more measure than in some of its predecessors" (October 25). After deciding that no new religion adapted to the needs of our age is possible, Renan gives a historical review of Christianity, a survey of its present state, and a forecast of its future possibilities. His one solution of every problem is liberty. "The division of the Churches will save the future from the excesses of too

---

suffered for political agitation, and in 1861, even so eminent a Catholic professor as Victor de Laprade was dismissed from his chair at Lyons for publishing "*Les Muses d'État.*"

[62] A note on this book, together with the preface, appeared in the *Débats*, May 21.

[63] A curious evidence of this reversion is a page from *Avenir* printed in the *Revue*, pp. 768, 769, but dropped in the reprinted essay. It would have come on p. 353 of *Questions contemporaines* between "*n'a point passé*" and "*Remarquons.*" The passage from p. 365, "*Enfin, l'Église romain,*" to p. 367, "*S'en séparer,*" does not appear in the *Revue*. There are, as always, other corrections, chiefly in the direction of definiteness of expression.

strong a religious power, just as the division of Europe must forever prevent the return of that *orbis Romanus,* of that closed circle, in which there was no possible recourse from the fearful tyranny that is always born of unity." [64] The future should, in his view, rest on the religious principles of Jesus without dogmatism. "The idea of a spiritual power opposed to the temporal power should be modified. The spiritual is assuredly not the temporal, but the spiritual does not constitute a 'power,' it constitutes a 'liberty.' " (P. 405.) The essence of Renan's conception is in the following passage:

Every prejudice is an error, and yet the man of prejudices is far superior to the nugatory man without character that our indifferent century has produced. Every abuse is blameworthy, and yet society lives only by abuses. Every dogmatic affirmation, shut up in a finite phrase, is subject to objection, and yet the day humanity should cease to affirm, it would cease to exist. Every religious form is imperfect, and yet religion cannot exist without forms. Religion is true only in its quintessence, and yet when you subtilize it too much, you destroy it. The philosopher who, struck by the prejudices, the abuses, the errors contained in its forms, thinks to obtain truth by taking refuge in abstractions, substitutes for the reality, something that has never existed. The sage is he who sees at once that all is image, prejudice, symbol, and that the image, the prejudice, the symbol are necessary, useful and true. . . . One can admit and love a symbol, since this symbol has had its place in the consciousness of humanity. . . . The problem of truth and justice is like that of the quadrature of the circle, approach as near as you may, you never reach it. (Pp. 414, 415.)

When Renan in Syria prayed in every Maronite church, he was not, as one who saw him thought,[65] trying to curry favor with the natives, or even simply continuing early habits; he was carrying his theory into practice.

---

[64] *Questions contemporaines,* p. 359.
[65] Édouard Lockroy, *Au Hasard de la vie.*

CHAPTER VII

October 18, 1860, Renan left Paris for Syria, where he was engaged in excavations and travels for nearly a year. After a trip to Jerusalem, he wrote his *Life of Jesus* at Ghazir. On September 24, 1861, his sister Henriette died at Amschit, while he too was suffering from fever. He reached Paris October 24. His only publications during his absence were reports in the *Moniteur*. Having been presented for the professorship of the Hebrew, Chaldaic and Syrian languages in the Collège de France by the Academy of Inscriptions and the Faculty, he was appointed by an imperial decree dated January 11, 1862. His inaugural lecture on February 22, published in the *Débats* February 25, created a disturbance and led to the suspension of his course by decree of February 26. On March 1, his daughter Noémi was born, and on March 16, Henri Scheffer, his father-in-law, died. In May Renan was in Holland and delivered an address before the theological faculty of Leyden. He was the subject of two essays by Sainte-Beuve in the *Constitutionnel*, June 2 and 9. In August, he entered the circle of the Princess Matilde at Saint-Gratien, having soon after his return from Syria also entered the circle of Prince Napoleon (Plon-Plon). His summer was passed at Chalifer near Lagny. In literary work, he had completed his discourse on French art in the fourteenth century for Vol. XXIV of the *Histoire littéraire de la France,* and he was busy with his *Life of Jesus*, his report of the Phœnician expedition, and a new edition of his book on Semitic languages. In September *Henriette Renan* was privately printed for friends. The great event of 1863 was the publication of his *Life of Jesus* on June 24. It aroused a storm and it ran through numerous editions. Renan passed his summer near Saint-Malo and on the Island of Jersey, diverting himself by writing out his philosophical views in the form of a letter to Berthelot, published in the *Revue des deux Mondes,* October 15. On his

207

return to Paris, he opened his Hebrew course privately at his home. On March 28, he entered the Magny dinners. A popular edition of *Jesus*, without notes, was published March 3, 1864. His dismissal from the chair of Hebrew was accomplished on June 12, preceded and accompanied by a journalistic controversy. At this time Renan procured a summer home at Sèvres, to which he resorted for several years. He wrote a few minor articles for the *Débats* and one on "Higher Instruction in France" for the *Revue des deux Mondes* (May 1).

I

LEAVING Paris, October 18, 1860, Renan and Henriette reached Marseilles the next day, where on the 21st they bade farewell to Berthelot and embarked for the Orient. In a week they were at Beirut, and Renan plunged into his task of excavation, assisted by soldiers of the army of occupation,[1] and having a naval steamer at his disposal for coastal trips. He was the first Syrian excavator on a large scale. From November 26 to February 9 he was at Byblos, then at Tyre, at Sidon, at Tortosa and other places on the coast, making excursions into the Lebanon mountains and even spending a week in the desert under a tent, which he found agreeable enough in good weather. He was often eight or ten hours in the saddle, undergoing all sorts of fatigues and hardships without complaint. His interest in what he saw eclipsed all sense of discomfort. "On my mule I ride whole days on the summits of Lebanon," he writes Berthelot (November 30), "on roads a foot broad, above deep-cut valleys whose bottom can scarcely be seen. . . . The roads are of an unimaginable break-neck sort; but you can trust your beast absolutely."

In spite of occasional remarks about the Syrian population or outbursts of enthusiasm over the flowers and the glory of the scenery, the letters of this period are far less

---

[1] Just after Renan's appointment, a massacre of Christians in Lebanon led to the occupation of Syria by French troops.

valuable to a student of Renan than those written ten years before from Italy. The thinker was now fully formed, and while he might still add much to his experience, while he might fill up some unoccupied spaces in the chambers of his mind, there were no new rooms to be unlocked and explored. He had come, moreover, to feel the irksomeness of letter-writing. "I am," he says, "the least epistolary of men." He felt it difficult to use in a free way for his friends the pen that was habitually employed with reflection for the public. Almost every letter of Berthelot utters a plaint over his friend's silence. Henriette is instigated to coerce her recalcitrant brother into performing his duty as a correspondent. Sometimes Renan is penitent, sometimes apologetic, sometimes refractory. At any rate, his experiences of this period are reflected in his books rather than in his correspondence.

In fact, every moment was occupied, and he was often too exhausted for mental effort after the day's work. He was busy from morning to night, traveling, planning, supervising. Four campaigns, Ruad, Byblos, Sidon, and Tyre, were inaugurated under his eye and then continued by assistants, the most competent of whom was Dr. Gaillardot. All sorts of negotiations had to be undertaken both with officials and with the populace, schemes of work had to be laid out, unearthed objects viewed and classified, larger monuments carefully studied and measured, and reports prepared.[2] Henriette writes that both she and her brother were of unusual strength and indeed for this task they needed all the strength with which they were endowed, for she too accompanied him on most of his expeditions, undergoing hardships and privations beyond the endurance

---

[2] A detailed account of his trips, with dates, will be found in the introduction to the *Mission de Phénicie*. A brief account of the whole expedition and a criticism of its results, is given in *The Development of Palestine Exploration* by Frederick Jones Bliss, pp. 242-254.

of most women, while also taking care of the accounts, copying and arranging the records, and relieving her brother of all material cares.

And she was happy, he tells us, though sometimes in her letters she hobnobs with Berthelot more than a thousand miles away over her brother's indifference. "His ambitions preoccupy him more than his affections," she complains (November 30). "It seems he can do everything for those he loves except devote time to them. I assure you I do not exaggerate in saying that during our two stays at Beirut he gave more time to the General and the Pasha than to his old friend who has abandoned everything to follow him to these distant shores. Literally, since we have been in Syria, I have scarcely seen him, and when I do see him, he is so absorbed by the work of his mission, so preoccupied with what it has already given him or what it promises, that I truly do not know if he is aware of my presence." And again she writes (February 11, 1861): "I cannot help thinking often that you and I seek in him one who is no longer there, the friend whose first thought we were, whose first confidants, and in whose soul we were accustomed to read without witness or interpreter. You and I have remained the same, while he is completely metamorphosed and we seek to seize in him what is only a phantom or a recollection."

Berthelot had been expecting to join the party in January, 1861, but he was detained in Paris, at first by his father's infirmities and later by professional engagements. In every letter he gives news of "Baby," his doings and sayings, his measles and scarlatina, his need of his father's personal influence. From early in the winter Berthelot importunately and insistently urges an early return to France, partly for his own sake, partly for the sake of "Baby," but above all on the grounds of the peril that lurked in the summer climate of Syria, a warning that was unfortunately not heeded. His marriage in May brought a new intimate friend into the Renan circle, for though his wife had not been previously acquainted with the Syrian travelers, she at once, in spite of distance, was adopted as one of them and with her Henriette began a cordial correspondence. "We shall make a nice little coterie (taking the word in its good sense)," writes Berthelot (May 31, 1861).

In December, 1860, Mme. Renan joined her husband at Beirut, leaving "Baby" to grandmother, cousins and aunts. Having taken the trip to Palestine, she returned to Paris in July, 1861, thus escaping the fatal fever. Lockroy, who made drawings for the expedition, says that Henriette suffered when the wife arrived. There was a sort of rivalry between the two in taking care of the common object of their affection, tying his necktie and seeing that he was properly dressed. Renan, on his part, was so absorbed in his work that he paid no attention to the ladies, and probably had no idea which of them had done his tie or attended to his wants.

He was, Lockroy reports, like a child in the hands of his sister, who looked after him, laid down the law to him and scolded him. He would then humbly excuse himself and beg her pardon. "The most seductive man I have known," is this observer's verdict. Already with a tendency to fat, which was at this time only a tendency, he had a large nose, small eyes, an ironical mouth, and the manners of a priest. When people talked, he sat thinking of other things, and when the talk ceased, he would exclaim: "Ah! how true that is!"[3]

In April and May the Renans spent thirty-four days on a trip to Jerusalem, visiting all the places associated with the career of Christ. Even if the legendary topography

---

[3] Édouard Lockroy, *Au hasard de la vie.*

were false, he felt, in pointing out any precise spot, the error was at most only a matter of a few yards; and there unmistakably were Bethany, the Mount of Olives, Gethsemane, and the road from Galilee, the very road trodden by the feet of Jesus. By June 1, the party was back in Beirut. The mission was ended by the withdrawal of the · French troops. The essential work was finished, though Renan ardently desired to return to Umm-el-'Awamîd; what remained was to close up the affairs, group results, ship home tons of antiquities, and visit some of the high parts of Lebanon, where relief could be found from the deadly heat of the plains. A new campaign of excavations in Cyprus was also in prospect for the autumn. Meanwhile, during the month of July, spent at Ghazir, Renan set eagerly to work on a book.

I have employed my long days at Ghazir [he writes Berthelot (September 12)] in composing my *Life of Jesus*, as I conceived it in Galilee and in the land of Tyre. In a week it will be finished; I have only the story of his last two days left to write. I have succeeded in giving all this an organic continuity which is completely lacking in the Gospels. I truly believe that the reader will have before his eyes living beings, and not those pale, lifeless phantoms of Jesus, Mary, Peter, etc., which have passed into the state of abstractions and mere types. As in the vibration of sonorous discs, I have tried to give the stroke that arranges all the grains of sand in natural waves. Have I succeeded? You will judge. But I ask you not to say a word about it outside our little circle. This big piece in my portfolio makes up my whole force. The wind must not be taken out of it. It will come forth in its proper time. Now that it is done, I have come to care little for the Collège de France and all the world. If I am allowed to publish it (and I cannot be refused), that will be enough for me.

The prudent Berthelot is eager to read the new book, but advises delay in publication, thinking that there will be enough to do in arranging the collections and giving out the results of the expedition (September 26).

Ghazir, Renan says, is one of the most beautiful spots in the world, surrounded by wooded valleys and grassy slopes. Here he and Henriette, who had suffered terribly from the hardships and fatigues of exploration, rested happily while her Arabian mare and his mule, Sada, "our poor traveling companions," found pasture close by their little house.

I resolved [says Renan][4] to write out all the ideas that, since my sojourn in Tyre and my trip to Palestine, were germinating in my mind about the life of Jesus. When reading the Gospels in Galilee, the personality of the great founder had vividly impressed me. In the midst of the deepest conceivable peace, I wrote, with the sole aid of the Gospels and Josephus, a *Life of Jesus,* which at Ghazir I carried forward up to the last journey of Jesus to Jerusalem. Delicious hours, and too soon vanished; oh, may eternity be like you! From morning to evening I was intoxicated with the ideas that unrolled before me. With them I went to sleep, and the first rays of the sun behind the mountain gave them back to me clearer and more vivid than the evening before. As fast as I wrote a page, Henriette copied it. "This book," she said, "I shall love." . . . Her joy was complete, and these moments were without doubt the sweetest of her life. Our intellectual and moral communion had never been so intimate.

Early in September the needs of his mission called Renan to Beirut, and the two left Ghazir "not without tears." On September 15, they went to Amschit, where he had to supervise the shipment of two large sarcophagi. She was indisposed, but they still worked on the *Life of Jesus* until her illness forbade further effort; then he too was seized with fever and, though still active, went about in a sort of trance. Unable to secure proper medical treatment, Henriette died, September 24, while her brother was semiconscious and delirious. Two days elapsed before he could realize his loss. The funeral was attended to by Dr. Gail-

---

[4] *Sœur Henriette*, pp. 60, 61.

lardot, and Henriette found her resting place in a native tomb near a pretty chapel amid the palms.[5]

Leaving Beirut October 10, 1861, Renan reached Paris on the 24th, still suffering from the effects of his fever, which probably, as Grant Duff surmises, laid the foundation of his later maladies. "Gloomy as an owl," Taine found him in February. During his absence two long reports addressed to the Emperor had been published in the *Moniteur*, the third and last report appearing after his return.[6] It is a curious fact that these reports, addressed to the Emperor in the respectful terms demanded by court etiquette, furnished the basis of opposition to Renan by the irreconcilable radicals, who thus strangely found themselves allied with the clericals. Letters from him to the Emperor and to colleagues were also read before the Academy of Inscriptions.[7] The material and often the wording of these official reports are reproduced in his immense *Mission de Phénicie*, the publication of which in parts was begun in March, 1865, and completed ten years later. Even in these archæological notices his style is vigorous and often charming. A letter read by Maury on July 12, 1861, which tells of numerous rock carvings of the Emperor Hadrian's name, adds the remark: "They are, I think, the visiting cards of this traveling Cæsar."[8]

In one interesting episode Renan showed himself decidedly

---

[5] All the details are given in *Sœur Henriette*.

[6] Report dated Amschit, January 30, 1861, in *Moniteur*, February 25 and 27; report dated Beirut, June 28, in *Moniteur*, July 8 and 11; and report dated Paris, January 20, 1862, in *Moniteur*, February 21, 22, 26. A final instalment was announced but not published. The first of these documents also was printed in the *Débats* July 15 and 16 and the *Journal de l'Instruction publique* July 17 and 20 and the *Revue archéologique*, first report March, 1861; second report July, 1861; third, March, April, May, 1862. All are given in full, though they occupied a disproportionate amount of space and crowded out other matter.

[7] See *Comptes rendus*, vol. v.

[8] *Comptes rendus*, vol. v, p. 177.

bellicose. Some inscriptions previously found and offered for sale were refused him, the owner having been scared by the threats of a little group of fanatics. Renan proposed to take them by force, though not without paying even more than their value, but the commander of his naval boat, the *Colbert,* was not willing to lend a hand in the marauding expedition suggested by the gentle scholar.[9] The objects were finally obtained, though we are not told how.[10]

II

During the period extending from the return to Paris to the War of 1870, we shall not be occupied as heretofore with an examination of the growth or modification of Renan's thought or style—for there was none of any serious import—but with the vicissitudes of his public career and the progress of his life work.

The first episode of this nature, an episode that made a great stir at the time, was his appointment to the Chair of Hebrew in the Collège de France. Upon this chair he had fixed his eyes in the earliest days of his career as a scholar, and for it he had prepared himself with the most arduous toil. On the death of Quatremère in 1857, he had made the customary visits to the members of the Academy and the Faculty of the Collège to solicit their support, but the Minister of Public Instruction, instead of calling for the usual presentations, had designated a substitute (*chargé de cours*) to carry on the instruction without the professorial title. While Renan was in Syria, the minister, sharing the general feeling that so distinguished a scholar could no

---

[9] *Ibid.,* vol. v, p. 97.

[10] In the Report to the Emperor published in the *Moniteur,* February 21, space is given to this affair at Ruad. An armed cruiser that accompanied the workmen changed the disposition of the people on the island to such an extent that the excavators were encumbered with too much assistance.

longer be kept in the inferior position he then filled at the Bibliothèque Imperiale, made certain advances, to which Renan replied that he could accept no place but the professorship of Hebrew.[11]

Finally, on December 13, 1861, the minister invited the Academy of Inscriptions to propose two candidates for the chair of Quatremère, at the same time indicating a change of title from Hebrew, Chaldaic and Syrian Languages to Semitic Languages. This change Renan and others opposed, and it was not effected. On December 20, the Academy designated as its first choice Renan and as its second Latouche. Renan was also the first choice of the Faculty of the Collège de France, and his nomination by the minister became almost an obligation. On Sunday, January 12, 1862, the Imperial Decree naming Renan Professor of the Hebrew, Chaldaic and Syrian Languages in the Collège de France was published in the *Moniteur*. It was preceded by a report to the Emperor by Rouland, Minister of Public Instruction and Worship, a report obviously addressed quite as much to Renan and to the public as to his Imperial Highness. It is at once a defense of the appointment and a warning to the appointee. The form, indeed, had been prepared by Renan himself, but the minister had cut out that part of the draft which expressly reserved "the right to treat freely from the standpoint of the historian, literary man, philologist and scholar, all religious questions brought up by the subject of the course," a fact stated in Renan's letter to the *Constitutionnel* dated February 28 and published March 2, 1862. This omission changed the entire implication of the report.

The books [it says] that furnish the texts for the lessons of the professor are largely holy books. Our religion finds in them

---

[11] On December 29, 1860, Renan had been made Chevalier de la Légion d'Honneur.

its origins and also its prayers and its inspiration. It is for this reason that, in faculties of theology, the study of the Hebrew tongue includes traditional and dogmatic explanations which are the source of the received beliefs of every Christian communion. But it is evident that discussions of this kind ought not to take place in the Collège de France, whose chair of Hebrew is, if I may so speak, entirely lay. There, the professor, like all citizens, should maintain the reserve and respect due to the sacred character of the Bible; he leaves to the theologian the field that belongs to him, and he occupies himself exclusively with literary and philological research. Keeping free from religious polemic, he should give himself wholly to investigations useful to the understanding and the progress of the important science of comparative Semitic languages.

Prudence would have counseled Renan, as his friends did, to heed the warning and to begin his course in a small room with his half-dozen pupils without the usual public inaugural lecture. He had attained the chief ambition of his life, and why should he sacrifice it by arousing public clamor?[12] He was, however, unwilling thus to sneak into his chair. As the champion of historical and philological science, he must enter upon his labors with all the customary ceremonies. Among the writers for the *Débats,* to mention no others, Saint-Marc Girardin, Baudrillart, Franck and others announced, delivered and published inaugural lectures. To open a course without one, simply because the situation was dangerous to face, would have been a cowardly slinking away on Renan's part and a triumph for his opponents. He announced his discourse for Saturday, February 22,[13] and all Paris prepared for an interesting occasion.

Bersot, writing to his family under date of February 23, says:[14] "I went yesterday to the inaugural lecture of Re-

---

[12] On January 28, he wrote to Michele Amari: "In any case, I shall face the storm. I shall give my first lecture without any reserve and with full publicity." Michele Amari, *Carteggio,* ii, p. 155.

[13] It was really given February 22, though the date in *Mélanges* is February 21.

[14] *Bersot et ses amis,* p. 180.

nan's course. It was uncertain how he would be received. The young men like him as a man of talent and a free-thinker in religion; but he had accepted the Syrian Mission from the Emperor, and they waited till the last moment to consult their leaders in order to know whether to hiss or applaud. In the end, for fear of being confused with the clericals, as in the About affair,[15] they applauded furiously. . . . Renan said some of the strongest things ever spoken in a professor's chair. In the tumultuous court, Bersot carried a policeman on his back.''

Taine's account is as follows:[16]

The Liberal students went to ask M. Despois whether they should hiss; the Catholics to ask M. Laprade.[17] There was a group that hissed, but those who applauded were in an overwhelming majority. When the torrent poured in, the crowd at the door was so violent that it tore down a lamp; the police had to clear the yard by force; I saw one man with a bloody head.

For three-quarters of an hour, there was a storm of vociferations, savage howls and laughter. "Long live Quinet, Michelet, Prévost-Paradol, Laprade! Long live Guéroult! Down with Guéroult! Down with the Jesuits!" Renan enters; all rise; there is a thunder of cheers, howls, waving of hats, a few hisses; then a louder thunder of applause; for twenty minutes he cannot say a word. He attempts by futile gestures to obtain silence. His gestures are a bit like those of a bishop (a bishop *in partibus infidelium*), and so are certain phrases of his lecture. It is published in

[15] About's *Gaëtana* had on January 2, 1862, been hooted off the stage at the Odeon by a combination of liberals and clericals, the liberals objecting to his complaisance to authority and the clericals to his writings on the affair of Rome. About the same time, a bitter personal, as well as clerical and anticlerical, quarrel ensued between Augier and Laprade. Laprade published in the *Correspondant*, ''La Chasse aux vaincus,'' a malignant attack in verse, and Augier answered in kind in *l'Opinion nationale* in prose. Both pieces are printed together—with regret—in the *Débats* for January 2 and 3, 1863.
[16] *Vie et correspondance*, ii, pp. 227, 228.
[17] Both Despois and Laprade had been dismissed from their chairs; the first for refusing to take the oath in 1852, and the second for his poem, ''Les Muses d'État,'' in 1861. In Laprade's case the Minister had spoken even more brutally about pay and obligations than was done at Renan's dismissal.

the *Débats*. He always talks as though pronouncing a benediction.

His lecture (on what the Semites have done for general civilization) is extremely good. Bold passages about Christianity and the Pope. The students applauded like readers of the *Siècle*, coarsely. After the lecture, an enormous column under umbrellas goes to cheer him at rue Madame.

Renan was not there, but his aged mother, proud of any honor paid to her son, showed herself to the crowd, accompanied by the faithful Professor Egger, and accepted their tumultuous plaudits.

As a matter of fact, there is in the celebrated address nothing that Renan had not said more emphatically in his published writings. It was indeed little more than a condensation of his views on general history and the Semitic character. The lecture is two-thirds over before he says a word about what all had come to hear. "We owe the Semites neither our political life, nor our art, nor our poetry, nor our philosophy, nor our science. What, then, do we owe them? We owe them our religion." In another five minutes comes the famous sentence:

An incomparable man—so great that, although in this place everything must be judged from the standpoint of positive science, I would not contradict those who, struck by the exceptional character of his work, call him God—brought about a reform of Judaism so profound, so individual, that it was truly a complete creation. Having reached the highest religious stage that ever man had attained, regarding God in the relation of a son to a father, devoted to his work with total oblivion of all else, and with an abnegation never practiced in so lofty a spirit, victim finally of his idea and deified by his death, Jesus founded the eternal religion of humanity, the religion of the spirit, disengaged from all priesthood, from all forms of worship, from all observances, accessible to every caste, in a word, absolute. "Woman, the time is come when they will adore neither on this mountain nor in Jerusalem, but where the true worshipers adore in spirit and in truth." [18]

---

[18] *Mélanges d'histoire et de voyages*, p. 18. Cf. *Avenir*, p. 474.

Among the strong things that Bersot speaks of is perhaps the following: "As I shall bring into my teaching no dogmatism, as I shall limit myself always to an appeal to your reason, setting before you what I consider most probable and leaving you perfect liberty of judgment, who can complain? Only those who believe themselves to have a monopoly of the truth. But they, indeed, must relinquish their position of masters of the world. In our days, Galileo would not kneel to beg pardon for having discovered the truth." [19] Or it may be such a remark as this: "David became king by the weapons of an energetic *condottiere*, yet this did not hinder him from being a very religious man, a king according to God's own heart." [20]

The conclusion presents, with little modification, the religious ideas of *The Future of Science*. "Our religion will become less and less Jewish; more and more it will reject political organization applied to things of the spirit. It will become the religion of the heart, the inward poetry of each. . . . We shall pursue the nuance, seeking delicacy instead of dogmatism, the relative instead of the absolute." Will science repay our sacrifice? The speaker cannot tell, but he is sure that we shall have done our duty. If truth is sad, we shall at least have deserved a better consolation. History shows that there is in human nature a transcendental instinct, and the development of humanity is inexplicable on the hypothesis of a finite destiny in which virtue is but refined egotism and religion a chimera. In spite of the author of Ecclesiastes, science is not the worst, but the best occupation given to the sons of men. If all is vanity, we are no more dupes than others. If, on the other hand, "the true and the good are really something, as we feel assured they are, then without contradiction he who seeks and loves them has followed the best inspiration."

[19] *Ibid.*, pp. 4, 5.
[20] *Ibid.*, p. 11.

After this conclusion, Renan added a few words called forth by the demonstration that had accompanied his address. In the next lesson he will plunge into Hebrew philology. The vivacity of his young auditors, praiseworthy in principle, should not be allowed to degenerate into frivolous agitation. "Turn to solid studies," he says; "believe that what is liberal in the highest degree is culture of mind, nobility of heart, independence of judgment. Prepare for our land a generation ripe for everything that makes the glory and the ornament of life. Beware of thoughtless enthusiasm, and remember that liberty is won only by seriousness, by respect for ourself and for others, by devotion to the public good and to the special task that each of us in this world is called upon either to found or to continue." [21]

The lecture, as published in the *Débats* (February 25), was introduced by Prévost-Paradol, who maintains that Renan had won a complete victory, having had more trouble from the enthusiasm of approbation than from marks of disapproval. On February 26, in announcing that Lévy would bring out the discourse on the following day, the *Débats* published the prefatory note, in which, after thanking his auditors for their kindness, Renan expresses the opinion that those who interrupt a thoughtful address which they have not been obliged to attend commit an illiberal act by imposing their opinion and suppressing the opinion of others by violence. In order that the public should not be deceived by the inaugural discourse, he further indicates that all future lessons will be entirely technical.

It is little wonder that Bersot wrote, February 25: "All goes well for you, and I am delighted. Your lecture is fine and decisive for the liberty of science." Indeed, according to the standards of the time, the occasion had been a success,

---

[21] *Ibid.*, pp. 24, 25.

and Renan's moderation was generally recognized. A considerable number of professors had, during the preceding quarter of a century, been prevented by turbulent students from giving their courses, among them Renan's friend, Sainte-Beuve, in 1855, nor did the practice cease. A little over a year later, Viollet-le-Duc was driven from his chair at the École des Beaux-Arts by a volley of pototes [22] and Taine, who replaced him with success, was received with a noisy demonstration that, as in Renan's case, followed him through the streets to his home. Adolphe Franck, too, in 1863, when speaking of de Maistre and de Bonald, encountered a row raised by their clerical defenders, which was suppressed by a counter-demonstration.[23] But in comparison with the affair of the professorship of Hebrew, these were as ripples by the side of ocean billows. Jules Simon testifies that the celebrated phrase was pronounced simply and naturally and furthermore that Renan never sought effects or did anything for notoriety. "The third day," says the victim, "certain persons, who ought to be well enough satisfied with their privileges not to be jealous of the liberty accorded to others, caused me to be forbidden to speak." [24] The course was suspended by imperial order on February 26, before a single lesson in Hebrew could be given, the grounds of the suspension being that "M. Renan has expounded doctrines injurious to Christian belief, and which may lead to regrettable agitations." [25]

The debate was continued in the press during the early days of March, the *Constitutionnel* accusing the professor of bad faith, a charge against which he vigorously defended

---

[22] As Viollet-le-Duc left the hall, he was accompanied by a hostile crowd of noisy, singing students. Théophile Gautier, who attempted to make a speech to them in favor of his friend, was arrested by the police who dispersed the mob. Maxime du Camp, *Souvenirs littéraires,* vol. ii, p. 240.

[23] *Débats,* January 27, 1863.

[24] *Questions contemporaines,* p. ix.

[25] *Débats,* February 28, 1862.

himself, though not to the satisfaction of his accusers.[26] Scholarship was almost unanimously in favor of the professor. Its judgment may be fairly represented by the following passage from the *Revue archéologique* (March, 1862): ''M. Ernest Renan began, Saturday, the 22nd, his course at the Collège de France. There was a large audience. It was feared that this was in part hostile. Some malevolent feelings were, indeed, shown at the beginning of the lecture, but they soon gave place to displays of approbation under the influence of the lofty and calm language of the professor. This first lecture was for M. Renan a real success, which will please every friend of science.''

Renan's feeling in the matter is well represented in a letter to Grant Duff.[27]

For my part, I do not feel wounded. I shall reopen in a few weeks; the course is therefore not threatened. On the other hand, the human species is so silly that those who govern it must be permitted to make concessions to its foolishness. The most that can be asked of the present government is that it should be inconsequent. The suspension was ordered on account of the reclamations of certain cardinals, which were almost threatening, and after most insistent efforts with the Empress by several bishops. The coincidence of the discussions in the Senate, of the speech of Prince Napoleon, of the Roman affair and of a certain agitation among the youth was of still more decisive weight. The Emperor is the one I most willingly pardon. His position amid the heated passions that tear the country is most difficult. Each act in the liberal direction recoils on him as a fault. In naming me in spite of the active opposition of the Catholic party, he performed an act almost courageous. As he did nothing but confirm the nomination made by the Collège de France and the Institut, it was certainly a liberal act. No other government in France would have done it. If the concession just made in the opposite direc-

---

[26] See *Débats* March 1 and 2, and *Constitutionnel*, February 28 and March 2 and 3. These latter articles are signed by Paulin Limayrac and P. de Troimonts. In a quotation from *le Siècle* and a nameless sheet published in the Latin Quarter it is said that ''not all the hisses came from Catholics.''

[27] March 10, 1862, *Memoir*, pp. 66, 67.

tion can aid in bringing about a liberal solution of the Roman affair, I shall very willingly forget.

Early in May Renan went to Dordrecht, Holland, to be present at the inauguration of the statue of Ary Scheffer, erected in his birthplace. The celebrated museum of oriental antiquities, as well as the distinguished body of professors, tempted him then to visit Leyden, and here, at the home of Professor Kuenen, a delegation of about thirty students of theology through one of their number chosen for the occasion greeted him in the name of the university as the champion of liberty in the realm of historical and religious studies. Renan, in his reply, expressed his deep appreciation of the spontaneous and wholly unexpected demonstration, and urged the distinction between religion itself and the supernatural, the one eternal, the other dying out through the spread of scientific and historical investigation. The incident was indeed gratifying in view of the organized opposition in Paris.[28]

In order to state his side of the case, Renan published on July 15 a pamphlet addressed to his colleagues at the Collège de France,[29] which ran through five editions before the end of the year. An equal popular demand greeted the inaugural lecture in pamphlet form. Instead of being suppressed, Renan actually addressed a wider audience than any that could have crowded into any amphitheater in existence. The whole episode is a glaring instance of the stupidity and flabbiness of Napoleon's government. If it had

---

[28] Correspondence from Holland, *le Siècle*, May 17, and *le Temps*, June 14, 1862. See *Questions contemporaines*, p. 220.

[29] *La Chaire d'Hébreu au Collège de France*, explications à mes Collègues, Michel Lévy, 1862. In the *Débats* for August 31, Prévost-Paradol published the last division of this pamphlet with an introduction in which he summarizes and approves the main points. Renan corrects one view of Prévost-Paradol in a letter dated July 31 and published in the *Débats* August 5 and reprinted in *Questions contemporaines*.

not been ready to meet opposition, it should never have made the appointment, for opposition was certain and readily to be foreseen; having made the appointment, it should undoubtedly have maintained Renan in his post.

The explanation to his colleagues is much more methodical than Renan's other writings. He has been reproached, he says, on four points: (1) Seeking an appointment that was bound to cause trouble, (2) giving an inaugural lecture, (3) the subject of the lecture, (4) the mode of treatment. Two divisions of his pamphlet are devoted to the first point: (1) It was his duty as a scholar to seek the chair, and "those who know me will have the justice to admit that what I have once conceived as a duty, I do not abandon''; (2) the chair is purely scientific and philological. The third division is occupied with the inaugural lecture: "If I had relinquished it, a special circumstance would have given my renunciation a color that I could not accept. . . . If the inaugural lecture had not been an established usage, I should never have invented it. But, since the custom existed, to relinquish it would be to retreat before a threat, to admit the justice of those who maintained that I dared not avow my principles.'' In the fourth division, he shows that the terms in which he had referred to Jesus had been used even by Bossuet and that the theological Faculty of the University of Leyden, by a spontaneous manifestation, had recognized his expression as truly Christian.[30] In the last two divisions he takes up the mode of treatment, maintaining that he spoke, not as a theologian but as a historian; that it is a fundamental principle of science that there is no supernatural event. "For science a supernatural explanation is neither true nor false; it is not an explanation.'' To

---

[30] Charles Ritter writes August 6, 1862, of ''an address of M. Renan to the Faculty of Theology of Leyden, in which he repeats what he has so often said about the necessity of separating the ever triumphant cause of religion from the lost cause of miracles.'' This is the address noted above.

separate religion from the supernatural, he continues, is not irreligious; it is rather, since belief in the supernatural is disappearing from the world, to render religion a service. "Bubbles of a moment on the surface of the ocean of being, we feel with the abyss, our father, a mysterious affinity. God does not reveal himself by miracles, but in the heart."

Renan does not argue; he simply states his case.[31] It is obvious that his appeal for liberty and for a purely scientific attitude toward his subject must fall on deaf ears. The differences between him and his opponents were irreconcilable, and both he and they were inflexible.

Still, for some time, Renan in his guileless way, believed that the course was only postponed, not finally prohibited. He even, as a further plea for the neutrality of the state in intellectual matters, urged the appointment of Adolphe Régnier, who had been recommended by both the Academy and the Collège, to the chair of Burnouf, vacant since 1852. As Régnier had been tutor to the Comte de Paris, he would for personal reasons refuse to take the oath of allegiance to the Empire; but should a mere question of politics interfere with the progress of Sanscrit studies?[32] Régnier was never appointed. He was first choice of the Collège de France for the new chair of comparative grammar, which was to be supported out of the appropriation for the chair of Hebrew,[33] but the Minister, instead of asking for the necessary nominations from the Academy of Inscriptions, designated the second choice of the Collège, Michel Bréal, as *chargé de cours*. It was not until April, 1866, that a can-

[31] The sort of argument involved in the case may be represented by the pamphlet, "Du discours d'ouverture de M. E. Renan" by François René Guettée, a widely known clerical editor and historian, who demonstrates Renan's ignorance of history and science by the fact that he does not know that all mankind is descended from the three sons of Noah.

[32] "La Chaire de Sanscrit au Collège de France," *Débats*, December 10, 1862; reprinted in *Questions contemporaines.*

[33] *Débats*, June 13, 1864.

didate was demanded of the Academy, and then Régnier, in a dignified letter, refused to stand, on the ground that, as the *chargé de cours* was admirably fitted for the post, there was no question of scholarship involved. Bréal, translator of Bopp,[34] and already noted for original investigations, was made first choice, and thereupon appointed by the Minister professor of comparative grammar. A history of the educational establishment under the Empire is quite as instructive as that of political events.

As early as March, 1863, Renan feels insecure; he may be dismissed, in which case he is ready to stand for election to the Corps Législatif from some radical Paris district, a duty, yet a great sacrifice, for his heart is set on a life of free and peaceful teaching.[35] "Do not think," he writes Berthelot, September 24, "that politics attract me; I swear in all sincerity that I should prefer to be a peaceable professor with ten pupils, making my books at leisure, and having some day as my supreme ambition to become the administrator of the Collège." By autumn he felt that some action on his part was required. All his friends told him that a renewal of his Hebrew course was hopeless.[36] The government could not permit the rows that would ensue. On September 29, he wrote to Bersot: "I am going to give at home the course I should have given at the Collège de France. My study is small, but, if necessary, I will hire another. I desire that no one in need of such teaching should be deprived of it. I believe, besides, that it is good to make the experiment for the sake of the general freedom of teaching." In the *Journal Asiatique,* November-December, 1863, appeared a notice signed J. M. (Mohl) to the effect that Renan offers a course in Hebrew to a limited number of pupils at his home and that he proposes to

---

[34] See long notice by Renan in *Débats,* May 3, 1866.
[35] *Carteggio di Michele Amari,* vol. ii, p. 163.
[36] Berthelot, September 3, 1863.

do this as long as he cannot give it in public at the Collège de France.

The whole procedure, though Renan found precedent for it in the sixteenth century and in Burnouf's action in 1848, was utterly irregular, and Victor Duruy, the new minister of public instruction, sought to end it, for, though to a large extent liberal, he wanted order. During the summer Taschereau, head of the library, had offered Renan a place as keeper in the department of manuscripts at 7,000 francs, which was more than the professorial salary, but Renan had declined, because as the law forbade holding a position in the library and at the Collège at the same time, to accept would imply his resignation of the chair of Hebrew.[37] At length an expedient presented itself to the minister on the death of Hase, who had held three positions, keeper of manuscripts at the Bibliothèque Imperiale, professor of comparative grammar at the Sorbonne, and professor of modern Greek and Greek paleography at the School of Living Oriental Languages. Duruy, in his report to the Emperor, dated June 1, 1864, proposed several changes, obviously in order that the transfer of Renan might be disguised as part of a general scheme. First, paleography was dropped from its association with modern Greek; then the chair of comparative grammar was transferred from the Sorbonne to the Collège de France as the more appropriate institution. To effectuate this transfer, since there were no appropriations in the budget, he suggested using provisionally the funds voted for the chair of Hebrew, Chaldaic and Syrian languages, a chair not occupied for two years. "It is against the interests of the service and the proper expenditure of public funds, as well as the dignity of the distinguished scholar forced to submit to this anomaly, that payment should be received when the functions are not performed."

---

[37] To Berthelot, September 8, 1863.

Renan had come from the library with the title of honorary librarian: he might now return as keeper and subdirector in the department of manuscripts, "where his special learning will allow him to render real service to the public." [38]

This whole clumsy report,—clumsy especially in its insistent reference to money—together with the imperial decrees, putting its recommendations in force, appeared in the *Moniteur* for June 2. Duruy apparently wanted to get out of an embarrassing situation in the easiest available way, but he merely succeeded in irritating Renan to the utmost. On the spur of the moment and burning with an indignation which he made no attempt to restrain, the transferred professor wrote the minister an open letter, in which even the friendly *Débats* found one expression "a little too vivacious." He flatly refused the library appointment and flatly refused to resign his chair, for he considered this particular task his scientific and moral duty. Since he had been assured that he could not reopen his course, he had given

---

[38] The chronology of the controversy in the *Débats* is as follows: June 2, a note by L. Alloury reserving judgment, and in another column, Duruy's report; June 4, Renan's letter with the statement that "M. Renan begs us to reproduce the following letter that he has just sent to the Minister of Public Instruction; June 5, editorial comment signed "The Secretary of the Editorial Board, F. Camus; June 6, a note questioning the legality of the call just issued for nominations to the newly established chair of comparative grammar at the Collège de France, to which the appropriation of the chair of Hebrew had been diverted; June 10, a long editorial by Edouard Laboulaye attacking the legality of Duruy's action. On June 11, *Le Constitutionnel* refutes Laboulaye's argument (signed L. Boniface) on the grounds that the decree of July 11, 1863, applied only to the University, of which the Collège de France was plainly not a part, an argument for strict construction as opposed to an interpretation of the spirit of the decree. If Renan's friends object to Duruy's indirect method and are so strangely eager for an explicit dismissal, "we see no reason why they should not receive this satisfaction." After the dismissal, on June 17, Paulin Limayrac editorially maintains that Renan's discharge has nothing to do with liberty of conscience. In a contemptible tone of journalistic superiority, he defends the government and belittles Renan as a man "not sufficiently master of himself for a public teacher," and as not earning his pay. All these articles in both journals occupy a prominent place on the first page.

instruction at his home. He still holds the professorial title and he will continue to teach without pay. It is the harping on money that chiefly arouses his wrath. "Science measures merits by the results obtained, not by the more or less punctual performance of any regulations, and, if you ever reproach a scholar who has done his country some honor with not earning the petty sum allowed him by the state, believe me, Mr. Minister, he will answer you as I do, and following an illustrious example; *Pecunia tua tecum sit."*

"Thy money perish with thee," is the English version of Acts, viii. 20. Renan's Latin, with the omission of *in perditionem,* is the sort of parliamentary language that actually sharpens the sting by innuendo. What in plain English is merely a gross vulgarism—"Go to Hell with your money!"—becomes amazingly effective when expressed in Biblical Latin. Moreover, the implication of the passage referred to—Simon trying to buy the gift of the Holy Spirit with silver—fits the case in hand to perfection and adds enormously to the effect. The occasion and the act were unique in Renan's career. This was his one blow delivered without premeditation or remorse straight in the face of his opponent. Holding the cause in question sacred, he never retracted or apologized or even softened the vivacity of his abusive citation. On June 12, the *Moniteur* published the decree revoking both appointments.[39] This was an act of arbitrary power, highly displeasing to the liberals,[40] and

---

[39] England was no less illiberal than France. Mrs. Ward went to Oxford in 1865, at which time Jowett's "salary as Greek Professor, due him from the revenues of Christ Church, and withheld from him on theological grounds for years, had only just been wrung—at last—from the reluctant hands of a governing body which contained Canon Liddon and Doctor Pusey." *A Writer's Recollections,* vol. i, p. 136, by Mrs. Humphry Ward. Taine found Jowett's liberalism "akin to Renan's"—Letter of May 27, 1871—*Correspondance,* vol. iii, p. 133.

[40] One imperial reason reads: "In view of the decree of March 9, 1852, ordaining that the Emperor names and dismisses professors at the Collège de France," thus going back to the oppressive days of the Coup D'État and disregarding in spirit the liberal decree of July 11,

the results could not have been thoroughly satisfactory even to the clericals. When candidates were asked for in December, the blind Salomon Munk, a prominent Jewish scholar,[41] was presented by Faculty and Academy, and he received the appointment the next June in spite of Duruy's scruples about having three Jewish professors in the Collège. Renan published the documents in a pamphlet, *The Dismissal of a Professor at the Collège de France,* to which he gave permanence in his *Questions contemporaines* (1868), and though expelled from his chair, he remained master of the field.

III

In this whole affair, the greatest scandal to Renan's opponents was the publication of the *Life of Jesus* on June 24, 1863. Though certainly not so intended, it seemed like a gage of defiance designed to insult and irritate. That Renan had such a work in hand was no secret. Taine, who saw much of him at Chalifer, writes:

He read me a long piece of his *Life of Jesus.* He constructs this life delicately but arbitrarily; the documents are too much altered, too uncertain. For the period of Nazareth, he puts together all the gentle and agreeable ideas of Jesus, removes all the gloomy ones, and makes a charming mystical pastoral. Then, in another chapter, he gathers every threat, every bitterness, and attaches these to the journey to Jerusalem. In vain Berthelot and I told him that this is putting a romance in place of a legend; that, by a mixture of hypotheses, he spoils those parts that are certain; that the clerical party will triumph and pierce him in the weak spot, etc. He will hear nothing, see nothing but his

---

1863, by which professors of the University could be dismissed only after a hearing.

[41] Grant Duff says that Renan placed Munk highest among the Jewish scholars of France. *Memoir,* p. 50. He was not, however, a native Frenchman, having been born in Silesia. His oriental studies begun at Bonn were completed in Paris and he became, like Mohl, a naturalized citizen.

231

idea, tells us that we are not artists, that a simply positive and dogmatic treatise would not reproduce the life that Jesus lived and must be made to live again, that he does not care if people howl, etc., etc. Lack of prudence and caution.[42]

Hints had even come to the general public. Sainte-Beuve had heard the substance of the work and let the readers of the *Constitutionnel* into his confidence in 1862, and on the verge of publication, in reviewing Dupanloup's *Avertissement à la jeunesse et aux pères de famille sur les attaques dirigées contre la religion par quelques écrivains de nos jours,* an attack on Littré, Maury, Renan, and Taine, Bersot suggests that, instead of paying any attention to these charges, Maury had better continue to busy himself with erudition, Taine with his *History of English Literature,* Littré with his dictionary, and Renan with the correction of the proofs of his *Life of Jesus.*[43] Even a distinguished foreigner like Senior noted (May 1) the substance of several long conversations held during the previous ten days with Renan on the subject of his unpublished, though already printed work, *Histoire critique des origines du Christianisme.*[44]

---

[42] Taine, *Vie et correspondance,* vol. iii, p. 245.

[43] *Débats,* April 27, 1863. Dupanloup's pamphlet consisted of a collection of citations from articles and books by the four writers. Bersot objects that to present such passages out of their context is unfair and that the appearance of the tract on the eve of the vote on Littré's candidacy for the Academy was an act of bad faith and against liberty of conscience. The following passage is quoted: "I will strip their works and tear away all their disguises. I wish to place them under the necessity of either denying my charges by affirming that they believe in God, the soul, immortality and religion, or of accepting publicly the title of atheists and materialists from which they shrink." (P. 9.) Dupanloup had been a member of the Academy since 1854. This time he was successful in defeating Littré, and in 1871, when Littré was finally elected, he resigned from the Academy, though his resignation could not be accepted and no successor was chosen till after his death in 1878. He did not live to see his two other abominations, Renan and Taine, take their academic seats.

[44] N. W. Senior, *Conversations with Distinguished Persons during the Second Empire.*

The advance notice in the *Débats* was written by the sturdy, but liberal-minded Jansenist, de Sacy,[45] and perhaps no fairer estimate of the work has been published. Out of the four Gospels and his own conjectures, Renan constructs, for this first volume of his *Origins of Christianity*, a sort of fifth Gospel, from which, to de Sacy's regret, miracles are absent. It is the "fruit of long labor and great inward agitations." The writer "seeks to conciliate the most exalted mysticism with the most hardy skepticism, the rigor of historical method with a transcendental imagination." The book is full of interest; the things have been actually seen, but de Sacy prefers the simplicity of the old Evangelists. "I believe in the Gospels of Matthew, Mark, Luke, and John; I do not believe in the Gospel of M. Renan." The remainder of the notice consists of an argument for liberty of criticism.[46]

The review in the *Débats* (August 28, 1863) was written by Bersot, who undertook the ticklish task unwillingly and against the advice of friends. He was not, indeed, a specialist in biblical studies. Thus the greater part of the article is taken up with a discussion of eighteenth-century skepticism as contrasted with the modern critical method. He imagines how the book might have been otherwise done, is surprised at the idea of a trick in the Raising of Lazarus, and realizes that the portrayal of Jesus as a delicate, charming young man, will wound, though not purposely. Jesus always hangs between science and art, and Renan, much in the manner of Ary Scheffer, has painted his picture. To this Renan privately answers, when thanking Bersot for his review:[47] "I assure you that I wrote the book with a

---

[45] Lévy feared that the edition might be seized by the government. Renan therefore requested de Sacy, Sainte-Beuve, and other liberal journalists to say that in their opinion such things had a right to be printed. See letter to Bersot August 28, 1863.

[46] *Débats*, June 24, 1863, the date of publication.

[47] August 28, 1863; *Bersot et ses amis*, p. 188.

sentiment far superior to petty vanity. . . . I do not believe that this way of trying to reconstruct the original physiognomies of the past is so arbitrary as you seem to believe. I have not seen the personage; I have not seen his photograph; but we have a multitude of descriptive details about him. To try to group these into something living is not as arbitrary as the entirely ideal procedure of Raphael or Titian.''

The Catholic party greeted the book with howls of rage and with calumnies for which Renan thought he had a right to bring legal action for slander.[48] The most innocent of these tales was that Rothschild had subsidized him with a million francs. The most virulent of the printed libels was a pamphlet, *Renan en famille*,[49] a series of pretended letters between Renan and a supposed Sister Ursule, introduced, with the obvious intention of inflicting as much pain as possible, by a letter from the spirit of Henriette, in which she is made to say: ''Blot out my name at once from that book, which is as badly written and heavy as it is abominable, and from that preface with its grotesque pretentiousness and its pitiable French.'' It is reported that the guests in a hotel at Dinard threatened to leave if Renan were allowed to remain there, and certainly a local newspaper published some malignant verses, beginning, ''Breton, no! Jew sprung from the blood of Judas Iscariot, what have you come here for?'' Even Jasmin published an offensive poem [50] in which ''he left his sphere and forced his

---

[48] Anti- and pro-Renan biographies were written. Carfort and Bazonge, *Biographie de Ernest Renan*, Paris, 1863, a pamphlet of about a hundred pages, dated December 10, 1863; E. Le Peltier, *Vie de E. Renan*, Paris, 1864, a pamphlet of thirty-one pages, dated October 10, 1863. Referring to the preceding brochure, Peltier says that, having learned that two fanatics in Brittany were falsifying Renan's biography, he had hastened to write his defense first. Neither is of any value.

[49] By Ch. de Bussy, Paris, 1866.

[50] Lou poèto del puple à mossu Renan, Agen, Août, 1864.

rustic pipe."[51] And the feeling did not soon abate. Taine tells with great glee the story of a young mistress of Plon-Plon, who complained bitterly that, on the trip to Norway in 1870, she had to sit at table with such an impious renegade.[52] Renan remained also a popular subject of caricatures, none of which seem to have been very brilliant.

Such was not, of course, the attitude of opponents of elevated sentiments, though their hostility was just as bitter. Cousin called the book an atheistical work.[53] Dupanloup and Gratry, among many, wrote opposition Lives of Jesus. The Empress with strange moderation said to Mme. Cornu: "It will do no harm to those who believe in Christ; and to those who do not it will do good."[54] She appreciated Renan's purpose. "No, indeed," he wrote to Sainte-Beuve,[55] "I have not wished to separate from the old trunk a single soul that was not ripe." What, on the other hand, the representative pious Catholic felt is perhaps best expressed in a letter written to Bersot by Montalembert (June 16, 1863?): "It must be easy for you to fancy what a Christian has to suffer in reading the *Life of Jesus*. Imagine what you yourself would feel if your father were treated publicly as a *charming impostor*. Just imagine that Jesus Christ is for us more than a father, that he is our God, that all our hopes and all our consolations are based upon his divine personality, and then ask yourself if there could be for our hearts a more deadly wound than that here given."[56]

---

[51] Sainte-Beuve, *Nouveaux Lundis,* vol. x, p. 170.
[52] Letter of August 31, 1870.
[53] Letter to Bersot, August 14, 1863.
[54] Grant Duff, p. 70. Such opposition Lives, written to counteract the effect of Renan's, were apparently addressed exclusively to the French public. I cannot find that they have been translated. The continued popularity of Renan's work contradicts the Abbé Freppel's prediction in his *Examen critique* that "no one would talk of Renan's book in three or four months."
[55] *Nouveaux Lundis,* vol. vi, p. 15, note.
[56] *Bersot et ses amis,* p. 19.

Renan seems, on the whole, to have been strangely obtuse to the offensiveness of his book to believers. He sent copies with an affectionate dedication to former comrades of Saint-Sulpice, some of them already bishops.[57] He was, indeed, so engrossed in his own idea that he could not sympathize with the opposite view, and seems to have felt the same naïve surprise at the rumpus over his *Life of Jesus* as he felt at the Abbé Cognat's refusal in early years to continue their discussions of Christianity.[58] In spite of all warnings, he went directly ahead, convinced that what he was doing was what needed to be done.

Meanwhile the book sold by the thousands, and during the latter half of '63, Paris talked of nothing else.[59] Renan did not utter a word in reply to attacks, a policy he had learned from the wise de Sacy. To a certain extent he had become insensible to abuse. "By character," he writes Bersot,[60] "I am entirely indifferent to such things; I do not believe they impede the progress of sane ideas. As for my book, it goes the better, and I might suspect my publisher of inspiring such opposition. Each edition of 5,000 is exhausted in eight or ten days and a letter from Lévy just received tells me that in this last period, the sale, far from slowing up, even goes faster. I say this without vanity, for it does not prove the book either good or bad. But it does prove that the means employed to smother it are not very efficacious." By November 60,000 copies had been sold, and translations had appeared in Dutch, Ger-

---

[57] Jules Simon, *Quatre Portraits.*

[58] Renan's letters to Cognat and Cognat's account in *Renan hier et aujourd'hui.*

[59] In his account of Renan's reception at the Academy, G. Valbert tells the anecdote of a lady who, after having devoured the *Life of Jesus,* said with a sigh: "I am so disappointed that it does not end in a marriage." *Revue des deux Mondes,* April 15, 1879, p. 941. As there are other similar anecdotes, e. g. of the English lady who wondered how the story would turn out—it is obvious that they are all apocryphal, a mere method of implying romance.

[60] August 28, 1863; *Bersot et ses amis,* p. 189.

man and Italian. The popularity of the most celebrated novels had, as Sainte-Beuve remarks, been surpassed.

Constructive criticism was furnished by Scherer in the *Temps* [61] and by Havet in the *Revue des deux Mondes* (August 1).[62] Another excellent criticism was that of Albert Réville.[63] After disposing of the dogmatic critics, including deists, Catholics and Protestants, Réville gives his own views, concluding that, on the whole, Renan has lessened rather than enlarged Jesus. The two main objections are Renan's confidence in the Fourth Gospel and his treatment of the Raising of Lazarus, which puts Jesus in the position of at least consenting to a pious fraud.[64] Both of these points Renan modified in the thirteenth, which was the first revised, edition, the Lazarus story being there regarded as a result of popular confusion, and the fourth Gospel being treated not as emanating from St. John, but as still containing incidents transmitted from an eyewitness of the crucifixion.

So far as the year 1863 is concerned, the whole matter is summed up in Sainte-Beuve's masterly *Lundi* of September 7.[65] Writing for the *Constitutionnel* and wishing to keep on good terms with the government, Sainte-Beuve was not, as he confesses to Renan,[66] entirely free, yet such re-

---

[61] *Mélanges d'histoire religieuse.*

[62] Havet's article, "L'Évangile et l'Histoire," gives a laudatory account of Renan's book with a few reflections, and then proceeds to the objections, which may be summed up in the general statement "that his criticism in detail is not always sufficiently firm and severe. M. Renan knows all that can be known, and no one has anything to teach him . . . he voluntarily refuses to follow his own criticism to the end."

[63] *La Vie de Jésus de M. Renan*, 1864, a reprint from the *Revue germanique et française.*

[64] These are also among the main objections of the Strassburg school, as set forth by Colani, *Examen de la vie de Jésus de Renan*, 1864.

[65] *Nouveaux Lundis*, vi, p. 1 et seq. Sainte-Beuve also republished from the *Constitutionnel* his note recommending the book on the day of publication.

[66] Letter of September 19, *Nouvelle Correspondance*, p. 183.

straint as he felt hindered him surprisingly little in conveying his liberalism and his sympathy.[67] Showing utter contempt for the corsairs of literature, who interrupt a scandalous tale to defend the divinity of Christ, he treats real opponents with a sort of respectful irony. These are personified in three objecting friends, a Catholic, a freethinker and a political opportunist, who call on him under the pretext of asking his opinion, but really to express their own, which is "what is generally done when one goes to ask an opinion." "Feeble and foolhardy," "surrender and concession," "dangerous agitation," such are the three judgments, summing up, minus the abuse, the attitude of the unfriendly press and public. Sainte-Beuve himself appreciates thoroughly, though with some few delicately expressed reserves, the artistic qualities of the book. Renan is not content to destroy, he builds, for he knows that nothing is destroyed until something is put in its place. The *Life*, addressed to the public, has reached its address. It is a narrative, not of absolute fact, but probable and plausible, "not very far from the truth." Renan, "to be historian and story-teller from this new point of view, had to begin by being above all a diviner,[68] a poet drawing inspiration from the spirit of times and places, a painter able to read the lines of the horizon, the least vestiges left on the slopes of the hills, and skilled in evoking the genius of the region and the landscape. He has thus succeeded in producing a work of art even more than a history, and this presupposes on the part of the author a union, till now almost unique, of superior qualities, reflective, delicate and brilliant."[69]

---

[67] Sainte-Beuve was a valuable asset to the *Constitutionnel*. His name is signed to his articles in type as heavy as the titles, a distinction accorded to no other contributor.

[68] In an essay on Ampère, Sainte-Beuve says, "In M. Ampère you always find one who divines beneath him who knows."

[69] Pp. 16, 17.

But what Sainte-Beuve chiefly praises is Renan's courage. It is true the author did not have to flee Paris, as Rousseau had done a hundred years before, but he had drawn upon himself a strife with "a notable and little amiable portion of humanity for the rest of his life," enough to intimidate one of less firmness. "Those of us who have the honor of M. Renan's acquaintance know that he has strength enough to face the situation. He will show neither irritation, nor bad temper; he will remain calm and patient, even serene; he will retain his quiet smile; he will preserve his loftiness by never answering. He will vigorously pursue his work, his exposition henceforth more solid, more historical and scientific; no cries or clamors will cause him to deviate a single instant from his aim." [70]

Such words seem bold enough, yet Sainte-Beuve wrote personally to Renan: "You have won for us the right of discussion on this matter, hitherto forbidden to all. The dignity of your language and of your thoughts has forced the defenses," [71] and again, at a later date, when thanking for an article on *Port-Royal:* "I place my intellectual honor in having my name associated with yours in this reform which is to be undertaken at the present period of the century. I have come too late and am about to finish. You are in full career, and you can long endure and fight. Your approval gives me the illusion that on some points my thought is entwined with yours." [72] Whatever may be the final judgment on the *Life of Jesus,* it was a resounding and ultimately triumphant blow for intellectual liberty in France.

Renan's conception is, without question, imaginative, but is controlled by experience and learning. He does not doubt; he affirms positively that Jesus was entirely human and that the miracles never took place. Neither materialistic

---

[70] Page 20.
[71] September 19, 1863, *Nouvelle Correspondance,* p. 185.
[72] November 17, 1867; *ibid.,* p. 246.

nor mystical, he is reverent, enthusiastic, original and individual. His own experiences in the East give an extraordinary life to his pictures of ancient times. "You could not believe," he wrote Berthelot (November 9, 1860), "how many things in the past are explained when one has seen all this." A new sentiment enveloped biblical scenes and personages. With *Le Génie du christianisme,* Chateaubriand had swept the great mass of half indifferent readers into orthodoxy; but now his direct influence was spent, and this same mass was aroused and moved with a totally different result by the *Life of Jesus.* What was particularly irritating to the clergy was the fact that the child wonder of Tréguier, who had been expected to charm the worldly into the church by his genius, was, instead, leading people into paths that they considered the paths of perdition. And all the world was reading and discussing the abominable book. The leaders sharpened their knives for the victim. Renan lost his professorship in the Collège de France, but he became one of the most celebrated men of the world. Henceforth, not a word he uttered was spoken unheard.

Far from believing that he was doing harm, Renan proceeded to publish (March 4, 1864) a cheap edition for the poor, "the true disciples of Jesus," so that they too might come to love the Master as he himself loved him, not as God, but as a man overflowing with the divine spirit. "The sweetness of this unequaled idyll" would be a consolation and a support to those who had to bear heavy burdens.[73] He indeed believed in his work. It was to be an antidote to brutal skepticism and arid indifference. As he says in

---

[73] This edition, the title of which is simply *Jesus* (*Jésus* par Ernest Renan, 1864, in-18, xii and 262 pp.), was sold for one franc 25 centimes. A notice, followed by the introductory essay, was published in the *Débats* for March 2. Here Renan omits his Introduction, all of Chapter I except the first paragraph, Chapters xvi, xix, xxvi, and xxvii, together with other scattered passages, particularly that about Lazarus and much of the last chapter, in fact, everything that might give rise to misunderstandings.

his dedication to the pure soul of his sister Henriette, "If at times you feared for it the narrow judgment of the frivolous, you were yet always persuaded that truly religious souls would in the end find it good."

Renan read all the serious criticisms of his work. No insult or calumny prevented him from profiting by what was urged. "As to those," he says, "who need to think in the interest of their belief, that I am ignorant, light-headed, or a man of bad faith, I shall not pretend to change their idea. If such an opinion is necessary to the repose of any pious persons, I should feel a real scruple about disabusing their minds." The thirteenth edition (1867)[74] is carefully revised; though the changes are not so extensive as would appear from the differences in pagination, which are largely a matter of typesetting. A preface and appendix are added, there are slight ameliorations of style, and many important modifications and additions to the notes. The Lazarus story, in particular, is so altered as to remove any suspicion of connivance in trickery on the part of Jesus,[75] and the Gospel of John is no longer treated as being the direct work of the Apostle.[76] No evidence that was produced was, however, strong enough to convince Renan that the fourth Gospel did not contain fragments that emanated from an eyewitness of the crucifixion. This thirteenth edition is the final form of the *Life of Jesus,* and, whatever the various schools may think of it, it is still a living book.[77]

---

[74] This edition is announced in the *Débats,* September 1, by Bersot, who notes the important changes and quotes the preface, almost four columns of the newspaper.

[75] Ed. 1863, pp. 359-364; ed. 1867, pp. 372-375. The criticism of this narrative cannot be understood by those who have read only the revised edition.

[76] In the text, for example, "John, who claims to have seen" becomes "The fourth evangelist, who here introduces the Apostle John as an eyewitness."

[77] An illustrated edition with a new preface—published in the *Débats,* February 21—was brought out in 1870. For critical remarks on the *Life of Jesus,* see the chapter on *The Origins of Christianity.*

IV

During this period of public turmoil, Renan pursued his scholarly labors with unremitting diligence. He was active in the Société Asiatique, of which he had been assistant secretary to Mohl since 1860, and in the Academy of Inscriptions, where he read philological papers and served on committees to award prizes. He worked also on his vast account of his Phœnician mission which ran to nearly 900 quarto pages. His dissertation on "The State of the Fine Arts in France in the Fourteenth Century," which had been more than half finished before he went to Syria, [78] was now completed and published in the *Histoire littéraire de la France,* vol. xxiv.[79] Of this volume the first 600 pages were occupied by the dissertation on the literature of the period by Victor le Clerc, who had been engaged on the task since 1842. Renan fills 150 pages with a detailed discussion of churches, castles, bridges and other edifices, together with a review of sculpture, painting and music, all associated in characteristic fashion with the social life and the politics of the time. Connected with this work was his later study of the politics of Philip the Fair, and here also are the roots of his intimacy with Avignon, shown in *L'Eau de jouvence.* Such thoughts as were most fit for the general public were attached to a review article in the *Revue des deux Mondes* (July 1, 1862), "The Art of the Middle Ages and the Causes of Its Decadence." [80]

---

[78] *Comptes rendus,* vol. v, 174.

[79] These official publications were unconscionably delayed. At the Académie meeting of July 11, 1862, the secretary states that the volume is in press. In January, 1863, he states that it has been printed for several months, but the indexes retard publication. A bit from Le Clerc's dissertation is given in advance in the *Débats* for March 6, 1863. The quarto, published by the Inprimerie Impériale, is nevertheless dated 1862; the octavo, in two volumes, was published by Lévy in 1865.

[80] While the article is a review of the *Album de Villard de Honne-*

Just about this time (June 2 and 9, 1862), Sainte-Beuve devoted to Renan two *Lundis* in the *Constitutionnel*. These were to be timely, as, when preparing them, he expected the new professor's course in Hebrew to be reopened after Easter.[81] As usual the great critic prepared his articles very carefully, getting his biographical information in this case from the subject himself. Renan, however, was in Holland when his friend called in May,[82] but he afterwards sent some missing publications and a letter giving the facts of his life. In thanking him for this letter Sainte-Beuve says: "I have lived with you, and I believed that I already knew you, but you have kept a surprise in store for me. It was a critic that I observed and pursued, the most delicate and attractive of critics, and lo! at the end of each avenue, I find an artist. It is this last side that strikes me most strongly when I study you. How difficult you are to grasp. What should be done about you should be a dialogue in Plato's manner; but who shall do it?" (May 26).[83] The idea is repeated in the essays, which are, as one should expect, and even after all the later critics have had their say, about the best things that have been written concerning Renan. In Taine's contemporary judgment, they are not frank, their aim being to bring about a reopening of Renan's course by saying what would be agreeable to the Emperor; but, though this purpose is almost unconcealed, particularly in the second article, it is not pervasive enough to injure the justice of either

court, this publication is chiefly an excuse for Renan's own opinions on the general topics, a point that Viollet-le-Duc emphasizes in *Revue archéologique,* February, 1863. Of this nature, in fact, are most of Renan's reviews. He writes, for example, to Berthelot (September 24, 1863) that, if the proposed philosophical letter does not seem fitting, he will "change the epistolary form and tack it on to a review article dealing with Littré's essay on Auguste Comte."

[81] Letter of April 8, in *Nouvelle Correspondance.*

[82] *Ibid.,* May 5.

[83] Where Sainte-Beuve feared to tread another venturously rushed in. The youthful Maurice Barrès unfortunately imagined himself the destined Plato, with melancholy results.

appreciation or dissent. The biographical part reads as though based on the *Recollections,* so keen is the critic's insight. That Renan is not negative, but essentially a religious spirit, that for the supernatural he substitutes the divine, that his view of progress toward an end presupposes God—such an analysis is fundamental, and not simply addressed to Napoleon III. "In him the impression is sometimes victorious over the idea itself"—have we not here the secret key to Renan? Add to this the delicate balance of critic and artist so skillfully traced and emphasized by Sainte-Beuve, and the reader cannot remain greatly puzzled by the intricacies of this unusual spirit, a spirit that is, in the '60's as in the '80's, "learned, profound, delicate, subtle, proud and somewhat disdainful."

On September, 1862, Renan distributed to friends a slender volume, *Henriette Renan, memorial for those who knew her.*[84] This begins and ends with his ideas of God and Immortality:

The memory of man is but an imperceptible stroke in the trace that each of us leaves in the bosom of the infinite. It is not, however, vain. The consciousness of humanity is the highest known reflective type of the total consciousness of the universe. The esteem of a single man is a portion of absolute justice. Thus, although a beautiful life needs no other remembrance than that of God, the attempt has always been made to perpetuate its image.

.   .   .   .

But God does not suffer his saints to see corruption. O heart, in which burned unceasingly so sweet a flame of love; brain, seat of thoughts so pure; charming eyes from which kindness radiated; long, delicate hand that I have so often pressed, I shiver with horror when I think that you are dust. But all here below is symbol and image only. The truly eternal part of each is his relation with the infinite. It is in God's memory that man is immortal. It is there that our Henriette, forever radiant, forever faultless, lives with a thousand times more reality than when she

[84] Paris, Impr. J. Claye, September, 1862, in-16, 77 pp. signed Ernest Renan. 100 copies printed. The work was first published as *Ma Sœur Henriette* in 1895, and then with the *Lettres intimes* in 1896.

244

struggled with her weak body to create her spiritual personality, and, thrown in the midst of a world that could not understand her, obstinately sought perfection. May her memory remain a precious argument in favor of those eternal truths which each virtuous life helps to demonstrate. For my part, I have never doubted the reality of the moral order; but I see now with full evidence that the whole logic of the system of the universe would be overturned, if such lives were but dupery and illusion.

The brief chapters that lie between contain recollections of early days, of Henriette's return from Poland, their life together, the anguish caused by his marriage, and then the Syrian trip ending in her death. He recalls her learning, her taste and skill in composition, her appreciation of beauty in art and nature, her simple goodness, her self-sacrifice, her retiring disposition, her forcible personality and her pure and lofty soul. The little book is, as Jules Simons says, a masterpiece. Privately printed in an edition of one hundred copies for intimate friends, it was not published, in spite of urgent entreaties, till after Renan's death. He felt that to put his appreciation of his sister in a book to be sold would be like sending her portrait to an auction room.

To the year 1863 belongs an enlarged and revised edition of the *Histoire général des langues sémitiques*, the second volume of which would have been finished, we are told, but for the Phœnician mission. Renan still expects to complete the work, and it will have the advantage of forming part of his course at the Collège de France, since one of his two hours will be devoted to this topic. Vain hope. In the meantime, he expects to publish a separate volume of *Semitic Studies,* made up of articles that had appeared in the *Mémoires* of the Academy of Inscriptions, the *Journal Asiatique* and other collections, "but long developments will have to be added." For this task, however, as well as for the *Débats* and the *Revue des deux Mondes,* Renan had now no time, his whole energy being spent on the *Life of Jesus.* "Since my return," he says,[85] "I have worked incessantly to complete and to control in detail the sketch that I had hastily written in a Maronite cabin with five or six volumes about me." All his care was demanded by art and truth, "two inseparable things, art holding the secret of the most intimate laws of truth." (P. ix.) Every statement was weighed, every citation verified, and the expression was worked over again and again till it was as perfect as his feeling and skill could make it.

As soon as the book was published revision was begun. In August, at Dinard, he was already at work on a dissertation on the Gospel of St. John. As a relaxation—the first of those literary diversions which later produced such masterly works as the *Recollections* and the *Dramas*—he wrote during the summer his letter to Berthelot, "The Natural and the Historical Sciences," published in the *Revue des deux Mondes* October 15. On November 15 appeared Berthelot's reply, "Ideal and Positive Science." Both essays [86] are highly characteristic.

Renan puts forth one of his favorite ideas (already in *Avenir* and in Herder), that the aim of all science is the history of the universe, from the atom, the molecule, the formation of planets, through geologic and prehistoric times to authentic human history. The evolution of the whole is an evolution of consciousness. "There is an obscure consciousness of the universe that tends to produce itself, a secret force that urges the possible to exist." (P. 178.) "There will come something that will be to present consciousness what present consciousness is to the atom." (P. 183.) The full development will be God, for in one sense God is synonymous with total existence, which is *becoming*. In another sense God is the absolute, the ideal, the living principle of the good, the true and the beautiful, eternal and change-

---

[85] Introduction, p. xcix.
[86] Republished much later in *Dialogues et fragments philosophiques*.

less. In this absolute, in the idea, we shall all live forever.

Berthelot, in contrast, is definite and methodical. Proceeding by way of example from a burning torch to chemical laws, he shows that positive science is based on observation and experiment, a method to be extended also to moral truths. Ideal science is legitimate because it results from an irresistible impulse in man to seek beyond; yet no reality can be reached by mere reasoning, and every system of philosophy represents merely the amount of positive knowledge of its time. Like Renan, he sees a law of progress in human society, progress in science, in material welfare, in morality. God is the center and the mysterious unity toward which the universal order converges and to an appreciation of which only sentiment can lead. In ideal science, though it rests on demonstrated facts, the largest share will always be contributed by fantasy.

It is illuminating to place beside these two essays the account by Taine [87] of discussions with Renan and Berthelot in 1862:

I have seen a good deal of Renan at Chalifer, and he also spent a whole evening with me.

He is, above everything, a passionate, nervous man, beset by his own ideas. He walked up and down my room as if he were in a cage, with the jerky tones and gestures of invention in full ebullition. There is a great difference between him and Berthelot, who is as quiet as a patient, laboring ox, chewing the cud of his idea and dwelling upon it. It is the contrast between inspiration and meditation.

Neither of them has, like Bertrand the mathematician, the analytical habits of Condillac. The one ferments slowly and obscurely, the other explodes. Neither of them goes methodically forward, passing from the known to the unknown.

Renan is perfectly incapable of precise formulas; he does not go from one precise truth to another, but feels his way as he goes. He has *impressions,* a word which expresses the whole thing. Philosophy and generalizations are but the echo of things

---

[87] *Vie et correspondance,* vol. ii, pp. 242-244.

within him; he has no system, but only views and sensations.

In metaphysics he is absolutely unstable, entirely lacking in proofs and analysis. Roughly speaking, he is a poetical Kant with no formula; exactly like Carlyle; I read him parts of the *Sartor Resartus*, which he thought admirable. He admits that he only perceives phenomena and their laws, that beyond lies an abyss, an x whence these are derived, that we suspect something, though very little, of it through the sublime sense of duty; we only know that in the beyond there is something sublime which corresponds to the sublimity of our sense of duty. In any case, that something is not a person; personality and individuality are only to be met with at the further end of physiology, at the final point of phenomena, and not at the beginning. Therefore there is no Personal God.

As to the soul, he does not believe in personal immortality; he only admits immortality of works. "My idea, the idea to which I have devoted myself, survives me. In it I myself survive in proportion to the love I have given it and the progress I have made with it."

Nevertheless he leaves a lacuna which Faith and Symbols alone can fill, though only with simple allegories and pure presumptions; this is the nature of that supreme x, and of the correlation between a noble soul and that x.

"A skeptic who, where his skepticism makes a hole, stops up the hole with his mysticism." Berthelot laughed, and called me a man of labels, when I told Renan that this was the definition of him.

For everything else, for psychological, historical and all other facts, he is a pure Positivist; he believes in natural laws only, and absolutely denies all supernatural intervention.

Of the three, I am the most truly Positivist and the least Mystical.

This eager, excitable man was nevertheless completely self-controlled in print. While his dismissal from his professorship was in the air, he published in the *Revue des deux Mondes* (May 1) an essay "On Higher Instruction in France,"[88] which is without a single specific reference to anything that could bear a personal hue.

---

[88] *Questions contemporaines.*

It is "not a criticism of any administration," but a plea for improvement. He stands for science in opposition to popular university lectures calculated to attract an audience. The Collège de France should furnish the great laboratory for discoveries; investigation, not rhetoric, should be its method; to form scholars, not to please the crowd, its aim. And so he hopes even for the establishment of a chair of Celtic—not that everything should be taught, but that the noble tradition of original research may be maintained. He is confident that democracy will support science, though not understanding it. "I am one," he expectantly exclaims, "who believes in the future of democracy." But popular prejudice should not be flattered. If a foreign example, such as that of German philology, is good, it should be inculcated. "To cultivate one's faults is not the way to be truly oneself." Indeed, in the things of the mind, exclusion has become impossible. "The intellectual culture of Europe is a vast exchange where each gives and receives in turn, where the pupil of yesterday becomes the master of to-day. It is a tree of which each branch participates in the life of the others and on which the only fruitless branches are those that are isolated and deprived of communion with the whole."

V

For the *Débats* after the Syrian expedition Renan wrote few contributions of importance. In fact, this journal, though still remarkable for its *Variétés,* felt the unhappy effects of political liberty in the loss of some of its superior literary skill. Often trivial parliamentary debates crowded out articles of permanent interest. Taine, Bersot and Saint-Marc Girardin, among others, continued to contribute freely. Prévost-Paradol was nothing less than astounding in the number and variety of his articles; there were also new writers, such as Karl Hillebrand, Maxime du Camp and

249

Viollet-le-Duc. But fatigue seems to have overtaken de Sacy and some others of the good old school. As for Renan, never a real journalist like Bersot, or Prévost-Paradol or Maxime du Camp, who turned everything into copy, during the early '60's only three or four modest notes of his on learned books appeared, and one long essay on the *Marcus Aurelius* of Desvergers (July 8 and 9, 1864), passages from which were afterwards embodied in his own volume on this emperor. He, however, kept up close relations with the editorial group and took part, we may be sure, in the discussions in the office around the chair of that successful artist and omnivorous reader, turned editor and newspaper proprietor, Édouard Bertin.[89] These discussions, Taine tells us, were chiefly on literature, history, philosophy and science. ''I do not know a place,'' he continues, ''excepting the dinner presided over by Sainte-Beuve, where all sorts of general ideas were handled with such tolerance and sincerity.'' [90]

The dinners here alluded to were the celebrated ''dîners Magny,'' of which Goncourt has left such an inadequate report. Founded November 22, 1862, by the eccentric artist Gavarni with the aid of Sainte-Beuve, they were held fortnightly at the Magny restaurant, rue Contrescarpe, in the Latin Quarter, and soon gathered to them the best literary and artistic intellect of Paris, including Gautier, Flaubert, Scherer, Nefftzer, Tourguénieff, Berthelot, and others of more transitory importance.[91] Renan entered March 28, 1863, but offended, perhaps by the noise, perhaps by the

---

[89] Bertin made over 3,500 paintings and drawings, the fruit of his travels in various regions of Europe and the Orient.

[90] *Derniers essais*, p. 262.

[91] The Goncourt *Journal*, vol. ii, p. 67, under date of Saturday, November 22, 1862, tells of the first dinner attended by six; and thenceforth there are frequent references to these meetings. On May 11, 1863, the day was changed probably to suit Sainte-Beuve, from Saturday to Monday, which was thenceforth adhered to. Many guests, including at times George Sand, are mentioned. There is an incomplete list also in Sainte-Beuve, *Souvenirs et indiscretions*, p. 149, note.

mockery that greeted his remark, "I admire Jesus completely" (July 20, 1863), he stayed away and had to be coaxed
back by Sainte-Beuve.[92] The Goncourt *Journal* repeats only
what was sensational, sexual or scandalous, causing Taine to
remark: "If we had exchanged nothing but such platitudes,
neither my friends nor I would have attended beyond a second time."[93] Undoubtedly there was much good talk, and
Renan's part, even in the scrappy Goncourt account, is always serious and elevated.

After his return from Syria, Renan became associated
with the circle of the dissipated and erratic, but highly intelligent Prince Napoleon (Plon-Plon).[94] He was further
in 1862 presented by Sainte-Beuve to the Princess Matilde
at Saint-Gratien (August 7),[95] where he was already much
appreciated,[96] as any one praised by the great critic was
sure to be. Renan frequented also the happy-go-lucky salon
of the lively Mme. Mohl (rue du Bac), where all sorts of
eminent political and philosophical opposites rubbed el-
bows.[97] At the more dignified house of Édouard Bertin (rue

[92] Letter, September 19, 1863.

[93] *Vie et correspondance.*

[94] Grant Duff.

[95] *Nouvelle correspondance.* In *Lettres à la Princesse,* there is question of this visit in a letter (viii) of August 4. The following letter
(ix) dated the 22nd, Tuesday, must be of August 12, as there was no
Tuesday, the twenty-second of any month of 1862 after the visit. We
learn from this letter that Renan had given a lecture at Saint-Gratien
on the Gospels, and, further, that he was charmed with the Princess.
"He is one of the few Frenchmen," says Sainte-Beuve, "who know
what is discovered elsewhere, and who not only know it, but improve
it."

[96] Sainte-Beuve's Letter to Renan of August 3, 1862.

[97] Senior, with his daughter, and Trevelyan met Renan at Mme.
Mohl's April 9, 1862, at breakfast, since, owing to the recent death of
his father-in-law, propriety forbade the more formal dinner: *Conversations,* vol. ii, p. 147, and M. C. M. Simpson, *Many Memories of
Many People,* p. 316. George Eliot had the same satisfaction December
31, 1866; *Life,* vol. iii, p. 1. Renan's relations with the Mohls were
very close, and he was very kind and helpful to Mme. Mohl after her
husband's death. The catalogue of Mohl's library is his work, *Catalogue de la bibliothèque orientale de feu M. J. Mohl,* Paris, E. Levoux,
1876. Mrs. Simpson tells a story, without date, of a mortifying ex-

des Saints-Pères), he found grace and charm in his host and art, music, and literature for entertainment. For the average social function, however, Renan was not adapted. He still suffered the inhibitions that he had portrayed in Hermann. "Renan is not a society man," writes Taine,[98] "he does not know how to chat with ladies; he must have specialists. He lacks skill in making and seizing opportunities. He is above everything else a man of his own idea, a priest absorbed in his God. On this fact he prides himself justly enough."

But his talk was extraordinary and fascinating. "Renan's appearance was against him," says Mrs. Simpson. "He was fat, his arms and legs were particularly short, his face was very pale, and the ultra-suavity of the seminarists still clung to him. But one forgot all these disadvantages when he began to speak. . . . He was entirely without airs, and often did not even lead the conversation; he was willing to talk on any subject suggested by his hearers."[99]

Of Renan's family life we hear very little. It is a subject on which, with true Breton secretiveness, he rarely expresses himself. A daughter, one of the great comforts of his later life, was born March 1, 1862, and named Noémi, after a playmate of his childhood. On March 16 died Henri Scheffer, whose part in the intellectual life of his son-in-law does not appear to have been of much importance. Chalifer, near Lagny, where the Scheffers had a little country place, was the vacation resort till 1863, when for repose after the publication of the *Life of Jesus*, he, with his wife and chil-

perience that befell Renan at the home of these friends. The Mohls had invited Cousin, Guizot, Prévost-Paradol and Mignet to meet Mme. Ristori. Renan, arriving after dinner and coming into the darkened room, did not see the actress and, regardless of the kicks Cousin gave him to warn him to stop talking, blurted out: "It is that Italian woman, that actress who plays on the boulevard, who degrades art." Whereupon Ristori exploded and left the house. *Many Memories*, p. 317.
[98] *Vie et correspondance*, vol. ii, p. 244.
[99] *Many Memories*, p. 316.

dren, spent nearly three months by the sea at Dinard, and later on the Island of Jersey and at Granville. The literary people of the age, Balzac, De Musset, George Sand, Sainte-Beuve, Flaubert, Gautier—the list could be indefinitely extended—seem to have been chronically hard up. This was not the case with Renan, poor though he was, and even to the end of his life in only moderate circumstances. Without superfluities, he managed by economy to have enough. In 1864 he secured a little place at Sèvres, with the Berthelots for neighbors, his city residence being an apartment in the rue Vanneau. His mother, whose image he was,[100] continued to be an honored member of the household. "Dear old Madame Renan," says Taine, [101] "is gentle and dignified; she is eighty years old; she made me tell the story of my patron, Saint Hippolytus, and, smiling, raised her hands toward heaven at the thought of what her son has become after his pious bringing up." Few indeed can believe that a good person with whom they live is going to be eternally damned.

---

[100] *Nouveaux Lundis,* vol. ii, p. 385.
[101] *Vie et correspondance,* vol. ii, p. 245.

CHAPTER VIII

From November, 1864, to July, 1865, Renan and his wife were traveling in Egypt, Syria, and Greece. After his return, he was very busy with his *Origins of Christianity,* publishing *The Apostles* in April, 1866, and *Saint Paul* in June, 1869. During his trip he sent the *Revue des deux Mondes* an article on Egypt; another article of the year 1865 being an introduction to a book. In 1866 he published a paper written many years before, and in 1868 a tribute to Le Clerc. His contributions to the *Débats* were also meager, consisting in book notes, articles on St. Francis and Galileo, 1866, a review of Sainte-Beuve's *Port-Royal,* third edition, 1867, and "The Cæsars," 1868. In 1867 he wrote an article on the Institut for the *Paris Guide.* In June, 1868, his mother died, and in September, after a trip to Germany, he revisited Tréguier and neighboring places. In erudition he worked persistently on the Report of his Phœnician Mission and on papers for learned societies. The monumental *Corpus Inscriptionum Semiticarum* absorbed much of his attention from 1867 on. In 1867, too, he became secretary of the Société Asiatique, and for fifteen years he made to that body an extended annual report on the progress of oriental studies. In 1868 he published *Contemporary Questions,* made up of various pamphlets and articles. Much time in 1869 was given to politics. From March to June he campaigned for a seat in the Corps Législatif from the second district of Seine-et-Marne, but was unsuccessful. In this connection, besides purely political speeches, he delivered three lectures: "The Part of the Family and the State in Education" (originally prepared for an educational society), "Turgot," and "The Services of Science to the People." He summed up his views of political conditions in an article on "Constitutional Monarchy in France" in the *Revue des deux Mondes* for November 1. In January, 1870, Renan was

254

elected president of the Academy of Inscriptions and Belles-Lettres and shortly afterwards he was a second time nominated for the professorship of Hebrew in the Collège de France. In July he went to Norway with the Prince Napoleon on a yachting trip which was interrupted by the declaration of war.

I

THE publication of the *Life of Jesus* was the first stage in the achievement of the life work, a history of the origins of Christianity, which Renan had proposed to himself in *The Future of Science* fifteen years before. He now proceeded uninterruptedly with this task as his main scholarly pursuit, producing a new volume at the average interval of three years. The doctrinal history that he had at first projected was changed to a study of personalities, as he became vividly aware that Jesus and Paul and Peter and countless lesser and even nameless individuals had made the Church, not so much by their creed, as by their lives. In order to add vital reality to his conceptions, he determined to visit all the important centers of apostolic activity.

Leaving the children in the care of the two grandmothers, he and his wife traveled from November, 1864, to the end of June, 1865, in Egypt, Syria, Asia Minor and Greece, enduring hardships of which he never complains, and enjoying new experiences with unfailing enthusiasm. Intense interest and eagerness to see everything significant or beautiful are the marks of Renan as a traveler. Every place that he is likely never to visit he regrets. The trip gets constantly extended, in spite of Berthelot's complaints and warnings. As travelers, indeed, the two friends were very different. Berthelot's letters from Egypt in 1869 give space enough to heat, insect pests and other discomforts; Renan barely mentions a sunstroke, a horrible Turkish boat, a trying journey over appallingly rough country. Sustained by the feeling of what he owes to his work, he is entirely absorbed in what

255

he learns and what he thinks, in the recollections of bible times, in objects that make the past alive.

Over a month was spent in Egypt, though this was not in the plans. With the archæologist Mariette for a guide, he went up the Nile to the Assouan cataract, and sent an article, "Ancient Egypt," in the form of a letter to the director of the *Revue des deux Mondes,* dated "The Nile, from Assouan to Cairo, December, 1864." This, the only published account of his trip, appeared April 1, 1865,[1] and was so well received that Buloz wanted more.[2] The piece is a sort of popular exposition of Mariette's discoveries, with high praise for that indefatigable worker. A new kind of life and history is opened to Renan, and he is almost overwhelmed with a chronology that takes him back 5,000 years before Christ. Of Thebes he writes: "I spent four days in this unequaled library, guided by M. Mariette, my admirable 'exegete,' from obelisk to obelisk, from chapel to chapel."[3] He habitually amalgamates ancient and modern: "Thebes is the Versailles and the Saint Denys of an Egyptian monarchy."[4] The Pharaohs are "Louis XIV's," a flattering inscription is "the eloquence of the *Moniteur,* the style of the official journalist." This ancient civilization, which seems to contradict the theory that history originates in mythology, fills him with astonishment, but he detects in it the absence of nobility. Egypt, lacking the ideal, was condemned to millenniums of mediocrity; it gave of its treasures to its neighbors, but, religion aside, Greece alone is "the land of noble origins."

From Egypt Renan proceeded to Syria, where he spent the month of January, 1865. His first care was to visit the tomb of Henriette, and here, in the adjacent chapel, he

---

[1] *Mélanges d'histoire et de voyages.*
[2] Letter of Berthelot, p. 361.
[3] *Mélanges,* p. 29.
[4] To Berthelot, December 17, 1864.

had a service celebrated "in that fine Maronitic liturgy, which is one of the oldest and goes back almost to the origins of Christianity." [5] He still hoped to make some excavations at Umm-el-'Awamîd, but in this project he was disappointed. His chief acquisition was Damascus. "I have fully fixed my background for St. Paul's conversion. It took place in a vast cultivated plain, thickly inhabited, and perhaps even in the midst of gardens. Every external accident must be dismissed; the phenomenon took place entirely in the soul of Paul." [6] His recollections of his own visions in fever completed his conception of Paul's experience.

From the middle of February to the end of March, the Renans were in Athens, and here he was in ecstasy. There was not a dull moment amidst all this glory. That the Greeks had always seemed to him models in art, philosophy, poetry and social life, the youthful notebooks and *The Future of Science* sufficiently testify, but his Semitic studies had somewhat clouded this impression. Now his early recollections came back upon him like a fresh and penetrating breeze from afar. It was, he says, the strongest impression he had ever experienced. Here was a place where perfection really existed, "the ideal crystallized in marble." By the side of the Jewish miracle, the Greek miracle took its place, "a type of eternal beauty, without local or national disfigurements." On the sacred hill, he wrote the "Prayer on the Acropolis," found many years later among his notes of travel and published in his *Recollections*. The "incomparable superiority of the Greek world, the true and simple grandeur of all it has left us" [7] was one of those permanent impressions that constitute his personality. [8]

---

[5] To Berthelot, January 12, 1865.
[6] To Berthelot, January 21.
[7] To Berthelot, March 19.
[8] The immediate effect is noted by Sainte-Beuve in a letter to the Princess, August 31, 1866: "A Renan, gay, lively, brightened by an indescribable ray of the sun of Greece, since he was there."

In April he visited Smyrna, whence he took a terribly rough caravan trip to Ephesus and the interior, and later a rougher sea trip to Patmos, where the boat tossed for fifty-two hours outside the harbor without being able to enter, experiences which are all reproduced in the journeys of St. Paul. From Athens, having seen the Argolid and Corinth,[9] he went to Saloniki by a coasting vessel that touched at every port; then through Macedonia and by an abominable Turkish boat to Constantinople, a place he was glad to see once, but only once. "Never has human baseness, shame, stupidity and self-satisfied emptiness created such an adequate portrayal of itself. . . . This city seems to me like a city of monkeys, a sort of perpetual capital founded by the worthy Constantine for ignominy, intrigue and stupidity."[10]

By June 30 he was back in his suburban place at Sèvres, amply provided with vivid impressions for his volumes on the Apostles and St. Paul. In these volumes the scene of Paul's vision near Damascus, the splendor and corruption of Antioch, the lonely paths amid the mountains of Asia Minor and Macedonia, are portrayed as only an eyewitness could paint them, while in all sorts of details a thousand life-giving touches were the result of these oriental experiences.

Renan's notions about the resurrection are saturated with his personal feelings on visiting his sister's tomb. To Berthelot he wrote (January 12, 1865): "We made the trip by short stages in lovely April-like weather. The mountain is already green and blooming as in spring. Each hollow of the rock is a basket of anemones and cyclamens. It was a great joy for me to see again that beautiful road she

---

[9] May 14? The date printed in the *Correspondance* is impossible, as he was at Smyrna May 6.
[10] *Ibid.*, June 13.

loved so much, and where literally each step recalled a remembrance of her." In *The Apostles* we read (p. 29):

It was near the end of April. The earth is then covered with red anemones, which are probably those "lilies of the field" from which Jesus loved to draw comparisons. At each step, his words came back to them, as though attached to the thousand casual objects of the road. Here was the tree, the flower, the field, each the source of a parable; here the hill where he spoke so engagingly; here the boat in which he taught. . . . They saw him in every spot where they had lived with him. . . . If all of us, once a year, in secret, for a brief moment long enough only for the exchange of a few words, could see again our lost loved ones, death would be no longer death. [And on another page (p. 37)]: It is a peculiar property of great and holy things always to grow greater and purer. The feeling for a loved one lost is much more prolific at a distance than on the morrow of death. The greater the separation, the stronger the feeling. The grief which at first mingled with it and, in a sense, lessened it, changes into a serene reverence. The image of the dead is transfigured, idealized, becomes the soul of one's life, the principle of every action, the source of every joy, the oracle consulted, the consolation sought in moments of dejection. Death is the necessary condition for every apotheosis. Jesus, so loved during his life, was even more deeply loved after his last breath, or rather, his last breath became the beginning of his true life in the bosom of his Church.

"The second life of Jesus," he continues after telling of the Ascension, "pale image of the first, is still full of charm. Henceforth all perfume from him is lost. Risen on his cloud to the right hand of his Father, he leaves us with men, and heavens! how grievous is the descent. The reign of poetry is past."

It is thus with regret that Renan takes leave of Jesus to proceed with a task that seems to him more commonplace. And indeed a certain ardor, a certain juvenile exuberance, which was in strange contrast with his mature and tranquil intellectual attainment, now disappears, or almost disappears, from his work. What Renan regretted was just what gave satisfaction to his friend Taine, who, in announcing the volume in the *Débats*,[11] expresses the opinion that "the author of *The Apostles* has surpassed the author of the *Life of Jesus.*"[12]

The memories of Henriette, indeed, in this second volume of the *Origins,* represent the final effort of certain strong sentimental influences from which Renan was fast getting weaned. *Saint Paul,* dedicated to his wife, marks the completion of his emancipation from his childhood and youth. He was henceforth fully developed and entirely himself. The friends he had made have taken the place of those among whom he was born. His dearly loved mother died in June, 1868, leaving him isolated from the past and morally self-sustaining in his own environment. To meet the evil days that he forsees, he goes forward hand in hand with the companion of his choice. Henriette was now a cherished recollection, not a directive force. The emotional agitations that dictated the *Life of Jesus* and the early chapters of *The Apostles* are no longer persistently active. The spectacle of the universe loses none of its interest, but it ceases to inspire a mystical exaltation.

The death of his mother led Renan to revisit Tréguier in the summer of 1868. On June 20, he wrote from Sèvres to her tenant, Le Bigot, to reassure him about his lease of the house.[13] All his dealings with these humble people exhibit his kindly and genial nature in a most attractive light. Though one of the world's celebrities, he was with them only one sweet human being dealing with another of his kind.

---

[11] April 13, 1866. After his brief notice, Taine quotes fourteen pages of the introduction, from "*Une chose unique,*" p. 1, to the end. Renan reciprocated with a notice of Taine's *Intelligence* in the *Débats,* March 28, 1870, where he quotes the Preface in full. "In the philosophy of realities," he remarks, "though there are plenty of obscurities, there are only two questions wholly mysterious, the origin of human consciousness and the supreme end of the universe."

[12] The review in the *Débats* was by Albert Réville, July 4, 5 and 6.

[13] René d'Ys, pp. 60-62.

After a trip to Germany, he came in the middle of September to his old home, visiting also Lannion, Paimpol, and the Isle de Bréhat, in all of which places he had relatives. His graceful expression of a desire to inspect his old collège met with a polite refusal. To many he was not at this time welcome, though later this intolerance was somewhat alleviated, when it was found out that he was not really the devil. Some of the neighbors sprinkled the chairs he had sat in with holy water, and children gazed at him with admiration and terror. The subject of these attentions could not fail to feel a trifle uncomfortable, and he did not come again to Brittany for sixteen years.

Saint Paul appeared June 9, 1869.[14] Here Renan feels himself on the firm ground of fact, though conjecture and imagination still have ample space. "Jesus and the primitive Church of Jerusalem seem like forms of a distant paradise, veiled in a mysterious haze."[15] And again, after Paul, there begins a profound darkness, "in which the bloody glow of the barbarous festivals of Nero and the lightnings of the Apocalypse alone throw some gleams of light."[16] Two further volumes, he thinks, will be sufficient for the task ahead of him. "I hope that within five years I may complete the work for which I have reserved the ripest years of my life. It has cost me many sacrifices, above all by excluding me from teaching in the Collège de France, which was the second aim I had set before myself. But we must not demand too much; perhaps he who has been permitted out of two projects to realize one, ought not to complain of his lot, particularly if he has looked upon these projects as duties."[17] Before the next volume could ap-

---

[14] The advance notice in the *Débats,* June 8, signed P. David, secretary of the board of editors, quotes the last chapter of the book. The review by Bersot appeared August 29 and 31.

[15] Introduction, p. iii.

[16] *Ibid.*

[17] *Ibid.,* p. lxxvii.

pear (1873), the professor was again seated in his chair of Hebrew.

Some by-products of Renan's studies appeared as notes —four or five a year—on learned books in the *Débats*.[18] Just after the publication of *The Apostles,* he again for a brief period took up book reviewing, producing "Francis of Assisi" (August 20 and 21, 1866) and "The Trial of Galileo"[19] (November 12, 1866), and out of friendship for Sainte-Beuve, a charming and much appreciated notice of the third edition of Port-Royal (November 15, 1867).[20]

The most important of these reviews, and one of the most perfect of Renan's essays, is that on Saint Francis, a saint who had always attracted him and of whose order he had wished to write the history.[21] The essay is, moreover, a commentary on the *Life of Jesus,* "an answer to certain objections." Francis of Assisi has, for religious criticism, an exceptional interest. He is, after Jesus, the man who has had the most limpid consciousness, the most absolute naïveté, the liveliest sentiment of his filial relation to the Heavenly Father. (P. 325.) "Francis of Assisi has always been one of the strongest reasons for my belief that Jesus was very nearly such as the synoptic evangelists have depicted him." (P. 326.) Renan's special sympathy with the saint is in the idea that possession of worldly goods is an imperfection, that it is nobler to be poor than to be rich, that we are to enjoy and not to own, that the finest things in life are indivisible. "Where a man's treasure is, there is his heart also; possession narrows the soul, makes it lose something of its lightness." Material compensation, moreover, is never adequate for spiritual activities. "Between

---

[18] The longest of these, on Beulé's *Auguste, sa famille et ses amis* (May 10, 1868), he republished with the title "Les Césars" in *Mélanges d'histoire et de voyages.*
[19] It is easy to see the bearing of this essay on his own case.
[20] All republished in *Nouvelles Études religieuses.*
[21] *Les Apôtres,* Introduction, p. liii.

the things of the soul and any payment whatsoever, there is such a disproportion that in such a case the money reward can never be regarded as anything but alms." Many years later Renan humorously compares himself with the saint. "Like the patriarch of Assisi, I have passed through the world without any serious bond of attachment to it, in the condition of a mere tenant, if I dare say so. Both of us, without having anything of our own, have felt rich. God gave us the usufruct of the universe, and we have been content to enjoy without possession." [22] And in the *Recollections*, he remarks with a whimsical smile, which many readers have failed to perceive, "I alone in my century have been able to understand Jesus and Francis of Assisi" (p. 148), this being but another way of saying that the materialistic spirit of the age is the reverse of his own spirit.

In connection with this article, Renan in 1876 told Grant Duff the story of the Capuchin friar who said to the Princess Matilde: "He has done very bad things, your friend, M. Renan—very bad things; but he has spoken very well of Saint Francis, and Saint Francis will fix all that." [23]

For the *Revue des deux Mondes* he wrote at this time practically nothing. His one article for 1865 after his return was prepared as an introduction to a translation of a book by Kuenen.[24] The one for 1866 was a study dating from 1852,[25] and the one for 1868 [26] was a tribute to his colleague

---

[22] *Nouvelles Études* (1884), Preface, p. iii.

[23] *Memoir,* p. 87. In the Introduction to *Nouvelles Études,* p. iii, the story is told in less lively form.

[24] November 1; "L'Exégèse religieuse et l'esprit français," a review of Hebrew studies in France, in the course of which he refers to Bossuet's suppression of Simon as "the rage of the rhetorician against the investigator." Obviously Renan had his own case in mind. The volume for which this introduction was written was *Recherches historiques et critiques sur la formation et la réunion des livres de l'Ancien Testament,* published by Lévy. Renan had a note on this book in the *Débats,* January 21, 1861.

[25] "Joachim de Flore et l'Évangile éternel," July 1.

[26] The single general essay of 1867, that on the Institut of France (*Questions contemporaines*) was written for the *Paris Guide,* which

and early patron, Joseph Victor Le Clerc, "the true Bene-
dictine of our century," the most laborious, the most devoted, the most learned collaborator, ever associated with
the *Histoire littéraire de la France*. It was written as an
introduction to the twenty-fifth volume of that collection. [27]
Renan here gives a full account of Le Clerc's immense contributions to French scholarship, with a detailed and laudatory review of the results of his medieval studies. Nor is
the professor's influence as Dean of the Faculty of Letters
overlooked, a post wherein, by raising the standard of examinations and theses for the doctorate, he had stimulated
erudition in the University. The character of the lonely
scholar is also presented, without much incident, but with
the skillful selection of just those particulars that give life
and reality to the portrait. A casual reader might not notice
that when, owing to eye-trouble in 1857, Le Clerc doubted
his ability to continue his vast study on the fourteenth
century,[28] he selected Renan to carry on the work: "He
feared for a time that he could not finish it, and made arrangements with the youngest of his colleagues (this was
Renan) to the end that, if he should die, the work should be
completed in the same spirit in which it had been previously
composed." [29]

II

To Renan pure scholarship was always a most precious
thing: he loved the foundations quite as much as the super-

---

was not an ordinary guidebook in the Murray or Baedeker sense, but
two very stout volumes of essays about Paris and things Parisian, contributed apparently by everybody who could hold a pen, from Victor
Hugo down. This astonishing publication was intended for visitors
to the Exposition.

[27] See *Histoire littéraire de la France*, vol. xxv, 1869. Renan's chief
contribution to this volume, however, was a thorough study of the
life and works of "Jean Duns Scot, frère mineur," pp. 404-467.

[28] *Histoire littéraire*, vol. xxiv.

[29] *Mélanges d'histoire et de voyages*, p. 506.

structure, and to the foundations he gave the greatest part of his time. In the country Taine can get along with only a few books, but, he says: "Renan and Berthelot for their work need, the one his laboratory and the other his library. They come from their country place at Sèvres every morning about nine o'clock to Paris, and shut themselves up to work till six in the evening" (May 22, 1868). A glimpse of the library at Renan's home is given by Goncourt:[30]

Visit to Renan. He has a fourth floor on the rue Vaneau,[31] a little bourgeois and fresh apartment, furniture in green velvet, on the wall heads by Ary Scheffer, and in the midst of some Dunkerque ware, the mold of a delicate woman's hand. Through an open door you perceive the library, shelves in white wood, disorder of big unbound books, tossed and piled on the floor, medieval and oriental utensils of erudition, all sorts of quartos, in the midst of which a fascicle of a Japanese dictionary, on a little table the proofs of *Saint Paul* slumbering, and through two windows an immense view, one of those forests of verdure hidden in the walls and stone of Paris, the vast Park Galliera, an undulation of tops of trees overshading the peaks of ecclesiastical buildings, domes, towers, that give somewhat the effect of the horizon of Rome. The man, always more charming and more affectionately polished as one comes to know him better. He is a type in his unfortunate physique of moral grace; in this apostle of doubt, there is the lofty and intelligent amiability of a priest of science.

Renan was an enthusiastic academician. He rarely missed one of the weekly meetings, and the moment he got back from Asia Minor, he is found in his place.[32] In these years he inaugurated two new tasks that occupied him to the day of his death. As early as 1864 he suggested to the Academy of Inscriptions as a topic for the *Histoire littéraire de la France*, the French rabbis of the fourteenth century,[33] and in 1867, with the support of three other members, he pro-

---

[30] May 25, 1868, *Journal*, vol. iii, p. 209.
[31] Spelled thus by Goncourt, and others, instead of "Vanneau."
[32] July, 1865; a fact noted in the *Revue archéologique* for the year.
[33] Report of Secretary in *Comptes rendus*, 1864.

posed the publication of the *Corpus Inscriptionum Semiti-carum*, a vast undertaking of which he remained to the end the heart and soul, and to which he devoted intense and conscientious labor. One may say that it occupied the first place in his life and preoccupations.[34] No member, moreover, was more frequently before the Academy to present reports and take part in the discussions, as well as to read technical memoirs, mostly dealing with inscriptions. One of his memoirs of more general interest, that on Faustine, which he was designated to read at the public meeting of the Institut held on August 14, 1867, is of special interest as showing how Renan worked simultaneously on various problems, the solutions of which were later to be incorporated in his *Origins*.

No less assiduous was his attendance at the monthly meetings of the Société Asiatique [35] and, as these often fell on a Friday evening, he must at such times have devoted the hours from eight to ten to the discussions here after a long afternoon at the Institut. Assistant secretary and librarian till January 12, 1866, when he resigned because his other occupations would no longer permit him to perform the duties of the office,[36] he was elected secretary for a term of five years on June 27, 1867, when Mohl became president in succession to Reinaud. As secretary, Mohl had been accustomed to present a long, and not very lively, annual report on the progress of oriental studies, a practice that Renan continued, though limiting his review to productions

---

[34] The proposal was made January 25, 1867; on February 8 a committee of six was elected to draw up a plan, which was presented in detail by Renan, April 12. See *Comptes rendus* and also *Journal Asiatique*. The first fascicle was issued in 1881.

[35] Renan must have belonged to a number of other learned societies. Of the Société des Antiquaires he was first vice-president in 1863 and president in 1864. See *Revue archéologique* for January in these years.

[36] He had been elected member of the editorial committee for the *Journal*, July 14, 1865.

by members. Into this arid task, however, he introduced a
new spirit and a new style. The artist supports the scholar,
and large views flash out amid dry details. In matters beyond his own competency, he calls upon all the specialists of
the society to aid him, so as to give scientific value to his
judgments. Nor is sentiment excluded from these annals.
In that part of his first report (July 9, 1868) in which he
chronicles the deaths of eminent scholars, his appreciation
of Bopp is followed by a loyal tribute to his old teacher, the
Abbé Le Hir,[37] and he concludes the general review with a
passage on philology closely modeled on one in *The Future
of Science*.[38]

For the next year (June 28, 1869) the secretary's report
is not a report at all. Instead of reviewing oriental studies,
it merely refers to the dangers of restricted specialization,
approves the division of labor in research, but not the isolation of workers, and points out that each branch of science,
which develops apart without regard to the others, becomes
narrow and egotistical and loses the lofty idea of its mission. In excuse for the brevity and incompleteness of this
document, Renan explains, what all his hearers knew, that
"particular and unexpected affairs have in the last few
weeks absorbed almost all my activities."

III

These "particular and unexpected affairs" were his ex-
ertions in his campaign for a seat in the Corps Législatif
from the second district of Seine-et-Marne, a compaign
which ended June 6 in his defeat. In the autumn of 1863

---

[37] A further instance of Renan's loyalty is furnished by Ollivier.
When he spoke to Renan about becoming a candidate for the Academy,
Renan answered: "Yes, provided that it does not involve a contest
with Mgr. Dupanloup, to which I would not consent, for I can never
forget the favors he has done me." *L'Empire libéral*, vol. vi, p. 347.

[38] This report covers pp. 11-164 of the *Journal*.

Renan had had an impulse to go before the electorate for some district of Paris, as a protest against the suspension of his Hebrew course,[39] but nothing came of these aspirations.

Several times he had been attacked in the Senate. On March 18, 1864, Mgr. de Bonnechose had demanded his prosecution for blasphemy in the *Life of Jesus* but, after a defense of liberty of thought by Delangle, who spoke from a legal point of view, the order of the day was voted.[40] The government had doubtless learned a lesson from the fruitless prosecution of Flaubert in 1857 for *Madame Bovary*.

Three years later a scene occurred in the Senate which does not give a favorable impression of the parliamentary procedure of the body.[41] The Comte de Ségur d'Agnesseau, a tedious and inconsequential speaker, whose attempts to address the house were apt to provoke cries of "Clôture, Clôture!" delivered a lengthy tirade, nominally on a law concerning primary instruction, but really wandering around amid all the grievances over which he had been brooding. Without any relevance, he turned to Rouland, ex-minister of public instruction, saying: "His conscience will always feel remorse for having made a certain nomination that caused a great scandal." "I protest," shouted Sainte-Beuve, "against personal imputations that have nothing to do with the question and that involve honorable men." "Don't interrupt, M. Sainte-Beuve," said the president. "If he refers to M. Renan," continued Sainte-Beuve, "I protest against an accusation that assails a man of conviction and talent, whose friend I have the honor to be." And the storm burst: "Atheism, irreligion, immorality, social conflagration!" But Sainte-Beuve went on: "There

---

[39] See Bertholet correspondence.
[40] Ollivier, *L'Empire libéral*, vol. vi, 496.
[41] *Moniteur*, March 30, 1867. Also Sainte-Beuve, *Premiers Lundis*, III.

are honorable and respectable philosophical opinions that I defend in the name of liberty of thought and will not allow to be attacked and calumniated without protest.'' ''You are not here for that,'' howled Lacaze; and another, ''Every honest person protests against such words''; and still another, ''It is the first time atheism has found a defender here.'' The quarrel was closed by Marshal Canrobert: ''One cannot in this assembly make an apology for him who has denied the divinity of Jesus Christ and set himself as the bitter enemy of the religion of our fathers, which is still that of the great majority of the French. As for myself, in allowing each the liberty of appreciating from his own point of view the book of this writer, I protest formally against the doctrines there set forth and I am persuaded that my voice will have many echoes here.'' (Prolonged approbation.) [42]

On June 25 Sainte-Beuve made his first speech in the Senate, the topic being a petition to exclude from a provincial library certain books, among which were works by Voltaire, Rousseau, Michelet, Renan, and George Sand. Of the two last he said, amid much disorder: ''The Emperor honors M. Renan with his esteem, as he honors George Sand with his friendship.'' [43]

These incidents are characteristic of the intolerance against which the friends of liberty were contending, and measure the extent of their ultimate victory. The clerical leaders and particularly the clerical press seemed always to have a chip on the shoulder. In 1868 Sainte-Beuve invited the Prince Napoleon to dine at his house and the Prince selected Friday, April 10. Among the guests was Renan.[44] It happened that April 10 was Good Friday, and

---

[42] Mérimée's correspondence abounds in remarks about the old generals in the Senate who trembled in fear for the future of their souls.

[43] *Moniteur*, June 26, 1867. Also *Premiers Lundis*, III.

[44] It was of course the Prince who designated what guests should be invited. See Sainte-Beuve's invitation to Renan, April 6, 1868.

a howl went up that an orgy had been held on purpose to desecrate the holy day. It was, as a matter of fact, no orgy, but a very good dinner, with good wines, and, we may be sure, an abundance of good talk.[45]

Anticlerical Renan certainly was, though by no means an extremist. A gradual separation of Church and State with full recognition of the interests of the clergy and their flocks and with no violation of their material and property rights —such was his program. He foresaw schisms that have not come to pass, but he also foresaw a time when the majority of believers would, by sacrificing the letter to the spirit, bring about universal toleration. "Let us remain in our respective Churches, profiting by their antique worship and their tradition of virtue, participating in their good works and enjoying the poetry of their past."[46] But the present will assert its rights. "Two things are evident: the first is that modern civilization does not desire that the old forms of worship should wholly die; the second is that it will not permit itself to be hindered in its task by ancient religious institutions."[47]

All of Renan's reflections on public affairs were collected from periodicals and pamphlets and given to the world in *Contemporary Questions*.[48] The main body of the book is made up of essays dealing with higher education, the Institut, the Collège de France and its professors, and the professorship of Hebrew. These are followed by three essays on religion and the Church, of which two are taken from *La Liberté de Penser*. (See ante, pp. 76, 81.) The first essay in the volume is on "The Philosophy of Contemporary History" (see p. 191), and the last on "The Theology of

---

[45] See the account, including the *menu* in Sainte-Beuve, *Souvenirs et indiscrétions*, p. 209 et seq.

[46] *Les Apôtres*, p. lviii.

[47] *Ibid.*, p. lx.

[48] Notice in the *Débats*, March 4, 1868, with about three columns quoted from the preface.

Béranger." (See p. 199.) As usual the preface is one of the most interesting of the disquisitions.

Renan insists on the necessity of higher education, not only for culture and progress, but also as the source even of primary teaching. "The instruction of the populace is an effect of the higher culture of certain classes. Countries that, like the United States, have founded a considerable popular education without serious higher instruction, will long expiate this error by their intellectual mediocrity, their grossness of manners, their superficial spirit, and their lack of general intelligence." (P. viii.) "It is said that the victor at Sadowa was the primary teacher. No; the victor at Sadowa was German science, German virtue, Protestantism, philosophy, Luther, Kant, Fichte, Hegel." [49] War has become a scientific and moral problem. "The final victory will lie with the people the most highly educated and the most moral, by morality meaning the capacity for sacrifice and the love of duty." (P. xxiii.)

From Orsay Taine wrote, May 22, 1868: "Renan is pessimistic about France and politics"; but this pessimism was not occasioned by the shadow of war, though the chauvinism of the reactionary party might give rise to some apprehension. It was internal troubles that Renan foresaw. "Our youth beheld sad days," he says in the dedication of *Saint Paul*, "and I fear that fate reserves for us nothing good before we die. Certain enormous errors drag our country toward the abyss; the persons to whom these errors are pointed out only smile." The nightmare that oppressed the philosophic observer was factional violence leading to revolution.

French history to Renan's view presented the conflict be-

---

[49] In "La Part de la famille et de l'état," *La Réforme intellectuelle et morale*, p. 310, he said: "It is said that the victory of Sadowa was the victory of the primary school-teacher; that is true, gentlemen," But here he was addressing a particular educational society.

tween Roman centralization and Teutonic autonomy, with a dynasty belonging to the nation, and an aristocracy both possessed of hereditary rights and burdened with hereditary duties. Centralization triumphed under Louis XIV and led inevitably to the Revolution. "Always great, sometimes sublime, the Revolution is an experiment highly honorable to the people that dared attempt it; but it is an experiment that failed." The State remained tyrannically supreme, the head of a centralized administration, while Paris gathered all the intellect of France, leaving the provinces a spiritual desert. In place of an aristocracy, the only inequality was that of wealth, and property was not treated as a moral thing, involving duties, but as a mere source of enjoyment. Meanwhile there were no colonies to which socialists could resort for their experiments. The result was unrest and frequent revolutions. The overthrow of the dynasty in 1830 introduced a new element of discord. France was divided into four factions, Legitimists, Orleanists, Bonapartists, and Republicans, leaving always three against any government that might be established, so that at a given moment the nation exerted only a fourth of its strength. If the radical republicans win, it leads to reaction, as in 1848, revolt inducing suppression and suppression inducing revolt. "In the fatal circle of revolutions, abyss summons abyss."

The ideal would be a constitutional monarchy with strict legality in descent and, as a restraint, a body of nobles who, standing for their own rights against the crown, would thus insure the liberty of all, as they had done in England. As this ideal was impossible of realization, Renan proposed to accept the Empire, on the ground that a government strong enough to maintain itself becomes in the course of years legitimate. Since 1859 the Emperor's personal views had inclined toward liberalism, and for a little good, Renan was willing to forget much evil.

POLITICAL CAMPAIGN

It was with such ideas that he entered the electoral campaign of 1869 for a seat in the Corps Législatif.[50] In a letter of March 7, M. Paul Cère of Meaux, a former prefect and the editor of a local journal, *L'Empire libéral*, suggested his candidacy to represent the Third Party, that is the party that accepted the Bonaparte dynasty, provided that it should transform itself into a constitutional monarchy. There were already in the field Paul de Jouvencel, radical; de Jaucourt, official; the Comte de Moustier, clerical; the Comte de Lafayette, who later withdrew; Jeoffroy and the Baron d'Avernes, who did not have much of a following. In order to feel out his constituency, Renan applied to the authorities for permission to repeat a lecture on "The Part of the Family and of the State in Education,"[51] given on April 19 in Paris, and when this permission was refused, he nevertheless proceeded to deliver it on the evening of April 26 as a political speech. Encouraged by his success, he spoke again on April 29 at Lagny on "The Services of Science to the People."[52] This address was so warmly received that he no longer hesitated to announce his candidacy, for though victory appeared doubtful, it did not seem at all impossible. At any rate, here was a call of duty to which he felt obliged to sacrifice his tastes and his comfort.[53]

Renan's first circular, which appeared May 6, presented

---

[50] See Gaston Strauss, *La politique de Renan*, p. 289 et seq., *Bersot et ses amis*, and the *Débats*, May 9, 17, 18, 22, 23, 26, June 5 and 9, 1869.

[51] Published in the *Débats*, also separately as a pamphlet, Lévy, 31 pp., 1869. The most vital point in the address is that instruction should be provided by the State, but that education should be given in the family, and especially by the women. As usual Renan's experience governs his views: seminary versus mother and sister.

[52] *Mélanges religieux et historiques.* The lecture on "Turgot," for which an admission fee was charged, was given in aid of a widow whose husband had lost his life in trying to save one of his workmen.

[53] The preface of *Questions contemporaines* opens with the words: "A serious man will not mingle actively in the affairs of his times unless he is called either by birth or by the spontaneous demand of his fellow citizens."

a program under four heads—no revolution, no war, progress, liberty. A new revolution would not only hinder material progress, but prepare a worse reaction than that which followed 1848. The country can realize its reforms and execute its own will. War is as bad as revolution; it arrests progress, leaves the destiny of the country to chance, and leads to exhaustion. A reduction of military forces is favored and distant expeditions are condemned; the immediate evacuation of Rome is demanded. Progress includes a vigorous control of the budget, publicity, reduction of unproductive expenditures, development of public education, a more equitable distribution of taxes so that incomes should bear their share as well as land. There should also be the greatest possible extension of liberty of the press, of public meetings, of association, of religion, and at some future time equitable arrangements should be made for the separation of Church and State. Renan's draft was much more expansive in the wording than his published circular, but it was doubtless blue-penciled by his political advisers.[54]

Very active in visits to constituents and in attendance at public meetings, the candidate underwent the usual attacks and slanders, the most effective of which was that, since he was a personal friend of Prince Napoleon and had received appointments from the Emperor, he was a veiled imperialist running on purpose to divide the opposition vote. When his supporter, *L'Empire libéral*, returned these slanders in kind, Renan wrote to the editor begging him to avoid personalities in his behalf. "I have accepted the candidacy," he says, "only from a sense of duty and because I did not wish it to be said that I shrank from the conditions of public life."

In Paris his candidacy was supported by Nefftzer in the *Temps* and by Bersot in the *Débats*. To the latter he wrote

[54] The circular was reprinted in the *Débats*, May 9.

the outline of an article (May 14) in which he said: "If M. Renan should some day become the representative of the liberal spirit as it is understood in the provinces, in opposition to the radical spirit of Paris, we should not be much surprised." Some of this matter Bersot employed in two editorials on the front page (May 17 and 18), adding that the second district of Seine-et-Marne, which had sent to the Chamber Lafayette and Portalis, now had the opportunity of sending M. Renan, one of the most distinguished men of our time, and that, while various parties had complaints against him, the party that had none at all was the party of liberty.

In a final circular of May 19, Renan maintained that the future belongs to what used to be called the Left Center, now the Third Party, representing the moderate opinion of France. "In voting thus, you do not make a threat, nor perform an act of complaisance; you do not, as they say, give the government a lesson, nor do you approve the conduct of the government. You perform an act of free citizenship; you declare that you wish at once respect and control, order and liberty, conservatism and progress."

The first ballot, cast on May 23 and 24, resulted as follows:[55]

de Jouvencel,	8650
de Jaucourt,	6621
Renan,	6010
de Moustier,	4097
Jeoffroy,	1654
d'Avernes,	524

By his friends Renan was now advised to withdraw, and at the same time he was threatened by his enemies. With characteristic obstinacy, he stuck to his guns and went into the second contest. In his address to the electors he repeats

[55] *Débats,* May 26.

his program, maintains that he is a liberal, a moderate, and not semiofficial as had been said, and explains that he stands anew because de Jouvencel had refused to agree with his early offer that the liberal candidate having the fewer votes should withdraw. On the second ballot, on June 6, only 876 new votes went to Renan, while, as was to be expected, the thousands were cast for the official candidate and the radical. The *Débats* for June 9 reports:

de Jouvencel,	10484
de Jaucourt,	9167
Renan,	6886

Easily consoled for his own defeat, perhaps even glad of it, Renan was yet saddened by the general results of the election. Moderation was thrown to the winds. On one side were the reactionaries; on the other, the exalted radicals, whose election promises urged them toward violence and revolution. Renan was haunted even more strongly than before with the premonition of evil days to come. "I become a sort of poor Cassandra," he writes, "may I prove a bad prophet!" [56] On the same day on which he wrote these words, there appeared in the *Revue des deux Mondes* his article "Constitutional Monarchy in France," [57] reprinted as a little brochure, [58] which immediately went into a second edition. Here, with great moderation but with great boldness, he condemns both the Revolution of '48 and the Coup d'État as crimes, although, still maintaining the principles of the Third Party, he looks forward to Napoleon as a constitutional monarch whose function it will be, less to continue, than to correct, the Revolution. The Revolution, indeed, he says, and here he speaks like Edmund Burke, proceeded philosophically in an affair in which it should

[56] To Berthelot, November 1, 1869.
[57] *La Réforme intellectuelle et morale.*
[58] Michel Lévy Frères, 1870.

have proceeded historically. A republic he does not believe possible, as monarchy answers the deepest needs of France. The radicals can prevent liberal government by provoking repression, but they cannot establish a stable state. Social democratic theories, indeed, inevitably make a state feeble. They involve political materialism, the idea of each for himself, whereas a great nation demands sacrifices, each in his own sphere doing his part toward the accomplishment of the divine aim of humanity. "Looking only at the rights of individuals, it is unjust that one man should be sacrificed for another; but it is not unjust that all should be subjected to the higher task accomplished by humanity."

He felt that the political preponderance of Paris must cease. "No one more than I admires and loves this extraordinary center of life and thought called Paris. Disease, if you please, but disease in the nature of the pearl, precious and exquisite hypertrophy, Paris is the raison-d'être of France. Source of light and heat, I willingly allow that it may be called also source of moral decomposition, provided you will admit that on this dungheap spring charming flowers, some even of the rarest. It is the glory of France to be able to support this prodigious permanent exhibition of her most excellent products; but we must not dissimulate at what a price this marvelous result is obtained."

The conclusion of the essay breathes the purest patriotism: "France can do everything but be mediocre. What she suffers, after all, she suffers for having dared too greatly against the gods. Whatever ills the future holds in reserve for her, even if her lot should arouse the pity of the world, the world will not forget that she made audacious experiments for the profit of all, that she loved justice even to the limit of folly, and that her crime, if it be a crime, was to have admitted with glorious imprudence the possibility of an ideal that the wretchedness of humanity will not allow."

IV

If Renan's love of France filled him with disquietude, his love of learning brought him peace. "I go to Paris every day," he wrote to Berthelot from Sèvres (November 1, 1869), "working with all my might to complete my *Mission*. I shall absolutely finish the manuscript by January 1." Moreover, he was honored by his associates in the Academy of Inscriptions et Belles-Lettres. On January 7, 1870, having been vice president for a year, he was elected president by thirty votes out of thirty-three.[59] The reparation of a wrong, too, seemed imminent. On Friday, March 18, a letter from the Minister of Public Instruction was read asking the Academy to designate two candidates for the vacant chair of Hebrew at the Collège de France. At the next meeting, Renan and Derenbourg presented themselves for selection in writing, neither being present, and Renan was named first choice by thirty votes out of thirty-four, while Derenbourg was named second choice with thirty-one votes, the same recommendation being also made by the Collège de France. Munk had died February 6, 1867, but naturally, with the assurance of Renan's nomination, no demand for candidates had been made so long as Duruy remained minister. Since January 2 Renan's friend Ollivier was at the head of affairs, with Segris as Minister of Public Instruction, and the occasion gave rise to the hope that the new liberalism of the Emperor would permit the reappointment of the expelled professor. At any rate, such was Renan's expectation. "It seems certain," says the *Revue archéologique* (April, 1870, p. 278), "that M. Renan will soon be restored to his chair."[60] At Easter, when Grant Duff took Sir John

---

[59] *Comptes rendus*, 1870.
[60] The Empress, however, was still, as might be surmised, irreconcilable. On August 15, 1870, while Regent, she with her own hand

Lubbock to see him, he said: "I shall begin my lectures as Luis de León did, when he resumed his, after having been silenced for years by the Inquisition, with the words, 'As I was observing at our last meeting.' " [61]

War was not yet in the mind of any one. On January 25, 1870, Taine and Renan signed a letter in the *Débats* urging subscriptions to a monument to be erected by the Philosophical Society of Berlin to Hegel, who "remains, in spite of what is hazardous and incomplete in his work, the first thinker of the nineteenth century." On March 18, furthermore, it was reported to the Academy of Inscriptions that certain army officers had been assigned to make a map of Palestine, completing the work done by the Mission in Syria in 1860-1861. Thus, without a dream of the impending catastrophe, Renan joined the Prince Napoleon on a yachting trip to Norway, a land he had long desired to visit, since it was attached to the memories of his childhood, the legends of the Breton race, the dreams of his imagination. [62] The Irish in his opinion had reached Iceland before the Northmen. [63] A letter to Berthelot from Storen tells of his delight in Inverness, which he had visited, and in the Norse fiords and the Scandinavian Alps with their cascades and pines. He wishes for his friend: "Why are you not here! I am so used to doing my thinking in company with you that every impression not shared with you seems incomplete." The Prince he finds charming: "He has entirely unexpected sides, a thirst for the unknown, a desire for the infinite, something romantic and profound, that is not apparent in Paris." The party is inclined to continue

crossed off Renan's name from a list presented by the Minister of Public Instruction, Maurice Richard, for the grade of officer in the Légion d'Honneur. The document is still in the archives, René d'Ys, p. 219.

[61] *Memoir*, p. 79.

[62] Cornélie Renan to Bersot, July 6, 1870: *Bersot et ses amis*, p. 252.

[63] Grant Duff, p. 53.

to Spitzbergen and Lapland. On July 19 war was declared. A telegram called the Prince home from Tromsö, and on July 22 Renan was again presiding over a meeting of the Academy of Inscriptions.

CHAPTER IX

During the siege, Renan, very much distressed, remained in
Paris, and presented his ideas on the situation in the *Débats* and
the *Revue des deux Mondes*. The exchange of open letters with
David Friedrich Strauss was part of this propaganda. He stood
in the elections of 1871, but again failed. In the fall of this
year, he published *Intellectual and Moral Reform,* a volume of
political tracts. During the Commune, he took refuge at Versailles, where he composed his *Philosophical Dialogues,* not published till 1876. In the meanwhile (November 17, 1870) he had
been reinstated in his chair of Hebrew at the Collège de France,
and he continued to busy himself with the *Histoire littéraire de la*
France and the *Corpus,* joining also (1873) the *Journal des Sa-*
vants. His annual reports as secretary of the Société Asiatique
were eagerly received. A committee on higher education also
occupied his attention. His autumns were mostly spent in Italy.
The Antichrist appeared in June, 1873, and various comparatively
unimportant essays were contributed from time to time to periodicals. Rheumatism began more and more to disable him, and he
sought relief at Ischia, where he began his *Philosophical Dramas.*
1876 was the year of a Sicilian trip and 1877 that of a great
speech on the unveiling of the Spinoza monument at the Hague.
The publication of *Recollections of Childhood and Youth* was
begun in the *Revue des deux Mondes* in 1876. *The Gospels* was
published in 1877, *Miscellanies of History and Travel* and *Caliban*
in 1878. On June 13, 1878, Renan was elected to the French
Academy, into which he was received at a notable session the next
April.

I

THE Franco-Prussian war was a crushing blow to Renan's
international idealism. Germany, as he repeatedly con-

fesses, had been his intellectual and moral foster mother. Of her he had constructed an image of uprightness, philosophic liberalism and devotion to lofty moral principles, to which the reality did not correspond. He had looked forward to an intellectual, and perhaps political, alliance of France, Germany and England to hold in check the Slavic hordes, which he regarded as a possible menace to European civilization. And now it was German brutality before which that civilization trembled. Nor did his condemnation spare the frivolous rulers and superficial patriots of his own country. Meeting Brandes on the street,[1] he burst into a violent denunciation of the politicians responsible for the war and parted from his Danish acquaintance with tears in his eyes. To others, referring to his defeat at the polls, he said: "They might have torn me in pieces from the tribune, but they would not have declared war before I had told them the whole truth."[2] And on August 19, he wrote from Sèvres to Grant Duff: "What an access of insanity! What a crime! The greatest heart-pain I have ever felt in my life was when at Tromsö we received the fatal telegram informing us that war was certain and would be immediate."[3]

Renan was, indeed, a better patriot than those who refused to see and those who were incapable of thought. The crowd at Brébant's[4] mocked him and howled him down, to the great satisfaction of the inert and shallow Goncourt, who grew sentimental over the woes of France, but never raised a helpful finger or uttered a stirring or a useful word. When Renan retires from the window in disgust over the acclamations of the crowd at the passage of a troop, and remarks contemptuously, "Not a man there is capable of an act of

---

[1] August 12, *Moderne Geister*, p. 88 et seq.
[2] Darmesteter, *Revue Bleue*, October 21, 1893, p. 523.
[3] *Memoir*, p. 81.
[4] After the death of Sainte-Beuve the Magny diners transferred their meetings to the Restaurant Brébant.

virtue;"[5] and when, after proclaiming the superiority of the Germans (September 6), he cries out against revenge: "No, rather let France perish; above country there is the kingdom of duty, of reason," he is giving momentary vent to passion over the broken ideals of a lifetime, an explosion which is in no sense inconsistent with the most ardent love of country. Renan was, to use his own words, one of "those whom a philosophic conception of life has raised, not indeed above patriotism, but above the errors into which one is drawn by an unenlightened patriotism."

It is in this spirit that he prepared for the *Revue des deux Mondes,*[6] his article on "The War Between France and Germany," a war that he had always regarded as "the greatest misfortune that could befall civilization," since by it "the intellectual, moral and political harmony is broken," and hatred is substituted for understanding. Prussia is hard, ungenerous and proud; France, superficial and presumptuous. It was her opposition that made the Prussian strength. The Unity of Germany is perfectly legitimate, and in spite of the fact that the Baltic nobles want to Prussianize the whole nation and then all the world, Prussia will gradually be absorbed in the German state.[7] "Prussia will pass, Germany will remain." Democracy will overwhelm militarism, a task in which it deserves assent and grateful sympathy. Once dynasties are renounced, there is no prin-

---

[5] August 23. For comment on this remark see the speech of Antistius (*Drames philosophiques,* p. 349): "Among those who take and give death, there are few who act from any motive! Man's arm is sinewed only by passion. There must be rules to act as a wolf among wolves. As to erecting into lofty morality that which is the negation of all morality, it is an exercise for which I have little taste. Let the people do without principles; but do not give them sophisms for truths."

[6] September 15, 1870: *La Réforme intellectuelle et morale.*

[7] A poet, Auguste Barbier, took a different view:
"Le venin de la Prusse en toi reste à jamais,
Et morte est l'Allemagne."
Revue des deux Mondes, October 1, 1870, p. 561.

ciple to apply to boundaries but the principle of nationalities. Without Alsace and Lorraine, France could hardly survive, and Europe without France would lack an essential element of life. But the principle of nationalities holds in it the germs of wars of extinction. "The end of war will be seen only when to this principle is added its corrective, the principle of a European federation, superior to all nationalities." Renan therefore calls for the intervention of all the neutrals, leading to a federal pact. To the Prussian naturalists who argue that the strong drive out the weak, he answers that the analogy of the animals does not hold: There is in humanity a sense of right, justice, morality. Never have several species of animals formed a coalition to fight an aggressor, as Europe did against Spain in the sixteenth century, against Louis XIV and against Napoleon. "The wise friends of Prussia whisper to her, not as a menace, but as a warning: *Væ Victoribus!*"

Of all Renan's writings on the war, this is the most complete. The same ideas, however, and often in identical words, are repeated in his letters to his "learned master," Strauss.[8] The first of these, dated September 13 and published in the *Débats* September 16, is an answer to a letter printed by the German scholar in the *Augsburg Gazette* for August 18, and by Renan in the *Débats* for September 15. In this communication, after a historical review of the steps toward the unity of Germany, Strauss places the blame for hostilities on France and invites Renan to reply through the press. Renan thus became the literary protagonist of the French nation before the world, a nation which he claims is pacific and not to be judged by journalistic declamation. Let the present boundaries remain. It is for the victor to

---

[8] Renan's letters are published in "*La Réforme intellectuelle et morale*"; those of D. F. Strauss in *Gesammelte Schriften*, vol. i. See also Maurice Muret, "La Querelle de Strauss et Renan," *Revue des deux Mondes*, 1915, tome xxx.

decide whether France is to resolve on revenge or to join an alliance with Germany and England. Let there be a Congress of the United States of Europe. "Up to our time, the central power of the European community has been shown only in temporary coalitions against any people who aspired to universal dominion; it would be good that a permanent and preventive coalition should be formed for the maintenance of the chief common interests, which are after all those of reason and civilization."

The reply of Strauss, dated September 29, also printed in the *Augsburg Gazette*, October 2, shows the baleful effects of the poison of Prussianism. The Hohenzollern tradition seems to him moderation, not arrogance, and he admires the Prussians as "political animals." In the new state, Prussia will provide bone and sinew, South Germany flesh and blood. The victorious army will bring back from France German unity and it will not lay down the sword till the purpose of the war is attained, though after that it will brandish the weapon no longer. The final pages are boastful and arrogant, even insulting. "If you had spoken so to your French people, O Ernest Renan, and converted them to your peaceful beliefs, our soldiers would not soon be drinking choice French wines in Paris." [9]

The conduct of Strauss in this correspondence was boorish. Renan had printed his opponent's first letter in the *Débats* before answering it; Strauss did not reciprocate this courtesy when he published his second letter in the *Augsburg Gazette*. Instead, he printed the three documents, presentation, reply and refutation, an obviously unfair proceeding, in a pamphlet, which was sold for the benefit of the German wounded. His misunderstanding of Renan's remarks about boundaries would be dishonest in one not blinded by an intolerant and supercilious patriotism. The

---

[9] Strauss, p. 339.

German professors of 1914 were his legitimate offspring.

Renan's comment is a model of urbanity combined with inflexible severity. Of Strauss he had written to Ritter: [10] "He is, I think, the man of this century for whom I have the greatest admiration and sympathy." But this high opinion, like so many of Renan's ideals, had received a rude shock. In his second letter to his "learned master," dated September 15, 1871, after rehearsing the story of the correspondence, he indicates "the difference between your way and mine of comprehending life," making perfectly clear the fact that this difference is one of good manners. Strauss had done him the honor of translating and publishing his letter together with two of his own, and the profits of the pamphlet had accrued to the German troops. "The work to which you made me contribute," says Renan, "is a work of humanity, and, if my humble prose has procured some cigars for the soldiers who pillaged my little cottage at Sèvres, I thank you for having furnished me the opportunity of conforming my conduct to certain of the precepts of Jesus which I believe to be the most authentic." He proceeds to utter a warning against exactly what has in our day finally happened. "The only vice that is punished in this world is pride." Moderation had not won the day. It was the right of Alsace to choose its nationality; "we do not admit the cession of souls." What has been introduced is a "zoölogical war." "You have raised in the world the flag of ethnographic and archæologic, in place of liberal, politics; that policy will be fatal to you. . . . Each affirmation of Germanism is an affirmation of Slavism." Renan would dislike a planet in which everybody was like himself. "If all the world were made in your German image, it would perhaps be a little gloomy and tedious. . . . This universe is a spectacle that a god has procured for himself. Let us

[10] September 3, 1869. *Charles Ritter, ses amis et ses maîtres: choix de lettres,* 1911.

carry out the intentions of the great Choragus in contributing to make the spectacle as brilliant and varied as possible.'' He has vainly counseled love; he will not counsel hate, but will be silent. Yet he concludes with quoting the words put by Æschylus into the mouth of Prometheus: ''Jupiter, in spite of all his pride, would do well to be humble. At present, since he is conqueror, let him sit on his throne at ease, trusting to the peal of his thunder and shaking in his hand his dart of flame. All this will not preserve him from some day falling ignominiously with a horrible crash. He himself, I see, creates his enemy, a monster hard to combat, who will find a flame superior to lightning, a peal superior to thunder. Vanquished then, he will understand by experience how different it is to reign or to serve.'' In particulars Renan was no better prophet than many another, but when he took the cosmic view, his sight was clear and just.

The second letter to Strauss was, of course, written after the treaty of Frankfort. During the Siege of Paris, Renan was pleading with his countrymen for reason and calm judgment. Convinced that an organized and disciplined force always defeats an unorganized and undisciplined one, he perceived the uselessness of continuing the war after the establishment of the new government on the fourth of September. The Government of National Defense, composed only of the Parisian deputation, together with certain republicans, was not representative of France. The country cannot be governed without the assent of the provinces. Unwilling to ask favors of the conquerors, he yet sees the possibility of electing an assembly from the departments not yet invaded, which constitutes three-quarters of the whole number, and to such members might be added a selection of the best men from the occupied districts. Let no exaggerated and pedantic considerations of regularity interfere; let every one forget party divisions, and constitute a unity in the presence of the enemy. There must be an assembly, and it must be distinct from the body that is to regulate the future political destinies of France. To save the people is the dire need in the hour of distress. Let party and personal ambitions be thrown to the winds. "Candidates, great heavens! for a mission of tears and grief!"

Renan's appeal for a national assembly was presented in three letters to the *Débats,* November 10, 13, and 28, 1870. To these, as might have been anticipated, the politicians paid no attention; they secured an armistice (January 28, 1871) so that regular elections might be held, they got into a fierce squabble over the exclusion of Bonapartist office-holders, in which Bismarck had to intervene, and the resulting assembly viciously clung to power for five years and at length voted the constitutional laws of 1875 which regulated the political destinies of France.

At the elections of February 8, 1871, for which there was no time to make a canvass, Renan allowed his name to be presented, but he was defeated. "I have no hope," he wrote Berthelot on February 27, "for I am the first to admit that the remedies I perceive are impossible, at least for the present, and even within a fairly distant future." Nevertheless, he insists on presenting his remedies to the public. On March 17, Taine writes: [11] "Renan has lent me four long political articles dealing with the situation, which he probably will not publish. They are loose, abstract, not very good. He is by no means at his best. He has always plenty of ideas, but his fundamental notion will repel; very clearly he is for the restoration of aristocracy, the better to follow the example of Prussia."

These four articles, made into one, form the title essay of *Intellectual and Moral Reform,* published in October, 1871.[12] Economic considerations, as usual, are none of

---

[11] *Vie et correspondance,* vol. iii, 59.
[12] The rest of the book is made up of the letters to Strauss, the 1870

Renan's concern. In the first part of this essay, headed "The Evil," he shows the general incapacity of France, resulting from universal suffrage. The materialism of the workmen and peasants, their moral debasement and indifference, and the selfish desire for comfort among the bourgeoisie, must result in mediocrity, while the absence of discipline and self-sacrifice had unfitted the country for war. "The group of statesmen and generals in command when France faced Prussia was the most inefficient any nation had ever had." On the other hand, Prussia had been preserved from industrial materialism by the old régime, which fostered subordination, the idea of duty and the military spirit. "Military organization is founded on discipline; democracy is the negation of discipline." The German victory, therefore, while a triumph of science and reason, was also a triumph of the old régime. After defeat, the Commune showed a wound beneath a wound, an abyss below an abyss. Yet "France renewed its life; the corpse disputed by the worms again developed warmth and motion."

The second part of the essay, headed "The Remedies," is based upon the idea that France must regain the lost provinces. Patriotism demands this restoration. If Germany had left the nation intact, she might have established permanent peace in Europe, but now even a philosopher cannot be deaf to the cry of two million souls. To accomplish the task a reform is essential. Penitence involves the correction of fundamental faults, and the fundamental fault of France has been a taste for superficial democracy. The model before it is the victor: Prussia after Tilsit became in fifty years the first power in Europe.

---

letters to the *Débats,* the lecture on family and state in education, and the two latest essays in the *Revue des deux Mondes,* that on constitutional monarchy and that on the war. It is entirely a book of circumstance.

At this point, for the first time, Renan employs imaginary speakers to express the opposite phases of his thought. A first citizen, who clearly represents the author's preferences, urges France to restore royalty and, to a certain extent, aristocracy, since duty is aristocratic and democracy with its indiscipline and disorder cannot make war. Then the nation should found a system of solid education and obligatory military training; it should become serious, submissive to authority, amenable to rule and discipline; and in twenty years it can avenge Sedan. The second citizen, on the contrary, who represents what is most likely to take place, considers such a program chimerical. France, in his view, will not change, but will continue in her course until she corrupts her neighbors to the same materialistic egotism and drags all of them down to a uniform plane of national feebleness.

The essay proceeds to devise plans for elections to two chambers, a common recreation for French publicists at that time. Three points in Renan's scheme are interesting: (1) There should be representation, not only of numbers, but of functions, such as army and navy, teachers, clergy, and chambers of commerce; (2) women and children should be counted, the vote being cast by the male members of the family, since "it is surely impossible that women should participate directly in political life"; (3) the publication of debates, since it leads to prolixity and declamation, should not be allowed.

In education Renan would leave the elementary schools to the Church, the university to the Liberals. Literary studies, which have been overemphasized, should largely give place to science, though this should consist of principles and not of practical applications. There should be half a dozen independent and autonomous universities.

Perhaps our defeat has been a benefit, he says in conclusion, for we might have proceeded in our folly. There are two types of society before us: the American, free, given to labor and to the pleasure of activity, but lacking distinction and the capacity to produce original works in art and science; and its opposite, the old régime, which can be developed and corrected by liberalism. Though France is not tending toward the American type, but rather toward an unstable socialism which leads to Cæsarism, yet she always does the unexpected and may do it again. At any rate, she has been generous, she is the salt of the earth, and without her the world would be tasteless. The last word of the essay, recalling Candide's, "We must cultivate our garden," is *Laboremus.*

II

Between the composition of these articles and their publication, the Commune, with its immense destruction of property and its horrible sacrifice of life, had inflicted upon Paris wounds in comparison with which the damage wrought by the siege was a mere trifle. To Renan the visions of the Apocalypse seemed almost realized and his experiences have marked their trail through *The Antichrist,* upon which he was then engaged. For his political counsels he expected no hearing, and he got none. He had worked for the intellectual, moral and political alliance of Germany and France, which would draw in England and constitute a force able to govern the world. But his early mistress, from whom he had derived the best that was in him, had mocked the ideal. "What we loved in Germany, her largeness, her lofty conception of reason and humanity, exist no longer." Yet he hopes. "May there be formed at length a league of men of good will of every tribe, of every tongue, of every people, who will be able to create and maintain above these hot conflicts an empyrean of pure ideals, a heaven where there will be neither Greek nor barbarian, nor German, nor Latin." [13] Though

---

[13] Preface, *La Réforme,* p. xii.

always interested, often agitated, by political events, Renan ceased to write upon the subject. In 1876, when asked to stand for Senator to represent the Bouches-du-Rhône, he allowed his name to be presented, but refused even to go to Marseilles to attend the caucus. When Jules Simon asked him if he would vote with his party, he replied: "Pretty often." [14]

It is fairly certain that Renan would not have been a successful political leader. His task was elsewhere, and his task was his delight. His venture into this field is, however, not to be regretted.

I will not hide the fact [he says in the introduction to *The Antichrist*] that the taste for history, the incomparable delight felt in seeing the spectacle of humanity unfold, has particularly captivated me in this volume. I have had too much pleasure in writing it to ask any further recompense. Often I have reproached myself for having enjoyed myself so much in my study while my poor country is being consumed in a slow agony; but I have a quiet conscience. When in the elections of 1869 I offered myself to the suffrage of my fellow citizens, all my placards bore in large letters: "No revolution; no war; a war will be as injurious as a revolution." In the month of September, 1870, I begged the enlightened minds of Germany and of Europe to think of the frightful misfortune that menaced civilization. During the siege, in Paris, in the month of November, 1870, I exposed myself to the greatest unpopularity by advising the calling of an assembly having power to treat for peace. In the elections of 1871, I answered to the overtures made me: "Such a mandate may be neither sought nor refused." After the reëstablishment of order, I applied all my attention to the reforms that I consider the most urgent to save our country. I have therefore done what I could. We owe our country our sincerity; we are not obliged to resort to charlatanism to make it accept our services or our ideas. (P. xlix.)

Many of the political ideas of Renan were held in common by Taine and others of what may perhaps be called

---

[14] *Quatre Portraits.*

the Whig group. In one way or another, they have not been without their influence. The scholar's services, however, belonged to his country, not in its parliament, but in its institutions of learning. On November 17, Jules Simon being Minister of Public Instruction, Renan was for a second time appointed to the chair of Hebrew in the Collège de France, and there he remained till his death.[15] At the Academy of Inscriptions and Belles-Lettres, which did not omit a single one of its weekly meetings during all this troublous period, he presided over every gathering for 1870, excepting the three already noted. In January, 1870, he was driven by the German shells from his home in the rue Vanneau to temporary quarters on the right bank of the Seine. In April he went to Sèvres, where sixteen persons lived in his sacked cottage. In spite of his "invincible repugnance to fleeing," the shells in the battle with the Commune again drove him out, and, terribly distressed, and assured that he could be of no service to the cause of reason, he took refuge on May 1 in lodgings at Versailles.[16]

During the four weeks spent here,[17] while separated from his books and his customary tasks, he made use of his forced leisure for a review of his fundamental philosophic beliefs. The form of dialogue was chosen as being undogmatic and presenting varying phases of problems without requiring any conclusion. The purpose is to arouse reflection, even at the expense of exaggeration, for the dignity of man demands that we should not be indifferent to such questions, though we cannot hope for conclusive answers. It is a

---

[15] Berthelot proposed to the Government of National Defense the reappointment of Renan. "You must see Trochu," said Jules Simon. Pelletan supported the request. Trochu said nothing, and the decree was signed: Speech of Berthelot at the unveiling of the statue of Renan at Tréguier, René d'Ys, p. 449. Jules Simon says in his jaunty way: "I gave him back his chair without his asking it." *Quatre Portraits.*

[16] To Berthelot, April 17, 29, 30.

[17] He writes to Berthelot again from Sèvres, May 28.

superficial mind that never casts a glance into the depths of the abyss it cannot hope to fathom.

It is hardly necessary for Renan to inform us that his interlocutors do not represent persons, either imaginary or real. He has not attempted to give them individuality. They are obviously, as he calls them, "the different lobes of his brain," freely talking together. Malebranche and Kant, to whose formulas all must return, are the metaphysical writers chiefly quoted, though Fichte, Hegel and Schopenhauer are also referred to.

In the first Dialogue, entitled "Certitudes," Philalèthe, Eudoxe and Euthyphron, philosophers of the school that has for fundamental principles the worship of the ideal, the negation of the supernatural and the experimental investigation of reality, starting from a passage from Malebranche, review their ideas on God and the universe, a practice that ought to be renewed every ten years.[18] The first certitude is that there is no trace of the action in particular cases of the will of any being superior to man. Prayer is but a mystic hymn; if employed for self-interest, it would be an insult to the Divinity. The second certitude is that the world has an aim and works toward a mysterious result; it develops from an inward necessity, an unconscious instinct, analogous to the blind efforts of plants and embryos. Everything tries to realize itself. All reality aspires to consciousness, and all obscure consciousness aspires to clarity. Up to the present the consciousness of the whole is so obscure, that it scarcely surpasses that of the oyster or the polyp; but it exists and rises toward its end with sure instinct. The doctrine of final causes is replaced by the doctrine of evolution. The secret spring that moves all is God. We are duped for

---

[18] Renan's own practice is, as usual, generalized: 1849, *The Future of Science;* 1860, "Metaphysics and its Future"; 1871, *Philosophic Dialogues;* 1880, nothing published; 1889, "Examination of Philosophic Conscience."

nature's purposes, and every desire, as soon as fulfilled, is seen to be vanity. We know this, and yet pursue our desires. Self-devotion and virtue among men are analogous to the maternal instinct among birds, a blind sacrifice to an unknown end. An ingenious providence takes its precautions to assure the amount of virtue needed to sustain the universe. For the true philosopher, to obey nature is to collaborate in the divine work. Morality reduces itself to submission. Immorality is revolt against this course of things.

For the second Dialogue, "Probabilities," Théophraste has joined the others, and becomes the principal speaker. In the immense activity of the world, he maintains, all rival egotisms cancel one another, but what is done for the ideal subsists and gradually accumulates as capital. It is by what little we add to this reserve of progress that we live eternally. All is born of matter, but it is the idea that animates. A symphony consists of physical vibrations and the idea of the composer, neither existing without the other. "The idea is a virtuality that craves existence; matter gives it concreteness, makes it a reality." Perfect existence is to be attributed only to the idea, or rather to the idea conscious of itself, the soul. The highest expression of consciousness known to us is humanity, and the highest expression of humanity is science, virtue, art. If these fail here, yet in some other world, through nature's profusion, perfection will be realized. The universal work of all that lives is to make God perfect, to contribute to the grand final resultant that will close the circle of things by unity. This work hitherto accomplished blindly by a tendency, reason will take in hand and, after having organized humanity, will organize God. Science may conquer what seem insuperable difficulties, and a small body of men, by scientific secrets inaccessible to common brains, may control the mass.

Théocist is now added to speak of "Dreams" in the third

Dialogue. He goes beyond humanity and assigns to the universe an aim superior to man's conception. The future consciousness of humanity may be infinitely superior to the present. Philosophically speaking, democracy has little chance of success. It is impossible to raise all to the same level, for this is contrary to the ways of God, which create summits, superior beings whom others are glad to serve. An élite of intelligence, masters of the secrets of reality, would dominate the world and make reason reign. Such men would actually possess the power claimed by the Church. Truly infallible, beneficent, all-powerful, they might have the means to destroy the planet. There might thus be developed a superior race. Or the universe might be reduced to a single existence, all nature producing a central life, the sum of billions of lives, past and present, like the cells in an organism. Sometimes he conceives God as the vast consciousness in which all are reflected, each having his part, artist, writer, saint, even the man of pleasure. The resurrection of the individual, a soul without the body, is chimerical. God, become perfect, will resuscitate the past. Those who have contributed to the work will feel its accomplishment; those who have made no sacrifice will go to nothingness. A sleep of a billion centuries and one of an hour are equal. The recompense will seem to follow death immediately. God is an absolute necessity. He will be, He is. As a reality, He will be; as ideal, He is. We reach a point where we must stop. Reason and language apply only to the finite. "It is about as the priests speak, only the words are different." The last phrase of the essay asserts: "In matters of virtue, each finds certitude in consulting his own heart."

The developments omitted in the foregoing analysis but slightly modify the current of the thought, though a few of them rather scandalized some readers. Such, for example, the remark that nature does not favor virtue; or

that the universe is the great egotist that catches us with
the grossest baits; or that criticism demolishes religion,
love, goodness, truth; or that there may come a time when
a great artist or a virtuous man will be an antiquated, almost useless thing. These, however, are but sallies by the
way; the fundamental thought is that of *The Future of Science,* systematically developed and with a few additional
side lights. Taine finds in Renan much of Plato, almost a
poet, which may be the truest philosophy. That the world
has an aim and labors toward a mysterious end, he would
range rather among the probabilities than among the certitudes, and he invites his friend to develop the thesis.[19] For
Renan, however, the time for absolute systems was past. He
traversed philosophies, but dwelt in none. He had, indeed,
no doubt regarding his own views, though ready to admit
that the opposite might be right. In his heart he knew
that love, universal goodness, is the law that does not deceive, and that goodness depends upon no theory conceived
by the intellect.

It was the same with his patriotism, which to some people
seemed occasionally to flicker. It was firm in his heart.
When rumor ascribed to Berthelot the idea of taking a
position in England, Renan wrote:[20] "For Heaven's sake,
reject that idea. You would fail in a matter of duty. The
more unhappy our country, the less we should think of quit-
ting it." Unless driven out, deprived of intellectual liberty
or left to starve, those who have benefited from its institutions and its past would defraud the nation of the capital
advanced for their good. Even if the Collège de France is
left without governmental support, he will continue his
work there without pay, however "shameful, stupid, infamous, repulsive" the Parisian mob may become.

---

[19] Letter of June 5, 1876.
[20] April 29, 1871.

III

"Science, like duty, is never dormant," said Renan in his presidential address on the occasion of bestowing the annual prizes of the Academy of Inscriptions, December 29, 1871. While not a single weekly meeting of the Academy had been omitted, the scholarly exercises proceeding even when a shell fell upon the building in which they were held, yet the annual public assemblage, a sort of fête, was felt to be an impropriety during such times. Two such meetings, therefore, were combined in one, at which both Renan and his successor, Delisle, presided in turn. Delisle, however, contented himself with distributing the prizes, leaving Renan the orator of the occasion, an occasion which may be regarded as opening the series of those felicitous speeches for which he later was in such demand.[21] Here he insists on the continuity and permanence of erudition, the superior value of serious intellectual work, and the honor rightly due to those who "attach an elevated, almost religious meaning to their studies."[22]

Erudition, indeed, was for a time, not only Renan's principal, but his sole productive occupation. Even his articles for the *Revue des deux Mondes* were merely the advance publication of memoirs prepared for the *Histoire littéraire de la France*.[23] For this collection he also pre-

---

[21] A previous brief address as president of the Academy had been delivered on May 10, 1870, at the funeral of Villemain. *Discours et conférences.*

[22] *Mélanges d'histoire et de voyages.*

[23] February 15 and March 1, 1871, "Un publiciste du temps de Philippe le Bel: Pierre du Bois," and March 15, April 1 and 15, 1872, "Un Ministre de Philippe le Bel: Guillaume de Nogaret." The first piece is surprising in a magazine addressed to the reading public, as it is not at all in popular form and contains detailed analyses of the author's works. The second piece, divided into "L'Attentat d'Anagni," "Les Apologies de Nogaret et le procès des Templiers," and "Le Procès contre la mémoire de Boniface," has a more general appeal; in fact, the story of Anagni is of absorbing

pared an article on "The French Rabbis of the Beginning of the Fourteenth Century," based on a vast assemblage of notes collected by Adolphe Neubauer, under-librarian of the Bodleian, who gathered them on missions to the various European libraries.[24] Another work for the Academy of Inscriptions was the *Corpus Inscriptionum Semiticarum*, the progress of which we learn from the secretary's reports in the *Comptes rendus*. On July 5, 1872, Renan presents for inspection a provisional specimen of the arrangement and typography; in January, 1874, the committee, having finished its preliminary discussions, is ready to pass to the final notices on each inscription;[25] in February, 1875, translation into Latin and final and uniform editing have been begun; and in a few weeks a chapter can be printed in proof for further discussions; in August, 1876, the Phœnician part, about one-half of the work, is practically finished; in January, 1877, the work is nearly ready and in July the first fascicle is complete, merely awaiting funds from the government; the following February, it is still awaiting funds; but on November 7, 1879, Renan in triumph placed on the table the proof of the first sheet of the *Corpus*, thus bringing to fruition the labors of twelve years.

---

interest. A further contribution to the same series appeared in the *Revue*, March 1, 1879, "La Papauté hors de l'Italie—Clement V." Published in vols. xxvi (1873), xxvii (1877), and xxviii (1881) of the *Histoire littéraire de la France*, they were, according to directions in his will, collected after Renan's death in a volume, *Études sur la politique religieuse du règne de Philippe le Bel* (1899). *L'eau de jouvence* is directly connected with these studies.

[24] *Histoire littéraire*, vol. xxvii, pp. 431-734. The work had been begun eleven years before. The copy was ready in 1874, but the volume did not appear till 1877.

[25] Concerning collaboration in interpreting inscriptions, Renan says: "What one does not see, is apparent to another; a letter ill-read by this one is rectified by that one; comparisons not dreamed of by the first investigators are clearly perceived by their successors; so that, at the end of three or four years, a text submitted to the examination of eight or ten persons capable of interpreting it, reaches a maturity, a degree of clearness in which it remains stationary till new discoveries are made." Report to Société Asiatique, June 30, 1874.

His favorite Société Asiatique did not get along so well as the Academy. From October 11, 1870, to February 24, 1871, no meetings were held and thereafter they were for some time very irregular. For some years much trouble was experienced in obtaining suitable quarters, until they settled in 1878 in the rue de Lille. According to Darmesteter, it was Renan's faith in science that carried the society through this troublous period.[26] Twice reëlected secretary, he inspired his colleagues by his eagerly awaited annual report. Though the founders of the society even during the Revolution were happy in comparison, the rule he enunciated was to continue the work whether or not it had a future. "In times like ours, despair is overcome only by a reflective determination to fulfill one's task of every day, even if the mind is distracted and the heart heavy." In continuing intellectual research, the members act as good patriots and good citizens, for there is no better service to their distracted country than to maintain the tradition of solid intellectual culture. "It is because France allowed the scientific spirit, the habits of precision and exact reasoning, the aptitude of keeping many things in mind at once, to perish in her heart, that she was first precipitated into a disastrous war, then vanquished, then delivered over to the most desolating of civil strifes. . . . It is in working for this reform of the intellectual education of France, far more than by agitations and sterile declamations that we shall contribute to raise her up again. Let us do our duty as scholars hour by hour, without seeking popularity, even without hope of reward, and we shall be assured that we have well served our country."[27]

His hopes grow as the years pass. Not every expectation has been realized, but what acquisitions, what discoveries!

---

[26] *Revue Bleue,* October 21, 1893.

[27] Report of June 29, 1871. All these Reports are found in the July number of the *Journal Asiatique* for the year.

The young men of the *Société de linguistique,* such as Bréal and Darmesteter, are welcomed. (1874.) His pupil, Philippe Berger, shows wonderful keenness in deciphering inscriptions. (1875.) "It is a true joy for the friend of fine and excellent things to see the ever more flourishing state of our studies, the zeal, the activity, the solidity, the vigor, the good method that our youthful scholars, imbued with the best philological and critical doctrines, bring to researches in which the only recompense is the service rendered to truth." (1877.)

While the major portion of each Report is devoted to the appreciation of deceased scholars [28] and a critical review of the French oriental works of the year, Renan is constantly drawing morals from his subject matter. When Julien and Pauthier, who had lived in a state of chronic quarrel, died within the year, he remarked: "It furnishes a lesson from which we should profit. Liberty of criticism is the fundamental condition of science; it must not be touched, but personalities of every kind must be severely banished. Beware lest rivalry degenerate into hatred and the career of an estimable scholar be hindered, because two persons engaged in the same studies are at the outset of their activity placed in opposition to one another. If the number of scholarly positions is limited, the field of public esteem is immense. To seek to deprive a rival of that recompense is a wicked act." (1873.) Scholars, he thinks, are generally too severe in their judgments of one another. Whoever gives himself disinterestedly to research is worthy of esteem. "To use in such a matter disdainful or malevolent expressions is to show a great presumption. Let him who has never made a mistake, cast the first stone." For charlatanism and bad work, silence is best, since he would not

---

[28] The most complete of these is the appreciation and biography of Jules Mohl. (1876.)

301

be a policeman of erudition. (1874.) Yet his criticism, though kindly, never fails to indicate the points of weakness, even in the works of his friends. While there should be no frivolous rhetoric, there is for the most special studies a style, a form, conditions of elegance and refined composition. . . . Making no sacrifice in the subject matter, let us do all we can not to repel any cultivated mind desiring to enter our domain. Obscure topics can be treated clearly, and a conscientious writer ought not to be satisfied until he has taken all the pains he can to avoid presenting difficulties to his readers.'' (1875.)

It is not only in his great histories, and in his general essays, but in his most technical writings as well, that Renan exemplifies the theories here propounded. Indeed, he can transfer a passage bodily from the one to the other, as he sometimes does.[29] In 1873 he entered the editorial board of the *Journal des Savants,* receiving, as he tells us, not a rich pension from Napoleon III, but 500 francs a year,[30] a sum which he more than earned by the number and importance of his contributions.[31]

Another interest in these years was the reform of higher education in France, a subject that had agitated his mind since the days of *The Future of Science.* Appearing before the Guizot Committee on Higher Education appointed by

---

[29] For example, ''La Société berbère,'' *Revue des deux Mondes,* September 1, 1873 (*Mélanges d'histoire et de voyages*), has a passage from the Report of 1873, and ''Le Théâtre persan,'' *Débats,* July 9 and 10, 1878, a passage from the Report of 1878 (*Nouvelles Études*).

[30] *Feuilles détachées,* p. xxiii.

[31] The Bureau of the *Journal des Savants* consisted of the Minister of Public Instruction, as president, and six assistants, of whom Renan was one, selected from various classes of the Institut, together with a group of regular writers, who were the most distinguished scholars of France. Printed at the Imprimérie Nationale, the periodical is a monthly journal devoted to reviews of learned publications in all branches of knowledge, such reviews being generally almost independent articles. Almost all Renan's articles deal with topics connected with his *Origins.* Many of them are of considerable interest to non-specialists, but only a few have been republished.

Segris in 1870, he had opposed granting to any group that wished it the privilege of establishing a school of university grade under the guise of freedom of teaching. Such freedom, he maintained, could be procured only by opening the regular courses in the state universities to any properly qualified teacher (ordinarily any one having the doctor's degree) and by putting such courses on a perfect equality with those given by the official professors; in other words, he advocated privatdocentism.[32] During the winter of 1872, he was one of a group of about a dozen scholars, which included Taine and Berthelot, who presented to Jules Simon a report advocating the decentralization of the universities.[33] The next year liberal hopes were dashed by the reaction which elected MacMahon and placed the clerical Batbie at the head of the education department. The law of 1875 allowed any group of citizens under fixed conditions to found establishments for higher education alongside of those controlled by the state, and Renan published in the *Débats* [34] his views as stated above, defending them from the implication of Germanism by showing that such was the constitution of the University of Paris in the thirteenth century. From a letter of Taine [35] we learn that the successor of the old extra-administrative committee was still holding meetings in 1876, and Berthelot in August writes of what seems to have been its last conference (August 28, 1876). A detailed report, embodying Renan's leading principles of decentralization—seven or eight local universities in cities instead of one State University, and freedom of teaching within these universities for all qualified persons —was presented to Waddington, Minister of Public Instruction, and he drew up a project of law somewhat on the lines

---

[32] Liard, *L'Enseignement supérieur en France,* vol. ii, p. 305.
[33] Taine, *Correspondance,* vol. iii, p. 160.
[34] July 4: see *Mélanges d'histoire et de voyages,*
[35] To G. Paris, May 17, 1876.

suggested; but all came to naught in the political agitations of the time.[36]

IV

Meanwhile Renan continued his work on his *Origins* without intermission. During July and August, 1871, he visited the Prince Napoleon at Prangins, on the Lake of Geneva, and after returning to Paris, made in October and November a trip through Provence, Nice, Genoa and other cities of Northern Italy to Venice, where he is again much occupied with art.[37] He has modified some of his judgments, however, since he has seen the supreme type of the beautiful, the Acropolis at Athens.[38] On his return, he at once wrote an introduction for Ritter's translation of the Essays of David Strauss, a favor promised in March, 1870, when he had expected to meet the German scholar through the good offices of his Swiss friend. In performing this task Renan not only said, but showed, that he did not believe in allowing a political break to injure scientific and philosophical relations.

In 1872, after again paying his respects to the Prince Napoleon late in September, he crossed the Simplon, was

[36] Liard, Vol. II, Book viii, Chapter II, and Appendix, where the Report, probably in part the work of Renan, and the Project are printed.

[37] See letters to Ritter and Berthelot. In the Berthelot *Correspondance*, letter ix, p. 411, ought to be dated 1871, as letter x, following, is clearly an answer to it. On the other hand, letter viii, p. 408, should precede letter iii, p. 428, which is an answer to it, and should be dated 1872. The route followed in letter viii is not to be harmonized with that of letter ix. In 1871, moreover, Renan was present and spoke at a meeting of the Académie des Inscriptions on October 13. He could not, therefore, have been in Florence October 7 and then gone on to Rome. Furthermore, he says he had been in Italy twenty-three years before, whereas, writing to Ritter in 1871, he says twenty-two years. The allusion in letter viii to Gambetta's speeches refers to that statesman's tour of 1872 and the reference to the meeting of the three emperors is decisive for this date, as the conference occurred in August, 1872.

[38] To Ritter, November 29, 1871.

enchanted with Lago Maggiore, and then passed on through the Apennines to Florence and Rome. At Rome he read the proofs of *The Antichrist*. "It will take me about four months to correct and retouch it all," he writes.[39] "It will not appear before April." In April, however, he was still busy with his work, writing Bersot (April 1, 1873), "For six weeks I shall be wholly given to my *Antichrist*. Impossible to steal an hour from it."[40] It was, in fact, June before the book appeared.

On June 18, 1873, Taine wrote:[41]

I have received *The Antichrist* of Renan; it is interesting, lofty, and the erudition is enormous; but the fault of the subject is always there; the documents are lacking, there are too many gaps and conjectures; he stretches a text like a metal wire until he makes it infinitely thin and fragile. And then, all those early Christians have such weak brains, so like the Methodists of the populace, the blubbering converted negroes of America, that one becomes weary of their jeremiads and their hallucinations. What a pity that he did not write the history of the Cæsars from Augustus to Nero. Here the documents are sufficient and the human element is interesting; the real interest in his book is in what he says of Nero, of Rome and of the taking of Jerusalem.

The admiration of Renan and Taine for one another did not hinder frank dissatisfaction with the character of each other's work.

The summer of 1873 was spent at Sèvres, but the next year Renan again took a trip through Switzerland to Northern Italy. From Venice he sent his "Letter to Flaubert concerning the *Temptation of Saint Anthony*,"[42] September 8, in which he expresses his scorn for the pedants who

---

[39] To Ritter, December 7, 1872.
[40] *Bersot et ses amis*, p. 267. To Ritter he had written, March 13, 1873, that the correction of the proof took day and night, and would occupy from six weeks to two months more.
[41] *Correspondance*, vol. iii, 231.
[42] *Feuilles détachées*.

demand moral and political aims from a work of imagination. The little that Renan published during these two years is not of much import. "Phœnician Art"[43] is nothing but the conclusion of his *Phœnician Mission* (1874); "Berber Society"[44] is a mere abstract from a book on Algiers. "The Religious Crisis in Europe,"[45] an essay on current affairs, is a clear statement of the conflict between the doctrine of papal infallibility and the Prussian idea of the state. Here the chief interest lies in Renan's solution, liberty for the individual, whether Catholic or non-Catholic. "Liberty," he says, "is reciprocal; when it is desired for oneself, it must be admitted for others." It is an end, not a means. And, though the liberal party is the most completely discredited in Europe, its policies must in the end be adopted, being the only just, nay, the only wise ones. One of the few features Renan ever finds to praise about the United States is its policy toward religion.[46]

In this article, as often elsewhere, Renan looks forward to a schism in the Catholic Church and the election of rival popes. The same motive appears in his eulogy of Athanase Coquerel,[47] for his effort to establish a less narrow Protestantism. The principal thought is here embodied in four propositions: (1) The appearance of a new religion is an impossibility; (2) the present religions are not destined to disappear, leaving humanity without religious forms; (3) the established worship cannot remain without reforms and new interpretations; (4) it follows that both Catholicism and Protestantism will give birth to churches which, without

---

[43] *Gazette des Beaux-Arts*, May 1, 1873.
[44] *Revue des deux Mondes*, September 1, 1873.
[45] *Ibid.*, February, 1874.
[46] "Berber Society" Renan thought it worth while to publish in *Mélanges d'histoire et de voyages.* The other two pieces were reprinted in the posthumous volume, *Mélanges religieux et historiques.*
[47] "Le protestantisme libéral," *Débats*, September 23, 1876; *Mélanges religieux et historiques.*

breaking with the past, will seek better to answer the needs of the present. Whether or not Renan was a good ecclesiastical prophet, the future only can tell.

In 1875 Renan, officially representing the Collège de France, delivered one of the main addresses and several subsidiary speeches at the tercentenary of the University of Leyden (February 18).[48] On March 1, he for the first time published a chapter of the *Origins* in the *Revue des deux Mondes*.[49] There are now several indications of the premature old age that was coming upon him, as it came upon so many of his friends. Both Taine and Sainte-Beuve were old men at fifty. In August he went to Houlgate on the coast of Normandy, suffering severely from rheumatism and unwilling "to accept a diminution of life." Here, as a diversion, he revised his *Philosophic Dialogues*, published, to the accompaniment of much objurgation at their supposed cynicism, the next May. In fact, there was nothing in them that he had not said before, though put in a different form.[50]

On the invitation of Michele Amari, scholar and statesman, and formerly a colleague at the Bibliothèque, Renan started from Normandy for Palermo to attend a philological congress, embarking at Genoa in company with Gaston Paris on August 24. After the meetings, he, with a company of others, was rushed over Sicily on a ten-day sleepless archæological expedition. Received everywhere with speeches and ovations, he was particularly singled out for popular enthusiasm, because, having been for years a subject of

---

[48] See *Revue des deux Mondes*, March 1, 1875.

[49] The article, entitled "L'Apocalypse de l'an 97—Le dernier prophète des Juifs," consists of a passage from the midst of Chapter xvi, provided with an introduction, a conclusion, and various inserted phrases and paragraphs to adapt it to its independent publication.

[50] In the preface he says: "I shall later publish an essay, entitled *The Future of Science*, that I composed in 1848 and 1849, much more consoling than this, and which will better please those attached to the democratic religion. The reaction of 1850-1851 and the Coup d'État inspired me with a pessimism of which I am not yet cured."

hostile sermons, he had become a sort of legend and people were astonished and delighted to see it alive. These experiences are related in an article in the *Revue des deux Mondes* in the form of a personal letter to the director, dated Ischia, September 20.[51] Although Renan had previously written rather intimate prefaces, this was the first published article in which he talked about himself to the public as frankly as he would to familiar friends. He tells of his rheumatism. "For the first time I thought of old age. I complained that it was premature, though realizing that, since my essential work was nearly completed, I ought to count myself among those favored by fate." "My stiff leg and dragging foot did not once refuse the hardest work. The malady was not cured, but forgotten." We approach the frankness and charm of the *Recollections*. What delightful descriptions, reminiscences, reflections, side remarks! What sharp eyes! What trained artistic appreciation! But Sicily does not, after all, offer the best in art. "Every trip, every investigation, every new study, is thus a hymn to Athens."[52] The trip was rounded out by three weeks in Ischia and the remainder of October in Rome.

Familiar talk with the public was continued in 1876 with the publication in the *Revue des deux Mondes* of the first two chapters of the *Recollections of Childhood and Youth*.[53] Like his mother, to whom he owed several of his stories, the aging Renan allowed his mind to voyage back to his early home, a region softened and beautified by distance, peopled with persons who become altogether attractive in the indulgent and good-humored view of a tranquil old age. The scenes are realized with consummate art, and yet poet-

---

[51] November 15: "Vingt jours en Sicile: le Congrès de Palerme." *Mélanges d'histoire et de voyages.*

[52] The same remark occurs in "Phœnician Art."

[53] March 15, "Le Broyeur de lin"; December 1, "Prière sur l'Acropole. Le Bonhomme Système et la petite Noémi." These are republished with no changes, excepting here and there a word.

ized by the detachment of revery. Most readers would be willing to sacrifice a volume or two of the histories for another group of these fascinating reminiscences. The moment was precious. Delightful as are the later papers on life at the seminary, they have not precisely the same touch as these.

Such literary recreations were never allowed to distract Renan's attention from his main task. In June, 1877, was published *The Gospels,* fifth volume of the *Origins.* He had expected this to be the last, but the work grew as he progressed, and one more seemed now to be necessary; two were actually required. After the climax of interest in *The Antichrist,* the present volume seems to mark a decline, from which we do not completely rise until we reach *Marcus Aurelius.*

For over three years after 1876, Renan contributed nothing to the *Revue des deux Mondes* but a brief tribute to the high-minded and sympathetic Queen Sophie of Holland,[54] who loved both France and Germany for what was noble in each and who suffered because her aspiration for German unity had been achieved by the brutal negation of every ideal principle. This little essay is one of a group of three, each a gem of chivalrous and intellectual homage, which celebrate remarkable women of Renan's acquaintance. The other two enshrine the rare spirit, noble heart, philosophic mind and rich nature of Mme. Hortense Cornu, beneficent and liberal influence on Napoleon III (June 17, 1875), and the sonorous soul of George Sand, whose works are the echo of the century and whose death seems to bring about a diminution of humanity.[55] An exquisite delicacy of feeling, a perfect appropriateness of touch puts these little compositions in a class by themselves.

---

[54] June 15, 1877, two and a half pages in the *Chronique,* without heading, between the political review and a book notice.
[55] Letter to the editor of *Le Temps,* June 11, 1876. All three in *Feuilles détachées.*

The death of the Queen of Holland closely followed the two hundredth anniversary of the death of Spinoza (February 12, 1877), at which Renan delivered the principal address.[56] This is a pæan to reason, liberty and the ideal, based upon the humble, pious, kindly life and the lofty and fearless thought of the man who in his age "had seen most deeply into God." All the qualities that Renan admired in a scholar and thinker—"his life was a masterpiece of good sense and judgment"—were united in Spinoza, and if this discourse is inferior to the essay on Saint Francis, it is partly because the author was hampered by the requirements of an oration for a specific occasion. Instead of attenuating his customary ideas on such matters as religion, dogmatism and the supernatural, he rather overemphasized them, though never offensively, and a certain formality interferes with his natural ease. The piece is nevertheless a noble tribute, and worthy to open the long series of eulogies delivered during the next fifteen years.

V

In every direction we thus find the beginnings of the activities that occupied Renan's final period. Unhappily we also meet the infirmities that tormented his physical decline. On March 24, 1877, Grant Duff saw him on the upper floor of the Hotel Prince of Monaco, suffering cruelly from rheumatism. In April Ritter, visiting Paris, finds him "aged in face, but always amiable, gracious and charming."[57] The Swiss disciple visits the lecture room: "Yesterday I heard Renan at the Collège de France: delightful, incomparable hour!" (April 26.) Later the master explained the sixteenth Psalm, an interpretation of "such scientific exacti-

---

[56] Published separately in pamphlet form by Calmann Lévy, as were many of Renan's addresses; then in *Nouvelles Études d'histoire religieuse*, 1884.
[57] Letter, April 25.

tude and psychological depth.'' (May 8.) All the testimony shows that, while Renan might easily have attracted crowds by giving as courses his books in advance of publication, a common professorial custom, he confined his appeal to a small number of real students by presenting strictly scientific and philological matter. He chose the small room of Burnouf and Silvestre de Sacy and with a little group seated around a table, he conducted what he called a laboratory, once a week explaining a Bible text, and giving his second lesson to inscriptions, in order to provoke the spirit of research. Though a kindly and encouraging teacher, he was also severe, being pitiless toward hardy and fantastic translation, and the explanation of the uncertain by the uncertain, *obscurum per obscurius,* as he said. Yet his criticism was not of the geometric order, but sprang from sentiment founded on full knowledge.[58]

In the summer of 1877, the previous vacation having been passed at Sèvres, Renan's rheumatism drove him to Ischia, to take the baths at Casamicciola, the trip being made by sea from Genoa. The next summer he traveled through the Vosges, and by Bâle, Constance, Innsbruck, the Tyrol to Venice and Florence, where he attended a congress of Orientalists presided over by his friend Amari. In 1879 he was again at Ischia, having visited Taine at his place on Lake Annecy on the way down. Taine had become too much of a country gentleman, incapable of judging the great things of the past. ''He read me parts of his Jacobins. Almost everything is true in detail; only this is but a quarter of the truth. He shows that all those things were wretched, horrible and shameful; it should be shown at the same time that they were grandiose, heroic, sublime.''[59] In their mu-

---

[58] Article by Philippe Berger in *Débats*, October 7, 1892, and ''Ernest Renan et la chaire d'hébreu au Collège de France'' by the same, in *Revue de l'histoire des religions,* vol. 28.
[59] To Berthelot, August 17, 1879.

tual criticisms Renan and Taine patently display their basic tendencies. They love and admire one another, but neither can be quite satisfied with the other's work.

The summers of 1877 and 1879 at Ischia inspired the last great original stroke of Renan's genius, the philosophic dramas, *Caliban* and *L'Eau de jouvence*. Of the first, he says: "I wrote it at Ischia during the morning hours, when the vines were covered with dew and the sea was like whitish watered silk. The philosophy appropriate for such hours of repose is that of the crickets and the larks, who have never, I think, doubted that the light of the sun is sweet, life a beneficent gift and the living earth a truly agreeable place of sojourn." [60] Two years later the same surroundings recalled the same thoughts: "I began to live again with Caliban, Prospero, Ariel. These loved images set about talking to one another anew within me; their dialogues made me pass an agreeable month; combined with the oven of the Eporneo and the pure air of Ischia, they almost delivered me from the pains each winter brings to seize upon me." [61] The delight with which these pieces were written, combined with the striking originality of the situations invented, constitute a major portion of their charm. [62]

In February, 1878, appeared *Miscellanies of History and Travel*, a collection of articles which had been published in periodicals during the previous thirty years. [63] The preface marks his reconciliation with the Republic, or rather, a general indulgence for a flabby government that will do nothing very good or very bad, and that will find its safety in a

[60] Preface, *Caliban.*

[61] Preface, *l'Eau de jouvence.*

[62] "I have finished my sequel to *Caliban,* which I name *l'Eau de jouvence,* so as not to call it l'Eau de vie. . . . I will read it to you when I come. At any rate, the composition of it has entertained me immensely." To Berthelot, September 12, 1879.

[63] 1847-1877. In a footnote Renan remarks that nothing worth publishing remains from the period preceding 1852 excepting *The Future of Science.*

sort of universal demoralization, the Americanism toward which the whole world is irresistibly tending. He repeats his counsel to young scholars, given in his annual reports to the Société Asiatique, summarizes the political ideas of *Intellectual and Moral Reform*, reviews the abortive attempts at the restoration of monarchy in France, and sees no possibility that things should be different from what they are. "Let us then enjoy and profit by the present," he concludes: "it is good and agreeable. Let us all endeavor to outdo ourselves. Let us not sulk at our country when she does not agree with us. Perhaps, after all, it is she that is right. Poor France! *malo tecum errare quam cum ceteris recte sapere.*"

Many of Renan's prophecies are neither better nor worse than those of others in his circle of friends, but when he contemplated great currents, instead of isolated incidents, he is worthy of attention. "Patriotism," he writes Berthelot (September 10, 1878), "as understood to-day, is a fashion that will last fifty years. In a century, after it has covered Europe with blood, it will be understood no more than we understand the purely dynastic spirit of the seventeenth and eighteenth centuries. All is vanity, excepting science; even art begins to seem to me a little empty. My impressions of twenty-five years ago seem marked by a sort of childishness."

It is interesting to observe how Renan's political discontent had varied with the occupant of the Ministry of Public Instruction. In 1873, he is glad he has no political responsibility; in 1875, both he and Berthelot are much discouraged over reaction; in 1877, they are almost in despair.[64] In 1878, Bardoux was appointed Minister and the University felt free again. On December 4, Renan wrote that things were going badly, particularly in the education

---

[64] See Berthelot letters.

department, but they get along somehow, adding: "After all that we have been through, we ought not to be hard to satisfy." The greatest danger lay in violent party conflicts leading to disruption. "I sincerely believe," he writes (December 24, 1878), "that the development of republican institutions is the only course possible for our country. But I believe also that the true mode of serving the Republic is to proceed with great moderation and with an ardent desire for conciliation. Concord, as far as it is possible, is what is most necessary for France." [65] The famous Article VII of Jules Ferry's education law, forbidding unauthorized congregations to teach, seemed to Renan "an enormous fault." [66]

VI

The contrast between bigotry and liberalism is strongly accentuated in two features of Renan's biography during the year 1878. On the one hand, Bardoux proposed him for Officer of the Legion of Honor, but MacMahon refused to sign the decree;[67] on the other hand, he was elected to a seat in the French Academy. This election was chiefly due to the efforts of his friend Ustazade Silvestre de Sacy. The spectacle of these contests is by no means edifying. Intrigue and influence of every kind were brought to bear on the members voting, and the discussion of the candidates' merits in general meeting sometimes degenerated into unseemly squabbles. At this time two seats were vacant, that of Thiers (died September 3, 1877) and that of Claude Bernard (died February 10, 1878). Alexandre Dumas had induced Taine to present himself for one of these places,

---

[65] Strauss, *Politique*, p. 321.
[66] To Berthelot, August 17, 1879.
[67] Renan was made officer July 12, 1880, and afterward became commander, grand-officer, and member of the council, *Débats*, October 3, 1892.

while Renan was to stand for the other, Taine, of course, being unwilling to enter the contest against his friend. When Henri Martin announced his candidacy for the chair of Thiers, Renan, on account of friendship, selected the other, though even here he disliked having Wallon, perpetual secretary of the Academy of Inscriptions, as his competitor. Both he and Taine, though making the customary visits, were utterly dissatisfied with the academic procedure. "It would be better for my success," said Renan, "if I had never written anything." [68]

At the discussion on June 11, de Sacy spoke in such a lively, frank and natural way, that his words were long remembered. "M. Renan, they say, is a heretic on certain points; I don't deny it. But who of you, I wonder, is not a bit heretical. You, M. de Montalembert, do you know that, if I were inquisitor, I could find in you, without looking very far, enough to burn you? You, M. de Broglie, is your belief in the supernatural perfectly orthodox? You, M. de Falloux, are you in the flock a perfectly docile sheep?" And his final words were: "Let us pardon one another our heresies." Such is Renan's report in 1889, based on what had been told him.[69] Montalembert, de Broglie and Falloux were probably not won over, but Renan had enough friends and colleagues in the Academy to secure his election on June 13 by nineteen votes against Wallon's fifteen.[70] De Sacy did not live to see his protégé's reception, as he died February 14, 1879.

By December Renan's speech for the Academy was completed and placed in the hands of Mézières, who was to deliver the address of welcome. Their subject, Claude Bernard, was beyond their usual field of study, and it is en-

---

[68] See Taine's letters of April and May, 1878.
[69] *Feuilles détachées*, p. 139.
[70] Taine was defeated by Henri Martin, but elected November 14 in place of Loménie, who had died April 2.

tertaining to observe the eagerness of both for Berthelot's return to Paris, from which he was then absent on a trip, so that they may submit their compositions to him for scientific rectifications. So good a tutor assures us that the statements in the speeches are technically correct.[71]

The reception which took place April 3, 1879, was a literary event of the highest importance. Victor Hugo and Jules Simon were Renan's sponsors. The public, of course, crowded the hall, leaving little space for the academicians. Fashion as well as intellect was represented; the feminine element was conspicuous, and spring toilettes were remarked by the reporters. The séance was very long, for Renan read for about two hours, yet Mézières was listened to and applauded to the end.[72]

Describing the occasion in the *Temps*, Scherer finds that it marks a change in the spirit that had dominated the Academy for thirty years and that it was characterized by an unaccustomed liberty, tolerance and courtesy. No longer ruled by political and religious passions, the majority was ready to open the doors to literary merit without asking its certificate of confession, quite in contrast to Mgr. Dupanloup's angry resignation because Littré had finally entered. And Renan did not have to conceal his views. He expressed himself with perfect freedom before his new colleagues. M. Mézières, too, had not felt obliged to enter a solemn protest against the heresies uttered. He discussed them simply, without declamation, as one who recognized in others the right to think otherwise than himself.[73]

The dominant tone is struck by Renan in the opening words of his address:

---

[71] Letters to Berthelot, December 4 and 17, 1878.
[72] *Débats*, April 4, 1879, report by Francis Charmes.
[73] *Études sur la littérature contemporaine*, vol. vii. A delightful account of the reception by G. Valbert in the *Revue des deux Mondes* also emphasizes the spirit of courtesy and conciliation displayed on this occasion.

The great Cardinal Richelieu, like all men who have left in history the mark of their passage, came to found many things that he did not dream of, and even some that he only half desired. I do not know, for example, that he cared much for what we to-day call reciprocal tolerance and liberty of thought. Deference for ideas other than his own was not his dominant virtue, and as for liberty, its place does not seem to have been indicated in the edifice he erected. And yet, after two hundred and fifty years, the rigid founder of French unity is seen, in a sense very real, to have been the instigator of principles that he would perhaps have vigorously combated, if he had seen them develop in his lifetime. . . . To bring men together is almost to reconcile them; it is at least to render the human spirit the most signal of services, since the pacific work of civilization results from contradictory elements, maintained face to face, obliged to tolerate one another, and drawn on to mutual comprehension and almost love.

Renan proceeds to express his entire self in the masterly discourse that follows: We find his view that civilization results from contradictory elements, but at the summits opposing forces make peace; his lofty conception of the Academy as the union of all talents, introducing a graceful word of thanks for his election; his conviction that seventeenth-century French is sufficient for all purposes and that style is thought; his fixed ideas of the function of the Collège de France as the nursery of science; and above all, his exaltation of science itself as the greatest achievement of man, the triumph of science being the triumph of idealism. The life of Claude Bernard, whose eulogy was his chief subject, is told in vivid incidents mingled with apt reflections. The technical scientific discoveries of the great physician are by rapid summary and metaphor rendered popular without losing their scientific exactness. "By the side of the central system, he found as it were provincial autonomies, local circulations." "In his bold march toward the final secrets of animated nature, he came to the confines of life, to the obscure sources of the organism. Little by little, the difference between animal and

317

vegetable physiology vanished before his eyes. The germ of life in both seemed to him the same." The determinism of Claude Bernard is insisted upon, as well as the happiness of the investigator. All Renan's pet ideas are here delightfully, as in some of his former essays, deduced from an individual personality. For example style: "Human intelligence is a combination so bound together in all its parts that a great mind is always a good writer"; or medicine as the advance guard of science: "If humanity had always enjoyed good health, science and philosophy would twenty times over have died of hunger."

In conclusion he expresses his faith:

Reality always surpasses the ideas we have of it; every effort of imagination is flat in comparison. As science, in destroying an infantile material world has given us a world a thousand times more beautiful, so also the disappearance of a few dreams will only serve to give the ideal world vaster sublimity. As for myself, I have invincible confidence in the goodness of the thought that has made the universe. . . . The purest worship of Divinity is often concealed behind apparent negations. . . . How many saints under the guise of irreligion! . . . Reason triumphs over death, and to work for reason is to work for eternity. . . . Such thoughts rejuvenate; they lend themselves to talent, create it and invoke it. You who judge things by the spark they fling off, by the phrases they provoke, you have, after all, a good means of discrimination. The talent inspired by a doctrine is in many respects the measure of its truth. It is not without reason that one cannot be a great poet without idealism, a great artist without faith and love, an excellent writer without logic, an eloquent orator without a passion for goodness and liberty.[74]

---

[74] Some journalists considered this final passage a mere piece of academic flattery, but it really expressed one of Renan's fixed ideas. Compare the following from *Averroës*: "As the syllogism excludes every nuance, and as truth resides wholly in the nuance, the syllogism is a useless instrument for finding truth in the moral sciences. Penetration, suppleness, varied culture of mind are the true logic. The form in philosophy is at least as important as the substance; the turn given the thought is the only demonstration possible, and it is true in a sense to say that the Humanists of the Renaissance, apparently occupied uniquely in saying things well, were more truly philosophic

To the author of *The Life of Jesus*, as Renan was then generally called, a subject of scandal, "a malefactor of the intellect," Mézières replied with a grace and delicacy that the subject himself could not have surpassed. He recalled the years when the young scholar lived with his sister in the rue du Val-de-Grâce: "Mlle. Henriette Renan who has left you the recollection of an exquisite writer and critic, deserves to be named along with you, the day when the brother she so loved and for whose glory she labored, receives the highest of literary rewards." In treating the *Origins of Christianity,* he introduced his criticism by saying: "It is the capital work of your life; I should disappoint the Academy if I spoke of it with too much reserve. Excessive precaution would be worthy neither of you nor of the company that did itself the honor to elect you. You will pardon me for approaching so great a subject with a frankness equal to your own." His dissidence is expressed with what the French call malice, a sort of roguishness without malignity: "If, to an extent more, perhaps, than is permissible, you allow poetry to enter into history, have we any right to reproach you on this account? Are we not all to a certain extent your accomplices? . . . Your method, Sir, may be defended on plausible grounds; it is even better defended by your rare talent." [75]

One bit of this friendly malice led Renan to reply. "One wonders," said Mézières, "in what unpublished memoirs, in what documents known only to yourself, you discovered so many details hitherto unknown. . . . Before you, much had been written about Saint Paul; but nobody had been admitted to his intimacy to such a degree as yourself. An

than the Averroists of Padua." (P. 323.) Renan's remarks are often exaggerated, but they are never wholly gratuitous.

[75] Both addresses are to be found in *Académie Française, receuil de discours*, 1870-1879. The *Débats* published Renan's piece April 4 and Mézières' reply the next day, as was their custom at this time. For Renan's discourse, see *Discours et conférences.*

eminent critic (Scherer) presumes that you had seen him; and it must be so, since you are the first to represent him as an ugly little Jew and to describe him from head to foot.''

Not wishing to appear to have drawn a caricature of the great apostle, Renan, in the *Débats* for April 9, presents the evidence that his portrait is not at all imaginative, but is based on very ancient and, as it seems to him, reliable tradition, which accords with what Paul actually said of himself. He refuses to abandon the probable and the possible in history, so long as they are indicated by phrases of doubt. ''What I never do is to add a material circumstance to the texts, a detail to the portrayal of manners, a stroke to the landscape. The whole I grasp in my own way; I do not introduce into it a single element that has not been furnished me.''[76]

Another outcome of the reception address was irritation in Germany. In the course of his praise of the Academy for bringing scholarship and literature into the currents of social life and great affairs, Renan had said: ''You are little troubled at the pompous announcement of the advent of what is called another *culture*, that can get along without talent. . . . A science pedantic in its solitude, a literature without joy, a churlish polity, an upper class without brilliance, a nobility without wit, gentlemen without polish, great captains without sonorous phrases, these will not, I believe, very soon dethrone the remembrance of that French society of old, so brilliant, so polite, so eager to please.''

The remark excited a somewhat presumptuous professor from beyond the Rhine, Gustav Solling, who published a little pamphlet, *M. Renan and Germany*, a piece of angry,

---

[76] Mézières' reply, sent from Nancy, appeared April 12; to this Renan added a statement that certain features in which Mézières had ''recognized his right of property'' were taken textually from Nicephorus.

insulting and arrogant Teutonism,[77] the tone of which is fairly represented by the following: "To conquer you required not only much courage, but much intelligence. This remark will perhaps show you, Sir, that we do not lack politeness, even toward the eternal enemy of our country." To this accusation that he was an enemy of Germany, Renan answered with perfect forbearance in a "Letter to a German Friend,"[78] that not all those reproached by him were Germans. The collaboration of France and Germany, the oldest illusion of his youth, had become anew the conviction of his maturity, but the military leaders of Berlin had entered upon an ungenerous course of repression and violence, hard, arid and arbitrary. "Harsh and rigid, regarding the state as a chain, and not as something beneficent, they think they understand the German character, but they do not understand human nature." They have suppressed the genius of the nation. "Where is your continuation of Goethe, Schiller, and Heine? . . . You were strong, and you have not established liberty. . . . To win men, you must please them; to please them, you must be amiable. Your Prussian statesmen have every gift but that. . . . The genius of Germany is great and powerful; it remains one of the principal organs of the human mind; but you have put it in a vice that tortures it. You are led astray by a dry and cold school, that seeks to suppress rather than to develop. We are sure that you will find yourselves again, and that some day we shall renew our collaboration in the search for all that can give grace, gayety, and happiness to life."[79]

[77] *Monsieur Renan et l'Allemagne,* lettre ouverte d'un allemand. Wiesbade, 1879, signed G. Solling.
[78] *Débats,* April 16.
[79] Remarkable as showing how German thinkers blinded themselves to their perils is an article on this controversy, "Ernst Renan und die deutsche Cultur," by Heinrich Homburger, which appeared in the *Rundschau* for June, 1879. The author readily concedes the truth

of Renan's restrictions, but denies that they are matter of reproach. The ideal Germany found by the Frenchman in the great writers had never been the real Germany, for among the Germans there always had been, and there still continued, a cleavage between life and literature, such as was not to be found in England and France. A Machiavellian state policy, realism, genius turned wholly to practical affairs, constituted a natural reaction from previous conditions. The Germans had grown more narrow-minded, but this was necessary to their progress. "We seek no longer to be a race of poets and thinkers, but of soldiers and business-men." (P. 475.) This tendency is, indeed, universal, though more complete and thorough in Germany than elsewhere. It is perfectly proper that all Germans should look to the State for everything, and Prussianism is welcomed as a necessary stage toward something better in the future.

CHAPTER X

During his last years Renan's occupations were very numerous
and he went much into society. His rheumatism grew upon him,
so that he was seldom without pain. For a cure he took baths at
Ischia (1879) and Plombières (1880), employing his leisure in
writing the *Philosophic Dramas* and the *Recollections*. He finished
his *Origins* with *The Christian Church* (1879), *Marcus Aurelius*
(1881) and the *Index* (1883). Renan spoke often in public, at
academic and other functions and before learned societies. At
the Academy, he received Pasteur and Cherbuliez (1882), de Lesseps (1885), and Jules Claretie (1889), and distributed the Prizes
of Virtue (1881). His most important lectures were the Hibbert
Lectures in London (1880), though "What is a Nation?" delivered at the Sorbonne (1882), seems to have been his own favorite.
In 1881 and 1882 he spent the summer near Taine at Talloires
on Lake Annecy and 1883 was spent at Sèvres. Elected Administrator of the Collège de France (1883), he moved into the official
apartment in the college buildings. His translation of *Ecclesiastes*
appeared in 1882 and his *Recollections* in 1883. The first fascicle
of the first volume of the *Corpus* was published in 1881, and the
first fascicle of the second volume in 1891. In 1880 he began
presiding at the Celtic Dinners in Paris, continuing this function
till the spring before his death. Out of these dinners grew the
Fêtes in Brittany, the first of which, at Tréguier in 1884, led him
to procure his summer home at Rosmapamon, where he passed
his summers from 1885 on. In 1884 he was elected president of
the Société Asiatique, to which he was very devoted. In this
year he brought out *New Studies in Religious History*. He also
wrote a few reviews for the *Débats*, though most of his work of
this nature was done for the *Journal des Savants*. Three feuil-
letons appeared in the *Débats* for 1886 and 1887, one of them
being a dialogue in honor of Victor Hugo, spoken at the Théâtre

323

Français. In 1887 came *Speeches and Lectures* and Volume I of the *History of the People of Israel*, on which he had been working for six years. His collected *Philosophic Dramas* and Volume II of the *History* appeared the next year. As a diversion he had written an "Examination of Philosophic Conscience," which he published in the *Revue des deux Mondes* for August 15, 1889. In 1890 appeared Volume III of the *History* and *The Future of Science* (1848-1849). The quarrel with Goncourt over the indiscretions of the *Journal* belongs to this year. Renan's health was now broken. He went south in November, 1891, but with meager results. *Scattered Leaves* appeared early in 1892. Having finished the last proofs for the "Jewish Rabbis" in the *Histoire littéraire de la France*, Volume XXXI, Renan went to Rosmapamon, but was unable to walk and almost unable to work. On September 17th he was brought back to Paris in a condition of utter exhaustion and he died October 2, 1892. The state gave him a public funeral. The last two volumes of his *History* and a collection of articles from the *Histoire littéraire* were published after his death. Still later came some of his correspondence, his "Youthful Notebooks," *Sœur Henriette*, some sketches, and a further collection of essays. Renan's library was purchased by Mme. Calmann Lévy and presented to the Bibliothèque Nationale.

I

"YOUR intellectual group is reached," said Renan to his fellow academicians, "at the age of the Ecclesiast, a charming age most fitted for serene gayety, when on begins to see after a laborious youth, that all is vanity, but also that a multitude of vain things are worthy of prolonged tasting with enjoyment." This note is so prominent in Renan's last years that it has colored the general estimate of his whole career. "In a man raised to the dignity of a symbol," he had once written, "we must always distinguish between his personal life and his life beyond the grave, between what he was in reality and what opinion has made of him."[1] What opinion made of Renan, the Renan legend, was the

---

[1] *Averroës*, p. 432.

creation of a group of young reviewers, Paul Bourget and Jules Lemaître especially, who presented the genial, ironical, instable skeptic without solid principles, the intellectual epicurean tasting delicate ideas and intoxicating himself with the flavor of endless contradictions, the dilettante reducing the world to a mere spectacle for his enjoyment, the inscrutable artist gayly playing with insubstantial fantasies which he had conjured out of the void. It is needless to say that this view, based on his recreations and not on his solid daily task, was by no means shared by the toilers, like James Darmesteter and Philippe Berger, who worked with him and after him in oriental scholarship. The enthusiastic Ritter applies to Renan some words originally written of another: "Noble and venerable, powerful and sweet, working without intermission, calm in the pursuit of truth, serious and firm, but with love in his heart and benevolence on his lips." [2]

There was no intermittence in his labors of erudition. His special portion of *The Corpus,* the chapter on Phœnician inscriptions, was ready for printing in 1880,[3] but the first fascicle did not appear till a year later.[4] Renan had not only taken the initiative, but he was, throughout, the soul of this work. What many had thought an undertaking so vast that it would never come to publication, he carried through successfully to its achievement. At the same time

[2] Letter of August 29, 1881. The Bourget-Lemaître view was not universal even among the literary critics. Gaston Deschamps, a philologist as well as one of the most copious writers for the *Débats,* protested openly against it as early as 1889 (see *La Vie et les livres,* vol. ii), and Paul Deschanel, in reviewing *Souvenirs* (*Débats,* September 18 and 28, 1883), shows how arbitrary is Bourget's use of the word "dilettantisme." These articles of Deschanel manifest the best understanding of Renan since Sainte-Beuve. Appearing before *L'Avenir de la Science* and the correspondence, they display a surprising quality of divination.

[3] Renan's Annual Report as Secretary of the Société Asiatique.

[4] Reviewed by Philippe Berger in the *Débats,* September 16, 1881; the second fascicle appeared July 27, 1883.

he continued his contributions to the *Histoire littéraire de la France,* his studies on "Christine de Stommeln" and "Clement V" (vol. xxviii, 1881) appearing also as essays in the *Revue des deux Mondes* (March 1 and May 15, 1880). Up to 1882 he continued his annual reports as secretary of the Société Asiatique, being then relieved by Darmesteter, after having performed this duty for fifteen years. It had at length grown to be an irksome task—for eight or ten months the books and pamphlets piled upon his table, while he kept wishing that he would not be obliged to go through them. Then, when in May he attacks the heap, he finds such pleasure in looking over the great variety of new and original investigations that he is full of thanks for a function so fruitful and so agreeable.[5] It is a pleasing spectacle to see one of the most famous men of the world not only contented but happy to act as secretary to this little group of oriental scholars. But he was soon to become their leader. At the meeting of the Société Asiatique of November 14, 1884, announcement was made of the death of Adolph Regnier, and Renan was elected by acclamation to succeed him as president, an honor highly appreciated, for this society was one of his first loves and it continued dear to him to the very end.[6]

Meanwhile, his life work was completed as far as it had been planned. *The Christian Church* appearing October 21, 1879, and *Marcus Aurelius* November 11, 1881.[7] Prepared from the days of his youth, the actual performance of the

---

[5] Report of June 29, 1881.

[6] In order to economize his time Renan had the hour of meeting changed from 8 to 4:30 P. M. so that, after finishing at the weekly meeting of the Académie des Inscriptions, he could attend this monthly meeting later on the same afternoon. He was very regular in his attendance here, as well as at both Academies, absence being usually an indication of ill-health or of remoteness from Paris.

[7] See *Débats,* October 20, 1879, and November 10, 1881, in both cases a chapter being published in the advance notice. In the *Revue des deux Mondes,* Chapters xiii-xv of *Marcus Aurelius* had been published February 15, and Chapters xxviii-xxx November 1, 1881.

task had occupied twenty years of Renan's life, an effort "sustained without fatigue."[8] He had prolonged his history to include Marcus Aurelius for two characteristic reasons; one of scholarship, because his studies had led him to transfer the epoch of Montanism from the reign of Antoninus to that of his successor; and one of art, the contrast between the futility of the efforts of the philosophic reformers and the fruitfulness of the tide of Christianity.

Having been allowed, "thanks to infinite goodness," to finish this task, he promised to consecrate what remained to him of strength and activity to writing the *History of the People of Israel*, a necessary introduction to the *Origins*; and as a matter of fact, he set to work immediately on his new book. Meantime, an index, which he had expected to bring out simultaneously with his final volume, proved a greater labor than he had anticipated. With the aid of his daughter, Noémi, he struggled valiantly for two years with this interminable, colossal and almost crushing undertaking.[9]

As early as 1873, Ritter had begged Renan to do for *Ecclesiastes* what he had previously done for *Job* and the *Song of Songs*,[10] and Renan, after making the book the subject of his course at the Collège de France for the year 1875, promises the translation. "The author is a true sage," he writes, "and on a multitude of points we cannot speak better than he."[11] In the summer of 1881, Ritter saw proofs of the translation at Talloires, where Renan was finishing the work, much to his own entertainment. It was done by September 2nd, the introductory study appeared

---

[8] See the admirable review by Boissier in the *Revue des deux Mondes*, March 1, 1882.

[9] To Berthelot, August 12 and September 2, 1881; also letter of Ritter October 5, 1881. It was not until June, 1883, that the index at length appeared.

[10] Letter of June 22.

[11] To Ritter, June 9, 1875.

in the *Revue des deux Mondes* February 15, 1882, and the volume itself was published a few days later.

Like his other translations, in fact even more than his other translations, since he here gives a complete summary of Jewish beliefs and their connection with revolutionary utopias, this was a sort of preliminary study for his history, and indeed several passages from the introduction, notably one about Heine as a descendant of Koheleth,[12] were transferred bodily to the later work. The text, too, is carefully and extensively corrected, and personal experience is brought to bear upon the explanations. It is a mistake, however, to consider Renan's remarks on *Ecclesiastes*, as some did,[13] a chapter of autobiography. He had, to be sure, much sympathy with this philosophy, but it was not altogether his own. Instead of a resigned fatalism, he continued to cherish his faith in science. "In the midst of the absolute fluidity of things, let us maintain the eternal." (P. 88.) Whatever we may think or say, the laws of the universe will persist. "Ring out, bells! The more you ring, the more freely shall I allow myself to say that your chiming signifies nothing very distinct. If I feared to silence you, then I should indeed become timid and discrete." (P. 89.) There is no doubt, however, that the stamp of approval placed upon "Vanity of Vanities" contributed to the formation of the Renan legend.

II

It is certain that Renan enjoyed his literary preëminence; he had also the satisfaction of achieving every ambition of his life. In 1863 he had written Berthelot that he should like to be "a tranquil professor with a dozen pupils, writing

[12] Objection to this portrait as a type of the contemporary Jew was made in the *Débats*, April 26, by Henry Aron, who maintained that the Hebrew idealists are not all dead.

[13] See review in *Débats*, November 23, 1882, by Edgar Zevort.

his books at his leisure and having for his supreme aim
to become Administrator of the Collège de France."[14]   In
this desire, too, he was gratified.   On May 24, 1883, Laboulaye died and in his place Renan's colleagues on the faculty
elected him their head.[15]   He moved into the apartment
provided for the Administrator two flights up in the college
buildings and remained there until his death.

In the same year was published in book form his *Recollections of Childhood and Youth*,[16] the most fascinating of
all his writings.   Begun with two rather fragmentary contributions to the *Revue des deux Mondes*,[17] these reminiscences were continued as a connected narrative of his
early education.   The third installment was part of his summer recreation of 1879, contributed to the *Revue des deux
Mondes*, November 1, 1880.   In due course the fourth, fifth
and sixth chapters appeared in the same periodical.[18]   There
could be nothing more frank, nothing more mellow and
genial than this collection of essays.   The old man—we
must remember that, as Renan himself regrets, he was ten
years older than dates would indicate—looks back through
the haze of intervening time upon youthful experiences from
which the sharp angles have disappeared and finds his past
not only interesting, but attractive.   The story is to be taken
cum grano salis, he warns us; and this grain of salt, which
all who heard him talk, found in his incomparable smile,
the reader will here discover for himself in the very mode
of the telling.   Those who tear up violets in hopes of finding potatoes or turnips at the roots have little patience with
this book.   It is egotistical, illogical in its philosophy, contradictory in its moral precepts; so be it.   Those who ap-

---

[14] September 24, 1863.
[15] He was twice reëlected.
[16] April, 1883; reviewed by Paul Deschanel in the *Débats,* September 18 and 28.
[17] Parts I and II, see p. 308.
[18] December 15, 1881, and November 1 and 15, 1882.

preciate the work will smile indulgently, find delight in
what is offered, and feel that there has actually been transmitted to them the author's "theory of the universe." There
is, indeed, abundance of seriousness here for those who are
willing to perceive it, but the touch is light. The final
words, often accepted as Renan's whole attitude toward
life, are by no means to be so regarded. They constitute
only the view from one window, and that a very agreeable
outlook. "The existence given me without my asking has
been for me a benefit. If it were offered anew, I should
accept with gratitude. The epoch in which I have lived has
probably not been the greatest, but it will doubtless be
counted the most entertaining of epochs. Unless my last
years hold in reserve for me very cruel sufferings, I shall
have reason, in saying farewell to life, only to give thanks to
the cause of all good for the charming promenade I have
been permitted to take in the midst of reality."

Cruel sufferings did accompany Renan's last years, and
he had experienced pain enough even before these words
were written. It never, however, subdued his good humor.
In June, 1879, Philippe Berger read to the Société Asiatique
those parts of the secretary's report that could be finished
before illness interrupted. The summer trip was to Ischia
for the cure, and later to Sorrento and home by way of
Venice. In 1880, having "suffered almost all winter with
rheumatism, which has attacked his left arm,"[19] he went
to Plombières for the baths, and then again to Switzerland
and Venice, where Mary Robinson first met him. But notwithstanding all these trips, he was never idle. From
Plombières he writes to ask Berthelot about alembics as
decoration for his *Eau de jouvence*, which he had begun
the year before at Ischia. Simultaneously, during these

---

[19] Taine, March 14, 1880. Renan himself writes Berthelot from
London, April 5, of "my eternal enemy in the right knee," which
was cured this time by a fine performance of *The Merchant of Venice*.

vacations, the *Recollections* are getting written, *Ecclesiastes* translated, the *Index* carefully constructed. The eighteenth centenary of Pompeii elicits a letter to the *Débats*,[20] which he calls "twaddle about the fête at Pompeii,"[21] but which is in reality a deft mingling of seriousness and humor in a delightful personal chat.

Mary Robinson's impression is one of the most vivid of those to be found in her entertaining book:[22]

It was at this moment that I made the acquaintance of M. and Madame Renan and their children. Well do I remember the day, the year, the season! It was in September, 1880. I was traveling in Italy with my parents. At Venice we fell in with a friend of my father's—Signor Castellani, the archæologist. He invited us to spend a day at Torcello with the Renans, Sir Henry Layard, and his wife. I was a young girl then, more familiar with the Nineveh Courts of the British Museum (for which I worshiped Sir Henry Layard) and with Signor Castellani's exquisite Bronze Mask in the same collection, than with any writing of M. Renan's. In fact, save for a lecture on Marcus Aurelius, which I had heard him deliver a few months before, I knew him only by repute, as a heretic (that was attractive), and a philologist (which seemed less interesting). But after the first half-hour in his company I saw that here, here was the Man of Genius! I thought him like the enchanter Merlin—not Burne-Jones' graceful wizard, but some rough-hewn, gnome-like, Saint-Magician of Armor. What a leonine head, with its silvery mane of soft, gray hair, surmounted that massive girth! What an elfin, delicate light shone in the clear eyes, and lurked in the sinuous lines of the smile! How lucid, how natural, how benign the intelligence which mildly radiated from him! M. Renan was at his best on that occasion. We all felt ourselves in the glad society of an Immortal. . . . I still see the little Italian gunboat cutting through the bright lagoon towards the desolate shores of Torcello, fringed with scarlet-dotted pomegranate hedges and wastes of lilac-tipped sea-

[20] Dated Sorrento, September 26, 1879; published October 14, *Feuilles détachées.*
[21] To Berthelot, September 28.
[22] *The Life of Ernest Renan,* by Madame James Darmesteter (A. Mary F. Robinson), pp. 246-248.

lavender! How brilliant the mother-island looked in her abandonment. The brown old church inspired M. Renan. At that moment, with a heart divided between the glory of Hellas and the spiritual grace of Christianity, few things, indeed, could have touched him nearer than that ancient Mosaic, where the Apocalyptic Angels pour the Wrath of God from vials shaped like the purest classic cornucopiæ. He stood long in front of it. He discoursed to the eminent archæologists who accompanied him; we all listened, we girls no less earnestly than they, if with less understanding. At first I had thought him ugly, I confess. But, as he spoke, he grew almost handsome. The great head, held on one side, half in criticism, half in propitiation, was so puissant in its mass; the blue eyes beamed with wit and playful kindness. How he savored, and made us savor, that image of the anger of the Eternal elegantly treasured in the horns of plenty. How he revived for us the soul of the mother-church of Venice—the handful of poor refugees; primitive people, ship-wrecked, as it were, upon that lonely island; yet, in their way, refined thinkers, with a command of art and image, as became the heirs of more than one immeasurable ideal.

In 1881 the Renans spent the summer at Talloires, on Lake Amnecy, in an old ruined abbey near Taine and other friends, going for October, by way of Venice to Rome. On this visit he for the first time saw Lake Nemi, the inspiration of his third drama. He was meditating another trip to the Orient to gather inspiration for his *History of Israel*, but health prevented, and the next year he was again at Talloires in a rustic house immediately adjoining the home of the Taines, though he had not yet entirely relinquished all idea of his trip to the Holy Land.[23] In 1883 Noémi was married to Jean Psichari, a young Greek scholar, who later became one of the most distinguished of French philologists, and a pioneer in Neo-Greek literature. This year Renan apparently spent the summer months wholly at Sèvres.[24]

---

[23] For these summers see correspondence of Ritter and of Renan and Berthelot.

[24] He made an address in Paris, August 8, and one in the Montpar-

III

It was the summer of 1884 that brought about his re-
visits to Brittany, and consummated the return to early
days so marked in his later writings. Some four years
earlier, Narcisse Quellien, a Breton journalist, educated at
the Seminary of Tréguier, had inveigled Renan to the
"Dîners Celtiques," founded by him and held on the second Saturday of each month at a café near the Montparnasse
Railway Station. These dinners, of which Renan attended
two or three each season, prolonged his life, he says, ten
years.[25] Quellien was a serviceable person, who paid his
idol all sorts of daily attentions, ran errands, looked after
the luggage, and made arrangements with cabmen and inn-
keepers.[26] For the summer of 1884, he arranged a great
festival at Tréguier, a dinner (August 2) under a tent in
the garden of the Lion d'Or, which was attended by two
hundred and fifty guests. Here Renan as guest of honor
made one of his characteristic speeches, the whole affair
being reported at length in the *Débats* for August 4. After
giving Renan's address in full, the writer adds: "What
we cannot reproduce is the familiar and touching tone in
which these words were pronounced, and the joyous and
slightly ironical smile with which they were, so to speak,
seasoned. M. Renan regrets in his *Recollections* not being
able sometimes to put in the margin of his book: *cum grano
salis*. When he speaks, it is his smile that replaces the marginal comment."

After the great celebration, Renan was entertained by

---

nasse cemetery August 23, and he attended a meeting of the Académie
des Inscriptions September 7. See *Débats*. His paradise at Ischia,
which had been visited by an earthquake, March 4, 1881, was totally
destroyed by a second visitation, July 28, 1883, a calamity in which
over 4,000 people lost their lives.

[25] *Feuilles détachées*, p. 74.
[26] René d'Ys, p. 222.

his tenant, Le Bigot, who sacrificed a family pet in order
to regale him. "You can see how we love you," said Mme.
Le Bigot. "We have had this hen six years, and we have
killed it in your honor." In spite of his protestations that
he was so sorry for the poor beast he had not the courage
to eat it, the guest was obliged to take two helpings.[27] We
can appreciate Renan's repugnance when we remember a
scene at one of the Magny dinners during the siege, recorded by Goncourt. The whole company was surprised to
see a roast breast of lamb appear on the table. When it was
discovered to be dog, and somebody began praising the
flavor of stewed rat, Renan grew pale, threw his payment on
the plate and bolted.[28]

The result of this visit to Brittany was that Renan found
at Louannec, Perros-Guirec, a typical three-story country
house called Rosmapamon among woods close by and within
sight of the sea, of which he took a six-year lease in December. Here, surrounded by his family and visited by
many friends, he passed his summers for the rest of his life.
"The garden and the neighboring woods are charming," he
writes Berthelot (July 6, 1885). "The house is small, *parva
sed apta mihi;* we shall find means of accommodating our
friends without too much discomfort." One of the bedrooms
was always called Berthelot's room, though other favored
guests were allowed to occupy it. When visitors were too
numerous for the house, they were lodged in a neighboring
inn. At last Renan had a home, and in Paris too he obtained a permanent abode.

With the years 1883-1884, indeed, we enter the last phase
of Renan's career. Academician, Administrator, President
of the Société Asiatique, he had completed his *Origins,* even
to the index, completed his *Recollections,* begun his dramas,
and put before the learned world a goodly specimen of his

[27] *Ibid.,* pp. 63, 64.
[28] *Journal,* vol. iv, 206, January 24, 1871.

Corpus. There were henceforth no new undertakings; he simply carried forward what had been begun and by rare good fortune completed it all.

At the Academy he was very regular in his attendance and he was several times elected director, an office which is renewed every three months. ''The Académie Française,'' says Taine (March 14, 1880), ''is a sort of club composed of very diverse people, but very polite, who chat familiarly with perfect equality; burning political and social questions cool off in the hall where the dictionary is made;[29] each presents only that part of himself which is acceptable to others, and you find there the urbanity of the last century.''[30] As Renan was already a member of the Institut munificently remunerated with 1,500 francs a year, he received no further compensation by reason of his membership in the Academy, excepting such portion of an annual allowance of 300 francs as he may have acquired from attendance at meetings.[31] Although his books sold by the thousands, we cannot wonder at his remark uttered during a council on domestic finance: ''Money shows no signs of rolling our way.''[32]

IV

Renan was during all these years a public character. His comings and goings were chronicled, and every word he spoke to an audience was preserved in newspaper reports. A considerable number of these speeches were gathered in his volumes, *Addresses and Lectures* (1887) and *Scattered Leaves* (1892), but a great many remain buried in the *Jour-*

---

[29] Renan became a member of the committee on the dictionary in 1888.

[30] Even the heated passion that prevented Ollivier from speaking at his reception cooled down to such an extent that he was later elected director and received others.

[31] For the practice of the Institut, see De Franqueville, *Le premier siècle de l'Institut de France.*

[32] Mme. Darmesteter, p. 246.

nal des Débats and other dailies. Such pronouncements should rarely be considered apart from the occasion on which they were delivered. Most of them indeed are serious enough, but a few are merely festive. It is really comical to see a savage moral philosopher tearing to tatters and tossing about an agreeable after-dinner talk. Perhaps such things were not worth preserving, but Lévy wanted to make another book and Renan complacently allowed himself to be persuaded.[33] On the whole, we cannot regret the preservation of this small harvest in Renan's lighter tone.

In the four addresses delivered at academic receptions (Pasteur, April 22, 1882; Cherbuliez, May 25, 1882; de Lesseps, April 23, 1885; Jules Claretie, February 21, 1889), Renan is at his happiest. Here we find as a background a repetition of all his principal ideas: Science, disinterested criticism, the ideal, liberty, aristocracy, history, the revolution, universal suffrage, the élite, the French language, the function of the Academy—and, as in his most attractive early essays, these ideas occur as reflections attached to the individuals about whom he is speaking. Every thought is presented with the utmost courtesy and tolerance, with an appreciation of the element of reason animating the other side. He draws portraits of personal friends—Littré, Cherbuliez, De Lesseps; he indulges in reminiscences such as those of the *Revue*, with Buloz, Sainte-Beuve, George Sand; of his experiences in Egypt or of his discussions with Jules Claretie at the home of Michelet; he tells charming little anecdotes; for example, one of Buloz exclaiming to Cherbuliez, who had eaten a doubtful mushroom: "Cherbuliez, what are you doing? You haven't finished your story for the *Revue* yet"; or one of de Lesseps amusing the Khedive by allowing his set of Sèvres china to be broken by a refractory camel and thus assuring the construction of the

---

[33] Preface to *Feuilles détachées*.

Suez Canal. The individual trait is always deftly chosen and given its full value. Above all, Renan is always wholly and nothing but himself. "Your address is charming," he said to de Lesseps, "for it is your very self." And these pieces have this same exceptional charm. He means what he says and he approaches everything with the freshness of unfeigned enthusiasm. As the Institut is the greatest of French establishments, Napoleon I becomes "our illustrious colleague, General Bonaparte." There are no empty generalizations, but always vivid associations, individual incidents, personal experiences. Even Pasteur's abstruse scientific discoveries are simplified and attached to interesting human emotions. Of the cure of rabies, he says: "Humanity will owe you not only the suppression of a horrible malady, but also that of a sad anomaly, the suspicion always mingled with the caresses of the animal in whom nature best shows us her benevolent smile."

These pages are thickly sown with unexpected side remarks, of which the following are specimens:

Truth is a great coquette, Sir; she does not like to be wooed with too much passion.

(Pasteur, p. 24.)

I am tempted to add to the eight beatitudes a ninth: "Blessed are the blind, for they have no doubt."

(Cherbuliez, p. 97.)

Surely no one in our century has been more persuasive than you, and consequently no one has been more eloquent.

(De Lesseps, p. 130.)

One passage, dealing with the general who will lead France some day to victory, has been looked on as a prophecy:

How we shall elect him by acclamation, without worrying about his writings! Oh! what a meeting when he is received! How eagerly seats for it will be begged! Happy he who shall preside!

(De Lesseps, p. 134.)

In general treatment, there is constant variety. Receiving Pasteur, Renan gives a brief review of the newcomer's discoveries and then devotes the bulk of his address to Littré as critic and scholar, with accompanying discussions of history and philosophy.[34] A month later, almost the whole speech is given to the life and writings of the candidate himself, Cherbuliez, with only a brief reference to his predecessor. De Lesseps, of course, takes practically all the space in the speech at his reception, and Henri Martin, whom he replaced, is scanted, as is justly remarked by Henry Houssaye, who reviewed this meeting in the *Débats*.[35] In its discouraged tone, the last address (1889) shows Renan's failing vitality. Neither Jules Claretie nor his predecessor, Cuvillier-Fleury, receives much attention. The subject is rather the character of the nineteenth century, the vanity of literary fame, the obnoxiousness of naturalistic novels and the failure of the Revolution, then celebrating its centenary. Renan had often expressed his political disenchantment and his fears for the future of France, but rarely had the tone of any public utterance been so discouraged. Yet, after all, this Academy is a pleasant place. Let us enjoy what remains to us of life. We have, indeed, been well treated by our age and our nation. ''Poor mother country!'' he concludes, ''it is because we love her that we are sometimes a little hard on her. You, Sir, have indeed well said that she will ever be the essence of our hopes and our joys.''

Another academic discourse, which Henry Houssaye, re-

---

[34] Renan wrote to Amari, April 22, 1882: ''Two addresses at the Académie Française in one month! that is a great deal. I am overwhelmed. But I hope Thursday to pay homage to our dear and great Littré, so unjustly confiscated by the blacks.'' *Carteggio di Michele Amari*, vol. ii.

[35] *Débats*, April 24, 1885. The speech of de Lesseps fills a little over a column; Renan's speech a little over five columns. Houssaye's complaint is that de Lesseps did not know anything about Henri Martin, but that Renan might have said more. All of these addresses are, of course, reported in the *Débats* and published in full.

porting it in the *Débats*, August 5, 1881, calls "a marvelous address," a triumph, was delivered in distributing the prizes for virtue for which the Academy is the legatee.[36] It is the talk of a man with a warm heart and a full mind, telling little stories of suffering, devotion and heroism, with a peculiar combination of intimate sympathy and genial detachment, to which he adds the reflections of a philosopher. Virtue and self-devotion were in Renan's view divinely implanted instincts, which no rewards could stimulate and no penalties uproot.[37]

Another group of important addresses consists of those delivered before learned societies. In 1880 Renan was invited to give the Hibbert Lectures on the history of religion at Langham Place in April. He had been in London twice before, in 1851, to study manuscripts in the British Museum, and in 1870, when the party from Norway spent a night at the French embassy;[38] but this was the first occasion on which he appeared as a celebrated and cordially welcomed guest. Widely entertained, he distinguished himself by his agreeable manners and his brilliant talk.[39] One week-end he visited Max Muller at Oxford and was delighted with the place, but surprised at the absence of scholarly work.[40] The whole trip occupied only a fortnight.[41]

The subject of the four Hibbert Lectures was "Rome and Christianity" (April 6, 9, 13, 14), and an additional discourse on "Marcus Aurelius" was delivered (April 16) before the Royal Institution. The English hearers particularly remarked the perfection of the speaker's enunciation. As

---

[36] *Discours et conférences.*

[37] An address as presiding officer of the Five Academies, October 25, 1887, though slight, is based on oft expressed ideas. It is reprinted in the posthumous volume, *Mélanges religieux et historiques.*

[38] Goncourt *Journal*, vol. iv, p. 268.

[39] We have glimpses of this visit in Mrs. Simpson's *Many Memories of Many People* and Mrs. Humphry Ward's *Recollections.*

[40] Letter to Berthelot.

[41] Renan was back in Paris April 18.

for the substance, it consists of nothing but selections, often verbally, from the *Origins*. The lecture on "Marcus Aurelius" might have been read from proofs of the book, for the brief introduction is the only part prepared for the occation. It is interesting to compare the last page of this lecture with the last page of the volume, for Renan has characteristically omitted every phrase that might offend his audience. These five lectures were published as *Conférences d'Angleterre*.[42]

Three of Renan's public lectures were given before the Scientific Association of France, a society founded in 1864 by Leverrier, which held meetings in the large auditorium of the Sorbonne. The first of these, March 2, 1878, on "The Services of Philology to the Historical Sciences,"[43] is a popular exposition of the results of comparative philology, concluding with a warning against applying the ideas of language and race to politics, the basis of nationality being free consent of people to live together. "A nation," says the lecturer, "is above all a soul, a mind, a spiritual family, resulting from common recollections, common glories, sometimes also common griefs. . . . Man belongs neither to his language nor to his race; he belongs first of all to himself, for he is first of all a free and moral being." This idea is developed historically and philosophically in the second of these lectures.[44] "What is a Nation?" a discourse to which Renan attached great importance,[45] actually repeating himself in the preface to *Addresses and Lectures*, in which most of these pieces are published. He sums up in the words: "Man is the slave neither of his race, nor his language, nor his religion, nor the course of rivers, nor the direction of mountain chains. A great aggregation of sane

[42] June 9, 1880. They had been reported in *résumé* in the *Débats*.
[43] *Discours et conférences*. In the *Histoire du peuple d'Israël*, vol. ii, p. 2, this piece is called "Les Langues et les races."
[44] March 11, 1882; reported in full in the *Débats*, March 12 and 14.
[45] See Preface of *Discours et conférences*.

and warm-hearted men creates a moral consciousness called a nation. So far as this moral consciousness proves its force through sacrifices demanded by the abdication of the individual for the profit of a community, it is legitimate, it has a right to exist. If doubts arise over frontiers, consult the populations involved. They surely have a right to an opinion on the question.'' (P. 309.)

In politics, as in religion, Renan is opposed to transcendental dogmatism, to the substitution of formulas for the living reality. His third lecture to this society, ''Islamism and Science,''[46] is a sort of popular review of a portion of the subject dealt with in his *Averroës*, the Mussulman's hatred of science. His own summary reads: ''During the first half of its existence, Islamism did not hinder the scientific movement in Mussulman lands; during the second half, it smothered this movement in its bosom and this to its harm.'' (P. 409.) The Afghan Sheik, Gemmal-Eddin, objected in the *Débats* to the notion that Islam was in this respect any worse than Christianity, and Renan answered, showing that, though the same antiscientific spirit animated both religious systems, the Christian lands had partially emancipated themselves while Islam had not, though he hopes that enlightened Mohammedans will secure a similar emancipation. The letter of the Sheik had been translated for the *Débats* from the Arabic, presumably by Renan himself. At any rate, the episode is a striking illustration of the great scholar's courtesy, tolerance, and faith in science. [47]

Two further lectures of 1883, ''Judaism and Christianity'' and ''Judaism as Race and as Religion,'' delivered respectively before the Society for Jewish Studies and the Cercle Saint-Simon, a noted historical association, deal with phases of the subject treated in his great books.[48] On August 7

---

[46] March 29, 1883; *Débats*, March 30; *Discours et conférences*.
[47] See *Débats*, May 18 and 19, 1883; also *Discours et conférences*.
[48] These also are fully reported in the *Débats*.

he presided at the distribution of prizes at the Lycée Louis-le-Grand. In March there had been on the part of the students of this school certain riotous demonstrations requiring the intervention of the police and leading to expulsions.[49] It was possibly for this reason that the Minister of Public Instruction assigned his most distinguished subordinate to this task. At any rate, Renan, who had just been elected Administrator of the Collège de France, performed his functions admirably. Nothing could be more lofty than the views he inculcated of science, of duty, of the necessity of strenuous endeavor; and yet, what charm, what good humor![50] Toward the close of the address, unable to resist a tendency to rascality, he imagines one of the young men before him writing in 1910 or 1920 a critical article on the occasion: "The idea of sending us a man, inoffensive without doubt, but the last who should have been chosen when it was a question of affirming authority, of showing firmness. . . . He gave us good advice; but what spinelessness! What lack of wrath against the age!" Truly, the authorities must have squirmed. But the orator concludes, with the utmost propriety: "There will always be good to do, truth to seek, a fatherland to serve and to love."[51]

Two lectures remain, both on subjects dear to Renan's heart, the French language a perfect vehicle for every idea and the dispersion of scholarly work throughout France instead of concentrating it in Paris. "Can one work in the Provinces?" (June 15, 1889), the last address delivered by him in the amphitheater of the Sorbonne, was pronounced before the general meeting of learned societies which gathered every year in the capital. While the great center must remain, Renan points out, not without humor, the advantages of a more secluded life and the various kinds of

---

[49] See *Débats*, March 13-17.
[50] See *Débats*, August 8.
[51] *Discours et conférences.*

tasks that can be perfectly well accomplished in the smaller towns. The year before (February 2, 1888) the Alliance Française had held a matinée in the Vaudeville Theatre under the patronage of Mme. Carnot and other distinguished ladies. Two little plays were acted and songs and recitations were rendered, the performers being the leading artists of the Opera and the Comédie Française. At the end of the long afternoon Renan spoke, and we may be sure that his address was not the least interesting part of the entertainment. His amusing picture of himself pleading for a mitigation of his penalties in the other world and thereby making the Eternal smile, together with the hope that he will not have to translate his petitions into German, is excellent wit for the occasion. To tack it upon the author's philosophy as some do, is an elephantine blunder.[52]

As Administrator and as member of the Institut, Renan was often called upon to pronounce speeches on funeral occasions, at inhumations or at the dedication of monuments in cemeteries or elsewhere. He developed a special aptitude for saying something appropriate and his ideas associated themselves admirably with the eminence of the characters who formed the subjects of his discourses. Only a half dozen of these pieces have been collected; many more are buried in the *Débats* or in pamphlets published by the Institut.[53] We doubtless have enough of them, though perhaps we may regret that the loyal tribute to Émile Egger has not been rescued.[54]

Other speeches were called for at the unveiling of statues in the home province, a task in which Jules Simon and Renan were often associated as the two most illustrious of the sons

---

[52] *Débats,* February 3, 1888; *Feuilles détachées.*
[53] For some of these pamphlets see Vicaire, *Manuel.*
[54] Obituary notice in *Débats,* September 4, 1884, and tribute at the unveiling of the monument in Montparnasse cemetery, *Débats,* May 31, 1886. ''In vacation, we were in the habit of exchanging Latin verses,'' is a fact we are glad to know.

of Brittany. Then there were banquets and festivals of various sorts, Quimper in 1885, a visit of some Welshmen in 1889, the Félibres and Bréhat in 1891, and innumerable Celtic dinners, often extensively reported. Two dinner speeches Renan has seen fit to preserve, his greeting to Berthelot at a banquet of the Scientific Society and his talk to the students at one of their annual feasts, over which he was, according to university custom, called to preside. The only reason for prolonging such things beyond the moment of utterance is to add another stroke to the portrait of the speaker.

V

Such book reviewing as Renan did during his final period was practically confined to the *Journal des Savants,* where he averaged one serious study a year, generally upon some work in Hebrew or on religious history.[55] In the *Revue de deux Mondes,* he published nothing but advance chapters of his *History of the People of Israel,* the only exception being the "Examination of Philosophic Conscience" in 1889. In the *Débats* two or three brief notices, and two longer essays, the discussion of Amiel's *Journal*[56] and of Janet's *Cousin,*[57] were his only efforts in the old manner. To Amiel he was led by his friend Charles Ritter, one of Amiel's literary executors, and the book on Cousin revived his own experiences of former years and elicited a really warm tribute to the half-forgotten master.

Few essays of Renan have received from the moralists more severe reprobation than has been bestowed upon the

---

[55] Though generally of sufficient interest, only a few of the most important of these have been collected. See *Nouvelles études d'histoire religieuse,* "Nouveaux Travaux sur le bouddhisme," and in *Mélanges religieux et historiques,* "Le Légende de Mahomet," and "La Topographie chrétienne de Lyon."

[56] *Débats,* September 30 and October 7, 1884.

[57] *Ibid.,* June 13, 1885.

reflections attached to Amiel's *Journal*. That drunkenness should not be suppressed, but should be rendered kindly, amiable and moral—a truly shocking idea; that only those who had contributed greatly to civilization should be entitled to resurrection, the rest being condemned to everlasting oblivion—the inhuman fancy of an aristocrat; that we should be ironically resigned to the deceptions we know to be practiced on us by God—the negation of all virtuous philosophy. Indeed, the revulsion against a certain morbidness in Amiel's thought had carried Renan a little too far in the opposite direction. It was all, however, a matter of emphasis, as the ideas themselves, in a somewhat more subordinate relationship, belong to his habitual thought. "We think a man is religious when he is content with the good God and with himself"—"The sum of happiness in human life should be increased. Man should not be told of sin, expiation, redemption, but of kindliness, gayety, indulgence, good humor, resignation." This is doctrine Renan had learned from experience, and his experience as a worker also led him to point out the instable foundation of Amiel's life. "He has not a sufficiently definite conception of the aim of the human mind, which gives a serious basis to life. He is neither a scholar nor a man of letters." In other words, the fundamental morality is purposeful labor.

Suddenly, in January, 1886, the readers of the *Débats* were shocked or delighted, according to their mode of taking things, by a *feuilleton*, "Prologue in Heaven,"[58] a little dialogue in which Gabriel reports to the Eternal various happenings on earth which have scandalized him. The form is irreverent, but the content is Renan's usual philosophy. Some two months later (February 27), appeared another *feuilleton*, "1802, Dialogue of the Dead," written at the request of Jules Claretie to be spoken at the Théâtre

---

[58] *Drames philosophiques.*

Français by the leading actors on the anniversary of Victor Hugo's birth.[59] It was the first time, said Lemaître, in his "Semaine Dramatique,"[60] that a professor of Hebrew at the Collège de France had worked for the House of Molière. In the representation the little piece proved a brilliant success. Renan's last appearance as a *feuilletoniste* was on January 1, 1887, when he published "Letter to M——, Minister," the recipient naturally being recognized by all as Berthelot, who for a few months held the portfolio of Public Instruction in the cabinet of Goblet.[61] The genial detachment of age, its recollections combined with a sort of sweet irony, could hardly be better voiced, while the application of certain miracles of Krishna and Buddha to the budget is in a manner that belongs to Renan alone.

One further article must be mentioned, "Recollections of the *Journal des Débats*," contributed to the book published to celebrate the centennial of that newspaper in 1889. To the new writers, Renan was a survivor from an age of giants; the regularity of his attendance at the monthly *Débats* dinners, where he treated even the novices as colleagues, was a glory and a joy to them; and every article he sent in was a momentous event. In these recollections, he pays generous tribute to de Sacy and other associates of bygone days. How frequently during these years he was compelled to live in the past!

So far as substance was concerned, Renan had in these occasional writings little that was new to say. "By repetition, the charm has diminished," said Scherer in reporting his reception at the Academy at 1879.[62]

We have too much nuance; the challenge to vulgar prejudice has somewhat lost its piquancy; the premeditated contradictions,

---

[59] *Ibid.*
[60] *Débats*, March 1.
[61] *Feuilles détachées.*
[62] *Études sur la littérature contemporaine*, vol. vii, p. 349.

destined to show the various aspects of truth, risk becoming a mere sport. . . . What has long struck me in M. Renan is the unexpected in his resources. I have just pointed out some repetition in his philosophic fantasies, but this is by no means true of his style. He has written so much that it seems he must be fatigued, worn out, condemned like all the rest to copy himself. But no: it is just at such a moment that one of the hidden springs of this rich nature bursts forth suddenly with a new stream of penetrating and sublime poetry.

These remarks are especially applicable to the *Philosophic Dramas* (July, 1888), the two Caliban pieces, having been supplemented with the *Priest of Nemi* (1885) and the *Abbess of Jouarre* (1886). Without any very good reason, the *Abbess* had shocked everybody excepting Jules Lemaître, whose notice in the *Débats* [63] was calculated rather to augment than to diminish the agitation of the righteous. When the little group of pieces appeared as a single volume, the critics hailed it as the author's most original contribution to literature.[64]

Renan had reached a point at which the philosophical dialogue was not sufficiently complex to express the nuance of his thought; he therefore added imaginative dramatic action, making his *Philosophic Dramas* a sequence to his *Philosophic Dialogues,* and predicting, at the same time, a development in which even such action would not suffice, but would need the addition of music, the music of ideas, not that of mere entertainment, to express the more impalpable shades of human meditation. As a matter of fact, every idea presented in these pieces is already familiar to the reader of Renan's previous works. The touch, however, is even lighter than before. These "recreations of an idealist," as he calls them, though serious in subject matter, are the production of leisure hours and the series was abandoned

---

[63] October 25, 1886; *Impressions de Théâtre,* vol. i, p. 255.
[64] In this view Brandes seems to have set the pace.

when all the writer's spare time was needed for the completion of his Jewish history.

In *Caliban*, a sequel, though in no sense a competitor to *The Tempest*, there is nothing new, except the form. It is, however, a remarkable concentration of Renan's views about the triumph of democracy. Far from being dramatically impersonal, practically every character, even the coquette, the schoolmaster, the Wandering Jew, speaks or at least represents the thoughts of the author. The plot is of the simplest, a mere series of episodes and conversations. Prospero, returned to Milan, resumes his studies and is overthrown by the populace led by Caliban. The triumphant leader occupies Prospero's bed and becomes an upholder of property rights, settled order, elegance and the arts. The Duke accepts his fate, reserving only the privilege of ironical laughter, but Ariel vanishes, absorbed into nature. The play is an allegory, as well as a direct expression of philosophical ideas. Each of the main characters becomes a double symbol: Prospero is both royalty and science; Caliban, vulgar humanity and the leader of the sans-culottes; Ariel, the idea and ideal beauty. Around these three are gathered many others to represent shades of opinion—aristocrats, scholars, artists, bourgeois, populace, churchmen, the Jew, and Gonzalo, who joins Caliban's council to aid the new government with his experience. The allegory is obvious. Sans-culottism triumphant puts on the garb of aristocracy, adopts, as far as possible, its manners, its pleasures, its science and art, and imitates its elegance. Meanwhile, the aristocrats persist, some joining the new ruling class, others continuing their diversions or their avocations; and the church, though powerless to persecute—the inquisition had demanded Prospero from Caliban and had been refused—retains its dogmas and its tendencies. Ideas, however, have lost all power over the masses, and ideal beauty fades into the general substance of the universe. It is Renan who speaks, expressing the varied nuances of his thought in the contrast and conflict of abstract personalities. The music he imagines—Gounod was to have composed one melody—has never been written. As it stands, the piece is perhaps the only worthy sequel to a Shakespearean drama.

The Elixir of Life possesses less unity than *Caliban*. The main theme is the progress of science in spite of theological, political, class and personal opposition, its escape from total suppression in ages of darkness resulting from its applications in medicine; but many prominent subsiciary ideas, even including copyright and patents, are embodied in incidents and personalities. The feminine influence upon human affairs is strongly stressed in the discarded and the actual mistress of the Pope and in two coquettish nuns. Prospero, who is partly identified with Arnaud de Villeneuve, continues his investigations under the protection of Pope Clement at Avignon, though assailed by the Inquisition, the Emperor, the nobles and populace of Milan, and a former reactionary mistress of the head of the Church. At the end he dies by a process of euthanasia induced by his own will, and his body is sunk in the Rhone, the officiating cardinal to announce his death as a case of suicide if the body is found, and, if it remains at the bottom of the river, to declare that he was carried off by the Devil. Prospero, who represents "the higher reason, momentarily deprived of its authority over the lower portions of humanity" (preface), is also Renan himself. Throughout he propounds ideas about the progress and functions of science enunciated in *The Future of Science* and other works. The author is also curiously impersonated on the imaginative side by an old Breton bard, who, on drinking the Elixir, dreams details of Renan's life with Henriette, even to the childish incident of his biting her arm. Ariel and Caliban appear only in the last act for the purpose of being reconciled by Prospero, an obvious allegory of Renan's reconciliation with the republican form of government, stated in the preface, and of the spread of ideas among the populace through the achievements of science; Ariel, symbol of ideal beauty, becomes flesh through his love for a young woman, an equally obvious allegory of the relations of beauty and love to the ideal in human life. Of all the personages the Pope is the most nearly human, being a typical freethinking Renaissance prelate. The German ambassador, Siffroi, and the German Emperor, in his demand for Prospero's extradition, speak the ferocious language only too bitterly known to Renan through the experience of 1870, and now familiar to all the world. The thirty or so remaining *dramatis personæ*, most of them easily recognizable types, it would be futile to discuss. It is interesting to note, on the other hand, that the dying Prospero utters the wishes of Renan at the time and place of writing:

Have them play melodies of Amalfi and the Bay of Naples. Take heed that I see no sad face and hear no sigh of grief.

Eternal and good Being, I thank thee for existence. I have collaborated in all thy works, I have served all thy ends. I bless thee.

The Priest of Nemi represents Messianism and its martyrdom,[65] together with the political law that "crime is often rewarded and virtue generally punished." It pictures "the egotism of the nobility, the silliness of the populace, the impotence of thinkers, the infamy of a lying and the weakness of a liberal priesthood, the errors into which patriotism easily falls, the illusions of liberalism, the incurable baseness of low-minded men." For this purpose Renan chose the old story of the Priest of Nemi, who gained his office by putting his predecessor to death. In place of this ancient assassin, the author has imagined an enlightened

---

[65] See preface.

priest, who discards antiquated traditions and practices, and devotes himself to the amelioration of humanity, to the service of reason, and to the worship of the infinite. All are opposed to him except two lovers, who have open hearts, and Liberalis, head of the republic, who has an open mind; but the lovers are without influence and Liberalis is compelled to yield to the mob. Antistius has gained the Temple without slaying his predecessor, and the people demand for the office a vile murderer; he has abolished sacrifices, and the people demand the immolation of human victims; he has substituted reason, justice and real worship for outworn superstitions, corrupt practices and senseless rites, and the people demand the customs of their fathers. On his death, his murderer succeeds him for a moment amid general rejoicing, and when he too falls, we are left to infer that his fellow brigand, Ladro, is to gain the appointment through subserviency to the leader of the aristocrats, though Ganeo, a despicable assistant to Antistius, who has lost all faith and virtue as a result of the too exalted teachings of his noble master, would be a fitter candidate for head of the temple. This overthrow, together with an insane declaration of war by Alba Longa against Rome, constitutes the entire plot. In their acts of folly the populace, led by a demagogue, a fanatic and a self-seeking nobleman, force their chief, Liberalis, to proceed against his better judgment. The application to modern conditions is sufficiently obvious. Although Renan wished to indicate that progress is ultimately triumphant, he has not been very fortunate in producing this impression. The success of evil, foolish and reactionary forces is emphasized so strongly that the reader is apt to overlook the dim indications of the workings of the eternal law of evolution. These indications are embodied in the prophecies of the Sibyl, who foresees both the future power of Rome and, though darkly, the coming of Christ. The piece is fitly terminated by the words of

351

Jeremiah (li. 58) : "Thus the peoples shall labor for vanity,
And the nations for the fire."

The *Abbess of Jouarre,* in spite of its stilted speeches, is
more dramatic both in situations and in character contrasts
than the preceding pieces. Indeed, the first three acts,
translated into Italian, were actually performed with success by Eleanora Duse, to whom the title rôle appealed.
Local color, scrupulously avoided in the other philosophical
dramas, is here profusely employed. The action, however,
is extremely simple. During the Terror, the Abbess of
Jouarre, Julie de Saint-Florent and the Marquis D'Arcy,
both condemned by the revolutionary tribunal to die the
next morning, meet in the du Plessis prison. The two had
loved one another, but, though to a large extent freethinkers,
they had been kept apart by respect for her position and
for the educational task she had set herself. At night he
enters her cell and she yields to his passion. On the following morning, instead of accompanying him to the scaf-
fold, as she expected and ardently desired, she is reprieved,
and he goes to his death alone. After a frustrated attempt
at suicide, she accepts a life of misery for the sake of her
child. Some years later, through the persuasion of her
brother, she consents to wed La Fresnais, a general of the
republic and the man who had secured her reprieve, and
they determine to devote themselves to the regeneration of
France. This is the piece that Matthew Arnold regarded
as pertaining to the worship of "the great goddess Lubricity." Such was certainly not Renan's intention, and
he defended himself against the charge by prefixing to the
twenty-first edition a pretended translation of a passage
from an ancient biography of Plato, in which the philosopher justifies the writing of *Phædrus.* It is needless to say
that Renan does not emphasize the physical aspects of passion. Lubricity implies an excessive preoccupation with
the reproductive act as a sensual pleasure. Renan, on the

contrary, treats the act as sacred, and motherhood as an expression of divine law. The sexual tendency is a fact of nature. For the ordinary course of human society safeguards are necessary, conventions and rites indispensable. The relations of D'Arcy and Julie are exceptional, for the imminence of certain death dissolves earthly obligations and sanctifies their union. It is with a philosophical discourse that D'Arcy overcomes Julie's scruples, and it is with a philosophical discourse that her brother, after her hard period of expiation, induces her to accept La Fresnais as her husband. The theory, expressed in the preface, that the whole world, if assured of immediate extinction, would give itself up to unrestrained license, is assuredly not a doctrine of human nature, but one of Renan's absolutely stated partial views, for which the reader must supply the qualifications. If Renan had not been the author of the *Origins of Christianity*, it is doubtful whether any one would have thought of lubricity in connection with this drama. Truly, the work contains about as much of this quality as the virtuous Richardson's *Pamela*.

Since Renan's philosophy consists of pictures presenting various phases of existence, rather than of abstract deductions, the dramatic form offered a very favorable vehicle for his ideas. The reader acquainted with his earlier works constantly comes upon familiar phrases in the mouths of the most diverse personages. Prospero and the Priest of Nemi think almost entirely in the author's mode, but others, even minor characters, are often his disciples, either in all they say, or in scattered passages, sometimes at somewhat inopportune moments. When not his disciples, they talk, not as such persons would naturally talk under the given circumstances, but as they might express themselves if they were thoroughly transparent and logical. Imagine one of the populace saying at a time of revolutionary excitement, "Legitimacy is the pole of religion. Merit doesn't count.

Externals are everything." The phrase, it is obvious, presents the logic of the situation, the interpretation of Renan, the crystallization of vague and confused mass opinion into definite formulas. Thus Renan can invent a situation—a revolution, a declaration of war, a reactionary environment for a progressive scientist or for a religious reformer—and set before us representatives of all shades of opinion in such characteristic postures as show his ideas of how things work out in actual practice. His own experiences of '48, of the Empire, both repressive and liberal, of the Franco-Prussian war and the Commune, are here bodied forth in pictures of varying aspects of humanity and of the political and religious motives of both crowds and individuals. Renan is nowhere more entire than in this collection.

VI

Meanwhile two volumes of miscellanies had been added to his great accumulation: *New Studies in Religious History* (1884) and *Addresses and Lectures* (1887), most of the articles in which have already been considered. The opening piece in the *New Studies,* however, deserves special notice on account of some enigmatical words in the preface. It was composed, Renan says, "under circumstances that I tell my friends when I wish to make them smile, and which I remember with pleasure because they rendered me for a moment the collaborator of Taine, Max Muller and Emerson." The amusing feature was, to use a term of the theater, that Renan came to be "circussed." Wallace Wood was what Swift would call a "projector," and he managed to involve a considerable number of distinguished men in his absurd and bombastic schemes. One of his projects was "The Iconographic Museum, Liberal Education through Eye and Hand," "the bride of the library," consisting of seven Halls of History labeled with the names of great men, the prospectus of which ends with the following: "Iconographic Museums will be furnished at a certain price and set up in any town or college. Special terms for S. Africa and Australia." The particular undertaking to which Renan alludes was *The Hundred Greatest Men, Portrait Collection,* with "an international corps of writers," being four volumes devoted to Poetry, Art, Religion, and Philosophy. Renan's introduction was to Volume III and Taine's to Volume IV.[66] This work is extolled as "a Universal History, a complete Encyclopedia, an Entire System of Education, a Gallery of Fine Arts," and "the publishers confidently believe that they are issuing the important work of the century."[67] Even without knowing any of Renan's personal experiences with Mr. Wood, we can gather enough from the preceding manifestos to understand his amusement at being caught with his eminent friends in this net of unconscious charlatanism.

Such an experience was not calculated to diminish Renan's repugnance to what he called Americanism, the greedy, pushing, self-advertising tendencies in daily life and in politics. In the eighties and nineties the United States, as was natural enough, got the credit for all the crudeness of the new democratic society.[68] The apparent instability of the French Republic, moreover, gave the political manifestation of these tendencies a menacing appearance. The correspondence with Berthelot is full of gloomy forebodings occasioned by the violence of the demagogues and the absence of moderation in the most respected leaders. In the seventies Gam-

---

[66] For Taine's essay, see *Débats,* February 11, 1880.

[67] Wood, though an Englishman, ended his career as a professor of art at New York University. A number of his curious books are to be found in our libraries. The above quotations are made from advertisements published with his "Catalogue of the Wallace Wood Portrait and Culture Gallery, for the liberal and art education of men and women."

[68] The letters of Mérimée, Doudan and others are full of the same complaints.

betta's lack of restraint was disquieting, in the eighties came Boulangism, and this was followed by extensive anarchist bombing activities. As life went on pleasantly enough in spite of politics, *carpe diem* came to be the maxim intermingled with the political plaints.

Life was, indeed, pleasant to Renan, and he often enough publicly expresses his gratitude. His family life, sweetened by a devoted wife and daughter and freshened by his sportive grandchildren—Noémi had been married in 1883, Ary the next year—was to him almost a proof of predestination. In society he was a great favorite. "Uncouth in frame and gait, as some gnomelike Breton saint, unworldly as the village *curé* he looked like, Renan became the arbiter of the more intellectual elegancies of Paris. Fair ladies slept happy when they had exhibited him in their salons; bonnets from Virot drooped a trifle disconcerted at the uncompromising scholarship of his lectures at the Collège de France; latter-day Magdalenes consulted him as to the state of their conscience, and music hall singers asked his opinion of their songs." [69] Every week he received at the Collège de France. "He used to sit in his armchair, talking as no one else could talk, giving equally kind welcome to all comers, surrounded by his family, whom he loved intensely, and by whom he was adored in return." [70] He was very fond of dining out, appreciating good food and drink, as well as good company. He had been one of the group that dined every fortnight with Thiers after that statesman's retirement, and though the Magny dinners, grown unwieldy and held at Brébant's, seem to have lost their attraction, he had innumerable occasions for meeting brilliant people around both public and private tables. "M. Renan talked marvelously well, and he loved talking. He had little of the ready give-and-take which is the most

[69] Mme. Darmesteter, p. 242.
[70] Simpson, *Many Memories*, p. 319.

usual form of wit, yet he had a colloquial magic of his own.
His conversation was an attentive silence, interrupted by
long pauses of solitary meditation, and by outbursts of
radiant monologue." [71]

There was nothing in his external appearance [says Gabriel
Monod [72]] which at first view seemed calculated to charm. Small
of stature, with an enormous head set in broad shoulders, af-
flicted early with excessive obesity that made his walking heavy
and was the cause of the illness that carried him off, he seemed
homely to those who saw him only in passing. But the instant
he spoke, this impression vanished. You were struck with the
power and breadth of his forehead; his eyes sparkled with life
and wit, and they had besides a caressing sweetness. His smile
above all spoke all his kindliness. His manners, in which there
had been preserved something of the paternal affability of the
priest, together with the gestures of benediction of his plump
hands and the approving movement of his head, possessed an urbanity that was never belied and in which was felt the native
nobility of his character and his race. But it is impossible to
describe the charm of his talk. Always simple, almost negligent,
but always incisive and original, it penetrated and enveloped at
the same time. His prodigious memory permitted him to bring to
all subjects new facts, original ideas; and at the same time, his
rich imagination mingled in his conversation, with turns that
were often paradoxical, flights of poetry, unexpected comparisons,
sometimes even prophetic views of the future. He was an incomparable story-teller. The Breton legends in his mouth acquired
an exquisite savor. No talker, except Michelet, has been able
so to unite poetry and wit. He did not like discussions, and the
facility with which he assented to the most contradictory assertions has often been the subject of jest. But this complaisance
toward the ideas of others, which had its source in a politeness
at times a trifle disdainful, did not hinder him from firmly maintaining his opinion whenever it was a really serious question.
He could be firm in defense of what he believed just.

---

[71] Mme. Darmesteter, p. 250. The recollections in this book give
a charming picture of Renan's last days.
[72] *Renan, Taine, Michelet*, pp. 35, 36.

Badly housed in the Collège de France,[73] he still had space for his books and could have the relief of not fearing another moving day. It might have been anticipated that he would have made an indifferent executive, but abundant testimony shows that his administrative abilities were unusual. He was perfectly familiar with every detail, and he devoted to practical matters concerning the Collège an attention he never deigned to bestow on his own affairs.[74] Whatever task Renan loved, he accomplished with marked efficiency, and his affection for the Collège de France equaled that which he gave to the Société Asiatique and the *Corpus*. Besides acting as Administrator, he was also the representative of the Collège, with Berthelot, on the Conseil Supèrieur de l'Instruction Publique,[75] where the two friends gave much attention to the development of the system of French universities, though naturally unable to accomplish all they desired.

VII

Renan as a public man, however, is not nearly so attractive as the great scholar in his study. Here Philippe Berger used to come to work with him on the *Corpus*. Arriving by appointment in the morning, he would find that Renan was still in bed. Soon hurried steps are heard coming down the hall; then apologies, the breakfast cup of chocolate is brought, and work is begun, gravely superintended by Coco, the parrot. A meow at the door, and Minet, the Angora

---

[73] Mme. Darmesteter gives a picture of the meager study facing north, the narrow bedrooms the salon adorned with Ary Scheffer's pictures, and quotes a paper found in Renan's desk: "I have known the grip of poverty, but never have I been so badly housed as in the Collège de France." He never, however, thought of asking for repairs. (Pp. 242, 243.) So far as we have accounts of Renan's other dwellings, he seems always to have sought a study that commanded a view of trees.

[74] Gaston Paris, *Penseurs et Poètes*.

[75] Elected May 1, 1884.

cat, has to be admitted, jumps on the master's shoulders, walks over the papers, scratches the backs of some *Transactions* on the bottom shelf of the bookcase, and then calls to be let out. Renan, we are told, was a night worker. In the mornings his mind slumbered, and only as evening approached did he gain full possession of himself. Then he often went on till long after midnight.[76] It is almost needless to say that the clearest order and method were characteristics of his work. An ingenious system of marginal references permitted infinite correction and retained every thought in its proper place.

In his course at the Collège de France Renan now departed from his earlier practice, and devoted one of the two hours to preparing the ground for his *History of the People of Israel*. As this course made a popular appeal and as he had become one of the curiosities of Paris, his little room was often thronged with the curious. The Saturday lecture on the Pentateuch became too often a gathering place for fashionable ladies. The professor's free and colloquial manner were vividly painted by Jules Lemaître [77] and notes of his course were presented to the public in the *Débats*.[78] "In his Saturday course," says this reporter, "M. Renan pursues the study of the sources of old Hebrew literature. He brings forth and discusses before a public ever more and more avid to hear him, the materials of the *History of the People of Israel,* allowing his hearers to see day by day the scientific elaboration, all trace of which is effaced the moment the book appears."[79]

No more riotous demonstrations or attempts at suppres-

---

[76] Berger, "Renan intime," *La Revue,* November 15, 1903, and also in *Débats,* October 7, 1892.

[77] *Les Contemporains,* vol. i, p. 195 et seq.

[78] August 17 and 23, 1887, "Notes d'un auditeur du cours de M. Renan."

[79] In *Penseurs et Poètes,* p. 333 et seq., Gaston Paris gives a luminous picture of these courses, their exactness and their inspiration.

sion. No universal howl of objurgation and anathema at
the appearance of his books. The progress in tolerance and
moderation noted in the preface to *New Studies* was actual
and permanent, and Renan himself had been the principal
factor in accomplishing this result. "We may see strong
religious reactions," he said; "we shall not see a return to
real fanaticism."

Little annoyed by controversy, his serenity was sometimes
troubled by personalities. He objected to some pretended
conversations published by Maurice Barrès in the *Voltaire*
for May, 1886; [80] but his chief irritation was excited by
the betrayal of confidence in the Goncourt *Journal*. The
Débats printed (December 6, 1890) from the Lannionnais,
a letter of Renan to his cousin M. Morand, in which he expresses his indignation over Goncourt's violation of propriety and proclaims the reported conversations "complete
transformations of the truth." "When I wish to express
myself," he continued, "I do it in the *Revue des Deux Mondes*, in the *Journal des Débats*, or in my books. . . . I do
not recognize in any other place the authentic expression
of my thought." Newspaper reporters, catching Renan off
his guard, instigated the protagonist to recriminations for
the sake of interesting copy.[81] The fundamental truth is
probably to be found in a letter of Taine, written before this
particular controversy arose, and dealing with Goncourt's
second volume:[82]

Once or twice I am made to say the opposite of what I have
thought or do think, but this is done with no ill intent; the author,
for want of sufficient culture, has not understood what was said
in his presence. I beg you to believe that, if the Magny Dinner
had been such as it is here represented, I should not have at-

---

[80] *Huit Jours chez M. Renan*, a bit of pretentious crudeness recently
republished.
[81] See preface to Goncourt's fifth volume, and list of papers in
Strauss, *Politique*, p. 197, note 1.
[82] To Georges Patinot, October 25, 1887.

tended it a third time; fortunately, however, besides the authors of this Journal, there were present Sainte-Beuve, Renan, Robin, Berthelot, Nefftzer, Scherer, Flaubert, and sometimes George Sand, people well versed in physical or natural or philological sciences, in philosophy or theology, acquainted with foreign languages and literatures, classical antiquity, the Orient and history; these are the subjects we talked about and the conversation was worth listening to. Unfortunately it was above the heads of the two stenographers; their horizon was limited to Gavarni, the minor artists of the eighteenth century and Japanese curios; beyond this limited sphere they found nothing, and even within this circle everything was filled up by their own egotism.[83]

The Magny meetings were, after all, Sainte-Beuve dinners. To Flaubert in 1874, Renan wrote: "Do you recollect those dinners with that great friend, whose loss leaves in me the same literary void as though he had dragged half the public into the tomb with him."[84] Over Goncourt's treatment of the great critic, Taine expresses indignation: he feels that the Princess Matilde ought to turn the scandalmonger out of her house: "Truly literary manners are getting dirty."

Such irritations were, however, but passing clouds of small magnitude. The enemy Renan now had always with him was physical pain. Morally and intellectually he had fitted himself admirably into the conditions of the universe, but health he had neglected. The days free from suffering were marked days. Rheumatism, intercostal neuralgia, and a weak heart were his chief afflictions, and walking was difficult. He sought relief in change of climate and in mineral baths, but his confirmed sedentary habits made such alleviations merely temporary. "It is exercise above all that

---

[83] *Vie et correspondance,* vol. iv, 256-258. After the publication of the first volume, Taine had requested Goncourt to omit all reference to him thereafter. Letter of October 22, 1887. After the second volume, he resolves never to accept any invitation if Goncourt is to be present.

[84] *Feuilles détachées,* p. 350.

does me good," he wrote Berthelot from Saint-Raphaël (March 21, 1884), "or rather the interdiction I impose on myself of sitting all day long at my desk." But as soon as he was back in Paris, the interdiction was raised, and, unfortunately for him, exercise of the mind could not answer for exercise of the body. The Easter holidays were commonly, though not invariably, spent in the South of France,[85] and he was always happy if he could combine some investigation with his search for health, as when, in 1878, he visited the scenes of the persecutions of Lyons under the guidance of local antiquaries,[86] and fixed some vivid pictures for his *Marcus Aurelius*. To Renan every moment stolen from intellectual pursuits was a moment wasted.

To this feeling on his part we owe those diversions, which are so often masterpieces. The last of these belongs to the summer of 1888. Looking over the manuscript of *The Future of Science* with a view to publication, Renan was led quite in the manner of pious Catholics in a retreat, to review his opinions and strike a philosophical balance, "between proofs," of this Hebrew History, as he wrote Berthelot (August 9), or "like a parenthesis," as he called it the next year (July 7, 1889). His friend was asked to look over the proof sheets to see that the technical scientific statements were not "too far behind the times." The article, entitled "Examination of Philosophic Conscience," appeared in the *Revue des deux Mondes* for August 15, 1889.[87]

The opening passage contains the clearest statement Renan ever made of his philosophical attitude, a passive observation of objective truth, distorting it as little as pos-

---

[85] In 1886, for example, the Renans were in Switzerland; Ritter and Berthelot, same date, April 24, 1886.

[86] *Mélanges religieux et historiques*, p. 307.

[87] With the exception of the brief notice of the Queen of Holland, this was the only independent essay of Renan's which appeared in this periodical after 1874. All his other articles were chapters from his books.

sible with rigid formulas. "The first duty of a sincere man," he says, "is to exercise no influence upon his own opinions, but to allow reality to be reflected within him as in the camera obscura of the photographer, and to be a mere spectator of the inward conflicts of ideas in the depths of his consciousness." [88] The fundamental results of this conflict in Renan's consciousness differ little from those hitherto presented—There is no intervention of a will superior to man's; the law of the universe is a *becoming* through internal development; our ideas of space and time are wholly relative, one infinity being zero to another infinity; absolute certitude is unattainable, but the highest probability is practically sufficient; God and the immortality of the soul are possible at the limits of the infinite, and the intervening sleep would seem but a moment; mystery surrounds us, but we hear plainly a voice from the other world, the voice that speaks in the four great follies of man—follies because denials of calculating egotism—love, religion, poetry and virtue; we work by instinct for the ends of the universe, the development of its general consciousness, hoping that God is good. "The world, now governed by a blind or impotent consciousness, may some day be governed by a consciousness more reflective. There will be reparation then for every injustice, and every tear will be dried."

Sometimes, in his later days, Renan adopted the practice of saying things in a striking way, so as to startle readers into attention. Of this practice there is an unfortunate example here. After picturing what a consciousness of the infinitely little might think if suddenly disturbed by man, he exclaims: "All things are possible, even God." If he had said "an anthropological God," the remark would not have been drawn out of its context and paraded as an impious Renanism.

---

[88] *Feuilles détachées*, p. 401.

On the other hand, a long passage on the sacredness of love and of the reproductive impulse, as displayed in flower and animal, and ennobled and ennobling in man, is a complete answer to frivolous scoffers and seekers for indecency, who so frequently found their ammunition in Renan's ingenuous absorption in his idea. Through a consideration of love is developed the conception of the attachment of each detail of existence to the totality of the vast movements of the universe.[89]

The guileless way in which Renan saw only his own idea, and not at all the effect it would produce on his hearers, is well illustrated by an episode recorded by Goncourt. At the Magny dinner, October 22, 1866, the talk turned to God, and each attempted to give voice to his concept. Renan, after a long pause and amidst a silence of breathless expectancy, announced that to him God resembled an oyster with its vegetative existence. This portentous comparison was greeted by an enormous roar of laughter from the whole table, in which Renan, after a moment of naïve stupefaction, politely joined.[90]

In the "Examination of Philosophic Conscience," the pearl oyster is again his image of the universe. A disease of this little living cosmos forms a secretion of ideal beauty, a precious thing sought by men. "The general life of the universe is, like that of the oyster, vague, obscure, singularly hampered and consequently sluggish. Suffering creates mind, intellectual and moral movement. Disease of the world, if you choose, but really pearl of the world, mind is the end, the final cause, the last and certainly the most brilliant resultant of the universe that we live in. It is highly probably that if there come ulterior resultants, they will be of an infinitely higher order." This tone, with which the little piece ends, may almost be called a note of faith.

---

[89] *Ibid.*, pp. 421-424.
[90] *Journal*, vol. iii, p. 78.

The ideas here expressed are essentially the same as those in *The Future of Science*, which Renan finally published in March, 1890. He had promised the book to the public twice before in notes to the prefaces of the *Philosophic Dialogues* (1876) and of *Miscellanies of History and Travel* (1878). He had expected, Grant Duff tells us, that the revision would take very little time, for he had determined to change nothing, only to correct proofs, amend inadvertencies, and here and there improve the style, but most of his leisure during the winter was given to it. The time must have been spent on the effort, afterwards relinquished, to cut out passages repeated in later works,[91] for obviously, as well as according to Renan's own statement, the book was published practically as written. It is one of the essential biographical documents.

VIII

Really all the efforts of the last five years were required for the completion of the principal life works. By the time the *Origins* was off the press, Renan was already at work on his *History of the People of Israel.* He wished to revisit Lebanon and Jerusalem, so as to sketch the book on the spot,[92] but in this hope he was disappointed. The task was accomplished entirely in his study. By September, 1885, it is well advanced, the essential parts being almost done. "The two months I shall have in Paris before the opening of my course will, I hope, suffice to put the whole work on its feet; although a year will be needed to bring it all to an end."[93] The single volume that seems to be indicated here was lengthened out to five. In the preface to volume one (1887) Renan says that after six years of labor he had finished the story as far as Esdras; the second volume would

[91] Preface, p. xi.
[92] To Berthelot, September 2, 1881.
[93] *Ibid.*, September 24, 1885.

come out in a year, the third in two years, and, if strength should be granted, he would add a fourth. Again, as in the case of his *Origins,* the work grew in the process of accomplishment. The second volume was almost ready in October, 1888, after a summer's hard work.[94] In 1889 the third volume was going well,[95] and his fourth was to be done the next year in December, though two years will be needed before publication, owing to the care taken.[96] On October 24, 1891, he was able to write at the end of his manuscript, "End of Volume V and last." But for this conscientious scholar, much remained to be done. "I hope to publish my two volumes that complete the History of Israel," he wrote Berthelot, April 26, 1892. "I have read part of my proofs at Marlotte, and I am not dissatisfied. A good corrector could without me publish all that; although, indeed, if from purgatory I should see this work of correction done by another, I believe I should have a good many moments of impatience."

The first volume was published October 25, 1887. It was preceded by four articles in the *Revue des deux Mondes,*[97] in which Renan gathered, with preparatory and connecting matter, "the principal passages of the second and third volumes that deal with the composition of the historical books of the Bible."[98] On October 15, 1887, the last five chapters of Volume I appeared in the *Revue,* while an extract from the preface was printed in the *Débats* for October 24, the day preceding publication. Of Volume II, the whole of Book III appeared in the *Revue* for July 15 and

---

[94] *Ibid.,* October 3, 1888.
[95] *Ibid.,* July 7, 1889.
[96] *Ibid.,* August 1, 1890.
[97] March 1 and 15, and December 1 and 15, 1886.
[98] Though Renan tells us this fact in his introduction to vol. i, these have been spoken of as independent articles. Comparison shows that they do not differ at all from the corresponding passages in the completed work, except for the additions noted. It is, however, a great convenience to have them in this separate form.

August 1, 1888, while the preface was given as usual in the *Débats* for December 11. The same thing happened for the remaining volumes, the last chapter in the *Revue des deux Mondes* coming out January 1, 1894,[99] and the three volumes themselves appearing October, 1890, and April and December, 1893. Renan had really completed his work. It was only the conscientious last touches that the final chapters failed to receive.[100]

At the meeting of the Academy of Inscriptions for February 13, 1891, Renan placed upon the table the first fascicle of Volume II of the *Corpus Inscriptionum Semiticarum*, in this case, also practically completing a piece of his life work. This child of his own conception, planned a quarter of a century before, a work he loved so passionately and one that seemed to him so important for the scientific glory of France, he was happy to see so far progressed that its future was assured.[101] "Of all that I have done," he wrote on a scrap of paper found in his desk, "I prefer the *Corpus*."

The other completed task, and again it was one that he had proposed and carried through by his own force of conviction, was the "Jewish Writers of the Fourteenth Century," for the *Histoire littéraire de la France*. The final installment appeared in Volume XXXI. On the eve of his departure for Rosmapamon in 1892, as he sat at his table with a bundle of proofs, he said to Philippe Berger with the utmost satisfaction: "There is the last sheet of my Rabbis. I imposed this task on myself; it is finished. Now I shall

---

[99] Of vol. iii, book v, chapters i-iv, appeared June 15, and chapters v-viii, July 1, 1890; vol. iv, book viii, chapters x-xii, March 15, 1893; of vol. v, book x, chapters v-viii, January 1, 1894. Of course for vols. iv and v there were no prefaces to print in the *Débats*.

[100] Even after publication in the *Revue*, Renan still made corrections in details of style, a fact revealed by a careful comparison of the two versions.

[101] The substance of words quoted by Berger from a letter, "Renan intime," *La Revue*, 1903.

put the last stroke on my *History of Israel.*" [102]   It was an arid and ungrateful undertaking carried through with absolute probity by sustained application.   True to his principles enunciated in early days, Renan did his full share of dull toil on the foundations of philological science. [103]

IX

In his last years Renan frequently expressed the thought that he was lingering beyond the fifth act. Yet he liked to live. Once, indeed, he said to Berger from his sickbed, that he did not think he could bear his sufferings if they lasted; it would be better to die. But there were periods of comparative comfort and his mind was often able to dominate physical pain. Even as late as 1889, he could walk his two kilometers a day in the country, which had been for some years the limit of his summer exercise. In the winter, he seems to have been contented with the trip from his apartment to the lecture room downstairs. At the November Celtic dinner of 1890, after talking about Saint Yves, he said whimsically: "You really rejuvenate me, and you seem so glad to have me at your table that I should be rather impolite not to be in the world next year to attend a similar meeting." [104] But the next November he had to go south for his health, to Cap-Martin, near Mentone. In returning to Paris in a draughty train, he had a chill which dissipated all the benefits of the sunny days he had enjoyed. When Berger called, instead of finding him at his desk, he saw him sitting exhausted in an armchair designed for him by Ary Scheffer. Still he managed to continue his work, though the Société Asiatique knew him no more. He at-

[102] *Débats,* October 7, 1892.
[103] The magnitude and the irksomeness of the task will be apparent to any one turning the pages of vol. xxxi; the memoir covers pp. 351-789.
[104] *Débats,* November 9, 1890.

tended some meetings of the Academy, however,[105] and, presiding at the Celtic dinner at the Café Voltaire on May 14, he gave a charming causerie in which, after referring to the fact that he had been suffering all winter, he expressed hopes that his health would return and that he would preside again next year.[106]

In May, 1891, Calmann Lévy paid a visit to Renan at the Collège de France to ask him for another volume of recollections, and, as the composition of such a volume would require too much time, he suggested a book made up of miscellaneous articles and speeches, the result being *Scattered Leaves*, which was published February 17, 1892.[107] Before its appearance Lévy had died, and in his preface Renan pays his friend a beautiful tribute. For occupying himself with things of no importance, instead of eternal verities, he excuses himself, on the ground that his serious work is finished, though he will need time for correcting the proofs. The work on the Rabbis is nearly ended and the *Corpus* is in excellent hands. "All this," he says, "gives me great inward satisfaction, and so I have come to believe that, after having thus paid almost all my debts, I might well entertain myself a little." This attitude of indulgent serenity permeates the preface and, indeed, a good part of the volume. Where he says to youth, "Amuse yourselves since you are only twenty, but also work," the intemperate sophists accuse him of falling from grace and pointing out the paths of wickedness. Let them keep their fierce righteousness. More pleasing is the judgment of Charles Ritter, who compares the new preface with the opening lecture of 1862, and finds in the former a great lesson of life, serenity. "The pessimists," he continues, "say that there is no mean

---

[105] He presided at a meeting March 24 and voted on June 2; see *Débats*.
[106] *Débats*, May 16.
[107] Preface in *Débats*, February 15.

between frivolity and despair. . . . But for thirty years, you have shown us, dear and venerable master, by word and by example, that there is a path of salvation, work, which on the one hand calms and pacifies, and on the other, gives us, in the obscurity of our destiny, its little gleam that guides and consoles us."[108] This Swiss scholar was one of the truest of Renan's disciples.

When Renan went to Rosmapamon in July, he was already under the shadow of death. "To end is nothing," he writes Berthelot,[109] "I have almost filled out the framework of my life, and, although I still can make good use of a few years, I am ready to depart. . . . I shall utilize the remnants of life, if I have any. At present I am working at the correction of the proofs of my fourth and fifth volumes of *Israel*. I should like to go over it all. . . . The will of God be done. *In utrumque paratus.*" To Berger, he was constantly sending references for verification. On August 21, he thanks him for an inscription and expresses pleasure at the progress of the *Corpus*. He has not walked a step, often cannot even speak, is able to work a little at volume five, but what a loss of time! Every one who saw him testified to his patience and fortitude.[110] In his last letter to Berthelot, he still has faint hopes, though weak and unable to take nourishment. "One would die more tranquilly, if one were alone; if one did not leave loved ones behind." He still works a little. The volume might well be called, "Benoni, *filius doloris mei*. Yes, I have passed sad days; they would have been less sad if you had been with me. My wife and children have shown me exceeding kindness, and it has consoled me."

On September 17, Renan was brought back to the Collège

---

[108] Letter, February 25, 1892.
[109] July 20; the last letter in his own hand.
[110] For the words of an eyewitness, see Jean Psichari, *Sœur Anselmine*, pp. 168-175.

de France to die. On October 2, the *Débats* announced that
he had arrived from Rosmapamon much fatigued, but was
better yesterday afternoon. His end was peaceful. His son,
Ary, wrote: ''On Sunday, at daybreak, when we were all
standing around him, we saw his breathing become feeble,
then cease, without movement, without pain, like a lamp going out.''[111] On October 3, came the announcement that
Renan had died Sunday at 6:20 A. M. from pulmonary con-
gestion complicated with heart disease. Besides the obituary,
there was in the *Débats* a special article by Gaston Deschamps. On October 5 appeared an article by H. C. (Henri
Chantavoine), ''Ernest Renan and the *Débats*,'' in which
we get a delightful picture of the great talker sitting on a
sofa after a *Débats* dinner, cordial, frank, serene, indulgent,
witty but never malicious. ''He gave us the impression of
a man, perfectly kindly, perfectly sincere, who did not fear
a little fun between two masterpieces.'' ''He had the art,
very delicate and very difficult, which, among people of
good breeding, obliterates distances without confounding
ranks; he had, in a word, true politeness, that of the heart.''
On October 7, appeared ''M. Renan, Familiar Recollections
of One of His Pupils,'' by Philippe Berger, who later succeeded his master both in the chair at the Collège de France
and in that of the Academy of Inscriptions. Meanwhile
every day there were notices of the coming funeral ceremonies, for to Renan was accorded all the dreary ostentation
of a public solemnity in the court of the Collège de France.
The speeches here delivered by Léon Bourgeois, Boissier,
Gaston Paris and Alexandre Bertrand, were published in
full on October 8, together with an account of the military
and civic procession which accompanied the corpse to the
Montmartre cemetery. Here Renan was laid in the vault
of Ary Scheffer. He could not repose, as he had wished,

---

[111] René d'Ys, p. 377.

in the cloister of Tréguier under a stone bearing the words
—*Veritatem dilexi.*

Mme. Renan died May 22, 1894.

On September 24, 1896, a plaque was placed, not without
opposition, on the house in Tréguier in which Renan was
born. In 1903, by international subscription, a statue was
erected in the market place. It was unveiled September 13,
with notable ceremonies at which Berthelot spoke, the succeeding generation being represented by Anatole France.[112]
Doubtless with no excess of politeness toward the order to
which the great writer owed his early training, the streets
leading past the Seminary at Issy and the Seminary at Tréguier have been each named rue Renan.

---

[112] For all these matters, see René d'Ys.

CHAPTER XI

I

In Renan's thought the world is a vast, indefinite organism with its constituent elements in continual flux, but with a constant general movement of the whole toward some far-off divine event. Within this universal organism operate subsidiary organisms of every variety in vigor, importance and direction—individuals, groups, races, nations, institutions, inventions, arts, ideas, philosophies—now uniting in harmonious combinations, now flying apart, again clashing in mutually destructive dissonance, growing, hardening, dissolving, but all functions of the general, irresistible current toward the ultimate development, a current which is conceived as the will of God. It is the function of history to deal with these subsidiary organisms, and the historian of any one of them will seek its origin, so far as this can be fixed in the uncertainty and flux of things, and will then trace its comparatively free early growth, until the organism becomes to a large extent fixed as a fully developed member of the body of human affairs. Naturally, the workings of institutions and their decay, the biographies of individuals, and all the multitudinous elements in the study of the past were included in Renan's conception, but it was not these that excited his own special interest. His attention was chiefly attracted by the origins and the growth to maturity of spiritual forces in the forward world movement; and individuals, institutions, philosophies, and all the rest, were valued only so far as they contributed to this result.

373

"If I had at my disposal," he says, "several lives, I should employ one in writing a history of Alexander, another in writing a history of Athens, a third in writing either a history of the French Revolution or a history of the order of Saint Francis." [1] Obviously what gives import to each of these subjects is not merely a personality or the interest of a series of incidents, but the influence of ideas upon the progress of humanity. And in the one life at his disposal Renan selected as his task the History of the Origins of Christianity because Christianity seemed to him the greatest force in the world tending to the expansion of the human soul toward the infinite, this expansion being in his view the highest aspiration of the individual and of the race, and the origins being the period of most intense interest because at the point of impact the movement is always most rapid and unhampered.

II

The "embryogeny" of Christianity is the subject studied in these seven volumes, the formative period, the period of plastic power; and when the child possesses all its organs, is detached from its mother (the Jewish Synagogue), and lives its own distinct life, Renan leaves the account of its later career to those who choose to write ecclesiastical history, a worthy task indeed, but not that to which he has dedicated himself. Under another image he presents the church as a river, vast as the Amazon, of which he seeks in the mountains the bubbling source and the dashing upper courses. Here we have an exploration which is attractive and interesting, but at the same time difficult, and, indeed, if we demand strict accuracy in detail, impossible. There are, moreover, two tasks involved, the purely scientific study

---

[1] *Les Apôtres*, Introduction, p. liii.

of "embryogeny," the weighing of the trustworthiness of texts, the examination of inscriptions and coins, the application of the comparative method; and beyond this the artistic, the poetic task of achieving a human grasp of the whole and of transforming literal truth into imaginative truth.

The author's guiding principles are sufficiently set forth in the prefaces to the several volumes. Absolutely fundamental is the dictum that no miracle, no formal derogation by an individual will from known laws, no intervention of the divinity with a special purpose in view, is to be admitted by the historian; nor are there in existence any inspired writings, true to the letter from beginning to end. The laws of the material world and of human psychology have been the same in all epochs, and in no authenticated instance has God been known to deviate from those laws.[2] But while the supernatural is excluded from individual incidents, there is yet in the world a mysterious purpose which conducts the whole toward some unknown event. God is permanently present in everything, particularly in every living thing. "Our planet labors toward some profound accomplishment." All history manifests the divine current in human affairs, and everything that furthers the ideal is a contribution to this current. "Hellenism is as much a prodigy of beauty as Christianity is a prodigy of holiness. The unique is not miraculous. In varying degrees God is in all that is beautiful, good and true, but never is he so exclusively in one of his manifestations that the presence of his breath in any religious or philosophical movement may be considered a privilege or an exception."[3]

The absence of the supernatural in human history is not theory, but fact; and consequently the rejection of miracles

---

[2] *Les Apôtres*, Introduction.
[3] *Ibid.*, p. 1.

does not fall within the scope of controversy. Polemical writing is indeed foreign to Renan's temperament. Either to attack or defend religious belief forms no part of his purpose. His researches are in the region of pure erudition. He seeks for truth without passion, without partisanship, in perfect liberty, and regardless of any effect upon faith or practice. "Science alone is pure. . . . Its duty is to prove, not to persuade or convert."[4] Orthodoxy has no bearing upon his opinions. He would execute his work with supreme indifference, as if writing for a deserted planet.[5] His sole devotion is given to truth and art.

On the scientific side he intends that his work shall embody the results and conform with the methods of the best recent critical scholarship. He proclaims his indebtedness to his predecessors, particularly to Baur and other German critics who followed him, but he wisely refrains in general from cumbering his pages with references to modern books, restricting his footnotes to citations of the original authorities. His colleagues at the Collège de France also collaborated with him on points of scholarly detail. From whatever source obtained, he has made the facts his own. It is not his purpose to introduce extensive critical dissertations on disputed points; these matters can be dealt with, so far as is necessary, in an introduction, an appendix, or a technical journal. He tries, however, to neglect no means of information or control; documents, coins, inscriptions, ruins, the results of psychology and linguistics, comparison of the records of history, experience of life and politics, personal visits to the places at which the events took place—all are at his service in his search for truth.

In respect to his documents his tendency is less skeptical than that of most freethinking critics of the New Testament.

---

[4] *Vie*, p. xxviii.
[5] *Les Apôtres*, p. liii.

He is inclined rather to favor authenticity than to reject ancient tradition. Even where doubts are too strong to be dismissed, he draws from apocryphal writings valid conclusions concerning general beliefs and states of mind at the epoch of their composition. When a writer is an advocate he makes allowance for his prejudice; when he is superstitious, he discounts his credulity; when he is a falsifier, he measures him by his purpose and by his audience. If this procedure be open to objection on points of detail, it is yet in no way injurious to the general fidelity of his portrayal, for he is dealing with a period about which, by common consent, certainty is unattainable. It is here that the man of erudition blends into the artist.

"The talent of the historian lies in forming a true whole from details that are only half true." [6] For obscure periods, he can rarely tell with precision how things really occurred, but he can often fashion the various ways in which they might have occurred. If the history of such times were confined to certainties, it would be limited to a few lines, but such mere naked fact is really more inexact than truth made expressive and eloquent by conjecture and imagination. "The texts, not being historical, do not give certitude; but they give something. They must not be followed with blind confidence; their testimony must not be rejected with unjust disdain. One must seek to divine what they conceal, without ever being absolutely sure of having found it." [7] In his authorities the scholar encounters fact mingled with fiction, legends full of inexactitude and errors, even systematic falsification; from such chaos he must extract historic truth by delicate approximation. When he has presented the certain as certain, the probable as probable, and the possible as possible, his conscience may be at rest.

---

[6] *Vie*, p. xx.
[7] *Vie*, p. xvii.

His evocation of the past is compared by Renan to the reconstruction of the pediment of the Parthenon. A few fragments, a few indications are given—pedantic learning might enumerate and describe these bit by bit, but could never combine them into a semblance of what they once had been. The artist who would accomplish this feat must be able first, with his knowledge, to recognize, and piece together the scattered members, and then, with his imagination, to seize the soul, the life of the original. It is not enough to add one detail to another; he must have a grasp of the whole in which each of these details performs its vital function. A Paul, a Luke, a Theophilus, is not a theological dogma or a logical thesis, but a mobile, susceptible, visionary, irritable human personality, and the movements of which these men were leaders were movements in which such personalities united or clashed in ever varying combinations. The result, of course, is not guaranteed to be an exact reproduction of the past. We must always repeat "perhaps," "it might be," "it is said." Even the current dates on each page are merely approximate. The warning given in the first volume, and repeated in others, as the work proceeded, seemed to Renan sufficient. But the reader is apt to neglect these cautions. The text is generally written without qualification, so that he finds himself unconsciously regarding the plausible narrative as a picture of indubitable reality. The scientific harm, however, is slight. Whatever alteration a competent student of the period might see fit to make in this or that incident or character, the justice of the general impression remains untouched, and the portrayal of the gradual solidification of the fluid elements of the early church into fixed forms is likely to be accepted as a permanent historical achievement. At any rate, we know that our guide is gifted with a rare combination of solid learning, philosophic judgment, poetic intuition and power of artistic expression.

III

The vast and complex pageant opens with idyllic scenes in Galilee, portraying Jesus, disciple and friend of John the Baptist, gathering about him The Twelve, announcing the Kingdom of God, healing, and charming the simple folk by the fascination of his personality and the loftiness and intensity of his idealism. The synagogue, open to any speaker who elected to comment on the scriptures, offered unsurpassed opportunities for the preaching of the Gospel, the novelty and power of which lay, not in the ideas propounded, but in the character of Jesus himself. Soon the joyous days of outdoor freedom amid the rural beauties of the region about the Lake of Tiberias give place to bitter disputes in the Temple at Jerusalem. In conflict with the Pharisees Jesus grows somber, his teaching deteriorates in the atmosphere of controversy, his conservative opponents hound him to his destruction, and the Messiah of the poor ends his life on the cross. (VIE DE JÉSUS.)

But the death of such a man seems to his simple adherents an absurdity, an impossibility. The love of the followers of Jesus performed the miracle of the resurrection. Mary Magdalene saw him near the empty tomb, the vision was contagious, all believed that he was risen. Then as the fever and exaltation declined, the visions grew rare; they were replaced by the presence of the Holy Ghost, manifested by trances, convulsions, incoherent ravings, called prophecy and the gift of tongues. Meanwhile, the disciples, gathered at Jerusalem, formed a communistic society, the primitive church. Judea and Samaria were evangelized; Stephen, the first martyr, was stoned; Paul was smitten by his vision on the way to Damascus; the Gospel reached Antioch, the center from which the great apostle was to issue to convert the Gentiles. Christianity, still little more than a germ, but now at least named, is thus brought into contact with

379

Hellenic culture and with the organization of the Roman state.

Christianity now reaches out beyond its natal land. In all the principal cities of the Mediterranean coasts, the Jews had established synagogues. In these Paul began his preaching, first to the Jews, then to the Gentiles. The Galatians, the Philippians, the Thessalonians, the Corinthians, the Ephesians, the Colossians heard his voice. In each city that harbored a Jewish community he met the hostility of the strict observers of Hebrew ritual, but skeptical and philosophic Athens smiled at the agitator and soon found him wearisome. Subsisting on his own labor, and braving the hardships and perils of travel and the enmity of foes, he preached the word and established churches, little confraternities that met in an upper room, not bound together by circumcision and the law, which the congregation of Jerusalem exacted, but united in freedom by baptism, the Eucharist and the spirit of Christ. To these beloved churches, and to the church of Rome, whose only known members, Aquila and Priscilla, indicate that very humble folk first brought the word to the ghetto in the Eternal City, he wrote letters, which later became the basis of theological dogma. But Jerusalem was still the Holy City and the rigid, communistic James the head of the church. Even though Paul may in Antioch sternly reprehend the timid and vacillating Peter, he is obliged to visit those still attached to the Temple and make concessions to the rite of circumcision. Seized, imprisoned and brought to judgment, at the instigation of the formalists, he appeals to Cæsar, journeys to Rome, and there vanishes from the light. (LES APÔTRES, A.D. 33-45.)

Rome now becomes the center of the story, and Nero, the dilettante, public singer, poetaster, comedian, madman, becomes the principal personage. Peter, constantly following in the trace of Paul to counteract his teachings on the abrogation of the Jewish law through the sacrifice of Christ, comes to Rome, the proud city unaware that this poor Syrian wanderer would dominate its destiny. In the persecution that follows the great conflagration, both meet martyrdom. John escapes to Patmos, where he gives forth his apocalyptic vision, filled with hatred of the Empire and the Emperor, the Antichrist, who rules the world until flames shall destroy iniquity and leave dominion to the just. Meanwhile James is stoned at Jerusalem, the little church he governed flees to the desert, where it fades into insignificance, the fanatics of the city revolt, and Jerusalem and the Temple are utterly destroyed by Titus. Civilization and reason have triumphed over theocracy, the West has vanquished the East, but the revenge is even now preparing. The great, unconscious artist, who presides over the apparent caprices of history, has made a masterly dramatic stroke. Freed from the shackles of Judaism and refounded by persecution, the church moves forward toward its ultimate conquest of the Roman Empire. (L'ANTÉCHRIST, A.D. 61-73.)

With the destruction of Jerusalem, the violent Jewish fanatics, as well as the Sadducees, became extinct; the tradition of the Pharisees persisted with the study and observance of the Law, petrified into the subtleties of the Talmud. To all this the Christians were hostile and a growing antagonism separated them sharply from the Jews. Even the Jewish Christians began to shrink in importance, and the communistic Ebionites of the East proceeded on their way toward insignificance and heresy. All the Apostles were dead, and Christ had not yet come in glory; the church must adapt itself to daily human life. The western churches tended toward unity; at Rome, Clement, almost a pope, showed a love of moderation and order, and in organization regarded the presbyters as preëminent. At the same time was felt the necessity of sacred books. The first generation had preferred oral tradition, but the second generation needed to fix the life and words of Jesus in writing. The anecdotes and groups of sayings that were in circulation soon acquired a normal form and arrangement. In constructing the life of the master, the accomplishment of Old Testament predictions had an important share. The general process was aided by the oriental unconcern for material fact. Mark, having often acted as Peter's interpreter, translating the Apostle's Syrian stories into Greek as he told them to the congregations, at length, now that his teacher was dead, wrote these stories out in the same dry, narrow and credulous spirit to which he had been accustomed. Soon followed the most valuable book ever written, the Gospel ascribed to Matthew, a treasury of sayings and a masterpiece of popular story-telling. The literary Gospel, on the other hand, based, not only on traditions, but on documents, is composed by the conciliatory Luke under the influence of the spirit of Paul. But in reality these brief legendary narratives are not to be credited to their reputed authors; whoever may have held the pen, Jesus is the actual creator, and next after his life itself, the composition of the Gospels is the capital fact in the history of Christianity. (LES ÉVANGILES, A.D. 74-117.)

Dogmatism and speculation begin with the fourth Gospel, which, though not authentic, presents a real tradition differing from that of the Synoptics. The words here ascribed to Jesus are, however, invented to support a thesis; Christ becomes the Logos, and the Holy Spirit is transformed into the Paraclete. The tone, too, is anti-Jewish. Soon the death of Jesus is laid to the Jews, Justin writes against the Law, and theological quarrels between Jews and Christians arise. There are also disputes among the Christians themselves. Gnosticism developed and built the bridge over which pagan practices entered the Church. The prevalence of sects, charlatanism and individual aberrations threatened anarchy, but this danger in the end strengthened authority, and learned bishops began to direct doctrine and practice. When the dispute about Easter threatened disruption, the aged Polycarp, soon after a martyr at Smyrna, journeyed to Rome in the interest of accommodation. In the face of fraudulent Epistles and Acts, of puerile Apocrypha, and uninspired Apocalypses, the four Gospels tended to become canonical, living tradition ceased to produce, and dead tradition was established and fixed. At the same time, the organization of the Church grew more settled and more aristocratic with the dominance of presbyters or bishops; orthodoxy came into being, and, with it, the idea of Catholicity. Meanwhile persecution continued under the law against associations and through popular hatred of "atheists" who scorned the national or local gods. The last revolt of the Jews was cruelly suppressed. Hadrian, restoring ancient customs and rebuilding ancient cities and temples as he traveled about, erected on the waste site of Jerusalem a new Roman city. But the ancient world is smitten with a fatal malady, and, even under the good emperors, a pervading sadness betokens its decline. (L'ÉGLISE CHRÉTIENNE, A.D. 117-161.)

All the perfection that Stoic philosophy could produce is exhibited in Marcus Aurelius, most pious of men, the boast of no particular religion, of no metaphysical system, but an honor to the human race. For over a generation, the world was ruled by philosophers, who fostered social and moral progress. Stoicism prompted a liberal policy, developed charity, and humanized law and administration. On the other hand, art declined, physical science was neglected, and the grossest superstition, fostered by oriental religions and astrology, prevailed even among the more intelligent. A popular demand perpetuated the persecution of the Christians, whose constancy was vividly testified by the martyrs of Lyons. This age, indeed, witnessed the full blooming of the youth of Christianity. There was an active correspond-

ence between the churches; apologists arose, some assailing
Greek philosophy, some attempting a reconciliation, some
even addressing the Emperor; lay theologians, then clerical
doctors, began to write, and schools, particularly that of
Alexandria, grew prominent. There were sects and heresies
innumerable, propagating every variety of excess and absurdity, but all were broken against the episcopate, Greek in
origin, but Roman in development, which saved and now
began to rule the church. Rome gave, not doctrine, but discipline, the spirit of practical organization. Geographical
divisions followed the boundaries established by Augustus;
the city was the unit to which the neighboring villages were
attached; over provincial councils presided the bishop representing the capital of the province; Rome became more
and more the ecclesiastical center, its bishop, Victor, even
threatening the excommunication of those who disagreed
with him on the subject of Easter. Authority had displaced
individual inspiration, and orthodoxy frowned on unlicensed
healing, prophecy and the gift of tongues. When death took
Marcus Aurelius, wearied with too much labor, contemplation and self-discipline, and gave the imperial power to his
unspeakable son, all the chief observances of the Church
were in existence, even if not yet completely fixed. Here are
found the mass, baptism, holy marriage, penance, hymns, the
cult of martyrs, reverence for the Virgin; Sunday had taken
the place of the Sabbath, and Easter and Pentecost were the
chief festivals. From the lowly life of Jesus, prolonged beyond death by the simple love and faith of a handful of
ignorant outcasts, had sprung a vast organism, fed from
countless streams of influence, humble at first, but expanding
step by step, growing so great that it will form a union with
the haughty power that had tried to crush it, and by insinuating the seeds of dissolution, will undermine and at last
destroy the proudest of world empires. (MARC-AURÈLE, A.D.
161-180.)

IV

Here is no completed action, with beginning, middle and end, but an expanding action in its initial stages, an action that goes on indefinitely with no visible termination and with no precise limits. There is no interruption of living continuity. The final situation concludes nothing; the subject has simply arrived at a state of relative maturity and stability. A series of episodes has brought about a condition that opens up and looks forward to a vast new series of future episodes. Nevertheless, the point at which the work stops is not merely accidental; it is felt to be inevitable. While there is no mechanical and regulated completeness, there yet presides here another sort of unity governed by the wider correspondences between the course of evolution and the human conception of design and purpose.

Although the main features of his history were outlined from the beginning, the plan of the artist changed considerably as the work progressed and he became more fully aware of the symmetry of his theme. At the moment when he had finished writing *Saint Paul,* he expected to complete his task with two more volumes, to be accomplished in the next five years; but the material grew as he advanced and, on ending *Les Évangiles,* the second of these projected volumes, he found another necessary to carry the story to about the year 160. But once more, at the close of this, his sixth volume, the artistic rounding out of his subject demanded a further extension. By carrying his story forward to the death of Marcus Aurelius, he was enabled to introduce a climax, the suppression of Montanism by discipline and orthodoxy, furnishing a supreme test of the stability and power of the Church, and, at the same time, he was enabled to include a most effective moral contrast, a demonstration also of the fact, so dear to him, that religion is a necessity for humanity, his elaborate study of the futile attempt of philosophy to save the world. In this epoch, indeed, he sees the end of ancient civilization, the exhaustion of the Hellenico-Roman principle and the approaching triumph of the Judeo-Syrian.

When Renan first published his *Life of Jesus,* he said: "The prior movements do not belong to our subject, excepting in so far as they serve to explain these extraordinary men, who naturally could not have been without some ties with what preceded them"; but, having completed his portrayal of the early Church, he felt that his work lacked that preparatory part which the epic poets treat as the main episode, the prehistory of their hero. Aeneas and Odysseus narrate the events that led up to the main action of the poem: Renan goes back eight centuries to explain the moral and religious conditions that underlay the life and teachings of Jesus and the development of Christianity. In strict logic, he admits, this part should have come first. "But life is short and its duration uncertain. I proceeded to what was most pressing; I threw myself into the midst of my subject and began with the life of Jesus, taking it for granted that the previous revolutions in Jewish religion were familiar to my readers."[8] In this case the demands of expediency had a fortunate artistic result, and the *History of the Jewish People* produces its proper effect when read after the *Origins of Christianity.*

As the hero of this epic, if the life work of Renan may be so regarded, is not an individual, but a vast complex of emotions, ideas, beliefs, institutions and personalities, so the principles of composition must be of a new order adapted to this abstract type of subject matter. The treatment is no longer obedient to rules, but is shaped by the requirements of historical fact and philosophical conception. The art is the art of adjustment. It demands a true sense of proportion

---

[8] *Marc-Aurèle,* p. vi.

and continuity. The unity results from the establishment of relations in the midst of seeming confusion and the reduction of the apparently accidental to an ordered whole. In addition, the portrayal must be true to life, and it must, at the same time, rest upon sound critical scholarship. Even if there can be no "material certitude," the inferences and divinations must be based upon a solid scientific foundation and the grand resultant must, in its general lines at least, be a correct representation of reality. In investigation, however, no startling innovations were any longer to be looked for; the critical point of view, whatever differences there might be in problems of detail, was already established and the chief results were accepted by a host of competent scholars. Here, without question, the Germans, Baur and his successors, had surveyed the route and pretty completely constructed the highway. A few rectifications and repairs were all that was left to accomplish. All that these workers had done and were doing Renan knew thoroughly well, but he had also himself covered the whole field of original authorities, and added to it, and on all points in controversy he was able to make up his own mind. His views are truly his own. What is even more conspicuously and characteristically his own, however, is his imaginative moulding of the whole conception into a work of art as personal in its own way as the *Divina Commedia* or the *Paradise Lost*.

V

When, for the first time, Renan conceived a history of the origins of Christianity, he conceived it as a history of doctrines, in which personalities should play but little part; even Jesus would hardly have been named. But he came to recognize that history is not a mere play of abstractions, that the real forces are men. "Parseeism, Hellenism, Judaism could have combined in every form, the doctrines of the resurrec-

387

tion and the Word could have developed for centuries, without producing that fecund, unique, grandiose fact called Christianity. That fact is the work of Jesus, of Saint Paul, of the Apostles. To compose the history of Jesus, of Saint Paul, of the Apostles, is to compose the history of the origins of Christianity.'' [9] The *Life of Jesus* is therefore a biography, and the biographical element is prominent throughout each of the seven volumes. And yet the portrayal of individuals is rarely graphic; the personality is there, indeed, but it is a sort of incarnation of a dimly striving cosmic force, half unconsciously operative in a great social and spiritual movement, this movement being utterly different from anything that the actors in it can purpose or even dream of.

No human character in the work is more real than Jesus. In addition to the story of the Evangelists, Renan had before his eyes ''a Fifth Gospel, lacerated but still legible,'' the landscape of Palestine, which transformed for him an abstract being into a figure that lived and moved.[10] The stony, narrow streets of Nazareth where Jesus played as a child; the splendid view from the plateau above the town, including nearly all the scenes of his activities; the encircling distant mountain ranges, beyond which his feet never strayed except on pilgrimages to the arid regions about Jerusalem; the smiling, flowery, well-shaded meadows of Galilee, where he lived an idyllic and joyous life amid the beneficent beauties of nature; the little canton at the head of the Sea of Tiberias, together with Gennesaret on the opposite side, where Jesus laid the foundation of his divine work; these are brought before our sight as a harmonious setting for a delicious pastoral, the birth of Christianity among the naïve fisher folk and artisans upon whom Jesus exercised his fascination. Here daily wants were insignificant; there was no need of taking thought of the morrow; life was simple, gay and free

---

[9] *Vie,* p. c.
[10] *Vie,* p. xcix.

from care; materialism had no power to cramp the soul. The gentle, ardent, lovable young Jesus, with the beautiful Jewish countenance, is indeed no absolute fact, but the creation of an artist, whose studies and meditations and visions became bodily form. Where the exact lineaments are unobtainable, we get an imaginative portrait, true to the spirit and costume of the age and locality, yet colored with every trait of the ideal. We see the little schoolboy repeating Bible texts in chorus with his comrades; learning nothing of Hellenic culture, of scientific progress or of the general state of the world, but conserving the fresh naïveté that would have been enfeebled by extended and varied knowledge; we see the youth, free from asceticism and the bizarre scholasticism of Jerusalem, not too much occupied with the Law, but nourished on the poetry and allegory of the psalms, the prophets and the Apocalypse of Daniel; we see the young carpenter, a man of universal charm, living in perfect liberty of soul, burdened with neither dogma nor system, but conscious of God, his Father, dwelling in the infinite sweetness and tenderness of his own heart. Disinterested absorption in the idea, disdain of material well-being, contempt of worldly greatness, exaltation of the humble, the downtrodden and the despised, tolerance, delicacy, tact, joyous simplicity, personal attractiveness—these are some of the qualities that make up the endearing personality. A mystic, ardent nature, he regards everything that concerns himself as ruled by God and sees a sign of the divine will in the most insignificant circumstances. Miracle is a normal condition resulting from the familiar relations of God and man. The exorcism and thaumaturgy of the healer are a natural outgrowth of untaught credulity. The superhuman claims of the self-conscious Messiah, the vehement blasts of the transcendental revolutionist who saw the kingdom of God at hand destroying and rebuilding, the exaggerations, the reproaches, the bitter invectives of the heated preacher, these seeming defects are touched by the artist in such a fashion as not to mar the harmony of the picture. Renan indeed feels distaste and regret when he is obliged to represent the disputes and denunciations at Jerusalem. The purity of the idea is soiled in the process of propaganda. Even here he always emphasizes the sweetness, amiability and social charm of Jesus, and delights to take him out of the narrow turmoil of the dreary city into the friendly retirement of Bethany.

The calm, objective narrative of the arrest, trial and crucifixion is vivid and natural, so real indeed as to fill the reader with distress; but the pang of pity for the victim soon fades in contemplation of the cosmic import of the sacrifice. If Jesus had been released, he might have worn himself out in a desperate contest with the impossible; or, still greater tragedy, grown old, dried and hardened by years and experience, he might have sunk into a maker of formulas, the master of a school. In either case he would have been impotent in the world movement. It was his mission to die in the freshness of life, leaving in the hearts of his followers a love that created the Resurrection and eternalized the figure of the Son of God. He had founded a kingdom not of this world, the kingdom of the pure in heart.

Throughout the remaining volumes of the *Origins,* there is a constant return to the personality of Jesus as the central theme: "Jesus alone always had, in the mysterious process of the growth of Christianity, the great, the triumphant, the decisive part. Each Christian book, each institution is of value in proportion to what it contains of Jesus.[11] Even those developments of the church which seem most alien to the ideas of the Galilean teacher are derived, often in some distorted way, from his personality and his career. And looking forward at the close of his work, Renan insists that, beyond a doubt, "whatever may be the religious future of

---

[11] *L'Antéchrist,* p. 477.

humanity, in that future the place of Jesus will be immense.''

In contrast with Jesus,—the active, germinating force—stands Marcus Aurelius, the weary fruit of a maturity verging toward decline. The one opens, the other closes the exposition. To Renan, the Stoic emperor is one of the heroes of the life of the spirit, and his *Thoughts* constitute a sort of Gospel no less divine in its way than the sayings of Jesus; yet he perceives that this most glorious representative of our race "exercised no durable sway over the world." Unsurpassed in elevation of soul, heroism, devotion, self-sacrifice, he exerted his vast power for humane ends, for public felicity, for the amelioration of character. A wicked son annihilated his accomplishment. "The religion of Marcus Aurelius, as occasionally that of Jesus, is absolute religion, the religion that results from a lofty moral consciousness placed face to face with the universe." [12] Such absolute religion is, however, a gift for the elect. This most pious of men mortified the senses, strove for the union of his spirit with an indefinite God, met every evil with complete resignation, every temptation with renunciation; yet he was sad, skeptical, disillusioned. Having attained perfect goodness and absolute tolerance, he looked upon wickedness and stupidity with an indifference tempered with pity and disdain. As emperor, he lived in inward solitude; a favorite of fortune, he could smile at mindless and insensible death. Calmly and steadfastly he endured the complete ennui that weighs upon the blasé soul of the clear-eyed philosopher. The *Thoughts*, incomparable book, can never grow old; yet history furnishes no more striking example than Marcus Aurelius of the fact that philosophy as a motive power upon the masses is utterly ineffectual.

Midway in the vast narrative appears, in all his ghastly monstrosity, that other contrast to Jesus, Nero, the Anti-

---

[12] *Marc-Aurèle,* p. 272.

christ, who also continued after his death so strangely to live on in popular belief. Romanticist, poet, singer, public histrionic performer, sculptor, madman, "he conceived the world as a horrible comedy in which he was the chief actor." Even in his most cruel enormities he was a dilettante, and his licentiousness was "the debauchery of perverse estheticism." No vulgar monster, he had traces of the soul of the artist; and he was not entirely devoid of heart, he loved and he was loved. All the varied contours of this abnormity are depicted, the little good and the immense evil, and the naked horrors of his crimes are unsparingly revealed; yet the recital is conducted without hatred or disgust, as a surgeon might describe a loathsome malignant growth. This method is more effective than loud declamation. It renders in all its stark reality this object of the horror of the early Christian —the Christ of Hell.

Both as personalities and as cosmic forces, two other characters appear prominently throughout the seven volumes, Peter and Paul. James, brother of the Lord, the ascetic chief of the church at Jerusalem, is individualized merely through his intolerant Pharisaism and stiff-necked adherence to circumcision and other Jewish rites. It is with a sigh that Renan notes the painful decline in passing from Jesus to the Twelve Apostles. They are virtuous mediocrities. John alone, to whom is ascribed the Apocalypse, displayed some invention. The frank impulsive Peter, who won the confidence and esteem of Jesus, is mildly attractive. His affection brings him visions of his risen Lord, but he is so narrow and credulous that his view is obstructed by miracles and his memory transforms his master into a great magician. The good man, though sincere, is also timid and suffers from the not uncommon weakness of wishing to content every one for the sake of peace. He is thus on both sides of the controversy about circumcision, and draws upon his head the wrath of Paul.

Paul is, after Jesus,—with whom, however, in Renan's judgment, he will not bear comparison—the most elaborate of the Christian portraits. Physically he is a typical Jewish figure; sickly, but of marvelous endurance, short, thickset, with stooping shoulders, homely countenance, bald head, thick beard, long nose, piercing eyes and black meeting eyebrows. In mind he is equally typical: ardent and exalted, imperious and authoritative, stiff and unbending, even rough and choleric, tending toward isolation and brooking no master or equal among his companions; yet just as often calm, polite, submissive, gentle, affectionate, disinterested. "One feels that his character, in moments when passion did not make him irascible and fierce, must have been that of a polished, eager, affectionate man, though at times susceptible and somewhat jealous.[13] He commands, blames, speaks of himself with the utmost assurance, even proposes himself as a model, and again goes just as far in conciliation and humility. He gained his own bread by labor as a canvasworker, he often traveled on foot amid the greatest perils, he suffered poverty and hardship for the love of souls. Like a modern socialist laborer, he journeyed from town to town, from synagogue to synagogue, to spread his doctrines. His zeal was unquenchable. With a cold temperament but an ardent brain, he employed all the fire of the persecutor in the work of the propagandist. An embarrassed and incorrect speaker, he was yet eloquent and inexhaustible before a small congregation, though timid and ineffectual before a large assembly. To cultivated Greeks his bizarre style, moulded on Syrian idiom, was barbarous and almost unintelligible and his ideas seemed contemptible. Like other exalted souls, Paul was subject to ecstatic visions, which he took for realities, and he enjoyed complete faith in his own power of performing miracles and speaking the word of

---

[13] *Les Apôtres,* p. 169.

God; yet he possessed also a solid fund of practical good sense. The Apostle to the Gentiles was indeed a product of his age and race, admirably suited to his task, as his task was admirably adapted to his nature and his powers.

In addition to the leading personages, we come to know, though not in such detail, a multitude of minor characters— the friendly self-effacing Barnabas, the gentle, docile Timothy, the modest, devoted Luke, and a host of others, who are transformed from mere names into realities. Who can forget, for example, the little slave Blandine, timid and feeble, but with a vigor that would shame an athlete, whose heroism fatigued relay after relay of torturing hangmen? But beyond such individuals, the mass itself acquires life— the destitute throng in the Ghetto at Rome, the women converts in Macedonia, the motley crowd at Corinth, the trade-unions of Ephesus. Aquila and Priscilla, vivified from a mere mention in Paul's epistles, grow into types of the nameless humble folk who constituted the little congregations of apostolic times, and from insignificant beginnings, irresistibly carried forward the destined world movement. In themselves they are real human individuals, and at the same time they are like energetic microbes isolated by the skill of the investigator and made visible by his microscope, microbes that will multiply beyond computation, till they undermine the old organism and establish a new one on its ruins. Renan thus avoids the extreme view that history is nothing but the biography of great men, and at the same time the opposite view, equally false, that history is nothing but the product of mass forces in which great men are merely floating straws that indicate the current. And his theory on this matter is embodied in an artistic product. He represents, at once distinctly and completely, both the potent sweep of the mass and the productive energy of the individuals, whether prominent or obscure, of which the mass is composed.

The landscapes are hardly less admirable than the portraits. The background is always sufficient for the action. In representing the sojourn of Jesus and the path traversed by Paul, Renan drew scenes his eyes had looked upon, but, when necessary, he freshened his pictures with the colors of a former age. What was, is imaginatively substituted for what is. Smiling Galilee, arid Jerusalem, vile and splendid Antioch, the gloomy passes of Asian mountains, the islands and seacoast towns of the Mediterranean are presented in such intimate aspects as must have greeted the Apostles. The reality of the setting adds to the reality of the figures. Moreover, sufficient allowance is made for the influence of climate upon conduct, of physical phenomena upon ideas; yet here too Renan avoids extravagant theory, and we are made aware that environment is only one of the varied and complicated forces that shape the man.

The Author's own experience is often drawn upon to clarify a situation or enforce a contention. The blow dealt to constituted authority by the story of the Passion is illustrated by the pious repulsion felt when he was a child by the people of Brittany toward the police as representatives of the officials who arrested Jesus. The vision that operated Paul's conversion is effectively equated with Renan's own hallucinations in fever at Byblos. In the light that colors the Apocalypse, he sees the yellow, unnatural tone, the dull pallor that he noted when, on May 25, 1871, he looked down on Paris in flames. In fact, his own experiences of persons and events furnish the realizing vitality, not only of touches here and there, but of the entire conception of the way in which incidents happen and history is made.

VI

In order to illuminate situations and personalities of the dim past, Renan makes liberal use of historical and contemporary comparisons. The biographies of Mahomet, Buddha

and Saint Francis show how the stories about Jesus came together. The speeches in *Acts* are like those in Thucydides,
and the episode of Nicodemus in the Fourth Gospel bears
the same relation to the real Jesus as the Dialogues of Plato
bear to Socrates. The ornamental buildings in Herod's
Sebaste form an insipid *rue de Rivoli*, and this is what Jesus
had in mind when he spoke of "the kingdoms of the world
and all their glory." John the Baptist substituting his private baptismal rite for the legal priestly ceremonies is a precursor of Jesus in the same sense as the medieval flagellants
prepared for the Reformation by taking from the clergy
their monopoly of sacraments and absolution. Saint Paul
in the Portico at Athens is like a humanitarian socialist de-
claiming in 1869 against English prejudices before the fellows of Oxford. The narrow church at Jerusalem in its
action against the disciples of Paul was like nineteenth century Rome expelling Lamennais, Hermes, Doellinger, Père
Hyacinth, all her successful apologists; and the benefits to
the church from the ruin of Jerusalem were as great as
those to be hoped from the Italian occupation of the Papal
City. (Written 1873.) Lamennais, with his alternations
of unbridled wrath and gentleness, illustrates John the Baptist, Jesus himself, and several saintly but violent apostolic
figures. Lucian is "the first appearance of that form of
human genius of which Voltaire was the complete incarnation." Such comparisons, though objected to as sometimes
conveying an incorrect impression, or as sometimes being
based on subjects of fugitive interest, nevertheless as a rule
throw a flood of light upon the author's conceptions, and
often, when the resemblances are based on the law of recur-
rent types and phenomena, establish what may be called a
spiritual connection between persons and between occurrences far removed from one another in time.

Renan's work, indeed, is very different from a mere account of men and events; the story is always connected with

the deeper purpose of things. You may use the label "Hegelian" if you choose, but the conception really has no individual owner, and moreover, Renan's mode of treatment is concrete, rather than metaphysical. In such matters logic will lead the thinker astray. What is requisite is the intuition of a rich and sympathetic mind. Here again we perceive the artist, for the ideas in which the history abounds are, as truly as the persons and places, not methodically constructed systems, but what the author sees.

These ideas are naturally identical with those expressed in his critical and philosophical essays, but they gain a special flavor from their connection with the various aspects of his theme. Each incident fits into a general framework of theory and suggests reflections. In general, Renan estimates men and movements according to a scale of values at the summit of which is the ideal and at the bottom the material. The intermediate degrees are never mathematically fixed, but their interrelations are for the most part fairly stable. The highest quality of the ideal as manifested in human life is the good, and only a little below float the true and the beautiful, which are also divine. A complete devotion to these qualities marks the highest efforts of the human spirit; and here Jesus is supreme. The great mass of humanity, however, are given largely to the material. Nevertheless, within this mass, the divine mysteriously moves and operates, evolving popular ideal creations, the only ones that are stable and effective, yet which inevitably bear the marks of their lowly origin in the crudeness of their forms and symbols, admirable so far as these express the ideal, defective and often obnoxious so far as they represent the material. Furthermore, these ideals sometimes seem to work themselves out spontaneously; at other times the inert mass has to be attacked by violence, the task of men of action, of propagandists (Saint Paul). But this propaganda induces compromises by which truth and virtue are distorted. The purest manifestations of the ideal, therefore, are not found in the dust and heat of conflict, but in those lofty regions of the mind inhabited by philosophers and saints, who devote themselves in godlike equanimity to elevated thoughts, with no regard to any practical effect these may have upon the actions or beliefs of mankind (Marcus Aurelius). Here alone is to be attained perfect liberty of soul; but poor human nature finds the atmosphere too rarefied for its daily life. Man is bound by the conditions of existence and can only obtain glimpses of the divine. Our faculties permit us only to approach, never to grasp, the mysteries of creation, and our language, our modes of action, our institutions, everything we do and are, must suffer the hindering imperfection.

The idea partakes of the infinite; that is its glory. And of all men, Jesus was the one most completely dominated by the idea. "His perfect idealism is the highest rule of a detached and virtuous life. He created the heaven of pure souls, where is found what is sought in vain on earth, the perfect nobility of the children of God, consummate saintliness, total abstraction from the defilement of the world, liberty, in fine, which actual society excludes as an impossibility and which has its full amplitude only in the domain of thought."[14] To worship the Father in spirit and in truth is for him true religion. "Devoted without reserve to his idea, he so subordinated everything to it that the universe no longer existed for him."[15] Despising the earth he took refuge in his own kingdom, and established "that grand doctrine of transcendent disdain, true doctrine of the liberty of the soul, that alone gives peace."[16] Among his disciples, the resurrection was the triumph of the idea over the actual. What is the body, once the idea enters upon its immortality? Love for Jesus lived on, the vital force that made and sustained the Church,

[14] *Vie*, p. 461.
[15] *Vie*, p. 476.
[16] *Vie*, p. 124.

with its "sublime contempt for reality," "a refuge for souls under the empire of brutal force." The very brutalities, indeed, of Roman imperialism aroused a more flaming ardor and demonstrated the "eternal puerility of penal repression applied to things of the soul." [17]

But materialism, egotism, bourgeois vulgarity and brutal force are not the sole hostile influences. The idea partakes of the infinite: to limit it is to do it harm. Embodied, it is no longer the pure idea; it is perverted by an alien companionship. Dogma binds and tortures it into material shapes, in which it is fitted indeed to do battle with other material shapes, but in which its true nature is obscured. To approximate this true nature, it must take on contradictory forms, none of which may be regarded as absolute, but all of which have their utility. "When one has come to know the Heavenly Father, adored in spirit and in truth, one is no longer of any sect, of any particular religion, of any school. One is of true religion; all practices become indifferent; they are not despised, for they are symbols that have been or still are respectable; but one ceases to lend them any intrinsic virtue." [18] In the moral and the religious order, it is furthermore indispensable to believe without demonstration. Here not certitude, but faith is requisite. "What need have we of those brutal proofs that have their application only in the gross order of fact, and which would hamper our liberty." [19]

There is an inexorable law that condemns the idea to abasement as soon as it seeks to convert men. Their touch degrades it to their own level; their fanaticism distorts it. Even Jesus did not escape this fatality. Crowds have never been charmed or roused by pure truth. For the accomplishment of a great revolution rough methods are needed, fixed ideas, prejudice, dogmatism, not reason. It is the force of

[17] *Les Apôtres*, p. 136.
[18] *Saint Paul*, p. 167.
[19] *Marc-Aurèle*, p. 265.

fanaticism, not intelligence and tolerance, that leads men to die for an opinion; and amid opposing fanaticisms, liberal spirits have no chance of success. Not to philosophers, but to zealots belonged the future of the Roman world. With success, too, the early enthusiasm cooled. The mass was moved, but the forces that moved it were largely spent in the effort. Propaganda is carried on by means of rigid doctrine and absolute faith, but it is only by making concessions that the resulting institution can live in the general current. It must assimilate itself to its environment; to secure its wider triumph, it must sacrifice ideas, even principles. "It happened to Christianity, as almost always in human affairs; it succeeded when it had commenced morally to decline; it was made official when it had become but a remnant of itself; it acquired vogue when its true period of originality and youth was past." [20] Pagan superstition became the substratum of many rites. Crowds entering the little Church brought their imperfections to soil its purity and transformed its simple faith to fit the needs of their alien imaginations and their more worldly hearts. Then the Church, of necessity, gave birth to the convent, where souls could dwell detached from earth. "When entire countries became Christian, the rule prevailing in the first churches became a Utopia and took refuge in monasteries. In this sense, monastic life is the continuation of the primitive churches. The convent is the necessary consequence of the Christian spirit. There is no perfect Christianity without the convent since the evangelical ideal can be realized only there." [21]

Yet, while religion is degraded by the people, it is itself a popular creation responding to a human need, a great instinctive truth, though mingled with illusions and chimeras, seen and expressed by the mass of men. All humanity collaborated in Christianity. "In these popular movements,

---

[20] *Saint Paul*, p. 273.
[21] *Les Apôtres*, p. 128.

the part of each is impossible to discern; it is the sentiment of all that constitutes the true creative genius."[22] Even the Jesus of the Evangelists is not what he actually was, but what he was thought to be. Yet Renan has too direct and lucid a mind to leave his readers with any hazy, romantic concept of the folk. "Legends, myths, popular songs, proverbs, historic jests, characteristic party calumnies, all this is the work of that great impostor, the crowd. Surely each legend, each proverb, each witty jest, has a father, but an unknown father. Some one speaks the jest, a thousand repeat it, perfect it, refine it, sharpen it; even he who said it was, in speaking, but the interpreter of all."[23] Such things, moreover, as well as the more important contributions to the human spirit, do not grow mysteriously out of vast abstract societies; they spring from little centers where individuals are closely crowded one against the other. Propagated from center to center, the force of the humble and the nameless grows unseen to an irresistible wave that wrecks the most splendid structures of pride and power, and substitutes an edifice unconsciously reared by these obscure agents. Thus came about the fall of the Empire and the rise of the Church. "Sprung from the hardy affirmation of a man of the people, spread before the people, first loved and admired by the people, Christianity was impressed with an original character which will never be effaced. It was the first triumph of the Revolution, the victory of popular sentiment, the advent of the simple hearted, the inauguration of the beautiful according to the people. Jesus thus opened in the aristocratic society of antiquity the breach through which everything will henceforth flow."[24] No impression left by the book is more vivid than that of the aggregate force of fermenting humanity.

---

[22] *L'Antéchrist*, p. 371.
[23] *Les Évangiles*, p. 93.
[24] *Vie*, p. 456.

Not every period, however, is adapted to the effective propagation of great movements. The soil must be prepared for the seed, the seed itself must be ripe for germination, and the surrounding conditions must be propitious for the particular kind of growth that is to flourish. ''Each branch of the development of humanity—art, poetry, religion—finds in traversing the ages a privileged epoch in which it attains perfection without effort and by virtue of a sort of spontaneous instinct. No labor of reflection succeeds afterwards in producing those masterpieces that nature creates in such moments by inspired genius.'' [25] It seems as though there were a sort of world mind, in which at the right moment arise certain inevitable thoughts, thoughts that are propagated almost like an epidemic, crossing frontiers and sweeping over the barriers between antagonistic races. It was for religion that the world was ready in the first and second centuries of our era. The spread of Christianity was no miracle; the conversion of the world was, in fact, inevitable. The political, social, moral, intellectual and religious condition of the Roman Empire furnished the fertile soil and the salutary climate; the preaching of the Hebrew prophets culminating in Jesus furnished the procreant seed. The period Renan treats, instead of being one of settled order, where the movement of life is regular and formal, is one in which the hidden forces that humanity holds in reserve are set free. Among these forces are even extravagance, hysteria, hallucination, states of nervous exaltation that sober reason calls insane; equilibrium is upset; for violence, by a law of nature, is essential to creation. Man's will seems insignificant; he acts as by some vaster power. ''Everything favors those who are marked by a sign; they hasten to glory as by a sort of invincible and fatal impetus.'' [26]

The same sort of fatality hangs over nations that bear a

[25] *Vie*, p. 472.
[26] *Vie*, p. 473.

gift to humanity. The sacred fire cannot be carried with impunity. The choice lies between tranquil obscurity, and a troubled, stormy career ending in extinction or servitude. Every country that dreams of a kingdom of God, that pursues a work of universal benefit, sacrifices its individual destiny. The vocation that ruined the Jews was their contribution to the general fabric of civilization. So it was also with Greece. "Land of miracles, like Judea and Sinai, Greece flowered once, but is not susceptible of blooming again; she created something unique, which cannot be renewed; it seems that, when God has shown himself in a country, he dries it up forever." Such a fate is the result of the law of compensation, which applies no less to nations and to ideas than to individuals. "The religious inferiority of the Greeks and Romans was the consequence of their political and intellectual superiority. The religious superiority of the Jews, on the contrary, was the cause of their political and philosophical inferiority." [27] Contradictory destinies are impossible; every excellence is expiated by some defect; and the more resplendent the excellence, the more fatal will be the defect. Judea, Greece, Italy, each has suffered for its gift to humanity; will the same Nemesis overtake France? [28]

Such are some of the more important general ideas embodied in the narrative. They seem, not like philosophy deduced from the facts or applied to the facts, but rather like a part of the facts themselves. For while the *Origins of Christianity* deals with men as the chief agents in the struggle, we still feel as though ideas were the real contestants, somewhat as the Olympian Gods determined the outcome of the battles on the fields of Troy. It is an artistic triumph to have presented this divine participation, without shock to

---

[27] *Les Apôtres*, p. 364.
[28] *L'Antéchrist*, p. 542. All these general ideas may be found in the *Conférences d'Angleterre*, which consists of nothing but selections repeated verbally from *Les Origines du christianisme*, with introductory and concluding remarks.

the best critical and scientific scholarship, under an aspect so completely in accord with modern spirit.

VII

There are, in addition, many remarks of a different type, generally reflections suggested by the narrative. These are often most interesting, both in themselves, and as a revelation of the author's mental personality. It would be rash to affirm that they are all true, or even consequent or consistent. They are *obiter dicta*, and are therefore not to be cited as authoritative. A brief disconnected collection, by no means pretending to be exhaustive in any direction, will give some notion of the riches of this sort intermingled with the more essential matter.

"Christianity" has thus become almost synonymous with "religion." All that may be done outside of this great and good Christian tradition will be sterile. Jesus founded human religion, as Socrates founded philosophy and Aristotle science. There was philosophy before Socrates and science before Aristotle. Since Socrates and Aristotle philosophy and science have made immense progress; but all is built on the foundations they laid. Similarly, before Jesus, religious thought had passed through many revolutions; since Jesus, it has made vast conquests. Nevertheless, we have not issued, we never shall issue, from the essential idea that Jesus created; he has fixed forever the necessary manner of conceiving pure worship. The religion of Jesus is not limited. The Church has had its epochs and its phases; it has shut itself within symbols which have been or will be transitory: Jesus founded absolute religion, without exclusion, and fixing nothing but religious feeling. His symbols are not settled dogmas; they are images susceptible of unlimited interpretation. In the Gospel a theological proposition would be sought in vain. All professions of faith are travesties of the ideas of Jesus, resembling the way in which medieval scholasticism, in proclaiming Aristotle the unique master of a completed science, falsified his mode of thinking. Had Aristotle been present at scholastic debates, he would have repudiated such narrow doctrines; he would have taken the part of progressive science against the routine that clothed itself with his authority; he would have applauded its antagonists. In the same way, if Jesus could return among us, he would recognize as disciples, not those who pretend to shut him up wholly in a few phrases of the catechism, but those who labor to perpetuate his spirit. In all orders of greatness, the lasting glory is to have laid the first stone. Possibly in modern works on physics and meteorology there is not a word from Aristotle's treatises with such titles; none the less Aristotle remains the founder of natural science. Whatever may be the transformations of dogma, Jesus will remain the creator of pure religious feeling; the Sermon on the Mount will not be outstripped. No revolution can detach us in religion from the great moral and intellectual family, at the head of which shines the name of Jesus. In this sense, we are Christians, even when separated on almost every point from the Christian tradition that has gone before us.

Vie de Jésus, pp. 462, 463.

All that it is permitted to say is that, during his last days, the enormous weight of the mission he had accepted weighed cruelly upon Jesus. Human nature was for a moment reawakened. Perhaps he came to doubt his work. Fear, hesitation, took possession of him and cast him into an infirmity worse than death. The man who to a great work has sacrificed his repose and the legitimate recompenses of life, always makes a sad return upon himself when the image of death presents itself to him for the first time and seeks to persuade him that all is vain. Perhaps some of those touching recollections cherished by the strongest souls and at certain times piercing them like a sword, came to him at this moment. Did he remember the clear fountains of Galilee, where he could have had refreshment; the vine and the fig tree under which he might have been seated; the maidens who perhaps might have consented to love him? Did he execrate his bitter destiny that had forbidden him the joys conceded to all others? Did he regret his too lofty nature and, victim of his greatness, did he weep that he had not remained a simple artisan of Nazareth?

Vie, p. 391.

If we were dealing with another nature and another race, we should try to imagine Paul, in his last days, coming to recognize that he had spent his life for a dream, repudiating all the holy prophets for a book he had never read till then, *Ecclesiastes* (charming book, the only agreeable book ever composed by a Jew), and proclaiming that the happy man is he who, after passing his life in joy till his old age with the wife of his youth, dies without having lost a son. It is a characteristic trait of great Europeans to give adhesion at certain times to Epicurus, to be seized with disgust although still laboring ardently, and after having succeeded, to doubt if the cause they have served was after all worth so many sacrifices. Many dare to confess in the very heat of action, that the day a man begins to be wise is the day on which, delivered from all care, he contemplates and enjoys nature. Few at least escape tardy regrets. There is no consecrated person, priest or nun, who at fifty does not bewail his vow, and nevertheless persevere in it. We do not understand the worthy gentleman who is without a trace of skepticism; we like to have the virtuous man say now and then, "Virtue, thou art but a word"; for he who is too sure that virtue will be rewarded has not much merit; his good actions seem no more than a profitable investment. Jesus was not a stranger to this delicate sentiment; more than once his divine rôle seemed to weigh upon him. Surely it was not so with Saint Paul; he had no agony of Gethsemane, and this is one of the reasons why to us he is less attractive.

L'Antéchrist, pp. 101, 102.

In a sense, all of us, in so much as we are scholars, artists, priests, laborers at disinterested tasks, have still the right to call ourselves *ebyonim.* The friend of the true, the beautiful and the good never admits that he receives pay. The things of the soul have no price; to the scholar who enlightens it, to the priest who improves its morals, to the poet and the artist who charm it, humanity never gives more than an alms, totally disproportionate to what it has received. He who sells the ideal and considers himself paid for what he has delivered is humble indeed. The proud *Ebyon,* who thinks the kingdom of God his, sees in the portion that falls to his share here below not a salary, but the penny put into the hand of a mendicant.

Les Évangiles, p. 74.

When modern individualism has borne its last fruits; when humanity, dwindled and saddened, becomes impotent and returns to great institutions and vigorous disciplines; when our contemptible bourgeois society, or rather, our world of pygmies, has been whipped away by the heroic and ideal among human beings, then a life in common will resume all its value. A mass of great matters, such as science, will be organized in monastic form, hereditary though not through blood. The importance our age attributes to the family will diminish. Egotism, the essential law of civil society, will not suffice for great souls. All, gathering together from the most opposite points, will be leagued against vulgarity. A real sense will then be found in the words of Jesus and the ideas of the Middle Ages on poverty. We shall comprehend that possessions may be considered a point of inferiority.

Les Apôtres, p. 132.

Philosophy had seen all, expressed all, in attractive language; but these ideas needed to be spoken in popular, that is to say, in religious form. Religious movements are made only by priests. Philosophy had too much reason. The recompense she offered was not tangible enough. The poor, the uneducated, who could not approach her, were in reality without religion, without hope. Man is such a born mediocrity that he is good only when he dreams. He needs illusions in order to do at all what he ought to do for the love of goodness. To accomplish his duty, this slave has need of fear and lies. Sacrifices are obtained from the masses only by promises of pay. Christian abnegation is, after all, only a clever calculation, an investment in the kingdom of God.

Marc-Aurèle, pp. 566, 567.

The anæsthesia of Blandine, her intimate conversations with Christ while the bull tossed her in the air, the hallucination of the martyrs, who believed they saw Jesus in the person of their sister at the end of the arena bound naked to the stake,—all this legend, which on the one side carries you beyond Stoicism and on the other touches on catalepsy and the experiences of *la Salpétrière*, seems a subject expressly made for those poets, painters, thinkers, all original, all idealists, who imagine they paint only the soul, but in reality are duped by the body. Epictetus did better; he showed in the battle of life as much heroism as Attala and Sanctus; but he has no legend. The *Hegemonikon* by itself says nothing to humanity. Man is a very complex being. Crowds have never been charmed or moved by pure truth; a great man has never been made of a eunuch, nor a romance without love.

L'Église Chrétienne, pp. 476, 477.

At each tack they approached that holy land, where perfection once unveiled itself, where the ideal really existed, that land which saw the noblest of races found at one time art, science, philosophy, politics. Without doubt Paul did not experience that filial sentiment which cultivated men then felt on touching that venerable soil. He was of another world; his holy land was elsewhere.

Saint Paul, p. 167.

Such marvels little touched the Apostle; he saw the only perfect objects that have ever existed, that ever will exist, the Propylæa, that masterpiece of nobility, the Parthenon, which crushes all grandeur other than its own, the temple of the Wingless Victory, worthy of the battles it consecrated, the Erectheum, prodigy of elegance and refinement, the Errhephori, those divine maidens, with a bearing so full of grace; he saw all this and his faith was not shaken; he did not tremble. The prejudices of the iconoclastic Jew, insensible to plastic beauty, blinded him; he took these incomparable statues for idols. "His spirit," says his biographer, "was embittered, when he saw the city filled with idols." Ah! beautiful and chaste figures, true gods and goddesses, tremble; here is he who will raise the hammer against you. The fatal word is pronounced: you are idols; the error of this ugly little Jew will be your sentence of death.

Saint Paul, p. 172.

The fault of Christianity here appears. It is too entirely moral; with it beauty is entirely sacrificed. Now, in the eyes of a complete philosophy, beauty, far from being a superficial advantage, a danger, an unfitness, is a gift of God, as virtue is. It equals virtue; a beautiful woman shows one face of the divine purpose, one of the ends of God, just as much as the man of genius or the virtuous woman. She feels this, hence her pride. She feels instinctively the infinite treasure she possesses in her body; she feels indeed that, without wit, without talent, without much virtue, she counts among the highest manifestations of God. And why forbid her to put into effect the gift she has received, to set the diamond fallen to her lot? In ornamenting herself, woman fulfills a duty; she practices an art, an exquisite art, in one sense the most charming of the arts. Let us not be led astray by the smile that certain words provoke among the frivolous. The palm of genius was awarded to the Greek artist who was able to solve the most delicate of problems, to adorn the human body, that is to say, to adorn perfection itself, and we, for our part, can see nothing but a matter of rags in an attempt to collaborate in the fairest work of God, the beauty of woman. Woman's toilette, with all its refinements, belongs in its way among the high arts.

Marc-Aurèle, pp. 554, 555.

The Roman police was not very hostile to him; but they acted in these circumstances according to the habitual principles of the police. As soon as there was trouble in the street, they considered every one a disturber and, without disquieting themselves about the rights of the person who had been made a pretext for the agitation, they ordered him to be quiet or to depart. At bottom, this is to justify the riot and to establish the principle that a few fanatics can deprive a citizen of his freedom.

Saint Paul, p. 164.

One of the things that most flatters the vanity of fashionable people who occupy themselves a little with art or literature is to imagine that, if they were poor, they could earn a living with their talent.

L'Antéchrist, p. 303.

A prince is a soldier; a great prince can and ought to patronize literature; he ought not to be a literary man. Augustus, Louis XIV, presiding over a brilliant intellectual development, are, after the cities of genius like Athens and Florence, the noblest spectacle of history; Nero, Chilperic, King Louis of Bavaria are caricatures.

L'Antéchrist, p. 315.

Honor to him who suffers for a cause! Progress, I hope, will bring about the day when those vast structures that modern Catholicism has imprudently erected on the heights of Montmartre and Fourvières, shall become temples of the supreme Amnesty, and shall contain a chapel for all causes, for all victims, for all martyrs.

Marc-Aurèle, p. 344.

Saint Paul's principle: "Every authority, whatever it be, comes from God," bore its fruit, and,—a thing that Jesus had not in the least foreseen,—the Gospel became one of the foundations of absolutism. Christ had come on earth to guarantee princes their crowns. In our day does not a Roman pontiff try to prove that Jesus Christ preached and died to preserve the fortunes of the rich and to reassure capital?

L'Église Chrétienne, p. v.

Throughout the work one of the most persistent of the modern topics is socialism. The anarchistic tendencies of Jewish fanaticism, recognizing no law but the will of God, and the antipatriotic communism of the early churches, defying the imperial law against associations, naturally suggest reflections on popular labor movements of the day. Here Renan's judgment seems politically sound. "Institutions founded on communism," he says, "have a brilliant beginning, for communism always presupposes great exaltation, but they degenerate rapidly, communism being contrary to human nature." [29] In fact, no basis other than religion will suffice to sustain so much self-denial. "It is clear that an association in which the dividends are according to the needs of each, and not according to the capital contributed, can repose only on exalted abnegation and on ardent faith in a religious ideal." [30] Socialism, too, with its dream of an ideal organization of society, presents analogies with the primitive Christian sects. It is doomed to failure, however, because it is besmirched with gross materialism. To found universal happiness on political and economic measures is an impossible aspiration. The great need now, as under the Roman Empire, is the small fraternal organization that gives consolation, affords social pleasures and appeals to the heart. It is in fact noteworthy that the great history concludes, after an eloquent peroration, with the astonishingly unexpected sentence: "During two hundred years, Christianity gave consummate models of these little free reunions."

[29] *Les Apôtres*, p. 242.
[30] *Ibid.*, p. 118.

VIII

This peculiar ending suggests a few observations about the style employed in the work. To say that the reader rarely thinks of it at all is perhaps its highest praise. It is marked in general by sobriety, ease and good sense. Often miracles and theological absurdities are related with an indulgent smile, by many called irony, but it is the sort of affectionate irony used by grown people toward children. There is no violence; for although both bad and good are characterized with suitable epithets, there is always an aloofness on the part of the writer, as of one not engaged in the affair, not overpraising or blaming the actors, never really indignant or excited, but interested in understanding the drama and in viewing the varied spectacle that his theme presents. Even the most vivid and sometimes painful passages do not much disturb the reader's tranquillity. This effect results largely from the neutralizing influence of intermingling the scientific with the imaginative in immediate sequence. We are never kept long on the same level. Often the mode of speaking is distinctly ecclesiastical, the eloquence of a sermon; the next moment it is familiar, the tone of a charming *causerie;* then again the rhythmical sweep of an apostrophe will elevate the movement, or some noble object or thought will clothe itself in appropriately ornate expression. There are indeed few pages that can be called dry, although the amount of intrinsic interest and the skill displayed certainly vary in different parts of the narrative.

From a scientific point of view, it is probably a fault that interpretation is not invariably distinguished from fact; but from a literary point of view, such a distinction insistently forced upon our attention would be intolerable. The warning Renan frequently repeats ought to have been sufficient, but such is the perversity of misunderstanding that, even after his plain statement that his dates are merely approximate, he was still blamed by his censors for printing them as though they were exact. Renan carefully studied his texts, weighed their value, applied all available subsidiary helps, such as archæology, coins, parallel cases, the character of the age and country—the comparative method, in short, with all the devices of modern critical scholarship: then he formed by his imagination a picture of how Christ lived and spoke and performed healing and was tried and executed; how the stories of his resurrection arose out of a mixture of ecstatic visions and self-deceptions; then he saw the life of the early church at Jerusalem and all the subsequent incidents of his history as something that had really happened. He would have been the last to maintain that his narrative was confined to established facts: it was, on the contrary, born of intuition exercising itself upon materials provided by research. How could he present his story otherwise than in the language of a man telling a thing he knows? If, in the course of his labors, he changes his judgment upon the Fourth Gospel, or the brothers of Jesus, or the date of Montanism, the matter is sufficiently expounded in introductions and appendices. Some little dependence surely might be placed on the intelligence of the reader. He might be trusted not to be led astray by positive statements employed to express uncertainties. Besides, what, after all, is certain in history? Even when we have copious documents, we do not know the exact detail of anything. It is the general lines, the grand resultant facts, that nevertheless remain true.

In this regard, the *Origins of Christianity* is a veritable history, and a great history; but it is even greater as a work of creative imagination. Such imagination is here applied both in the interpretation of detail and in the perception of the general scope of a world movement. The whole course of human events forms a sort of setting in which this movement proceeds, sometimes coming into the foreground, sometimes receding, according as its influence upon the particular stream is increased or diminished. As the author moves on, he now looks backward to the past, now forward to the future, in order to enlarge the significance of the moment at which he pauses. Detail is added to detail, ever growing, ever developing, each rising out of the preceding in a fatal sequence. The little starting point in Galilee recedes into the far distance, Jerusalem is overtaken and left behind, then all Judea, all the ancient East, as the stream flows inevitably forward to absorb and to be absorbed by Rome. Here we have indeed what we may call a vast spiritual epic, its hero being the religious idea, and its fable one of the most significant episodes in the life progress of humanity.

CHAPTER XII

I

THE fundamental idea of the History is that Israel had a mission. To Renan there are only three national histories that are of prime interest as contributing to the world's heritage of civilization, those of Greece, Israel and Rome. From Greece we receive all our rational and progressive humanism, every intellectual, moral and artistic gift, excepting religion. Religion, with the ideal of social justice, was the contribution of Israel to the common fund, the founders of Christianity being direct continuators of the prophets, and the churches being nothing but synagogues open to the uncircumcised. Neither of these creations, however, could have conquered the world without the force of Rome, unlovely but founded on civic virtue, a force that leveled the nations and fitted the world for the propagation of Greek culture and Hebrew religion. The work of all three was thus providential; that is, indispensable for human progress.

The part of Rome does not attract Renan. While recognizing the utility of force, he finds it brutal and repulsive. The value of this contribution, moreover, is sufficiently recognized in the *Origins of Christianity*. As to Greece, however, he becomes ecstatic. "In art, O heavens, what a new apparition! What a world of gods and goddesses! What a celestial revelation! Here, above all, Greece showed herself creative. She invented beauty, as she invented reason." [1]   Al-

---

[1] Vol. iv, p. 197.

though Renan does not confess regret for the Nazarite vow
that early attached him to Jewish and Christian problems,
he yet rather envies the future historian of Greek genius.
"Happy he who at the age of sixty shall write this history
with love, after having employed his whole life in studying
the works consecrated to it by the learned." [2] One seems to
detect here a moment of such revulsion as the author imagines
in those who have renounced the world for some high calling.

This fleeting impulse does not weaken his devotion to his
task. His theme is the world mission of Israel. This mission
is conceived as the creation of Christianity, after which there
remained no important function for this race to perform.
"The man who has a vocation is good for nothing else.
Israel carried within it the religious future of the world. As
soon as it was tempted to forget itself in the vulgar paths of
other peoples, a sort of somber genius directed it toward
something entirely different, and, with accents of bitter
irony, proclaimed that justice of the ancient sort ought never
to be sacrificed." [3] Christianity was the outcome, but everything developed in Christianity had its roots in the Judaism
of the first and second centuries B. C., and the Judaism of
these centuries is a clear result of a process of development
that can be historically traced.

Not that we are dealing with certainties. The beginnings
of Judaism take us to the dawn of civilization, a region of
conjecture, centuries before the earliest documents. Even
for later epochs, there is no precision of detail. Fortunate
are the Arab historians who, after giving several versions of
an incident, can tranquilly add: "God knows how it really
was." We are warned that the chronology, so far as it is
indicated, is only approximate, the error from the time of
David on, being perhaps no more than twenty years. Exact

---

[2] Vol. i, p. vi.
[3] Vol. ii, p. 265.

dates are printed merely to help fix ideas and aid the imagination in properly spacing the succession of facts.[4] There is hardly a sentence that should not contain the word "perhaps." If the reader does not find it often enough let him suppose it throughout scattered profusely in the margin.[5] Yet, in spite of all uncertainties, the author is confident of the correctness of his final result. "Even if I should have conjectured ill on certain points, I am sure I have understood in its ensemble the unique work that the breath of God, that is to say, the soul of the world, has realized through Israel."[6]

This unique work is the achievement of the prophets, and it embraces the entire religious endeavor of mankind, since both Christianity and Islam are its offspring. "The origin of Christianity goes back to the great prophets, who introduced morality into religion toward 850 B. C.; the prophetism of the ninth century itself has its roots in the ancient ideal of patriarchal life, an ideal party created by imagination, but which had some reality in the distant past of the Israelitish tribe."[7] All the ideas of Israel were born in a way so inevitable that they seemed predestined. The product was a natural evolution, step by step, from nomadic life, through the broils of petty tribes, to Jerusalem, the Temple and the Law, on the one hand, and on the other, to the prophets, the Apocalyptic vision, the Messiah. In this evolution there are three main threads which, though often historically intertwined, may be conveniently disentangled and considered separately; the conflict between the tribal and the universal idea of God, the conflict between social ideals and political power, and the conflict between free inspiration and the sacerdotal system.

---

[4] Vol. ii, p. iv.
[5] Vol. i, p. xv.
[6] Vol. i, p. xxix.
[7] Vol. i, p. vii.

In the primitive age are found Elohim or spirits, also spoken of in the singular as a collection of spirits or the great spirit. Then God got a proper name, Jahve, which, from the religious point of view, marked a great decadence, for a proper name is the negation of the divine essence. About 1000 B. C. Jahve was a tribal god, cruel, unjust, revengeful, differing little from the god of Moab or of Edom. In the next century began the line of the prophets, the legendary Elias and Elijah, then Amos, Hosea, Micah, and, greatest of all, Isaiah, the classic genius of Judaism, who gave definitive form to Hebrew ideas. By a series of thrusts, continuous and always increasing in vigor, these enthusiasts returned to the primitive patriarchal Elohim. In their speech the local and provincial Jahve was transformed into the God who made heaven and earth and whose will is justice and righteousness. This movement is the essential fact in Hebrew history. All that preceded led up to it, for monotheism required as its basis the protecting god of a little tribe, a paternal god, not too far off for intimacy, not too abstract and absolute for personal contact. And all that followed this age only consolidated and gave organization to the prophetic impulse, so that opposition and hardship, exile and massacre, served merely to make conviction more obstinate.

Closely associated with the development of the idea of God is the conflict between social ideals and political power. No people plays two rôles at the same time. National and religious greatness are incompatible. The performance of a signal duty to humanity involves the sacrifice of little mundane hopes. While, from the patriotic point of view, the tribal god with a name marks a progress, every step toward the national idea, beneficial as it might be if it had been Israel's destiny to found a nation, was a decline in its theology. Happily, each impulse in this direction was but a passing error. There was something in Israel superior to national prejudice. This people had a mission, and until its mission was fulfilled nothing could distract it. The prophets, true depositaries of the spirit of the race, expel the exclusive god and return to the patriarchal unpatriotic idea of a just and good father, One for the whole human race. To them the events of world history were the politics of Jahve, and the conquering despot who overthrew a faithless king at Jerusalem and slaughtered his faithless subjects was hailed as Jahve's instrument. Furthermore their theocratic democracy undermined the bases of civil order. Always in conflict with royalty, they destroyed the state, but by so doing they created the originality and the historic importance of Israel.

The history of ancient Judaism furnishes the best example of the opposition between social and political questions. The thinkers of Israel are the first who revolted against the injustice of the world, who refused to undergo the inequalities, the abuses, the privileges without which there can exist no army or strong society. They compromised the existence of their little nation, but founded the religious edifice which, under the names of Judaism, Christianity, Islam, has served as a refuge for humanity to this day. Herein there is a lesson that the moderns cannot meditate enough. Nations that give themselves to social questions will perish; but if the future belongs to such questions, it will be fine to die for the cause destined to triumph. All sensible people in Jerusalem about 500 B. C. were furious at the prophets, who rendered all military and diplomatic action impossible. What a pity, however, if these sublime fools had been checked! Jerusalem would have succeeded in being a little longer the capital of an insignificant kingdom; it would not have become the religious capital of the human race.[8]

A similar conflict was waged between the prophets and the priestly order. Israel had within it two opposite currents, the alternating predominance of which constitutes its entire religious history. On the one hand, we find the spirit of the closed sect, exclusive, intolerant, antisocial, given to

---

[8] Vol. iii, p. vi.

formalism and sacrifices, buying favors from Jahve by strict observance of the Law. God becomes, in a certain sense, their private property. This perversion of religion is Pharisaism. On the other hand, we find the idealism of the prophets, their affirmation of a future of justice to humanity, their protestation against gross ritualism, and their propagation of a worship of inward feeling instead of outward sacrifices. Their God is the God of all, to whom legal impurities are as nothing compared with the impurity of evil deeds. Yet, just as the tribal god, enemy of the universal Father, was a necessary stage in the development of this idea, so the Thora, enemy of universal religion, was a necessary structure to preserve the prophets. It was, in fact, partly their creation. In its construction three periods are marked: "The first, characterized by a grandiose genius, expressed in simple formulas that the whole world might adopt (this is the age of the ancient prophets, of the Book of the Alliance, of the Decalogue); the second, stamped with a severe and touching morality, partly spoiled by a very intense fanatical pietism (this is the age of the Deuteronomist and of Jeremiah); the third, sacerdotal, narrow, utopian, full of chimeras and impossibilities (this is the age of Ezekiel and of Leviticus)."[9] The precepts of the Thora, often excellent as hyperbolic expressions of lofty moral sentiments, became senseless when regarded as a practical code. Its greatest misfortune was that it should be applied, as happened from the Asmonean revolt to the fall of Jerusalem in 70 A. D. For a time, indeed, it won a complete victory. Jerusalem belonged to Pharisees and Sadducees, to the rigid formalists and to the proud, aristocratic, irreligious priesthood. Yet, of every disinterested endeavor, something is left. The spirit of the prophets awoke again in Jesus, and the power of the Thora was broken forever.

---

[9] Vol. iii, pp. 432, 433.

While, at this time, all official glory was awarded to disputes on the Law, certain other influences were working in the direction of the new evolution. These included the rise of the synagogue in the Diaspora, the popularity of apocalyptic visions, and above all the growth of Messianism. An ancient prophet compensating himself in imagination for the deceptions of reality, had traced his ideal of a kindly, pacific king, thus for the first time presenting the traits of the Messiah, who should realize all the hopes of the nation. Each generation added its hopes and its visions, until the portrait was complete. The time was ripe for the coming of the Christ.

Such are the main threads running through this history.

II

The work is divided into ten books, two to a volume. Each book completes a topic and a period, and the interest varies with the subject matter. Book I deals with the origin of civilization and with Israel as a nomadic tribe, hardly distinguishable from other wandering groups of Semites. Their religion is the religion of the tent, a sort of Monotheism. As the epoch lies centuries before written records, we are here in the region of speculation, assisted by folklore, philology and psychology. The picture is uncertain, but not wholly undecipherable. Even though Abraham, Isaac, Jacob and the rest are mere creations of fiction, "the patriarchal age really existed; it exists still in those countries where nomad Arab life has retained its purity." [10] In Egypt the tribe became a nation, and El or the Elohim, a sort of universal divine spirit, was supplanted by Jahve, the national god with a personal name, cruel, unjust, a product and minister of national egotism. The wanderings in the wilderness are reduced from the impossible forty years to as many months, or less, and

---

[10] Vol. i, p. x.

the revelation on Sinai to a vague and awful recollection attached to this anti-human mountain, fruitless, waterless, seat of everlasting desolation, haunt of terrors and home of raging tempest, "from which, it is said, came the Thora, but never a particle of life." As the Beni-Israel was preparing to fight for a settled home in Palestine, Renan looks with a certain regret to the past. "The patriarchal era was ending; nations began; human society lost in nobility and goodness; it required a larger and stronger structure." [11]

Book II is filled with the ferocious combats of insignificant tribes, inspired by their national gods. Jahve, Camos, Dagon, are equally patriotic, and demand of their adherents equally horrible atrocities. Here, too, the details are doubtful. Perhaps Joshua has no more historic reality than Jacob. But songs were made, though not yet written, the pearls of Hebrew poetry. "The finest pages of the Bible are to spring from these verses of children and women who, after each victory, received the conqueror with cries of joy to the sound of the tambourine." [12] Meanwhile, the Ark became a faint precursor of the Temple and the tendency toward monarchy produced King Saul. After him came David, the brave, hardy, adroit bandit, capable at the same time of the worst crimes and of the most delicate sentiments. Unconscious agent of the forces of the world, he built a fortress on Mount Sion and thus founded Jerusalem.

Book III continues the story of David's reign, carries us through the age of Solomon and ends with the political severance of the northern from the southern kingdom. In this narrative there stand out from the petty details three points of supreme importance for the history of Judaism, the establishment of the exclusive worship of Jahve, the building of the Temple, and the separation of Israel from Judah. The success of Jahve's servants was of course the success of

---

[11] Vol. i, p. 210.
[12] Vol. i, p. 305.

Jahve himself. If David was cruel and deceitful, it was Jahve who commanded this cruelty and deceit. When the king punished crimes at which he had connived and thus succeeded in ridding himself of troublesome accomplices, he acted as the divine avenger. In return for his devotion and his burnt offerings, Jahve, according to contract, awarded him victory, bestowed upon him power and fortune, and maintained his descendants upon the throne. As a result of this belief, the national god became firmly established in the consciousness of the people. Moreover, when the king brought the Ark to its tent on Sion, he unwittingly performed a decisive act in the history of the world. Solomon, just as unwittingly, in building the Temple, as a purely royal undertaking, a plaything, a domestic sanctuary, established a permanent center for the worship of the tribal divinity who grew into a universal god. On the other hand, the secession of the northern tribes, by destroying the political power of the government, procured freedom for the prophets, and thus assured the transcendant destiny of Israel.

With Book IV we enter upon the most significant epoch in the evolution of Hebrew religious ideas. Here are discussed the earliest compositions which entered into the construction of the Bible, patriarchal idyls, and heroic legends, first written in the northern kingdom about 900 B. C. Like a breath from the springtime of the world, uniting exquisite freshness with grandiose crudity, these writings, still discernible within later compilations in which they are imbedded, preserve half the poetry of humanity. To the same period belongs the first written form of the Law, which later developed into the inflexible Thora. But most important of all are the prophets, who maintained a reactionary ideal of pastoral or agricultural life, without a regular army, central authority or court with princely aristocracy, without temple or fixed altar or priestly caste. Royalty was conquered, and the future was placed in the hands, not of wise kings and sensible states-

men, but of visionaries, utopians, inspired democrats, who made and unmade dynasties, preached limitless theocracy, established religion and ruined the state. Here we meet Elias and Elijah, real individuals, indeed, but so overlaid with legend that they have become mere personifications of the prophetic ideal; Amos and Hosea, who proclaimed that God loves goodness rather than sacrifices; and greatest of all, Isaiah, the classic genius of Judaism, who gave definitive form to the Hebraic ideas of Providence and social justice, which Jesus and the Apostles had only to repeat. Sad to say, the prophets are to such an extent soiled by hatred and barbarism that, in reading the hideous stories of their vengeance and cruelty, we are glad to think these the mere inventions of later admirers; but, in spite of the prophetic maledictions and blood-thirstiness, Jahve becomes with these fanatics the God who has created heaven and earth and who loves justice and righteousness. Prophetism is thus the most decisive event in Jewish history, "the beginning of the chain that in nine hundred years finds its last link in Jesus." [13]
The Fourth Book ends with the fall of Samaria.

Thenceforth Judah pursued alone the work laid upon Israel as a whole. It pursued this work with a consecutiveness far superior to that which the tribes of the north had been able to put into it. Half a century, indeed, before the capture of Samaria, almost the whole activity of the Hebrew genius had been concentrated in Judah. Prophetism had arrived at its essential results; monotheism, God (or Jahve) being the sole cause of the phenomena of the universe; the justice of Jahve, the necessity that this justice should be realized on earth and for each individual within the period of his life; democratic puritanism of manners, hatred of luxury, of profane civilization; absolute confidence in Jahve; worship of Jahve consisting above all in purity of heart. The vastness of such a revolution is astonishing, and, on reflection, we find that the moment of this creation is the most fecund of all religious history. Even the initial movement of Christianity

---

[13] Vol. ii, p. 329.

in the first century of our era must yield to this extraordinary movement of Jewish prophetism of the eighth century before Christ. Jesus is in Isaiah all complete. The destiny of Israel in the development of humanity is as clearly written towards 720 B. C. as was that of Greece two hundred years later.[14]

Book V continues the story of the monotheistic prophets, who solidified the work so that it survived the destruction of Jerusalem by Nebuchadnezzar. The little city of David, exalted by the fall of Samaria, developed a new intensity of religious life, manifested in an unparalleled creative activity. Moral and social problems became the essence of this religion. The ideal is a theocratic republic, and to serve Jahve is the first duty of the state. The friends of Jahve, the élite, are the poor and humble. They are just, faithful and righteous, while the rich are hard, violent and impious. The reign of Ezechias is the classic epoch of Hebrew literature and its masterpiece is the Book of Job. But the great figure of the age is Jeremiah, whose terrible fanaticism concentrated the energetic germs of Judaism into an indestructible force and gave to a local worship the capacity to become universal. This somber genius, a radical destroyer in politics, rejoicing in the extermination of peaceful citizens and, sympathizing with the fierce heathen agent of Jahve's vengeance, was yet a powerful creator in religion, who cast his spell upon Jerusalem and determined the religious destiny of humanity. Without him there would have been no Christianity. Then come the fantastic visions of the exiled Ezekiel, source from which all apocalyptic imagery has been drawn. At this moment Judah is transplanted from Palestine to Mesopotamia only to redouble the intensity of its Judaism within the walls of Babylon.

Book VI covers the exile. In captivity the worldly were absorbed, the saints alone remained separate, sustained by

---

[14] Vol. ii, pp. 538, 539.

trust that Jahve would keep his word and reëstablish his
worship in a rebuilt Jerusalem under an ideal David who
would cause justice to reign. The old books were again rewritten with the addition of a priestly Law, not fitted to
realities, but speculative, chimerical, socialistic. Ezekiel continues his labors, but the great progressive thinker, the culmination of three centuries of religious effort, was the anonymous prophet (the second Isaiah) who saw that Israel's
mission was the establishment of true religion for the whole
human race. For the first time, a voice proclaimed that all
peoples have only one God, whose temple is the universe and
whose ritual is justice. "With him we are on the top of a
mountain from which Jesus is seen on the summit of another,
and between the two lies a great hollow." [15] Meanwhile
Cyrus has overthrown Babylon and the little caravan starts
across the desert.

Cantate Domino Canticum Novum, this was the inaugural chant
of the era now opening. Poor humanity needs to affirm that it
intones a new song when often it only repeats the old tunes.
No people has ever lived on hope so much as the Jews. Judaism
and nascent Christianity are religions of obstinate hope, per-
sisting in spite of all appearances. The return from Babylon
was hope pushed to folly, and here again folly was found to be
a good counselor, at least so far as concerns the general interests
of the world. In the history of Judaism this can be called the
solemn hour, the hour that decides death or life. If the return
had not taken place, Judah would have had the fate of Israel; it
would have been absorbed in the East; Christianity would not
have existed; the Hebrew writings would have been lost; we
should have known nothing of those stories that charm and console us. The little troop that crossed the desert indeed carried
with it the future; it founded definitively the religion of humanity.[16]

Throughout the next four books we are in the hollow between the two mountains. The great creative epoch is past,

---

[15] Vol. iii, p. 502.
[16] Vol. iii, pp. 523, 524.

and effort is now absorbed in solidifying, amplifying and working out details, the most prominent of which concern the development and application of the Thora.

Book VII: By a miracle of faith and hope, the Jahvists, returned to Judea, reëstablished their worship and rebuilt Jerusalem. In this city the high priest becomes the real ruler and the new Temple becomes the seat of an elaborate liturgy. The Levitical code prescribes ceremonies, holy feasts, pilgrimages, sacrifices, fasting, penance, purification, expiation, all legal, exterior, the materialism of religion. If a prophet finds himself in the midst of the priesthood, he no longer speaks to the crowd words of fire, but in retirement writes apocalyptic visions. In fact the prophets have passed away; they must be brought back from Sheol. In the stories told of Elias and Jonah appear the first traces of the resurrection of the dead. It is in the fifth century, too, that the form of the Hebrew Bible is definitively fixed. The editing is incoherent, but so much the better. "Thus was formed in about four centuries, by the commixture of the most diverse elements, this strange conglomeration where are found intermingled fragments of epopee, débris of sacred history, articles of customary law, ancient popular songs, tales of nomads, utopias or pretended religious laws, legends stamped with fanaticism, bits of prophecy, the whole implanted in a pious veinstone that has made of a heap of profane débris a sacred book, the soul of a people." [17] At this time too the chain of the Thora is forged, a bondage that Israel has never broken. The doctor versed in the Law rises to eminence. Indeed the Thora absorbs the whole intellectual effort of the race. It is all they desire to know, their entire philosophy and science, a source, not only of happiness, but of pleasure, "a sort of game of solitaire for poor old decrepit Israel." [18]

Book VIII: With the conquest of Alexander, we arrive at

[17] Vol. iv, p. 112.
[18] Vol. iv, p. 186.

the first contact with western civilization. The glory of Greece, with its science, philosophy and art, spreads over the Orient. Palestine, though in spirit untouched by this culture, is yet subjugated politically, until the Maccabees arise and establish national autonomy. Nevertheless, residence among the Greeks in Alexandria and Antioch, which now become important Jewish centers, leads to far-reaching developments. As there could be but one Temple, and sacrifices were forbidden elsewhere, there grew up, afar from sacerdotal Jerusalem and particularly in Alexandria, a religion without altar and without priests, somewhat resembling that of which the prophets had dreamed. Here we find the germ of the later synagogue, the most original and fecund of Jewish creations, a little group meeting to sing hymns and to read and discuss the Law and the Prophets. For those who had forgotten their Hebrew, as well as for outsiders, a translation into Greek was made, the Septuagint, a version full of errors. This became the Bible of the early Church and it is often from its downright blunders that Messianic ideas were destined to grow. Meanwhile, persecution produced martyrs, and, since the Jews had no conception of a soul as distinct from the body, these martyrs, whom a just God was presumed to reward, strengthened the notion of the resurrection of the just in the flesh to enjoy the future Kingdom of God on earth. Such is the inspiration of the Book of Daniel, which, ill-written, flat, prolix, incorrect, often untranslatable, marks the passage from the monotheistic to the Messianic age. It became the model for all later apocalyptic visions, which repeat its images and which must in the same fashion gain credence by coming forth under the celebrated name of some ancient prophet or sage.

Book IX: The long narrative is drawing to its close; we are coming to the conditions into which Jesus was born. The whole secret of Jewish history from this time forth is found in the opposition of Pharisee and Sadducee. On the other hand, something much like Christian monasticism is exhibited in the communistic communities of the Essenes, with their rigorous discipline, their special rites and their sacred repast in common. The first of the series of apocalyptic poems attributed, not to a Hebrew prophet, but to the everliving Sibyl, makes its appearance in Alexandria. And now we are taken for a time out of the current to enjoy the admirable pages devoted to Ecclesiastes, the work of an incredulous man of the world calmly viewing the absurdities of human fate, one who finds his modern counterpart in Heine. In the midst of the Bible, this book is "like a little composition of Voltaire astray amid the folios of a theological library."

Book X: At last the Roman power enters into possession of the East. Herod needs its support for his tyranny. Horrible as this was, his most famous massacre is yet fictitious. "The list of Herod's real crimes is long enough to need no amplification from those that are apocryphal. Jesus was not born when Herod died at Jerusalem. Yet, in a sense, it is true that Herod tried to kill Jesus. If his idea of a profane Jewish kingdom had prevailed, there would have been no Christianity." [19] But a permanent secular state could not be established in Jerusalem; it was contrary to destiny. Several insurrections were suppressed by Varus. "Two thousand unfortunates were crucified; order reigned anew." [20] Judea became a Roman province under a procurator, an office later filled by Pilate. At the same time, Jews spread throughout the cities of the Mediterranean, forming the Diaspora and conducting a propaganda that prepared the way for Paul and other Christian missionaries. In Alexandria Philon attempted to reduce Judaism to a sort of deism or natural religion and the *Book of Wisdom* enunciated the doctrine of the immortality of the soul. The age was naïvely credulous; assertions were made and accepted with-

[19] Vol. v, p. 303.
[20] Vol. v, p. 306.

428

out reason, one could lie and believe his own lies. It produced *Enoch, The Assumption of Moses, The Little Genesis,* books that belong to the same group as the synoptic Gospels and the Apocalypse named of John. There were in Judea opposed tendencies, groups and coteries of many sorts, Pharisees, Sadducees, Essenes, Zealots, and also Apocalyptists and Apocryphists. Among these latter what may be called the mythology of the Messiah became fixed. Everything was ready for the new movement. "The remote cause of Christianity was the ancient prophets of Israel. The mediate cause was the eschatological movement which, since the Book of Daniel, so strongly agitated the Jewish spirit. The proximate cause was the Messianic school of Judea, whose manifestations are the *Book of Enoch* and *The Assumption of Moses.* The immediate cause was John the Baptist." [21]

The last chapter, the link with the *Origins of Christianity,* is headed *Finito libro, sit laus et gloria Christo.* The lowlands, where we have been traveling since the days of the prophets, have led us to the second mountain, on top of which stands Jesus. Christianity is the end, the final cause of Judaism, the résumé of its evolution, the masterpiece by which it has conquered the world. In Jesus all the messianism since Daniel arrived at its minority. "The prophets, vanquished by the Thora after the return from captivity, are now definitively victorious. . . . Jesus, the last of the prophets, puts the seal on the work of Israel. . . . Dreams of the future, the Kingdom of God, hopes without end are to be born under the guidance of this divine enchanter and to become for centuries the nourishment of humanity." [22] For Jesus is a real personality, and not only real, but great and beautiful. He inspired in a little circle a love so miraculous that it produced the resurrection and, being spread abroad, inspired the adoration of the world.

---

[21] Vol. v, p. 413.
[22] Vol. v, p. 415.

III

The subject matter here is of slighter interest than that in the *Origins of Christianity*. The period covered in five volumes is so long that the incidents are sometimes overcrowded, and the incidents themselves are for the most part insignificant, the interminable battles of little tribes led by obscure captains and kings, sieges, burnings of towns, pillage and slaughter. What do we care for the tediously reiterated broils of Israel, Judah, Edom, Moab and Ammon? They were once dignified by being placed under the patronage of the Almighty; Renan finds a different element of interest. "This trivial history of a little people, without great military institutions, without political consequence, without splendor in art, would hardly merit telling if, along side of a profane life in no wise superior to that of Moab or Edom, the Israelites had not possessed a series of extraordinary men who, at a time when the idea of right hardly existed, stood as defenders of the weak and oppressed.[23] But the prophets themselves become, it must be confessed, a little tedious. Their outbursts of hatred and vengeance, their invectives and woeful warnings, even their pictures of the ideal future, full of joy for the righteous, but also full of punishment for the wicked, who are to be exterminated in a sea of blood, are not attractive in themselves and, when often repeated, become monotonous. The topic, indeed, could not be treated as history without displeasing repetitions. Perhaps a narrative of half the length would have been more successful.

Moreover, the learned discussion, which Renan in his earlier work had taken pains to conceal, is here forced upon the attention. The text is encumbered with a multitude of Hebrew words, phrases and proper names. Often the treatment is either not sufficiently detailed to present all the

---

[23] Vol. ii, p. 420.

steps in the argument, or too detailed to be followed without looking up references. The reader is supposed to be familiar with the works of Reuss, Graf, Kuenen, Noeldeke, Wellhausen, Stade, where he "will find the explanation of many points that could not be treated in detail without repeating what had already been well said." [24] The author even states that, if he should not live to finish the fourth volume (the original plan was for four volumes), he would ask his publishers to have one of the numerous German works on that part of his subject translated to complete the story.[25]

The artist is obviously somewhat oppressed by the scholar, and yet imaginative power is by no means lacking. In spite of the inferiority of the material, such imaginative power appears both in the general scheme and in the vivid interpretation of individual facts.

As might be expected, striking characters do not furnish so prominent a feature as in the *Origins of Christianity*. The patriarchs and such early leaders as Moses and Joshua, wrapped in the mist of legend, are too shadowy for the grasp of fact; the prophets, too, though they furnish the central theme of the work, have little distinctness of personality; and the oriental despots, big and little, who abound throughout, give the impression of a gloomy sameness of crime, tyranny and cruelty. Perhaps the most individual figure is David, the bold, rough warrior and adroit politician, the graceful, elegant and intelligent hero, bandit and king, a ruler who could profit by every crime without ever directly committing one. Of Solomon the outline is even more frankly a result of intuition. "Some thousand years before Christ there reigned in a little Syrian acropolis a petty sovereign, intelligent, free from national prejudices, understanding nothing of the true mission of his race, wise according to the opinion of his age, without being morally superior to the average of oriental

---

[24] Vol. i, p. xx.
[25] Vol. i, p. ix.

despots of every epoch.'' [26] A greater king than Solomon was Ahab, so grievously calumniated by the Jahvist historians, for he was ''brave, intelligent, moderate, devoted to the ideas of civilization.'' [27] We thus get a few sketches, no finished portraits, for the traits of the subjects are indistinct and the colors faint from distance.

For vividness modern comparisons are freely employed. Rameses II is an Egyptian Louis XIV; David's limited racial sentiment was like that of Abd-el-Kadir; the history of the world is the history of the murderer, Troppmann, who, if he had escaped to America, would have become a conservative and made a brilliant use of his plunder.[28]

[26] Vol. ii, p. 174.

[27] Vol. ii, p. 301.

[28] Troppmann, a twenty-year-old Alsatian, was the chief figure in a sensational murder trial in 1869. On September 20, six corpses, those of a mature woman, of a youth of sixteen, of three young boys and a little girl, were found buried in a shallow trench in a field between the railroad station of Pantin and a place called Quatre Chemins. Every aspect of the case was exploited by the newspapers, columns being given to stories, letters, interviews and identifications. It was ascertained that the bodies were those of the family of Jean Kinck, of Alsace, who had himself mysteriously disappeared. Three or four days after the murder, Troppmann was arrested at Le Havre while attempting to embark for America under the name of Fisch, and on his person were found bonds, deeds, watches and other property belonging to the Kincks. The evidence was gradually concentrated upon him as the criminal, but, being an inventive liar, he kept up interest in the affair by mystifications to the very day of his condemnation. It developed that he had murdered Jean Kinck at Wattwiller, in August, robbed him and forged his name to deeds. Shortly after, by forged letters, he had lured the family to Paris, killed the sixteen-year-old son first, and then on the final night butchered the mother and the four younger children. He was tried December 28-31 in the Cour d'Assises de la Seine, in the presence of unprecedented crowds, including even members of the diplomatic corps. All Paris was agog. The sober *Débats* itself gave as much as two pages a day to the testimony at the trial and a whole page to the speeches of counsel. Troppmann displayed the utmost coolness throughout and lied tenaciously to the very end. Conviction, however, required only ten minutes' deliberation, the culprit was condemned to death, and on January 18, 1870, he was executed. The execution is recorded in the Goncourt *Journal* under date of January 19, 1870. By 1894 Troppmann was so far forgotten that the allusion to him is omitted by the editor when printing a portion of Book X in the *Revue des deux Mondes* (January 1).

Jahve came to be identical with God just as Christ took on God's functions in the Middle Ages and just as to-day God is said to have been taken out of the schools because the crucifix was removed. The tales about Solomon, together with the *Song of Songs,* constitute the divertissement and the humorous part in the great somber opera created by Hebrew genius. The Levitical Thora is not practical law, but consists of general indications, such as might be elaborated among the companions of the Comte de Chambord or discussed in Socialist clubs.

Such expressions may be considered mere ornaments or asides to relieve the author's mind; but there is a group of comparisons which are of the essence of the subject, and it is these that, in the preface to his third volume, Renan upholds against adverse criticism. He, for example, constantly equates the prophets with modern journalists and finds in their teachings the essence of modern Socialism.

On the first point, one quotation will suffice. "Prophetism has real analogies with modern journalism, which, like it, is an individual force (and on the whole, beneficial) along side of the government, the higher classes, the clergy. Jewish prophetism was a journalism speaking in the name of God. By turns it saved and destroyed dynasties. The prophets are at once a model for patriots, and the worst enemies of their country." [29]

The relation of prophetism to socialism is based upon the preoccupation of each with moral and social questions. Both grow furious over abuses that are inevitable in a great organized society. Both declaim against the army, jeer at patriotism, proclaim justice for the people to be the sole desirable end. For both, where the poor are victims and the rich enjoy privileges, there is no fatherland. In such a régime as they conceive there could be no culture, no art, no

---

[29] Vol. ii, p. 486.

science, no philosophy. The welfare of the individual in his little group is all that is sought. And who is to protect this welfare? Neither prophet nor socialist has found a practical answer, but such visionaries are incapable of disillusionment. "After each failure, they begin again; no one has yet found the solution, but it will be found. The idea never comes to them that the solution does not exist." [30] These fanatics may succeed in destroying their state, as the prophets destroyed theirs, they may succeed in bringing upon the world a new medievalism, but equilibrium will finally be restored. "The movement of the world is the result of the parallelogram of two forces, liberalism on the one hand, and socialism on the other—liberalism in origin Greek, socialism in origin Hebrew—liberalism impelling toward the largest human development, socialism taking account above all of strict justice and of the welfare of the greatest number, which is often sacrificed in reality to the needs of civilization and of the state." [31]

The contrast between Hebraism and Hellenism here indicated greets us on the first page of the preface to volume one and is still before us on the last page of the final volume. If there were anything that could have attracted Renan from the glory of Israel, it would have been the glory of Greece. "Greece raised the eternal framework of civilization; to this Israel brought an addition, a capital correction, the care for the weak, the obstinate demand for individual justice." [32] Yet sometimes Israel seems mean in comparison. "Esdras and Nehemiah coincide with the age of Pericles. They are contemporary with Herodotus, Æschylus, Socrates, Hippocrates. While Israel accepts with joy the yoke of the Achemenides, while Jahve is fully occupied in turning the heart of a great king to favor his people, while a Jew is proud to

---

[30] Vol. iii, p. 497.
[31] Vol. ii, p. 541.
[32] Vol. iii, p. 251.

be cupbearer, valet, spy to the king of Persia, Greece resists to the death, defeats Darius, Xerxes, Artaxerxes, and saves civilization.'' [33] But Israel, too, had its heroic age, and furnishes one of the two streams from which the refreshment of mankind has been drawn.

Israel had, like Greece, its epic collection in this primitive book (*The Wars of Jahve*) of heroic songs and deeds, certain parts of which, recognizable still in the later books, have made the literary fortune of the Bible. Answering the same ideal, the Bible and Homer have not been supplanted. They remain the two poles of the poetic world; from them the plastic arts will continue indefinitely to choose their subjects; for the material detail in them, without which there is no art, is always noble. The heroes of these beautiful stories are youths, strong and healthy, a bit superstitious, passionate, simple and great. Together with the exquisite stories of the patriarchal age, these anecdotes of the period of the Judges constitute the charm of the Bible. The narrators of later epochs, the Hebrew romancers, even the Christian annalists, take all their colors from this magic palette. The two great sources of inconscient and impersonal beauty were thus opened at about the same time, 900 B. C., among the Aryans and among the Semites. Since then, we have lived on them. The literary history of the world is the history of a double current which descends from the Homerides to Virgil, from the biblical story-tellers to Jesus or, if you wish, to the Evangelists. These old tales of patriarchal tribes, along with the Greek epopee, have remained the great enchantment of later ages, formed esthetically from a less pure clay.[34]

IV

Such are the main currents of thought in these volumes. A few quotations will illustrate the nature of the *obiter dicta* in which our author is so inexhaustibly rich.

Generally in history man is punished for the good he does and rewarded for the bad. (Vol. i, p. 411.)

---

[33] Vol. iv, p. 192.
[34] Vol. ii, p. 235.

In consequence of the enormous egotism of men, giving to one what has been stolen from another is a game that nearly always succeeds. (Vol. i, p. 437.)

Order, as I have often said, has been created in the world by the brigand turned policeman. (Vol. ii, p. 16.)

The Bible is believed because of an appearance of infantine candor, according to the false idea that truth comes from the mouths of children; what in reality comes from the mouth of the child is falsehood. (Vol. ii, p. 221.)

Those paid by drafts on a future life suffer more patiently than the disillusioned the iniquities inherent in human society. (Vol. ii, p. 434.)

Each human development has its hour of perfect accord, when all parts of the national genius strike their highest note in unison. (Vol. iii, p. 68.)

Not only is virtue not rewarded here below; it may almost be said that it is punished. It is baseness that is rewarded; for it are all the profits; if this were not so, the clever would turn their backs on it. Heroic virtue, steadfast unto death, finds in such heroism itself the exclusion of all possible remuneration. (Vol. iii, p. 80.)

There are men before whom popularity runs, almost without being sought, whom opinion takes, so to speak, by the hand and whom it orders to commit crimes in view of a program it imposes on them. Such was Bonaparte; such was David. The criminal, in this case, is primarily the crowd, a true Lady Macbeth, who, having chosen its favorite, intoxicates him with the tragic words: "Thou shalt be King." (Vol. i, p. 415.)

Among peoples devoted to an idea, the law is made by a minority; the French Revolution was the wager of a small number of fanatics, who succeeded in creating the belief that they had carried the nation. They alone are spoken of; the flock of sheep serves but to add numbers. History concerns itself merely with the ambitious and the passionate. (Vol. iii, p. 391.)

Liberty is a creation of modern times. It is the consequence of an idea not possessed by antiquity, that of the State protecting the most opposite forms of human activity and remaining neutral in matters of conscience, taste and feeling. (Vol. iv, p. 82.)

The final purpose of France was the Revolution. Those who contributed to the making of France, even the least revolutionary of men, labored for the Revolution. (Vol. iv, p. 132.)

In costly governments the populace sees the tax it pays, not the result obtained from the tax. (Vol. v, p. 283.)

The ordinary tactics of clerical parties is to drive the civil authority to its last hold, and then to represent as atrocious violence the acts of firmness they have provoked. (Vol. ii, p. 293.)

All were massacred and the city was burnt. Very odious indeed. But there is no race whose ancestors have acted better. (Vol. i, p. 353.)

A humble military man is a contradiction. (Vol. iii, p. 279.)

When a nation has made the Bible, it may be pardoned the Talmud. (Vol. iv, p. 129.)

The enemies of the clericals have no right to die without the intervention of heaven. (Vol. iv, p. 388.)

Germany, by her lofty philosophy, by the voice of her men of genius, proclaimed better than any other race the absolute, impersonal, supreme character of the Divinity. When she became a nation, she was led by the way of all flesh to particularize God. The Emperor William I often spoke of *unser Gott* and of his confidence in the God of the Germans. Nationality and philosophy have indeed little in common. The national spirit, among other pettinesses, has the pretension of possessing a god. . . . A nation is always egotistical. It wants the God of heaven and earth to have no other thought than to serve its interests. . . . Strange contradiction, frightful blasphemy! God is the possession of no people, of no individual. As well say: *My absolute, my infinite, my Supreme Being.* (Vol. i, p. 264.)

Poor humanity is so formed that it obtains good only at the cost of evil, truth only by passing through error. (Vol. ii, p. 291.)

Human things are composed of matter and spirit. Liberty and chains, that which excites and that which restrains, the sublime and the commonplace are equally necessary to construct a grand combination that will live. (Vol. iii, p. 214.)

Century after century we perceive such transformations. We see the brigand of Adullam and of Siklag take little by little the qualities of a saint. He is made the author of the Psalms, the sacred singer, the type of the future Savior. Jesus must be a son of David. The Evangelical biography is falsified on a multitude of points by the idea that the life of the Messiah should reproduce the traits of that of David. Pious souls soothed by the sentiments of resignation and tender melancholy found in the most beautiful of liturgical books, believe themselves in communion with this bandit; humanity believes in final justice on the testimony of David, who never thought of it, and of the Sibyl, who never existed. *Teste David cum Sibylla!* O divine comedy! (Vol. i, pp. 450-451.)

Budding Christianity was soiled with these chimeras. We regret the fact, but who knows if it would have succeeded without them? Weakness is the condition of strength; popular achievements are never accomplished without follies and excesses. (Vol. iv, p. 170.)

In religious history the import of a text is, not what the author meant to say, but what the needs of the time made him say. The religious history of mankind is made up of mistranslations. (Vol. iv, p. 193.)

Mankind is so made that the diverse elements of its composition are reciprocal enemies. When one part rises, another declines. A moral people is almost always hostile to science; I fear, on the other hand, that what we scholars accomplish does not much serve the moral progress of the masses. The morality of the populace demands enormous sacrifices of the reason; the progress of reason is injurious to the morality of the masses, who are ruled by instinct. (Vol. iv, pp. 359, 360.)

No one knows what he founds. Jesus thought he was founding the religion of the spirit; the religious system sprung from him has been as superstitious as any other; the Jesuits have named themselves the Company of Jesus. (Vol. iv, p. 130.)

Pietists are essentially persecutors; they loudly complain when they are the victims; and yet they find it very bad to be hindered from persecuting others; they are so sure they are right. (Vol. iii, p. 120.)

The Protestants suppressed masses and indulgences, but retained and even exaggerated the inspiration of the Bible and the merits of the blood of Jesus Christ. These distinctions, which seem naïve to us, are the conditions of active force. Poor human species! How it longs for the good! But how ill, on the whole, it is made for truth! (Vol. iii, p. 189.)

He who fears self-deception and calls no one blind; who does not know precisely what is the end of humanity and yet loves his fellow-men; who seeks truth, yet doubting, and says to his adversary: "Perhaps you see better than I"; who, in short, allows others the full liberty he takes for himself; he can sleep tranquilly and await in peace the day of judgment—if there be one. (Vol. iii, p. 280.)

He had no right to kill one less heroic than himself. Each is judge of his own conscience; he should not impose his principles on others. But, let us hasten to say, there would be no religious hero under such circumstances. Godefroy de Bouillon, Simon de Montfort, Charles d'Anjou needed to believe their enemies destined to hell. We are too liberal and too well-bred to express ourselves so absolutely. I believe that M. de Mun is at least five-sixths wrong. But my philosophy teaches me that he must be right for the other sixth, and if I were confronted with one of his partisans, my good manners would oblige me to seek this sixth, where I could agree with him. Judas Maccabeus did well not to be so well-bred. (Vol. iv, p. 339.)

All religions, just as all philosophies, are vain; but religion is not vain, nor is philosophy. (Vol. i, p. xxviii.)

Philo and Josephus were men of letters, and men of letters accomplish little. (Vol. v, p. 365.)

A prince is necessarily a man of the world, following the fashions and making them; he cannot live with gross, ill-educated people; he is constrained to belong to high society. . . . More than one evolution of this sort has occurred among the parvenus of present-day democracy. Power is a civil and polished thing; whatever the road by which a man reaches it, he becomes at once well-bred; at least he feels the need of living with well-bred people. (Vol. v, p. 50.)

Religion is a necessary imposture. The grossest means of throwing dust in the eyes cannot be neglected with such a silly race as the human species, created as it is for error, so that, even when it admits the truth, it never admits it for good reasons. (Vol. v, p. 106.)

The impatience of men can do nothing to advance the progress of things. At bottom the *beni elohim* are right; the creation is good and does great honor to the Eternal; the objections of Satan against the works of God are essentially misplaced; but milliards of centuries will probably be necessary in order that a just God should be a reality. Let us wait. (Vol. iii, p. 86.)

Each answers (i. e., in favor of liberalism or socialism) according to his moral temperament, and that is enough. The universe, which never says its last word to us, reaches its end through the infinite variety of its germs. What Jahve wills always happens. Let us be tranquil; if we are among those who are deceived, who work against the grain of the supreme will, it is not very important. Mankind is one of the innumerable ant hills in space in which the experiments of reason are being carried on; if we fail, others will succeed. (Vol. ii, p. 542.)

The objections to materialism will never be silenced. There is no case of a thought or feeling without a brain, or with a brain in process of decomposition. On the other hand, man will never be persuaded that his destiny is like that of animals. Even if it should be proved, he would not believe it. This is a thought that should give us courage to think freely. Our necessary beliefs are beyond reach. Mankind will listen to us only so far as our systems fit its duties and its instincts. Let us say what we think; woman will none the less continue her joyous song, children will not for our words be oppressed with care, nor will youth be less intoxicated; the virtuous man will remain virtuous; the Carmelite nun will continue to macerate her flesh, the mother to sacrifice herself, the bird to sing, the bee to make honey. (Vol. v, pp. 182, 183.)

The immediate future is obscure. It is not certain that it shall have assurance of light. Credulity has deep roots. Socialism, with the complicity of Catholicism, may introduce a new Middle Age, barbarians, churches, eclipses of liberty and individuality, of civilization, in short. But the final future is sure. The future certainly will believe no longer in the supernatural; for the supernatural is not true, and all that is not true is condemned to die. Nothing lasts but truth. This poor truth seems indeed abandoned, served as it is by an imperceptible minority. Be tranquil; it will triumph. All that serves truth is added together and preserved like a small capital, but it is held; no part of the little treasure is lost. All that is false, on the contrary, falls to pieces. The false founds nothing; while the little edifice of truth is of steel and rises forever. (Vol. v, pp. 420, 421.)

V

By the time Renan had completed his work, the views of Hebrew history held by him had ceased to excite surprise by their novelty. Biblical criticism, in its general outline, had already reached the public. The distinction between sacred and profane history could no longer be maintained. The violence of antagonism was quieted. "Since I began forty years ago to speak to the public of religious history, serious changes have taken place. There is no longer dispute on the foundation itself of religion, and that, in my opinion, is a very sensible progress. It is to recognize that in the infinite there is room for every one to shape his romance." [35]

Whatever Renan's dreams of the infinite may be, this work is not a romance. Yet it is, as has already been said, a creation of the imagination. The author is even more detached from his subject than he was in the *Origins of Christianity;* he stands outside and observes. Sometimes his view seems pessimistic, but he more often dwells on the good than on the bad. If, toward the end, the old man sometimes murmurs "Vanity of vanities," he does it in a genial, rather than in a somber tone. In fact, the last two volumes are rather more lively in style than the first three. We are left with an overwhelming impression of fatality in the course of events, an impression caused, as in a Shakespearean tragedy, by a

[35] Vol. i, p. xxv.

series of apparent accidents. If a single step in the action were missing or were different, the result could not have been attained. The future of humanity rests so frequently on a cast of the dice, and yet the winner of the cast is pre-destined. What Jahve wills always happens. There is a vast, inexplicable purpose in human affairs.

Renan felt that, in order to be consequent, he ought to have begun with the *History of the People of Israel*. We are glad that, attracted by Jesus and charmed by the dream of a kingdom of God whose law should be love, the historian plunged into the midst of his subject with the *Life of Jesus*, and treated the first century and a half of Christianity before taking up the earlier epoch. The order in which the books were written is the order in which they should be read. It is the story of the final achievement that gives significance to the evolution that precedes. And while the real climax of the whole is the *Life of Jesus*, the first of the series, it nevertheless seems entirely appropriate that the old scholar should joyously chant his *Nunc Dimittis* after he had written the final words of his less vivid, but by no means shrunken, history. These final words look to the future of the world he was ready to leave: "Israel will not be vanquished unless military force should once again take possession of the world, and found anew servitude, forced labor, feudalism. This is by no means probable. After centuries of struggles between national rivalries, humanity will be peacably organized; the sum of evil will be greatly diminished; with very few exceptions, every one will be content to live. With some inevitable modifications, the Jewish program will be accomplished; without a compensating heaven, justice will really exist on the earth."

CHAPTER XIII

CONCLUSION

AFTER Renan had ripened, the principal features of his character were amiability and benevolence. He could turn a blackguard out of his house with the utmost severity, but his general rule was, in spite of unhappy experiences, to regard every man as meritorious until he was proved otherwise. Even in poor scholarship, he could forgive everything but arrogance and charlatanism. Always using his influence toward concord and tolerance, he sought to eliminate personalities and violent polemic. "We seem to see him still," said Barbier de Maynard,[1] "seated in the same place, putting his almost universal knowledge at the service of our scientific discussions, and when, by chance, though rarely, they became a little too lively, intervening with words full of good humor and delicacy, often even with a smile, that kindly smile that seemed to say to the antagonists: 'Softly, dear colleagues, beware of treating one another as ignoramuses; the public will perhaps take you at your word, or at least laugh at your expense.'"

The charm of old age is its mellowness, its indulgence shown to others, its placidity in the midst of the world's turbulence, its tranquil acceptance of things as they must be. To some, this charm, which permeates most of Renan's later writings, seems a relaxation of moral fiber. They prefer the eager and strenuous youth of *The Future of Science* and the "Theology of Béranger." Even in his latest days, Renan

[1] Société Asiatique, November 11, 1892.

was occasionally an excitable talker. Brandes in 1870 found in him no nuance, but animation, vigor, abundance; and Mary Robinson presents for the final period an almost passionate dinner-table outburst against spiritualism. In his public utterances this volcanic nature is suppressed by reason, and even in talk it largely subsided as he grew old.

In any man's character it is only fair to separate what is voluntary from what is capricious, and in his thought the fundamental and habitual from the fugitive, variable and accessory. In Renan we find an almost complete neglect of the things he did not care for. About the professorship, the *Corpus,* the administration of the Collège, he was inflexible; money-getting, society, popular opinion, such things were treated with negligence. A permanent feature of Renan's life was his devotion to the ideal, with a corresponding aversion to the mechanical, the material, the merely useful. Accessory to this was a spirit somewhat akin to that of the juvenile Romanticists when they sought to "épater le bourgeois," a late example being furnished by the *Prologue in Heaven.* Much of his caprice, indeed, is to be laid to the account of a revulsion which drove him from any distasteful excess toward its opposite, so that, while by principle moderate, he is apt to express extreme and unconditional opinions. Scherer objects to his practice of making an unqualified statement and then an unqualified statement of the opposite, a practice that excited the public, but at length wearied it. This mode of expression Renan might have defended as according with his theory, but it doubtless had its roots in his mental constitution.

Some readers, as a result, got the idea that he was unstable in both character and opinions. They were fond of quoting his maxim: "Woe to him who does not contradict himself at least once a day." The maxim obviously applies to the limbs and outward flourishes of truth, and not to essentials, in regard to which Renan was as obstinate as a granite

rock. His main conceptions are iterated a hundred times
and are no more uncertain or wavering than the answers
in a catechism.

It is clear that Renan started upon his career with the
intention of becoming the apostle of a new religion, which
was to substitute the results of scientific investigation for
dogma. The old formulas might be retained, but they were
to submit to a new interpretation, and none of them was
to be considered more than an approximation to the truth.
God was the universe in the process of *becoming*, striving
blindly toward full consciousness. Negatively considered,
God was not a magnified man, and did not interfere in the
working of the laws of things. Providence was a general
evolution toward some far-off, inscrutable, divine result,
not the manipulation of particular persons and units. Immortality was not individual, but the permanence of ideas
and achievements. Religious exercises might be replaced
among the highly intelligent by scientific investigations, and
the laws thus discovered would reorganize society and bring
about the greatest possible elevation and spiritual development of the human race.

In these ideas Renan never varied. The impossibility
of propagating a new religion, and particularly *this* new
religion, became obvious to him even in the course of his
first Italian journey. An apostolate was thereafter unthink-
able. But the ideas remained, and they were expounded,
with their corollaries and connections, in his periodical essays. Duty and all disinterested endeavor for beauty and
truth are uniformly regarded as divine instincts, impulses
that reveal the infinite to man. These are permanent, and
independent of creeds or reasonings. The doubts expressed
on this subject in two or three late compositions constitute
the only serious contradiction in Renan's thinking.

That he should utter diametrically opposed statements is
by no means evidence of inconsistency. Formulas are merely

the means by which our minds do their work. In each there may be truth, but never the entire truth, for truth is infinite and as a whole inexpressible. A man who clings to a dogma simply blinds himself to the contradictions his dogma involves. He, indeed, is the truly inconsistent thinker. In a similar way, logic is useful only in a limited sphere, and within this limited sphere Renan's logic is inexorable. Applied to universals, our syllogisms lead us inevitably to A=A. Abstract philosophy, therefore, provides mere partial hypotheses, and religion is nothing but a feeling for the indefinite expressed in symbols. Let us view such part of reality as our organism allows us to perceive, appreciating always that we see only one side of a small part at a time, and that therefore, when we speak about it, our expression must be partial, and, to that extent, false. Opposites are necessary, there must be no exclusion, except for the moment, and truth, so far as we can attain it, will lie in the nuance.

To a mind so open and eager as Renan's, every phase of reality was attractive. He could have devoted himself to physical science as readily as to history, and the history of Greece would have been as attractive as the history of the Jews. His strong determination is nowhere more evident than in his voluntary limitation of his main endeavor to the one subject. He selected his life work and then he performed it without the slightest deviation. In his other writings, he either responded to what he considered the passing call of duty or he let his mind play by way of relaxation. It is perfectly legitimate for a man to be a dilettante, but Renan was not a dilettante.

He apparently devoted little time to current literature. It would be hard to find a celebrated author who digresses so widely over so many fields and who at the same time refers to so few contemporary works, whether of poetry, drama, fiction, history, politics or philosophy. His correspondence, too, contains hardly a reference to any general reading; of this sort one book only is mentioned to Berthelot, Quinet's *Merlin,* and when Berthelot opens his friend's copy, he finds many leaves uncut.[2] If Renan dreamed of a period of old age in which he might give up work and doze away his hours over the novel of the day,[3] that period never came. The slight attention he gave to such matters is a striking manifestation of his self-centered concentration. Perhaps his early distaste for the literature of the salon persisted, but it seems more likely that his interest was so intently fixed on his own group of topics that he had none left over for a great variety of things that might interest other people. If he had been gifted with three or four lives, the French Revolution, Athens, Brittany, Chinese literature, might have attracted him; a history of his own times, never.

History, in his view, presented a section of the evolution of the consciousness of the universe, an evolution beginning with the atom and continuing through the formation of the planetary system down to the present. Humanity, like matter, was a vast homogeneous mass, containing germs that operated through their own inner forces to bring about diversified results. Some such germs grouped themselves in Greece to give birth to poetry, philosophy and art; some in Rome to develop law and politics; some in Palestine to produce the agitation that made religion. These germs destroyed the nations in which they fermented, but they penetrated and permeated the entire mass. It was the beginnings of this fermentation that Renan preferred to study, beginnings that were obscure, the individual facts being uncertain, but the general character of the epoch being visible to the diligent, enlightened, and sympathetic seeker. Here, indeed, conjecture often takes the place of fact and the artist triumphs over the scholar, but nothing is gratuitous and we are glad to have such competent rearrangement of confused frag-

[2] October 4 and November 8, 1860.
[3] *Feuilles détachées,* p. 123.

ments and such ingenious filling of blank spaces, even if absolute certitude is lacking.

It might seem as if this use of conjecture and divination were out of harmony with the rigid scholarship which Renan professed. But the limits of scholarship have a general resemblance to the limits of logic; there is a region beyond, and this is to be reached only through the poetic faculties. The recent science of comparative philology opened such marvelous vistas into untraveled realms and so changed received ideas that Renan was enraptured. He was seized with a passion for the primitive. He knew well enough how small a handful of dry facts he possessed, but they seemed to him sufficient for an artistic reconstruction. At the best, the results must be uncertain, and a critical procedure that takes the middle path between accepting everything and rejecting everything has the chances in its favor. At any rate, it was the method in harmony with Renan's nature, a nature which sought moderation in life and politics, as well as in erudition.

An intelligent reader who has no special knowledge can readily discount hazardous statements. A fair example from the *Life of Jesus* is the story of the Samaritan woman at the well of Jacob. (P. 243.) In a note Renan points out that no one, unless it were either Jesus or the woman, could have reported the words there spoken and that the anecdote (John, iv. 21-23) is probably (others would say certainly) not historical, though correctly representing the attitude of Jesus. On the following page he treats the anecdote as a fact. But it really makes no difference. The conclusion drawn, that this is "absolute religion," does not depend on the truth of any incidents. Few doubt that Jesus taught his disciples to worship "in spirit and in truth," rather than to respect Jerusalem or Samaria as holy places. The general impression stands, even if groups of details may have no basis in fact.

The process of measuring Renan with a yardstick is wholly

unsatisfactory. The two tests most commonly applied are the metaphysical and the philological. The results could readily have been foreseen, if Renan's warnings had been heeded. In metaphysics we are certain that all our solutions are uncertain, we know that ultimate truths are unknowable, we see that all our views are distorted and partial. Limited microbes in the midst of immensity, we can comprehend our immediate environment, the things we bump against, but the farther we reach out, the more vague become the details, then the masses, until distinctions fade in universal obscurity. Why all this passionate rage and contention about dogmas and theories? Science shades off by imperceptible changes of tint into the unknown. Still the fact that we are not wholly egotistical, that there is such a thing as duty and self-sacrifice, indicates a moral order, inexplicable by any known physical laws, an order which mankind has personified as God, and represented by sacred symbols. Meanwhile, we use such capacities as we possess, and through scientific research widen the field of knowledge, complaining of the limitations of mental sight no more than of the limitations of physical sight. Having exhausted the strictly scientific methods, we are at liberty to apply imaginative conjecture, fully aware of what we are doing and never admitting imagination where scientific processes are applicable.

Our vision is similarly bounded when we look back upon the past. Indeed, even the present can be known to us only through imperfect indications of what really takes place. A strict analysis shows that we know hardly anything with certitude, and yet we have a comfortable assurance that our information is sufficient. The picture as a whole is possible, even probable, when based on the best information available; and it must suffice, for it is all that is within our reach.

The moral and practical yardsticks are also applied to Renan with equally unsatisfactory results. Nature is immoral, nature does not prescribe that the male should be chaste, nature is anti-patriotic—such remarks embody observation of neighboring facts, not precepts to govern conduct. Stronger than animal nature is what Renan calls the ideal, an effluence of the infinite. The man animated by this sentiment needs no ten commandments or ten thousand commandments. Here is the basis of Renan's affinity with Jesus, "the greatest of men, because he developed this dim feeling (i.e., the infinite which is in the heart) with an unprecedented, an unsurpassable power."[4] Such morality may not be practical except among the élite, and indeed for the scrimmage of life the Church was obliged to substitute definite rules more or less derived from the lofty precepts of the Master. Renan himself, though one of the élite, felt that his life had been dominated by the rules and examples presented to him in his early education, and he wondered what standards a generation deprived of such training could obtain for its guidance. As has been already remarked, this doubt seems to have been his only important infidelity to his principles. Faith should have assured him, as it undoubtedly did substantially, that the ideal would suffice for every higher need of humanity.

If we measure practical ability, as is commonly done, by success, Renan was one of the most practical men of his time. He achieved everything he set out to achieve. And he did this by a procedure entirely in harmony with his whole attitude toward things, by tenacious adherence to what was in sight and comparative neglect of unessentials. The professorship of Hebrew, the *Origins of Christianity*, the *Corpus*, upon these he concentrated, and fame and social position and money came of themselves. In politics he was not practical, and he was not successful. In this field he knew more of world movements than he did of the limited sphere in which an actual participant must work. Vast results he

---

[4] *Questions contemporaines*, p. 150.

could foresee accurately, not minor constituents of such results. Omitting his views about republican France, an example from his early life will furnish a sufficiently good illustration. He thinks Italian unity impossible, because each city—Florence, Venice, Genoa—would reclaim its independence and call for outside help against the others as in the Middle Ages. On the other hand, he sees truly that the future of Italy cannot be based upon its past.

No one can tell what poison an imbecile or a person of evil tendencies will suck out of a book. There are some who have made Kant responsible for 1914. The artist, as Renan remarked, is not responsible for misinterpretations of his work. "If a clumsy fellow swallows a perfume given him to smell, he has no one but himself to blame for his stupidity." [5] If such characters as the Richardet of Cherbuliez—and it is said that there were many of this type—extracted from Renan a flabby theory of life, solid heads like Charles Ritter, Gabriel Monod, Gaston Paris, to mention only those who were not orientalists, found a nourishment of quite different character. Upon young scholars, in particular, his influence was wholly good, encouraging disinterested, laborious and accurate research. How often, in reading his correspondence, do we find him working night and day on one of his self-imposed tasks! This in itself is a high morality.

The world is a place for serious labor and for serious reflection; it is also a spectacle, and we are called upon to enjoy and admire it. Some who claimed to be disciples of Renan regarded it as exclusively a spectacle, but the very word "exclusive" shows that they had no real affinity with him they claimed as a guide. The world, then, is also a spectacle, and something inexcusable from the spiritual standpoint may yet have its appropriate place in this varied panorama. It may even arouse admiration, provided it is

---

[5] "Réponse à Claretie," *Feuilles*, p. 236.

not entirely vulgar. Nero himself excites curiosity rather than hatred. His insanity, cruelty and viciousness are fully exposed in words that are adequate to the horrors he committed, yet the saving grace of artistic or semiartistic sensibility is not denied the monster. If the specimen is repulsive on account of its capacity for evil, it is nevertheless attractive as an object of study and comprehension. And the same may be said of the conditions that originated and nourished a monstrosity so unique. Perversion and excess may properly arouse the wrath of the moralist; they may also, with equal propriety, be examined by the thinker without excitement and be explained rather than judged. In his writings, Renan is not much given to praise or blame. He does not enter into his personages, or even stand aside and applaud or hiss them. He rather places them in the current and by his unimpassioned statement leaves the admiration or the horror excited by individuals to the sentiments of his readers. He had indignation enough, but he kept it out of his books.

There was, indeed, no irritation so violent that its current would not be absorbed in his placid tolerance;[6] and this tolerance was not indifference or indolence, but the fruit of a kindly nature and of a sincere love of justice and liberty. The rights he demanded for himself he also demanded for his opponents. It is impossible to find in his published works a single expression of personal hatred. Even his irony is uttered with a benevolent smile. His superiority he certainly knew, but he never imposes it upon others, his writings being as free from arrogance as his relations with men, both the most exalted and the most humble. Assuredly, the dominant trait of Renan is benevolence.

This benevolence is, indeed, not only a trait of character,

---

[6] "O what a fine tolerance, and of a wholly new kind, which has its source, not in contempt for everything, but in a profound faith in something!" Sainte-Beuve, *Nouveaux Lundis*, vol. ix, p. 199.

but a literary quality. It appears in his engaging way of putting things, and especially in his fraternal spirit toward all mankind, his humanity that recognizes an essential likeness under every superficial variation of conditions and appearances. Most people tend to regard an ancient Egyptian, a Chinaman, a Bedouin, as differing in character from themselves. Not so Renan. His sympathies emphasized the fact that his relationship with men of every age, of every land, of every manner of life, was one of kind. The motive of a flattering hieroglyphic inscription is the same as that of a note about the Emperor in the *Moniteur,* the Chinese government is such as would be the rule of the Académie des Sciences Morales et Politiques, the courtesy and taste of an illiterate nomad in his desert tent differs in no respect but fashion from the delicacy and refinement of a Parisian salon. The much abused modern parallels are in truth nothing but a bookish modification of the same tenderness of heart that found its personal expression in charitable acts, kindly demeanor, and manners of exquisite dignity and charm.

It has not been the purpose of this study to defend Renan or even to propagate any of his ideas—neither procedure being appropriate in the case of a writer who himself refused to be a controversialist or a propagandist—but to exhibit the intimate relationship of his work to his life. In such a view, the much heralded contradictions largely vanish. Each remark of his is to be taken in its context, and the context of every remark is not such or such a page, but his whole work. His philosophy is not a system but an organic unity. It fits itself into the varying experiences of the hour. In his earliest writings, he is a little overstrenuous; in his latest, he appeared a little less serious than he actually was; but he has not really changed, either in the mode or substance of his thought, or in his laborious habits of performing his daily task, or in his earnest devotion to duty and to the ideal. If in *The Future of Science,* forty years has made a difference between the text and the preface, we merely feel that the tone of the aging voice shows signs of fatigue. The sentiment is the same though the eagerness of anticipation has, as might be expected, been left behind.

In fact, we find in Renan, what Sainte-Beuve was so fond of seeking in the subjects of his studies—the unity of a fine life. If externally this life is especially characterized by benevolence, internally it is characterized by joy, joy of a sort that begets and is in turn begotten by, benevolence. Of this happy state the gayety for which Renan has been reproached is but a manifestation. He had joy in his thoughts, joy in his travels, joy in his human relationships, and above all joy in his work. He never got far from nature; even in Paris his study, when he chose it, always looked out on trees. A fine view never failed to elicit his enthusiasm. When the contemplation of the universe gives us delight, we should not deprive ourselves of this element of harmless happiness.

It is not any particular idea, but the unity of a great man's life and the variety and perfection of his expression of it that constitutes the originality of genius. Others perceived the fluidity of existence, others broke through rigid formulas, others substituted thorough learning for superficial declamation; the belief in science as the universal solvent was general about the middle of the century; the intermingling of poetry, erudition and philosophy was no invention of Renan's; an intense concentration on a limited field, together with views into the vague distance, is a method that can, without wide search, he paralleled; but nowhere else can be found the special combination, the resultant of thinking, in short, the personality that we call Renan. He belonged to no school, and he formed no school. In fact, no school was in his case possible. The very idea is self-destructive.

The general influence of his attitude toward existence, however, is peace of spirit. After being nourished on his works, one is enabled readily to translate into nontheological terms the famous line of Dante:

> In la sua voluntade è nostra pace.
> (In his will is our peace.)

"Let us submit to the laws of nature," he said, "of which which we are one of the manifestations. The earth and the heavens remain." Those who need abstract formulas and definite promises can readily find elsewhere all that they desire. It is unreasonable for them to complain that such things are not among the offerings of Renan. What he does present is given with fullness and sincerity. Such was the picture reflected in his intellectual retina. To debate its correctness is, as he would be the first to admit, utterly futile. For all readers it has elements of interest; for those who have a somewhat similar vision, it furnishes an enrichment of outlook which they will find of serious import and not without charm.

INDEX

No references are made to the chronological outline in the chapter headings and only the principal passages are indexed.

461

(1)